Advances in Infrared and Raman Spectroscopy

VOLUME 2

Advances in Infrared and Raman Spectroscopy

VOLUME 2

Edited by

R. J. H. CLARK
University College London

R. E. HESTER
University of York

London · Philadelphia · Rheine

Heyden & Son Ltd., Spectrum House, Hillview Gardens, London NW4 2JQ
Heyden & Son Inc., 247 South 41st Street, Philadelphia, PA 19104, USA
Heyden & Son GmbH, Devesburgstrasse 6, 4440 Rheine, West Germany

ISBN 0 85501 182 3

Set by Eta Services (Typesetters) Ltd., Beccles, Suffolk.
Printed and bound in Great Britain by Mackays of Chatham Ltd.

CONTENTS

CHAPTER 1: Vibrational Energy Levels in Matrix Isolated Species—
J. K. Burnett, M. Poliakoff, J. J. Turner and
H. Dubost

CHAPTER 2: Vibrational Information from the Electronic Spectra
of Transition Metal Coordination Compounds—
C. D. Flint

v

CHAPTER 3: Industrial Plant Applications of Infrared and Raman
Spectroscopy—
H. A. Willis

CHAPTER 4: Time-Resolved and Space-Resolved Raman
Spectroscopy—
M. Bridoux and M. Delhaye

CHAPTER 5: The Vibrational Spectra of Ionic Vapours, Liquids
and Glasses—
J. P. Devlin

CHAPTER 6: Raman and Infrared Spectral Studies of Electrolytes—
D. E. Irish and M. H. Brooker

LIST OF CONTRIBUTORS

M. BRIDOUX, Service de Spectrochimie Infrarouge et Raman C.N.R.S., Université des Sciences et Techniques de Lille, B.P. 36 59650, Villeneuve d'Ascq, France (p. 140).

M. H. BROOKER, Department of Chemistry, Memorial University, St Johns, Newfoundland A1C 5S7, Canada (p. 212).

J. K. BURDETT, University of Newcastle-upon-Tyne, Newcastle-upon-Tyne NE1 7RU, United Kingdom (p. 1).

M. DELHAYE, Service de Spectrochimie Infrarouge et Raman C.N.R.S., Université des Sciences et Techniques de Lille, B.P. 36 59650, Villeneuve d'Ascq, France (p. 140).

J. P. DEVLIN, Department of Chemistry, Oklahoma State University, Stillwater, Oklahoma 74074, U.S.A. (p. 153).

H. DUBOST, Laboratoire de Photophysique Moléculaire C.N.R.S., Université de Paris-Sud, 91405 Orsay, France (p. 1).

C. D. FLINT, Department of Chemistry, Birkbeck College, University of London, London WC1E 7HX, United Kingdom (p. 53).

D. E. IRISH, Department of Chemistry, University of Waterloo, Waterloo, Ontario N2L 3GI, Canada (p. 212).

M. POLIAKOFF, University of Newcastle-upon-Tyne, Newcastle-upon-Tyne NE1 7RU, United Kingdom (p. 1).

J. J. TURNER, University of Newcastle-upon-Tyne, Newcastle-upon-Tyne NE1 7RU, United Kingdom (p. 1).

H. A. WILLIS, Plastics Division, Imperial Chemical Industries Limited, P.O. Box 6, Bessemer Road, Welwyn Garden City, Herts., United Kingdom (p. 81).

PREFACE TO VOLUME 1

There are few areas of science which have not already benefited from the application of infrared spectroscopic methods, and progress in this field remains vigorous. Closely related information on chemical and biological materials and systems is obtainable from Raman spectroscopy, though there also are many important differences between the types of information yielded and the types of materials and systems best suited to study by each technique. The close relationship between these two sets of spectroscopic techniques is explicitly recognised in this Series. Advances in Infrared and Raman Spectroscopy contains critical review articles, both fundamental and applied, mainly within the title areas; however, we shall extend the coverage into closely related areas by giving some space to such topics as neutron inelastic scattering or vibronic fluorescence spectroscopy. Thus the Series will be firmly technique orientated. Inasmuch as these techniques have such wide ranging applicability throughout science and engineering, however, the coverage in terms of topics will be wide. Already in the first volume we have articles ranging from the fundamental theory of infrared band intensities through the development of computer-controlled spectrometer systems to applications in biology. This integration of theory and practice, and the bringing together of different areas of academic and industrial science and technology, constitute major objectives of the Series.

The reviews will be in those subjects in which most progress is deemed to have been made in recent years, or is expected to be made in the near future. The Series will appeal to research scientists and technologists as well as to graduate students and teachers of advanced courses. The Series is intended to be of wide general interest both within and beyond the fields of chemistry, physics and biology.

The problem of nomenclature in a truly international Series has to be acknowledged. We have adopted a compromise solution of permitting the use of either English or American spelling (depending on the origin of the review article) and have recommended the use of SI Units. A table on the international system of units is given on p. xiii for reference purposes.

August 1975

R. J. H. CLARK
R. E. HESTER

PREFACE

In accordance with the general aims of this series, Volume 2 contains a set of up-to-date review articles covering a wide range of topics in infrared and Raman spectroscopy. The selection of authors and topics is intended to provide material of interest not only to vibrational spectroscopists but also to other scientists and technologists with problems which may be solved with the aid of these versatile tools. Some indication of the range of such problems is provided by the contents of this volume.

Much has been written elsewhere about the powerful technique of matrix isolation in conjunction with infrared and Raman measurements so that we feel justified in presenting here a more specialized article than usual, dealing with a few specific problems. The emphasis of the first review is on transition metal carbonyls, but the methods described for studying these as trapped species in inert matrices are very generally applicable.

In the Preface to Volume 1 we indicate our intention to extend the coverage of this series to topics which, although not strictly within the title areas, yield results which are closely related to those obtained from infrared and Raman spectroscopy. The second review in this volume deals with such a topic: vibronic spectroscopy. The vibrational fine structure in electronic spectra from molecular or crystalline species may be determined from luminescence, absorption or excitation spectra, and all three methods are examined here. As is illustrated for transition metal coordination compounds, the vibrational data obtainable are complimentary to those given by direct vibrational methods.

Infrared spectrometers have for many years found widespread use in industrial laboratories as well as in fundamental research institutions. A more recent development has been the movement from the laboratory into the industrial plant situation of several types of analytical infrared instruments. The many aspects of this development are treated in the third review. Readers will find this topic covered in a very practical, down-to-earth way, with many illustrations of successful plant applications of infrared and an indication of the potential for Raman spectrometers.

At the more fundamental level of basic physics and research instrument development, the topic of time-resolved and space-resolved Raman spectroscopy is covered in the fourth review. Our authors have been the world leaders in instrumentation for very fast recording of Raman spectra and they describe here the impressive state of the art. The considerable advantages of multichannel spectroscopic techniques are described and illustrated with examples of pico-second spectra, microanalysis and Raman microscopy. It appears likely that these methods will find much more widespread use in the future when the forms of instrumentation described here become available in commercially packaged units.

The final two reviews in this volume treat different aspects of vibrational spectroscopic studies of ionic species. In the fifth review the emphasis is on ionic vapours, liquids (as in molten salts) and glasses, while aqueous electrolyte solutions constitute the major topic reviewed in Chapter 6. These areas have been subjected to vigorous investigation by both infrared and Raman methods in recent years. Our authors, all leading contributors to the progress made in these areas, have produced timely and complementary reviews which will be found valuable by workers with interests in electrochemistry, liquid structures, solvation phenomena and matrix-isolated ionic aggregates.

As in Volume 1 we have had to find a compromise between the different systems of nomenclature, of units for physical qualities, and even of spelling used by our international authorship. However, we have favoured IUPAC nomenclature and the use of SI units and expect to progress further in this direction in future volumes as the use of these systems becomes more widespread. To aid the reader a table of SI units and conversions from other systems commonly in use is included on pages xiii–xv.

June 1976   R. J. H. CLARK
                                                                 R. E. HESTER

THE INTERNATIONAL SYSTEM OF UNITS (SI)

Physical quantity	Name of unit	Symbol for unit

SI Base Units

length	metre	m
mass	kilogram	kg
time	second	s
electric current	ampere	A
thermodynamic temperature	kelvin	K
amount of substance	mole	mol

SI Supplementary Units

plane angle	radian	rad
solid angle	steradian	sr

SI Derived Units having Special Names and Symbols

energy	joule	$J = m^2\,kg\,s^{-2}$
force	newton	$N = m\,kg\,s^{-2} = J\,m^{-1}$
pressure	pascal	$Pa = m^{-1}\,kg\,s^{-2} = N\,m^{-2} = J\,m^{-3}$
power	watt	$W = m^2\,kg\,s^{-3} = J\,s^{-1}$
electric charge	coulomb	$C = s\,A$
electric potential difference	volt	$V = m^2\,kg\,s^{-3}\,A^{-1} = J\,A^{-1}\,s^{-1}$
electric resistance	ohm	$\Omega = m^2\,kg\,s^{-3}\,A^{-2} = V\,A^{-1}$
electric conductance	siemens	$S = m^{-2}\,kg^{-1}\,s^3\,A^2 = \Omega^{-1}$
electric capacitance	farad	$F = m^{-2}\,kg^{-1}\,s^4\,A^2 = C\,V^{-1}$
magnetic flux	weber	$Wb = m^2\,kg\,s^{-2}\,A^{-1} = V\,s$
inductance	henry	$H = m^2\,kg\,s^{-2}\,A^{-2} = V\,s\,A^{-1}$
magnetic flux density	tesla	$T = kg\,s^{-2}\,A^{-1} = V\,s\,m^{-2}$
frequency	hertz	$Hz = s^{-1}$

SOME NON-SI UNITS

Physical quantity	Name of unit	Symbol and definition

Decimal Multiples of SI Units, Some having Speical Names and Symbols

length	ångström	$\text{Å} = 10^{-10} \text{ m} = 0.1 \text{ nm}$ $= 100 \text{ pm}$
length	micron	$\mu\text{m} = 10^{-6} \text{ m}$
area	are	$\text{a} = 100 \text{ m}^2$
area	barn	$\text{b} = 10^{-28} \text{ m}^2$
volume	litre	$\text{l} = 10^{-3} \text{ m}^3 = \text{dm}^3$ $= 1000 \text{ cm}^3$
energy	erg	$\text{erg} = 10^{-7} \text{ J}$
force	dyne	$\text{dyn} = 10^{-5} \text{ N}$
force constant	dyne per centimetre	$\text{dyn cm}^{-1} = 10^{-3} \text{ N m}^{-1}$
force constant	millidyne per ångström	$\text{mdyn Å}^{-1} = 10^2 \text{ N m}^{-1}$
force constant	attojoule per ångström squared	$\text{aJ Å}^{-2} = 10^2 \text{ N m}^{-1}$
pressure	bar	$\text{bar} = 10^5 \text{ Pa}$
concentration	—	$\text{M} = 10^3 \text{ mol m}^{-3}$ $= \text{mol dm}^{-3}$

Units Defined Exactly in Terms of SI Units

length	inch	$\text{in} = 0.0254 \text{ m}$
mass	pound	$\text{lb} = 0.453\,592\,27 \text{ kg}$
force	kilogram-force	$\text{kgf} = 9.806\,65 \text{ N}$
pressure	standard atmosphere	$\text{atm} = 101\,325 \text{ Pa}$
pressure	torr	$\text{Torr} = 1 \text{ mmHg}$ $= (101\,325/760) \text{ Pa}$
energy	kilowatt hour	$\text{kW h} = 3.6 \times 10^6 \text{ J}$
energy	thermochemical calorie	$\text{cal}_{\text{th}} = 4.184 \text{ J}$
thermodynamic temperature	degree Celsius[a]	$°\text{C} = \text{K}$

[a]Celsius or "Centigrade" temperature θ_C is defined in terms of the thermodynamic temperature T by the relation $\theta_C/°\text{C} = T/\text{K} - 273.15$.

OTHER RELATIONS

1. The physical quantity, the wavenumber (units cm^{-1}), is related to frequency as follows:

$$cm^{-1} \approx (2.998 \times 10^{10})^{-1} \, s^{-1}$$

2. The physical quantity, the molar decadic absorption coefficient (symbol ε) has the SI units $m^2 \, mol^{-1}$. The relation between the usual non-SI and SI units is as follows:

$$M^{-1} \, cm^{-1} = 1 \, mol^{-1} \, cm^{-1} = 10^{-1} \, m^2 \, mol^{-1}$$

3. It appears that for many years to come a knowledge of the 'electromagnetic CGS' unit system will be a necessity for workers in various fields of spectroscopy, but for practical purposes it is usually sufficient to note that for magnetic flux density, 1 gauss (G) corresponds to 10^{-4} T and for electric dipole moment, 1 debye (D) corresponds to approximately 3.3356×10^{-30} C m.

The SI Prefixes

Fraction	Prefix	Symbol	Multiple	Prefix	Symbol
10^{-1}	deci	d	10^1	deca	da
10^{-2}	centi	c	10^2	hecto	h
10^{-3}	milli	m	10^3	kilo	k
10^{-6}	micro	μ	10^6	mega	M
10^{-9}	nano	n	10^9	giga	G
10^{-12}	pico	p	10^{12}	tera	T
10^{-15}	femto	f	10^{15}	peta	P
10^{-18}	atto	a	10^{18}	exa	E

Chapter 1

VIBRATIONAL ENERGY LEVELS IN MATRIX ISOLATED SPECIES

J. K. Burdett, M. Poliakoff and J. J. Turner

Department of Inorganic Chemistry, The University, Newcastle-upon-Tyne NE1 7RU, England

H. Dubost

Laboratoire de Photophysique Moléculaire C.N.R.S., Université de Paris-Sud, 91405 Orsay, France

1 INTRODUCTION

The object of the matrix isolation technique, developed largely by Pimentel,[1] is to trap an unstable species in a large excess of inert rigid matrix and examine its spectroscopic properties at leisure. There have been several reviews[2] of the technique and applications, and we do not propose to repeat such an exercise here. Rather, we have selected some specific problems involving vibrational energy levels of trapped species and attempted to cover them in some depth. However, before even outlining these topics a few words of introduction are appropriate.

The matrix-isolated sample can be obtained in a variety of ways: condensation at low temperature from the gas phase with a large excess of inert gas (e.g. $XeCl_2$ from a discharge in Xe and Cl_2,[3] or monomeric UO_2 from a furnace containing uranium(IV) oxide);[4] co-condensation of two reactive species with excess of the matrix gas on a spectroscopic window at low temperature (e.g. $Ni(CO)_x$[5] from Ni atoms and CO, or CCl_3[6] from Li and CCl_4); or generation by *in situ* photolysis of a parent species already isolated at low temperature in a matrix (e.g. OF from OF_2[7]). Each of these techniques has its proponents and its appropriateness depends on the particular application and to some extent on personal prejudice.

In all cases the main problem is the positive identification of the trapped species. Although e.s.r. and u.v.-visible methods have been used, it is much more common for infrared and, more recently, Raman methods to be employed. The first task is the assignment of vibrational bands to *a single species*; this involves accounting for bands due to dimers and higher polymers, the understanding of split bands due to so-called matrix effects and the use of 'growth

1

and decay curves'.[8] Having assigned, say, four infrared (i.r.)-active bands to a single species the next problem is to use i.r./Raman spectroscopy to establish the structure of the molecule. 'Structure' here can mean simply its molecular formula (e.g. CCl_2 or CCl_3), or its symmetry (e.g. is MgF_2, when trapped in solid argon, linear or bent? Is $Cr(CO)_5$ square pyramidal or trigonal bi-pyramidal?), or its geometrical structure (e.g. what is the bond angle in the C_{2v} radical anion SO_2^-?). Of course, *proof* of molecular formula may well involve a detailed structure determination so that these points are not different problems but merely represent three different degrees of sophistication of the same one.

In practically every case, it is essential before making any use of vibrational data to answer the two questions: what is the effect of the matrix environment on the vibrational energy levels of a trapped species, and what is the effect of the matrix environment on the actual structures of molecules? After all, there is little point in proving that, say, CCl_2 in argon is bent with an angle of $\approx 100°$ if this is totally irrelevant to the structure of the species in the gas phase. Anticipating some of what follows we can *generally* conclude that, with genuinely inert matrices (e.g. Ne to Xe), both effects are small and certainly not enough to make any significant difference to the structure of the trapped species.

What kind of structural information can be obtained from vibrational spectra? Since, in all except a very few cases[8] there is no molecular rotation in the matrix, the information has to be extracted from the pure vibrational bands. Fortunately, these bands are usually very narrow ($\approx 1 cm^{-1}$ halfwidth), in the absence of rotation. Two different methods have been used to extract this information. The first is to use band patterns and selection rules; this can vary from the trivial (e.g. the deduction that a species giving five infrared-active bands, all attributable to fundamentals, cannot be triatomic) to the more subtle (e.g. the use of Raman polarization data for the identification of totally symmetric modes). The second is to use isotopes; this can also be simple (e.g. if a band shifts on producing the species from a starting compound containing deuterium rather than hydrogen, then the species must contain hydrogen) or complicated (e.g. ^{12}C—^{13}C isotopic shifts demonstrate that $Pd(CO)_4$ is tetrahedral).[9]

A major part of this chapter is concerned with a detailed analysis of the structural information which can be obtained from the vibrational spectra of transition metal carbonyl and related species. However, rather than start with these molecules it seems appropriate to consider some much simpler molecules, bearing in mind comments and approximations appropriate to the carbonyls. Indeed most of our early examples involve triatomic species, which we use to investigate the following problems. How accurately can the bond angle in bent symmetric XY_2 species be determined? Are intensity measurements of any value? What information can be extracted from isotopic frequency and intensity patterns? The answering of these questions allows us to look closely at the structures of transition metal carbonyl fragments.

One of the great successes of matrix isolation in metal carbonyl chemistry is the detailed information which has been obtained about the mechanisms of photochemical reactions; this topic is discussed at length elsewhere.[10] However, in such discussions a question of very general interest arises viz. how is the photochemistry affected by the matrix? How, for example, is energy transfer in the matrix relevant to this problem? Thus, in the later part of this chapter we examine recent work on this topic; most of the work involves the use of infrared lasers and the study of infrared emission spectra. Finally, it is our belief that matrix isolation will have much to contribute to the rapidly expanding field of infrared and laser-induced photochemistry. We conclude the chapter with some thoughts on this topic.

2 THE DETERMINATION OF BOND ANGLES IN SYMMETRIC BENT (C_{2v}) TRIATOMIC MOLECULES

In principle, this problem may be solved straightforwardly using isotopic substitution. Assuming a general quadratic valence force field for the C_{2v} molecule XY_2, the asymmetric stretching frequency is given by [11]

$$\lambda_3 = 4\pi^2 c^2 \omega_3^2 = \left(1 + \frac{2M_Y}{M_X}\sin^2\phi\right)\frac{f_r - f_{rr}}{M_Y} \tag{1}$$

(see Fig. 1), where ω_3 represents the harmonic frequency. M_X and M_Y are the masses of atoms X and Y respectively, and 2ϕ is the Y—X—Y angle. It is worth commenting that the angle dependence arises because in general these G matrix elements contain terms involving ϕ. In force fields of more complex molecules (e.g. metal carbonyls) with greatly simplified G matrices, this dependence may be lost so that bond angles cannot be determined directly from the force field. Assuming that f's and ϕ do not change on isotopic substitution, and that the

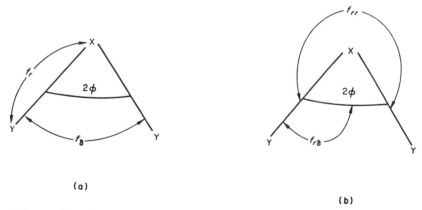

(a)

(b)

Fig. 1. General quadratic valence force field parameters in a symmetrical XY_2 molecule. (a) Diagonal and (b) off-diagonal force constants.

substitution is symmetric, i.e. $XY_2 \rightarrow X\bar{Y}_2$, $\bar{X}Y_2$ or $\bar{X}\bar{Y}_2$ where $\bar{M}_X > M_X$, $\bar{M}_X > M_Y$, then for $X\bar{Y}_2$

$$\bar{\lambda}_3 = 4\pi^2 c^2 \bar{\omega}_3^2 = \left(1 + \frac{2\bar{M}_Y}{M_X}\sin^2\phi\right)\frac{f_r - f_{rr}}{\bar{M}_Y} \tag{2}$$

$$\therefore R_\lambda \equiv \frac{\lambda_3}{\bar{\lambda}_3} = \frac{M_Y\left(1 + \dfrac{2\bar{M}_Y}{M_X}\sin^2\phi\right)}{\bar{M}_Y\left(1 + \dfrac{2M_Y}{M_X}\sin^2\phi\right)} \tag{3}$$

and hence, knowing ω_3 and $\bar{\omega}_3$, ϕ can be determined. In the absence of data for λ_3 then that for λ_1 and λ_2 can be used. Alternatively, and more satisfactorily, if a full range of isotopic data is available then a full quadratic valence force field can be obtained by minimizing the calculated–experimental differences.

The question is: how accurate is the information likely to be? The accuracy will depend on four factors:

1. Anharmonicity, i.e. the use of observed rather than harmonic frequencies
2. The fractional changes in isotopic mass
3. The sensitivity of R_λ to small changes in ϕ, at particular values of ϕ
4. Matrix perturbations.

In a classic paper, Allavena et al.[12] made a detailed analysis of the infrared spectrum of SO_2 isolated in a matrix of krypton; they calculated the bond angle to be 119° 37′—compared with the gas-phase microwave value of 119° 19′. Thus, in this case at least, matrix perturbations are virtually zero. Since a whole range of spectroscopic data for all isotopic species of SO_2 is available it was also possible to consider the effect of anharmonicity in some detail.

For the asymmetric stretch, ν_3, of the XY_2 molecules they showed that, by using *anharmonic* frequencies, the substitution $XY_2 \rightarrow \bar{X}Y_2$ produces a lower limit, $2\phi_1$, to the true angle, whereas the substitution $XY_2 \rightarrow X\bar{Y}_2$ produces an *upper* limit, $2\phi_u$, i.e. $2\phi_u > 2\phi > 2\phi_1$ where 2ϕ is the true value; for SO_2 (Table 1) the values are 122° 2′, 119° 37′ and 116° 18′ respectively. For the symmetric modes the limits to the values obtained depend on the value of the interaction constant between stretching and bending internal coordinates ($f_{r\delta}$). If $f_{r\delta} \geq 0$, then for *harmonic* frequencies

$$2\phi_0 \geq 2\phi$$

i.e. the angle, ϕ_0, calculated from ω_1, ω_2, $\bar{\omega}_1$, $\bar{\omega}_2$, assuming $f_{r\delta} = 0$, will be an upper limit, the equality holding when $f_{r\delta} = 0$; for SO_2 (Table 1), the values are 123° 54′ and 119° 37′, respectively. If anharmonic frequencies are used then for $XY_2 \rightarrow \bar{X}Y_2$ the ordering $2\phi_0' > 2\phi_0 > 2\phi$ is found, where the prime represents the angle calculated using anharmonic frequencies. For SO_2 (Table 1) the value of $2\phi_0'$ is 125° 19′. The error in $2\phi_0'$ compared with 2ϕ will generally be greater than $2\phi_u$ compared with $2\phi_1$ because of the error introduced by assuming $f_{r\delta} = 0$. For the $XY_2 \rightarrow X\overline{Y}_2$ substitution the relationship between $2\phi_0$, $2\phi_0'$ and 2ϕ is less well defined and depends on a balance between the $f_{r\delta}$ and anharmonicity constants.

Thus for $XY_2 \rightarrow \overline{X}Y_2$ the 'best' estimate of 2ϕ using *anharmonic* data is obtained by taking the average, $2\phi_a'$, of $2\phi_1$ and $2\phi_0'$

$$2\phi_a' = (\phi_1 + \phi_0')$$

Table 1 summarizes some of the data for SO_2 obtained by Allavena *et al.*;[12] the predictions are in remarkable agreement with experimental observations. In

TABLE 1
Apex angle of SO_2 from observed and harmonic frequencies (Ref. 12)

	$2\phi_1$	$2\phi_u$	$2\phi_0'$	$2\phi_a'^a$	$2\phi_0^b$	$2\phi_a^c$	$2\phi^d$
$^{32}S^{16}O_2-^{34}S^{16}O_2$	116°18′	—	125°19′	120°49′	123°54′	120°6′	119°37′
$^{32}S^{16}O_2-^{32}S^{18}O_2$	—	122°2′	123°12′	122°42′	—	—	119°37′
			SO₂ gas phase—microwave data				119°19′

^{a} $2\phi_a' = (\phi_1 + \phi_0')$.
^{b} The values of ω_1, ω_2, $\overline{\omega}_1$, and $\overline{\omega}_2$ required for this calculation were obtained by assuming that the anharmonicity corrections $[\nu_i = \omega_i(1 - \alpha_i)]$ are related by $\alpha_1 = \alpha_2$, $\overline{\alpha}_i = \overline{\omega}_1 a_i / \omega_1 \approx (\overline{\nu}_i / \nu_i)\alpha_i$, and then applying the product rule relationships.
^{c} $2\phi_a = (\phi_1 + \phi_0)$.
^{d} Value obtained by estimating the anharmonicities then varying the force field to minimize the difference between the theoretical and experimental data.

view of their significance, it is worth summarizing the conclusions. For SO_2 in a krypton matrix:

1. The apex angle determined by the best use of isotopic results and anharmonic corrections is 119° 37′, very close to the gas phase value of 119° 19′; thus
2. matrix perturbations are *very* small, and
3. certain useful limits can be set on bond angles determined from *anharmonic* frequencies.

Before considering some examples of the application of such measurements to previously unknown systems it is worth considering sources of error other than anharmonicity, particularly when using the $\overline{\lambda}_3 / \lambda_3$ method.
From the $XY_2 \rightarrow \overline{X}Y_2$ data for ω_3 and $\overline{\omega}_3$ we have

$$\sin^2 \phi = \frac{\overline{M}_X \left(R_\lambda - \dfrac{\overline{M}_Y}{M_Y}\right)}{2\overline{M}_Y \left(\dfrac{\overline{M}_X}{M_X} - R_\lambda\right)} \qquad \left(R_\lambda = \frac{\overline{\lambda}_3}{\lambda_3}\right) \qquad (4)$$

If

$$\delta\lambda = \lambda_3 - \bar{\lambda}_3, \ \delta M_X = \bar{M}_X - M_X, \ \delta M_Y = \bar{M}_Y - M_Y$$

$$\delta\lambda = \left[\frac{1}{M_Y} - \frac{1}{\bar{M}_Y} + 2\sin^2\phi\left(\frac{1}{M_X} - \frac{1}{\bar{M}_X}\right)\right](f_r - f_{rr}) \tag{5}$$

$$\therefore \ \frac{\delta\lambda}{f_r - f_{rr}} \approx \frac{\delta M_Y}{M_Y^2} + \frac{2\delta M_X}{M_X^2}\sin^2\phi \tag{6}$$

$$\therefore \ \frac{1}{f_r - f_{rr}}\frac{\partial(\delta\lambda)}{\partial\phi} = \frac{2\delta M_X}{M_X^2}\sin 2\phi \tag{7}$$

Since

$$R_\lambda = \frac{\lambda + \delta\lambda}{\lambda} \tag{8}$$

$$\delta R_\lambda \approx \frac{1}{\lambda}\delta(\delta\lambda)$$

So

$$\frac{\partial R_\lambda}{\partial\phi} = \frac{\dfrac{2\delta M_X}{M_X^2}\sin 2\phi}{\dfrac{1}{M_Y} + \dfrac{2\sin^2\phi}{M_X}} = \frac{\dfrac{2\delta M_X}{M_X}\sin 2\phi}{\dfrac{M_X}{M_Y} + 2\sin^2\phi} \tag{9}$$

For a small error in the calculated bond angle, $\partial R_\lambda/\partial\phi$ must be large. Since δM_X is usually only 1 or 2, the bond angle precision will be low for large M_X. Secondly, if $M_X/M_Y \gg 1$ the first term in the denominator will dominate and $\partial R_\lambda/\partial\phi$ will again be small.

An important point is that $\partial(\delta\lambda)/\partial\phi$ tends to zero as $2\phi \to 180°$. Thus there will be large errors, even for small M_X, if the molecule is nearly linear.

Finally there follows a comment about matrix perturbation in general. The fact that vibrational frequencies are usually shifted in going from gas phase to matrix by up to $\approx 1\%$ indicates that there must be some perturbation of vibrational energy levels. The interpretation of such shifts has been discussed extensively elsewhere.[8] The use of isotopes for structure determination assumes that the matrix shift will be 'linear with isotope' so that the correct structure will be determined. This is clearly the case for SO_2/Kr, but it may not be generally true.

There has been a very detailed and exhaustive study of hydrogen cyanide, HCN, trapped in argon matrices, with careful frequency measurements for all possible isotopic species and a comparison with gas phase data.[13] Allowing for some difficulties in extracting the isotopic shifts from the gas phase spectra there is a surprising discrepancy. Substitution of hydrogen by deuterium gives *different* shifts in gas and matrix. The fundamentals of $H^{12}C^{14}N$ in an argon matrix are ν_2 (bend) 720.96 cm^{-1} and ν_3 (C—H stretch) 3305.66 cm^{-1}; ν_1 (C—N stretch) is too weak to observe for HCN in a matrix. The shifts observed for some isotopic substitutions can be summarized as follows:

Molecule	$\Delta\nu_2$/cm^{-1}			$\Delta\nu_3$/cm^{-1}		
	matrix	gas	δ	matrix	gas	δ
$H^{12}C^{14}N \rightarrow D^{12}C^{14}N$	144.94	143.21	1.73	679.18	681.11	-1.93
$H^{12}C^{14}N \rightarrow H^{12}C^{15}N$	1.22	1.05	0.17	1.00	1.32	-0.32

Since $\omega_2/\bar{\omega}_2$ for a linear XYZ molecule is given by

$$\frac{\lambda_2}{\bar{\lambda}_2} = \left(\frac{\omega_2}{\bar{\omega}_2}\right)^2 = \frac{\left[\dfrac{r_{YZ}^2}{M_Z} + \dfrac{r_{XY}^2}{M_X} + \dfrac{(r_{XY}+r_{YZ})^2}{M_Y}\right]}{\left[\dfrac{r_{YZ}^2}{\bar{M}_Z} + \dfrac{r_{XY}^2}{\bar{M}_X} + \dfrac{(r_{XY}+r_{YZ})^2}{\bar{M}_Y}\right]} \tag{10}$$

where r_{XY} is the X—Y bond length, the ratio r_{CN}/r_{CH} can be determined from $\lambda_2/\bar{\lambda}_2$ for the various isotopic pairs. Correcting for anharmonicity (*not* a trivial process), the ratio is sensitive to the particular isotopic substitution *in the matrix*, particularly for H-D substitution which is, on the face of it, rather alarming.

There are various ways of interpreting the discrepancies, viz. inaccurate anharmonicities, extreme sensitivity of the ratio r_{CN}/r_{CH} to the data, or some sort of matrix interaction. It is generally agreed that the discrepancies are only to be expected for isotopic substitution involving very light atoms and then of course only if the calculation of the structure involves normal coordinates with a substantial motion of the light atom. But such errors could make a considerable difference to the calculation of bond angles of XY_2 systems. For MH_2 with $M = 50$, ω_3 at 1000 cm^{-1}, and $2\phi = 120°$, $\bar{\omega}_3$ should be at 717.3 cm^{-1}; if there is, for some reason, an error so that 715 cm^{-1} is used, then the calculated bond angle is $\approx 100°$. It is thus important to realize that most determinations of bond angles in matrices only seek rather approximate values.

We shall now briefly consider the application of these calculations to some *unstable* matrix isolated species.

2.1 SO_2^-

In view of the importance of the results for SO_2 above, it is appropriate first to consider the anion SO_2^- obtained by Milligan and Jacox[14] via co-condensation of SO_2-argon with alkali metals.

The authors assumed a valence force field with no interaction force constants. From the band assigned as ν_3 of $^{32}S^{16}O_2^-$, f_r is obtained as a function of 2ϕ;

the expressions for $\nu_1+\nu_2$ and $\nu_1\nu_2$ involve f_r, f_δ and 2ϕ so that f_δ is obtained from the ν_2 data as a function of 2ϕ. The values were then predicted for $\nu_1(^{32}S^{16}O_2{}^-)$ and ν_1, ν_2, ν_3 ($^{34}S^{16}O_2{}^-$ and $^{32}S^{18}O_2{}^-$) with 2ϕ being allowed to vary so as to minimize the differences between calculated and experimental frequencies. The value obtained for 2ϕ was $110\pm5°$.

An alternative is to use the Allavena approach.[12] The ν_3 isotopic data allow the calculation of the following angles:

$$2\phi_1 = 108°, \; 2\phi_u = 110°$$

Thus the species $SO_2{}^-$ appears well established as having a bond angle very close to $109°$.

2.2 $SrCl_2$ and $MgCl_2$

These are two of very many Group IIA halides that have been formed in matrices by condensation from a furnace with an excess of the matrix gas. The interest is in establishing whether such species are linear or bent and, if the latter, the bond angle. These data can then be compared with those derived from gas phase electric deflection experiments. The observation of a band assigned to ν_1 in the infrared spectrum of $SrCl_2$ is already evidence of a bent structure, but White et al.[15] have obtained data for ν_3 and ν_1 for all possible ^{86}Sr, ^{88}Sr, ^{35}Cl and ^{37}Cl species. Thus, $2\phi_u$ and $2\phi_1$ can immediately be estimated from the ν_3 data for the symmetrically substituted species;

$$2\phi_u = 128° \; 16' \; (86/35\text{–}86/37); \; 123° \; 58' \; (88/35\text{–}88/37)$$
$$2\phi_1 = 110° \; 2' \; \; (86/35\text{–}88/35); \; 118° \; 36' \; (86/37\text{–}88/37)$$

Thus the average value of 2ϕ we calculate to be $119\pm9°$ with a slightly worse error than the authors claim. (Previous workers[16] had obtained $130°$ on the basis of Cl isotopic work alone, which as we have seen gives only an upper estimate.) With this value of 2ϕ, force constants can be estimated and theoretical spectra computed for all isotopic species. The agreement with experiment is very close.

The difficulties of the simple approach via R_λ when $2\phi \approx 180°$ are illustrated by the same authors[15] for $MgCl_2$; that the molecule is not substantially bent is shown by the absence of any band attributable to ν_1 in the infrared spectrum.

Band	$^{24}Mg^{35}Cl_2$	$^{25}Mg^{35}Cl_2$	$^{26}Mg^{35}Cl_2$
ν_3/cm^{-1}	590.03	580.98	573.09

(The ν_3 band of $Mg^{37}Cl_2$ is too weak to be observed.) The pairs $^{24}Mg^{35}Cl_2/$ $^{25}Mg^{35}Cl_2$ and $^{24}Mg^{35}Cl_2/^{26}Mg^{35}Cl_2$ provide two estimates for $2\phi_1$ of $155°$

and $2\sin^{-1}$ (1.0450) respectively. The bond angle, however, is indeed shown to be very near to 180° by the correspondingly good fit of observed and calculated frequencies via a force field analysis. It is worth mentioning that, in the force field analysis, the high frequency approximation can be used with considerable success because ν_1 and ν_2 are very well separated.

2.3 SnO₂

Another linear molecule, SnO_2, was obtained by Ogden and co-workers[17] by co-condensing a stream of tin atoms with a gas stream of N_2 or Kr doped with $\approx 10\%$ O_2. The isotopic pattern of bands in the 850 cm^{-1} region (Fig. 2)

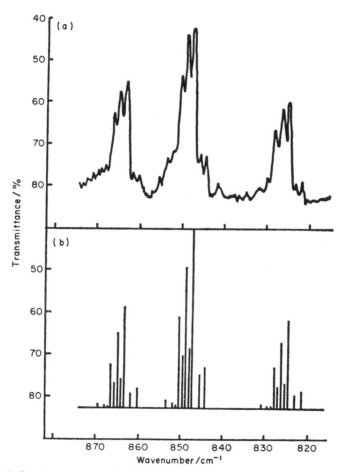

Fig. 2. (a) Infrared spectrum obtained on co-condensing Sn atoms with ^{18}O-enriched Kr (90% Kr, 2.2% $^{16}O_2$, 5.3% $^{16}O^{18}O$ and 2.5% $^{18}O_2$). (b) Calculated spectrum. (Ogden *et al.*, Ref. 17.)

clearly shows that the species contain one tin atom and two oxygen atoms (but see later). Detailed analysis shows convincingly that SnO_2 is linear but it is interesting to use the ν_3 data again to illustrate the difficulties which arise when $\phi \approx 180°$.

Band/cm^{-1}	$^{116}Sn^{16}O_2$	$^{124}Sn^{16}O_2$	$^{116}Sn^{18}O_2$
ν_3 (N_2 matrix)	881.0	874.8	841.6

From the first pair, $2\phi_1 = 2\sin^{-1}(1.0035)$, and from the first and third species, $2\phi_u = 164°$.

2.4 GeH₂

In some elegant photochemical studies of germane and deuterogermanes, Smith and Guillory[18] have obtained convincing infrared evidence for GeH_3 and GeH_2. However, GeH_2 is a further example for which all the difficulties of obtaining an accurate bond angle are present. There are no germanium isotopic data, anharmonicities are probably large due to the presence of the light H atom, M_{Ge}/M_H is large, and 'matrix perturbations' (cf. HCN) may be substantial. In spite of several different ways of attempting to handle the data the authors conclude that a reliable bond angle cannot be determined from their experiments.

3 INTENSITIES

Since we shall be making considerable use of intensity measurements to determine the detailed structures of metal carbonyls, it is appropriate to examine why quantitative considerations are of very limited use for determining structures for bent XY_2. In principle, since ν_1 is i.r.-inactive for linear XY_2 but active for bent XY_2, the ratio of the intensities of symmetric to asymmetric stretching vibrations for bent XY_2 might be expected to be a means of calculating the bond angle.

Assuming both mechanical and electrical harmonicity (the 'double-harmonic' approximation), the intensity of an i.r. band is given by[19]

$$I_k \propto \sum_g \left(\frac{\partial \mu_g}{\partial Q_k}\right)_0^2 \tag{11}$$

($g = x, y, z$; $(\partial \mu_g / \partial Q_k)_0$ is the change in molecular dipole moment, with normal coordinate Q_k, along the gth molecule-fixed axis, all other Q's held constant and the value determined with all Q (including Q_k) at their equilibrium values).

Since symmetry coordinates (S), normal coordinates (Q), and internal co-ordinates (R) are related by

$$S = L Q \quad \text{and} \quad R = U^{-1} S$$

$$I_k \propto \left[\sum_i L_{ik} \left(\frac{\partial \mu_g}{\partial S_i} \right)_0 \right]^2 \tag{12}$$

Then

$$I_k \propto \left[\sum_i \sum_j L_{ik} U_{ij} \left(\frac{\partial \mu_g}{\partial R_j} \right)_0 \right]^2 \tag{13}$$

For a bent XY_2 molecule the three symmetry coordinates are

$$S_1 = \frac{1}{\sqrt{2}} (\Delta r_1 + \Delta r_2)$$

$$S_2 = \Delta \phi$$

$$S_3 = \frac{1}{\sqrt{2}} (\Delta r_1 - \Delta r_2)$$

where Δr represents a change in bond length and $\Delta \phi$ a change in ϕ. All terms involving μ_y are zero (the molecule lying in the xz plane with z being the symmetry axis) and clearly, because of the symmetry, the only derivatives involving internal coordinates are

$$\frac{\partial \mu_z}{\partial \Delta r_1} \left(\equiv \frac{\partial \mu_z}{\partial \Delta r_2} \right), \frac{\partial \mu_z}{\partial \phi}, \text{ and } \frac{\partial \mu_x}{\partial \Delta r_1} \left(\equiv -\frac{\partial \mu_x}{\partial \Delta r_2} \right)$$

If we can now assume that $\partial \mu_z / \partial \Delta r_1$ and $\partial \mu_x / \partial \Delta r_1$ are the components in the z and x directions of $\partial \mu / \partial \Delta r_1$ along the X—Y bond then the derivatives are

$$\frac{\partial \mu}{\partial \Delta r_1} \cos \phi \left(\equiv \frac{\partial \mu}{\partial \Delta r_2} \cos \phi \right), \frac{\partial \mu_z}{\partial \phi} \text{ and } \frac{\partial \mu}{\partial \Delta r_1} \sin \phi \left(\equiv -\frac{\partial \mu_x}{\partial \Delta r_2} \sin \phi \right)$$

Since Q_3 involves only S_3, I_3 depends on $\partial \mu / \partial \Delta r$ and ϕ; Q_1 and Q_2 each involve S_1 and S_2 so I_1 and I_2 depend on $\partial \mu / \partial \Delta r$, $\partial \mu / \partial \phi$, ϕ, and the degree of mixing between S_1 and S_2 in the normal coordinates (i.e. the four L matrix components).

In matrix experiments it is generally impossible to measure absolute intensities because the total amount of compound in the matrix is unknown. Thus we have for bent XY_2, *two* experimentally determinable intensity ratios I_3/I_1 and I_3/I_2 (or, say, $I_3/(I_1 + I_2)$ and $I_1/(I_1 + I_2)$), and *seven* unknowns.

There are, however, the well-known relationships[19]

$$\sum_k I_k \propto \sum_{i,j} \frac{\partial \mu}{\partial S_i} \frac{\partial \mu}{\partial S_j} G_{ij}$$

$$\sum_k \frac{I_k}{\lambda_k} \propto \sum_{i,j} \frac{\partial \mu}{\partial S_i} \frac{\partial \mu}{\partial S_j} F_{ij}^{-1} \tag{14}$$

(where the sums extend over all vibrations belonging to the same symmetry species). These do not really help; for instance, suppose we don't know the force field and hence the L vectors, we can obtain $(I_1 + I_2)$ as a function only of the dipole moment derivative and structure (ϕ) but we now only have effectively *one* observable $(I_3/(I_1 + I_2))$ which is independent of the force field, and there are still three unknowns.

Moreover, even if we knew the four L matrix elements (which means that the structural problem would have been solved already as ϕ is required to calculate the G matrix) we still have only two observables and the three unknowns, $\partial\mu/\partial\Delta r$, $\partial\mu/\partial\phi$, and ϕ.

Any progress, therefore, depends on making even more assumptions. If, for XY_2, the symmetric stretch (ν_1) and bend (ν_2) are completely uncoupled, then ϕ may be determined: I_1 will depend only on $\partial\mu/\partial\Delta r$ and ϕ, and the ratio I_3/I_1 will depend only on ϕ, since $\partial\mu/\partial\Delta r$ will cancel out. It is not perhaps surprising that the method has not been widely applied, but it is instructive to look at the approximation in some detail.

3.1   Double Harmonic Approximation

This assumes that in the expansions

$$\mu_g = \mu_g^0 + \sum_k \left(\frac{\partial\mu_g}{\partial Q_k}\right)_0 Q_k + \left[\frac{1}{2}\sum_{k,l}\left(\frac{\partial^2\mu_g}{\partial Q_k\partial Q_l}\right)_0 Q_k Q_l + \frac{1}{6}\sum_{k,l,m}\left(\frac{\partial^3\mu_g}{\partial Q_k\partial Q_l\partial Q_m}\right)_0 Q_k Q_l Q_m\right]$$

and   (15)

$$V = \frac{1}{2}\sum_{i,j}\left(\frac{\partial^2 V}{\partial Q_i\partial Q_j}\right)_0 Q_i Q_j + \left[\frac{1}{6}\sum_{i,j,k}\frac{\partial^3 V}{\partial Q_i\partial Q_j\partial Q_k}Q_i Q_j Q_k + \ldots\right]$$ (16)

all the square-bracketed terms can be ignored. The intensities of fundamentals, overtones, and combination bands involve such integrals as $\langle\psi_i|\mu_g|\psi_j\rangle$. In the double harmonic approximation the fundamental occurs in first order and overtones (O) and combination bands (C) do not occur at all. O and C bands derive from either 'Q^2' terms in μ, or 'Q^3' terms in V (or both). However, if the vibration is mechanically harmonic but electrically *an*harmonic, the 'Q^2' terms in μ do not contribute to the intensity of the fundamental; if the vibration is mechanically *an*harmonic but electrically harmonic the 'Q^3' terms in V do not contribute to the fundamental intensity either. A contribution to the intensity of the fundamental can only arise from 'Q^3' terms in μ *or* 'Q^4' terms in V *or* 'Q^2' terms in μ *plus* 'Q^3' terms in V. That is, if the intensity of the fundamental (double harmonic approximation) occurs in *first* order, the O and C bands occur in *second* order, and the *an*harmonic contributions to the fundamental intensity occur only in *third* order.

Thus, considering the coefficients of the contributions to the intensity from the various terms, the double harmonic approximation for fundamentals is usually a good one, particularly where overtone and combination bands are weak. For metal carbonyls the O and C bands associated with the CO stretching vibrations are $<1/100$ of the intensity of the corresponding fundamentals and the approximation is likely to be very good. This point is discussed at length elsewhere.[20]

3.2 Contribution from Rotation

This has, so far, been tacitly ignored. In fact it can be very important and has been elegantly discussed by Overend,[19] and other approaches have been discussed by Person and Steele.[21]

In going from Eqn (11) to Eqn (13) in the reduction of infrared intensity from a normal to an internal coordinate basis it is assumed that Q_k involves *only* the $(3N-6)$ internal coordinates of the molecule. In fact, of course, many vibrations involve rotation. For example, in XY_2 the atomic displacements for ν_3 cannot be described in terms of bond stretching alone (Fig. 3) but require a partial

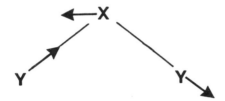

Fig. 3. Motion of X and Y atoms during the asymmetric X—Y stretching vibration of an XY₂ molecule showing the rotational contribution.

rotation of the molecule. This has to be included to keep the mass centre of the molecule unchanged on vibration. In general, the rotational motion involved in the real description of a normal coordinate can contribute to the intensity of the absorption if (a) the molecule has a permanent dipole moment, (b) the symmetry species of the vibration is the same as that of a rotation of the molecule which moves this permanent dipole. Before calculating bond angles from band intensities this rotational contribution must be subtracted. It can be surprisingly large. For instance,[19] for the 'CF$_2$ rock' of CH$_2$CF$_2$ the rotational contribution is *greater* than the vibrational contribution. This means that, since the molecular centre of mass is near the carbon atom of the CF$_2$ group, the real motion is not really a 'CF$_2$ rock' but a rocking of the rest of the molecule.

For the kind of simple molecules studied in matrices, this correction could therefore be quite large and, since its estimation depends on the moment of inertia and hence the geometry, we have a circuitous situation with respect to structure determination. It should be noted that this correction is totally unconnected with the overall rotation of the molecule described (for the linear molecule) in terms of the parameters B and J.

Where the molecules are large and hence have large moments of inertia this correction will be very small and almost certainly less than the errors involved in measuring the intensities.

3.3 Bond Dipole Moment Changes

It may be invalid to assume that, for example in XY_2, $\partial\mu/\partial\Delta r$ is collinear with the X—Y bond and that an incorrect bond angle would therefore be calculated. This point is considered in detail by Person and Steele[21] in their excellent review of infrared intensities. How bad the assumption is depends on the system under consideration. For a large number of metal carbonyl compounds the evidence suggests[20] that any deviation is small, but for some other systems the deviations are large.[21]

3.4 Force Field Approximation

There has been considerable interest[22] in molecules of type MA_2 where M is a metal and A_2 can be O_2, N_2 or even CO. These species can be prepared by co-condensation of M with A_2 or A_2/argon mixtures. One structural question relating to such molecules is whether the ligand is bonded sideways, with the A's equivalent, or end-on.

$$M<\begin{matrix} A \\ | \\ A \end{matrix}$$

Isotope intensity patterns (Section 4) can be of great help in deciding between these alternatives, but some care is needed. For example, for $Cu(O_2)_2$, Ogden's[23] isotopic data are consistent with a sideways-bonded species but the O—O stretching vibrations are *very* intense. It is difficult to see how this can be reconciled with a sideways model. The observations contrast with those for LiO_2,[24] where the isotope pattern also suggests sideways O_2 but for which the O—O stretch is very weak.

4   ISOTOPIC FREQUENCY AND INTENSITY PATTERNS

Since structural deductions are most reliable when based on complete force fields there has been extensive use of isotopic results to provide such data. Recently, for example, Müller and co-workers[25] have examined in great detail matrix infrared data for tetrahedral molecules (e.g. $SnCl_4$) and have obtained very complete force fields. Asymmetric isotopic substitution is often of value. To consider a trivial example: in linear XY_2, ν_1 is infrared-inactive and ν_2 and ν_3 are not coupled, being of different symmetry. Symmetric substitution provides no new information, so from the two observables two of the three force constants

(f_r and f_{rr}) cannot be separately determined. Asymmetric substitution activates ν_1 which can then couple with ν_3 (both modes transform as Σ^+ in the $C_{\infty v}$ point group) to give more information and the ready determination of f_{rr} and f_r.

The frequencies of all the isotopic molecules can obviously be calculated if the molecular structure and the force field are known, but simply the pattern of bands can often give valuable information. The isotopic frequency sum and product rules[19] link the frequencies of parent and substituted molecules. As an example consider again a bent XY_2 system. For the harmonic frequencies the rules simplify to:

$$\frac{\bar{\lambda}_3(\overline{XY}_2)}{\lambda_3(XY_2)} = \left[\frac{\bar{M}_Y M_Y}{\bar{M}_X \bar{M}_Y}\right]\left[\frac{(\bar{M}_X + 2\bar{M}_Y \sin^2 \phi)}{(M_X + 2M_Y \sin^2 \phi)}\right] \tag{17}$$

$$\frac{\bar{\lambda}_1\bar{\lambda}_2\ (\overline{XY}_2)}{\lambda_1\lambda_2\ (XY_2)} = \frac{M_Y^2 M_X(\bar{M}_X + 2\bar{M}_Y)}{\bar{M}_Y^2 \bar{M}_X(M_X + 2M_Y)} \tag{18}$$

$$\lambda_3(XY_2) + \lambda_3(\overline{XY}_2) = \lambda_3(\overline{X}Y_2) + \lambda_3(X\overline{Y}_2) \tag{19}$$

$$(\lambda_1 + \lambda_2)\,(XY_2) + (\lambda_1 + \lambda_2)\,(\overline{XY}_2) = (\lambda_1 + \lambda_2)\,(\overline{X}Y_2) + (\lambda_1 + \lambda_2)\,(X\overline{Y}_2) \tag{20}$$

and with asymmetric substitution, since ν_1, ν_2 and ν_3 may now mix together,

$$\frac{\lambda_1\lambda_2\lambda_3(XY\overline{Y})}{\lambda_1\lambda_2\lambda_3(XY_2)} = \frac{M_X M_Y(M_X + M_Y + \bar{M}_Y)^2(M_X + \bar{M}_Y)}{M_X \bar{M}_Y(M_X + 2M_Y)^2(2M_Y)} \tag{21}$$

$$(\lambda_1 + \lambda_2 + \lambda_3)\,(XY_2) + (\lambda_1 + \lambda_2 + \lambda_3)\,(X\overline{Y}_2) = 2(\lambda_1 + \lambda_2 + \lambda_3)\,(XY\overline{Y}) \tag{22}$$

LiO_2 illustrates well the application of these relationships. By co-condensation of lithium atoms and oxygen (or O_2/Ar mixtures), Andrews[24] has provided detailed and convincing evidence for molecular LiO_2 with overall C_{2v} symmetry. Thus this is a rather unusual example of the XY_2 class.

The ^{16}O, ^{18}O isotopic intensity pattern shows a 1:2:1 triplet suggesting that the oxygen atoms are equivalent (but see later). This is confirmed by the detailed force-field analysis which is consistent with $Li^+ (O-O)^-$. We can use the isotopic data for ν_3 as before to estimate upper and lower limits for 2ϕ.

Band	$^{16}O^6Li^{16}O$	$^{16}O^7Li^{16}O$	$^{18}O^6Li^{18}O$
ν_3/cm^{-1}	507.3	492.4	492.0

These data lead to the result $48° > 2\phi > 42°$ which compares with Andrews' value of $45° \pm 3°$.

With the wealth of isotopic data available for $LiO_2(^6Li, ^7Li, ^{16}O, ^{18}O)$ Andrews has performed extensive product-rule calculations using the relationships given above for various assumed geometries and the best agreement is obtained with $2\phi = 44.1°$ and a Li—O distance of 177 pm.

To distinguish between (a) M—A—A and (b) $M\diagdown\!\!\!\diagup\begin{smallmatrix}A\\|\\A\end{smallmatrix}$ the isotopic pattern derived from A_2, $A\overline{A}$ and $\overline{A}_2$ will obviously be of help since a given molecular vibration should occur at a different frequency for M—A—$\overline{A}$ and for M—$\overline{A}$—A, whereas it will occur at the same frequency for $M\diagdown\!\!\!\diagup\begin{smallmatrix}\overline{A}\\|\\A\end{smallmatrix}$ and $M\diagdown\!\!\!\diagup\begin{smallmatrix}A\\|\\A\end{smallmatrix}$. This situation has been demonstrated by Ozin[26] in work on MN_2 complexes. Figure 4 shows clearly the $1:1:1:1$ pattern for $\nu(NN)$ of $Rh^{14}N^{14}N$, $Rh^{14}N^{15}N$, $Rh^{15}N^{14}N$, $Rh^{15}N^{15}N$ units, thus demonstrating that the nitrogen atoms are inequivalent and therefore that the N_2 is probably bonded end-on in this rhodium complex.

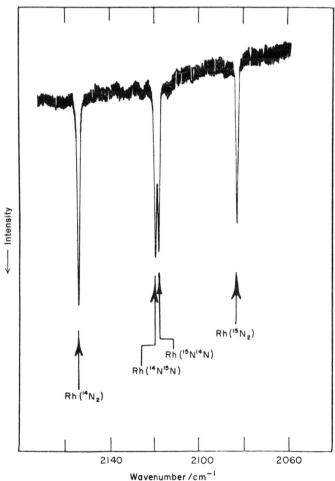

Fig. 4. The matrix infrared spectrum of the products of the co-condensation reaction of Rh atoms with $^{14}N_2:^{14}N^{15}N:^{15}N_2:Ar \approx 1:2:1:2000$ at 10 K. (Ozin and Van der Voet, Ref. 26.)

The converse is not necessarily true. Under the high frequency approximation, where the vibrations of the A—A bonds are assumed to be totally uncoupled from the other vibrations of the molecule, the A—A stretching bands of M—A—Ā and M—Ā—A should occur at the same frequency. The splitting of the band into a doublet is a second-order effect and it is possible for the splitting to be substantially less than the halfwidth of the infrared bands, and hence to escape detection. This argument was used by Darling et al.[23] to explain the absence of a splitting in the isotopic band of $Cu(O_2)_2$, even though the O_2 is apparently bonded end-on.

Is any useful information obtained from a comparison of the intensities of various bands of molecules of different isotopic composition? In Section 3 we noted that

$$\sum_k \frac{I_k}{\lambda_k} = \sum_{ij} \frac{\partial \mu}{\partial S_i} \frac{\partial \mu}{\partial S_j} F_{ij}^{-1} \tag{23}$$

Both F^{-1} and $\partial \mu / \partial S$ are isotopically invariant (provided of course the symmetrized F^{-1} matrix is constructed from symmetry coordinates appropriate to the isotopic molecule with the lowest symmetry). Therefore $\sum I_k / \lambda_k$ is isotopically invariant, and this intensity sum rule is analogous to the frequency product rule.[19] (There is also a further relationship analogous to the frequency sum rule.[27])

The value of these relationships is illustrated by a comparison of the infrared spectra of SnO_2[17] and UO_2.[4] Figure 5 shows schematically the matrix infrared spectra of these species.

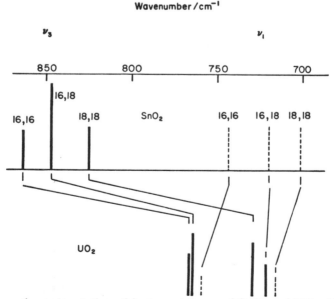

Fig. 5. Schematic representation of isotope patterns of SnO₂ and UO₂. (Ogden and co-workers, Ref. 17 and Gabelnick et al., Ref. 4 respectively.)

In order to include $^{16}OM^{18}O$ in the sums we must consider *all* the isotopic linear molecules to have the low symmetry $C_{\infty v}$ so that

$$\frac{I_3}{\lambda_3}(16, 16) + \frac{I_1}{\lambda_1}(16, 16)\ (=0)$$

$$= \frac{I_3}{\lambda_3}(18, 18) + \frac{I_1}{\lambda_1}(18, 18)\ (=0)$$

$$= \frac{I_3}{\lambda_3}(16, 18) + \frac{I_1}{\lambda_1}(16, 18) \equiv \frac{I_3}{\lambda_3}(18, 16) + \frac{I_1}{\lambda_1}(18, 16)$$

It will be clear from Fig. 5 that the intensities of the infrared-active bands of both SnO_2 and UO_2 qualitatively obey these sum rules (and more detailed measurements confirm this quantitatively), thus greatly assisting the band assignment for UO_2. One striking point is that the characteristic $1:2:1$ pattern for the infrared-active bands of the equivalent oxygen atoms in SnO_2 is not repeated in UO_2. This is obviously a consequence of the force field and of the large mass of the uranium atom. Gabelnick et al.[4] have neatly shown how the $I_3(16, 18):I_1(16, 18)$ ratio can be estimated from the eigenvectors obtained from a full analysis. For $^{16}OU^{18}O$,

$$Q_1 = 0.04\,\Delta r_1 + 0.34\,\Delta r_2$$
$$Q_3 = 0.36\,\Delta r_1 - 0.06\,\Delta r_2$$

i.e. the ^{16}OU and $U^{18}O$ halves are almost decoupled vibrationally from each other. Using the assumptions about intensity comparisons made before, we calculate

$$\frac{I(\lambda_3)}{I(\lambda_1)} = \frac{\left(0.36\,\dfrac{\partial\mu}{\partial\Delta r_1} - 0.06\,\dfrac{\partial\mu}{\partial\Delta r_2}\right)^2}{\left(0.04\,\dfrac{\partial\mu}{\partial\Delta r_1} + 0.34\,\dfrac{\partial\mu}{\partial\Delta r_2}\right)^2} \qquad (24)$$

However, $\partial\mu/\partial\Delta r_1$ and $\partial\mu/\partial\Delta r_2$ can be rewritten in terms of $S_1\ [\equiv(1/\sqrt{2})(\Delta r_1 + \Delta r_2)]$ and $S_3[\equiv(1/\sqrt{2})(\Delta r_1 - \Delta r_2)]$; the normal coordinates become

$$Q_1 = a_1(\Delta r_1 + \Delta r_2) + b_1(\Delta r_1 - \Delta r_2) = 0.19(\Delta r_1 + \Delta r_2) - 0.15(\Delta r_1 - \Delta r_2)$$
$$Q_3 = a_3(\Delta r_1 + \Delta r_2) + b_3(\Delta r_1 - \Delta r_2) = 0.15(\Delta r_1 + \Delta r_2) + 0.21(\Delta r_1 - \Delta r_2)$$

The coefficients a and b have been normalized in the sense that $L\tilde{L} = G$, and thus

$$\frac{I_3}{I_1} = \frac{\left(0.15\,\dfrac{\partial\mu}{\partial S_1} + 0.21\,\dfrac{\partial\mu}{\partial S_3}\right)^2}{\left(0.19\,\dfrac{\partial\mu}{\partial S_1} - 0.15\,\dfrac{\partial\mu}{\partial S_3}\right)^2} \qquad (25)$$

which, since $\partial\mu/\partial S_1 = 0$ gives $I_3/I_1 = 1.96$, in good agreement with the experimental value of 1.84. The reason for this agreement is that the approximations discussed in Section 3 are valid. The double harmonic approximation is generally reliable; the dipole moment changes associated with ν_3 and ν_1 *have* to be collinear. The force field is known and there needs to be no assumption about uncoupled vibrations. Thus in these terms it is clearly seen that I_3/I_1 for SnO_2 $\approx \infty$ because the form of ν_1 is almost exactly S_1; hence the denominator of Eqn 25 is zero for SnO_2.

5   APPLICATION TO TRANSITION METAL CARBONYLS AND RELATED SPECIES

The study of transition metal carbonyls in matrices is interesting for two reasons; first, these compounds have an extensive photochemistry[28,29] and the matrix isolation method provides an excellent means of studying primary photo-chemical processes; secondly, there is a growing interest in the bonding in these compounds, and the unsaturated carbonyl fragments produced in matrices have proved to be excellent tests of rival molecular orbital models.[30-32] The aim, in either case, is to determine the structures of carbonyl fragments, and in this section we describe the basic strategies for, and pitfalls of, such structural determinations.

There are two aspects of the problem. For species expected to have high symmetry one is seeking to distinguish between possible structures, a classic example being whether $Pd(CO)_4$ is tetrahedral or square planar. In such a case *qualitative* arguments *may* suffice, viz. isotopic patterns of intensity and frequency and infrared/Raman selection rules and Raman polarization data. On the other hand, we may wish to determine the bond angles of a fragment which is not highly symmetrical—the infrared spectrum of $Fe(CO)_4$, for instance, shows that the molecule belongs *neither* to the T_d nor to the D_{4h} point group.[33] In this case we shall need quantitative arguments. In either case we need first to look at the force fields for these species in order to consider what simplifications are valid.

5.1   Force Field Calculations

The classic assumption in examining the very intense C—O bands of metal carbonyls is that the vibrations are completely uncoupled from the rest of the molecule.[34] The absence of 'mechanical' coupling means that the **G** matrix is diagonal and consists simply of terms in μ_{CO} (the inverse reduced mass of the CO group)*; the absence of 'potential' coupling means that, in the **F** matrix, only C—O stretching force constants and interaction constants between C—O stretching coordinates will be included. Isotopic substitution ($^{12}C^{16}O \rightarrow {}^{13}C^{16}O$

---

* This immediately shows that no quantitative structural data will be obtained from *the force field* since there are no terms involving bond angles (see Section 3). We shall need *intensities* for this.

or $^{12}C^{18}O$) produces a complex pattern which is analysed by the usual Wilson GF method* following the pioneering work of Haas and Sheline,[35] Darling and Ogden,[36] and others.[37] The most striking aspect is the numerical fit of the ν_{CO} isotope band frequencies (and intensities—see below).

Consider first, however, some general points. Transition metal carbonyl compounds are excellent molecules for matrix isolation. They are, in general, highly volatile ($Ni(CO)_4$ boils at about 42 °C, and even $Os_3(CO)_{12}$ can be readily sublimed under vacuum) and have intense u.v. and i.r. bands. This allows very dilute matrices (carbonyl:matrix, $1:10^4$ or $1:10^5$) to be used, thus avoiding the possibility of dimer formation, while maintaining a high spectral signal-to-noise ratio. The compounds have high quantum yields for loss of CO which means that large quantities of unstable molecules can be generated by even a brief photolysis. Their chief drawback is that they are poor Raman scatterers, and can easily be photolysed by a laser beam.

Two contrasting methods have been used to generate unstable carbonyl fragments; the photochemical destruction of stable carbonyls[10,38] and the co-condensation of metal atoms and carbon monoxide which react together in the matrix.[22] Although both methods have their advantages and drawbacks, the basic problem of assigning a structure to a particular carbonyl is the same, namely that the number of infrared-active C—O stretching bands is rarely unique to a particular structure. For example, $Cr(CO)_4CS$ with four infrared-active bands could have either a square pyramidal (C_s) or a trigonal bipyramidal (C_{2v}) structure.[39] Alternatively, one band may be too weak to be observed (e.g. as in the case of $Fe(CO)_4$,[33]) or a band may be split into several components by 'matrix effects' (e.g. as in the case of $Mo(CO)_3$[40]). Thus, it is essential to have additional spectroscopic data before a unique structural assignment can be made. In principle, this extra information could be obtained from the Raman spectra of the fragment but the poor scattering and high photosensitivity of the molecules often makes it impossible to record such spectra. There has been some success in obtaining spectra of fragments synthesized from metal atoms, notably $Co(CO)_4$[41]; this will be discussed below.

For the majority of fragments, the additional information is provided by the infrared spectra of species containing isotopically enriched carbon monoxide, ^{13}CO or $C^{18}O$. Let us consider a specific example: $Fe(^{12}CO)_3$ has two bands[42] (at 2040.1 and 1930.4 cm^{-1}) which may be assigned to C—O stretching fundamentals of different symmetry species. This carbonyl may be made by photolysis of matrix-isolated $Fe(CO)_5$ via $Fe(CO)_4$. The spectrum of $Fe(^{13}CO)_3$ will provide no additional information since the frequencies of its bands will be directly related to those of $Fe(^{12}CO)_3$ by the relative reduced masses of ^{12}CO and ^{13}CO. On the other hand, $Fe(^{12}CO)_2(^{13}CO)$ and $Fe(^{12}CO)(^{13}CO)_2$ have lower symmetry than the parent molecule and they will thus give rise to more bands and

---

* When the eigenvalues of GF are determined using computer methods it is simpler to diagonalize $G^{1/2}FG^{1/2}$ rather than GF. $G^{1/2}FG^{1/2}$ is necessarily symmetric (Ref. 35) while GF is not, and this fact greatly simplifies the matrix diagonalization.

extra data with which to fix the geometry and force field (see Fig. 6). It is essential that the isotopically different carbon monoxide molecules be 'scrambled', if the experiment is to do anything more than confirm that the compound contains CO. In atom experiments, this scrambling is achieved by simply co-condensing the metal atoms with the appropriate mixture of ^{12}CO and ^{13}CO,[22] while in

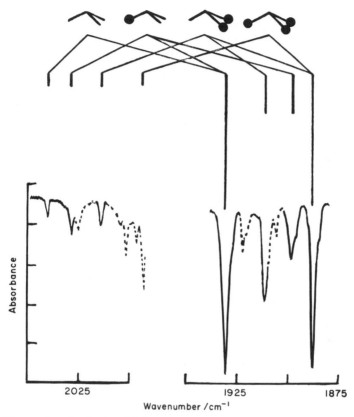

Fig. 6. Observed and calculated infrared spectra for a mixture of $Fe(^{12}CO)_{3-x}(^{13}CO)_x$ molecules ($x = 0$–3) in a CH_4 matrix at 20 K. Band intensities are calculated for a C_{3v} M(CO)₃ fragment with a bond angle of 109.4°. Bands drawn in broken lines are due to Fe(CO)₅ and Fe(CO)₄. The black circles represent ^{13}CO molecules.

photolysis experiments it is necessary partially to enrich the stable carbonyl precursor, in this case Fe(CO)₅. Fortunately, most carbonyls can usually be enriched by photolysis under an atmosphere of ^{13}CO in the gas phase or in solution.[43] $Fe(^{12}CO)_3$ has two infrared-active bands assignable to C—O stretching fundamentals; this eliminates a planar (D_{3h}) structure, which should give rise to only one infrared-active band (e'), and leaves a pyramidal (C_{3v}) structure (cf. NH₃) which has two infrared-active bands ($a_1 + e$) and a series of structures of lower symmetry, for example a T-shaped (C_{2v}) structure (cf. ClF_3) with three infrared-active bands, $2a_1 + e$. Let us consider the pyramidal C_{3v} geometry and apply the frequency-factored force field. Since all the C—O groups are equivalent, there will be one C—O stretching force constant, f_{CO}, and one interaction constant, $f_{CO,CO}$. In this case, all the matrices will be 3×3. (In general, for $M(CO)_n$ the matrices will be $n \times n$). The $\mathbf{F}$ matrix has diagonal terms, f_{CO}, and off-diagonal terms, $f_{CO,CO}$.

The two force constants, f_{CO} and $f_{CO,CO}$, can be calculated from the two frequencies of $Fe(^{12}CO)_3$ and can then be used to predict the frequencies of the three isotopically substituted molecules. Once the bands have been assigned to the appropriate isotopic molecule, a 'least squares refinement' can be performed on the force constants to minimize the error between all the observed and calculated frequencies. The results of such a calculation are shown in Table 2, and it can be seen that the agreement is remarkably good.

It is perhaps worth considering why the fit should be so close when we have made the gross assumption that the C—O stretches are uncoupled from the other vibrations, and we have had to use anharmonic frequencies (i.e. observed ones). The reasons are more clearly understood by considering the rather simpler case of a monocarbonyl, M—CO, and *including* the coupling of the M—C and C—O stretches. In this case

$$\mathbf{F} = \begin{bmatrix} f_{MC} & f_{MC,CO} \\ f_{MC,CO} & f_{CO} \end{bmatrix} \quad \text{and} \quad \mathbf{G} = \begin{bmatrix} (\mu_M + \mu_C) & -\mu_C \\ -\mu_C & (\mu_C + \mu_O) \end{bmatrix} \tag{26}$$

TABLE 2
Wavenumber (cm⁻¹) of
^{13}CO-substituted [Fe(CO)₃] species
in CH₄ matrix at 20 K

Species	Observed	Calculated
[Fe(CO)₃]	2040.1	2039.8
	1930.4[b]	1930.1
[Fe(CO)₂(^{13}CO)]	2027.9	2028.1
	1930.4[b]	1930.1
	1897.9	1898.0
[Fe(CO)(^{13}CO)₂]	2013.9	2013.9
	1911.3	1911.3
	1887.1[b]	1887.1
[Fe(^{13}CO)₃]	[a]	1994.3
	1887.1[b]	1887.1

Average error in the wavenumbers is 0.007%;
$f_{CO} = 1562.7 \pm 0.2$ N m⁻¹;
$f_{CO,CO} = 58.6 \pm 0.2$ N m⁻¹.

[a] Region obscured by [Fe(CO)₄] band.
[b] Wavenumbers included once only in 'least squares' refinement, despite the fact that the fundamental is degenerate. Ref. 42.

where $\mu_X = 1/(\text{mass of atom X})$. Note that there are now non-zero off-diagonal terms in the **G** matrix since we have included mechanical coupling between M—C and C—O bonds. If the relationship between normal coordinates Q and internal coordinates R is written $\mathbf{R} = \mathbf{LQ}$ (in this example the symmetry and internal coordinates are identical) then the solution for the predominantly 'C—O stretching' mode (Q_2) can be written

$$\lambda_{CO} = \frac{L_{12}}{L_{22}} [f_{MC,CO}\, \mu_{CO} + (f_{MC,CO} - f_{MC})\, \mu_C] + [f_{CO}\, \mu_{CO} - f_{MC,CO}\, \mu_C] \tag{27}$$

Ozin and co-workers have recently synthesized the monocarbonyl CuCO by co-condensation of Cu atoms and CO in an argon matrix[44] and observed ν_{MC} at 320 cm^{-1} and ν_{CO} at 2010.4 cm^{-1}. From the isotopic frequencies, they have calculated $f_{CO} = 1667$ N m^{-1}, $f_{MC} = 117$ N m^{-1} and $f_{MC,CO} = 63$ N m^{-1}. Substituting these values in the equation above gives $L_{12}/L_{22} = -0.4$, which confirms that there is considerable mixing of the M—C and C—O stretches. The minus sign arises because the M—C bond is compressed as the C—O bond stretches, and the vibrations are necessarily out of phase to preserve the position of the centre of mass during the vibration. The contribution to λ_{CO} by terms containing f_{CO}, f_{MC} and $f_{MC,CO}$ can also be calculated.

$$\Sigma \text{ terms containing } f_{CO} = 243131 \text{ s}^{-2}.$$

$$\Sigma \text{ terms containing } f_{MC} \text{ and } f_{MC,CO} = -5014 \text{ s}^{-2}.$$

Thus the f_{MC} and $f_{MC,CO}$ contribution to λ_{CO} is only 2.1% of the terms containing f_{CO}, in spite of the substantial mixing of M—C and C—O stretches. Since ν_{CO} is proportional to the square root of λ_{CO}, the f_{MC} and $f_{MC,CO}$ contribution to ν_{CO} is only about 1%. Since this contribution to ν_{CO} is so small, slight changes in M—C coupling between different isotopic species will have little effect on the overall frequencies.

The effect of neglect of the M—C part of the molecule on the vibrational force constants and the role of the frequency-factored force field is readily seen by calculating the difference between the size of λ_{CO} calculated (a) using the GQVFF force constants describing the stretching modes (f_{MC}, $f_{MC,MC}^x$, f_{CO}, $f_{CO,CO}^x$, $f_{MC,CO}^x$ where $x = cis$ or $trans$) and (b) using the f_{CO} and $f_{CO,CO}^x$ of the GQVFF only. The results are shown in Table 3, using the anharmonic force constants for Cr(CO)$_6$ calculated by Jones et al.[45] where $\Gamma_{vib,CO} = t_{1u} + e_g + a_{1g}$. It is clear that, as in the monocarbonyl case, λ_{CO} is determined to within about 3% by the terms f_{CO} and $f_{CO,CO}$ alone. However, we also see that the difference between the values in the first and second columns depends markedly on the symmetry species of the vibration concerned. Thus the same values of the C—O stretching GQVFF constants cannot be used to fit *all three* symmetry modes in the frequency-factored force field approximation. The frequency-factored force constants for the three vibrations are[46]

$$
\left.
\begin{aligned}
F(a_{1g}) &= f_{CO} + f^t_{CO,CO} + 4f^c_{CO,CO} \\
F(e_g) &= f_{CO} + f^t_{CO,CO} - 2f^c_{CO,CO} \\
F(t_{1u}) &= f_{CO} - f^t_{CO,CO}
\end{aligned}
\right\}
\tag{28}
$$

where c refers to cis, and t to $trans$ CO groups.

TABLE 3
Force field parameters for Cr(CO)$_6$

Contributions to $\lambda_{CO}/10^5$ s^{-2}	$\Sigma f_{MC} + f_{MC,CO} + f_{CO}$ terms	Σf_{CO} terms	Difference
a_{1g}			
12/16	2.693 36	2.635 57	0.057 79
13/16	2.568 83	2.519 37	0.049 46
12/18	2.573 63	2.509 77	0.063 84
e_g			
12/16	2.473 76	2.460 54	0.013 22
13/16	2.360 22	2.352 07	0.008 15
12/18	2.362 66	2.343 10	0.019 56
t_{1u}			
12/16	2.453 45	2.510 13	-0.056 68
13/16	2.344 82	2.399 47	-0.054 65
12/18	2.337 32	2.390 32	-0.053 00

In order to describe the three C—O stretching modes with only these **three** force constants, corrections must be applied to the GQVFF force constants used above. The corrections are calculated from the series of differences in the last column of Table 3.

Isotope pair	Δf_{CO}/N m^{-1}	$\Delta f^c_{CO,CO}$/N m^{-1}	$\Delta f^t_{CO,CO}$/N m^{-1}
12/16	-9.81	5.09	29.06
13/16	-11.73	4.94	27.46
12/18	-6.72	5.32	31.44

For the Cr(^{12}C^{16}O)$_6$ molecule the new force constants become

Force field	f_{CO}/N m^{-1}	$f^c_{CO,CO}$/N m^{-1}	$f^t_{CO,CO}$/N m^{-1}
GQVFF	1674	21	22
corrected	1664	26	51

The corrected values are identical to the frequency-factored force constants calculated for this molecule from Eqns (28). Small changes are found in f_{CO} and $f^t_{CO,CO}$ with a much larger change in $f^c_{CO,CO}$. Thus, most of the errors of the frequency-factored force field are absorbed by the interaction force constants, principally the *trans* CO—CO interaction force constant. It is interesting to note that this force constant, which has the largest calculated errors,[37] changes most on going from matrix to solution. The precise values of these absorbed errors will depend on the geometry of the carbonyl molecule being analysed and the individual values of the GQVFF constants. Therefore, the force constants cannot be transferred from cne molecule to another of different geometry. We can immediately see that the corrections to f_r and f_{rr} increase in the order $^{12}C^{16}O < ^{13}C^{16}O < ^{12}C^{18}O$. This gives us a ready explanation of the apparently widespread observation that the differences between observed and calculated frequencies are generally larger for data obtained via $^{12}C^{18}O$ substitution of $M(^{12}C^{16}O)_n$ species than for $^{13}C^{16}O$ substitution.

The slightly different values of the corrected force constants, calculated for the three CO isotopes, also imply isotope shifts that are not exactly in the ratio of the square roots of the respective inverse reduced masses, as predicted on the basis of the frequency-factored force field,
e.g.

$$\frac{\nu_{^{13}CO}}{\nu_{^{12}CO}} \neq \left(\frac{\mu_{^{13}CO}}{\mu_{^{12}CO}}\right)^{\frac{1}{2}} \tag{29}$$

As Braterman[34] has pointed out this may be allowed for by use of an 'effective reduced mass' for the isotopic CO groups. His suggested value compared with the value calculated from atomic weights, and the difference in shift of a $(^{12}C^{16}O)$ carbonyl band at 2000 cm^{-1}, is given below.

Ratio	Calculated (**G** Matrix)	Effective (Braterman)	Shift (Eff. − Calc.)
$\left(\dfrac{\mu_{^{13}CO}}{\mu_{^{12}CO}}\right)^{\frac{1}{2}}$	0.977 71	0.977 28	$+0.86$ cm^{-1}
$\left(\dfrac{\mu_{C^{18}O}}{\mu_{C^{16}O}}\right)^{\frac{1}{2}}$	0.975 90	0.976 68	-1.56 cm^{-1}

From this it is clear that bands of the ^{13}CO-substituted molecule are shifted further ($+0.86$ cm^{-1}) than expected on the basis of the reduced mass ratio and those of the C^{18}O molecule less (-1.56 cm^{-1}). The exact shift depends on the details of the GQVFF for the molecule.

Anharmonic (i.e. observed) frequencies are used in such studies since, in general, anharmonicity constants are obviously not known for these (previously uncharacterized) fragments. There is evidence[47] that the anharmonic effects give rise to the need for another correction to the frequency-factored force constants from the 'true harmonic GQVFF' ones. Thus agreement between observed and calculated frequencies is found for parent and asymmetrically isotopically substituted molecules.[47]

A large number of isotopic CO spectra of matrix-isolated metal carbonyls has been analysed using the CO-factored force field. The molecules include $Cr(CO)_6$,[37] $Fe(CO)_4$,[33] $Ni(CO)_3^-$,[48] $Cr(CO)_5CS$,[39] etc., and in all cases the frequency fit has been of the order of 0.4 cm^{-1} or even better. Ozin and co-workers have carried out similar analyses of metal carbonyl dinitrogen complexes (e.g. $Ni(N_2)_2(CO)_2$)[50] and dinitrogen complexes (e.g. $Ni(N_2')_4$),[49] but with somewhat poorer agreement than that indicated above. It is not clear whether this reflects a genuine difference between the carbonyl and dinitrogen compounds or merely the difficulty in obtaining accurate data for the dinitrogen systems.

In these force constant calculations it is not merely the number of force constants which determines the symmetry of a molecule but also the way that these force constants are distributed in the F matrix. An $M(CO)_n$ species has n C—O stretching force constants and $n(n-1)/2$ interaction force constants, all of which would be different for a species with C_1 symmetry. It is by making some of these force constants the same that the symmetry is defined. Thus, although both C_{4v} and D_{3h} $M(CO)_5$ have five different force constants (two stretching and three interaction constants), completely different isotopic frequencies are calculated for them, because in the C_{4v} F matrix there are four equivalent and one unique CO group, but in the D_{3h} F matrix there are two distinguishable sets of equivalent CO groups containing two and three groups, respectively.[37]

Before leaving this section, it is worth stressing that the force constant calculations show the number of equivalent CO groups in a carbonyl species, and the highest *possible* symmetry of the molecule, provided that all interaction force constants are non-zero. Thus, the frequencies of the species $Pd(CO)_4$, prepared by Pd atom/CO co-condensation, could be fitted using only two force constants (one stretching and one interaction constant). The molecule was deduced to have a tetrahedral (T_d) geometry.[9] However, it would be indistinguishable from a square planar, D_{4h}, structure where the two interaction constants (f_{CO-CO}^c and f_{CO-CO}^t) happened to be equal, or any other lower symmetry structure, where a sufficient number of force constants were accidentally equal. As will be explained below, these structures are also indistinguishable from the point of view of intensity patterns of the isotopically enriched molecule. Furthermore, Raman spectra and polarization data are of no help either, since they are much less sensitive to molecular distortion than infrared spectra (see below). Thus, in all studies of matrix-isolated metal carbonyl fragments there is the tacit assumption that the species has the highest possible symmetry consistent with the observed spectra.

5.2 Band Intensities of Metal Carbonyls

From Section 3 we appear to have all the information we need to calculate the intensity of carbonyl bands. The double harmonic approximation is almost certainly a good one (but see later), the high-frequency separation of C—O stretches from the rest we have just seen to be an excellent approximation, and we have an accurate force field describing coupling between the CO groups. Moroever, the rotational correction to the intensity is close to zero. Thus, the intensity of a carbonyl band is expected to be given by

$$I_k \propto \left[\sum_i \sum_j L_{ik} U_{ij} \left(\frac{\partial \mu_g}{\partial R_j} \right)_0 \right]^2 \tag{30}$$

where the L_{ik} are taken from the frequency-factored force field, and the U_{ij} relate the symmetry coordinates to the internal coordinates R_j (which are simply changes in C—O bond length). Since the dipole moment change is probably not far from collinear with the C—O bond, $\partial \mu_g / \partial R_j$ can be expressed as $\partial \mu / \partial \Delta R_j$ $h(\theta, \phi)$ where $\partial \mu / \partial \Delta R_j$ is the change in dipole moment along the C—O bond with change in C—O displacement and the $h(\theta, \phi)$ represents the appropriate geometric correction to obtain the change in μ along x, y, z axes. If all the CO groups are chemically equivalent all the $\partial \mu / \partial \Delta R_j$ terms are identical and the intensity ratio will be independent of $\partial \mu / \partial \Delta R_j$ and depend only on the L vectors and bond angles. Darling's and Ogden's[36] calculations use exactly this model and hence predict the intensity patterns as well as frequency patterns of simple carbonyls with equivalent CO's.

By taking care about the percentage isotopic enrichment, the spectrum can be calculated by standard methods.[37] Figure 7 shows the fit of band intensities for a molecule known to have all CO groups equivalent, viz. $Cr(CO)_6$, and where the bond angles are known to be 90° and 180°. The fit is very encouraging. Figure 8 shows the fit for $Pd(CO)_4$, assumed to be tetrahedral, and which had been generated by co-condensation of Pd atoms with CO.[9] It should be stressed that this spectrum does not give any more structural information than the force constant calculations (q.v.) and the identical pattern would be predicted for a square planar D_{4h} geometry, or any D_{2d} structure, provided that the two interaction force constants were equal.

For $Fe(^{12}C^{16}O)_3$ the a_1 and e C—O stretches do not mix and we can estimate the bond angle from this intensity ratio without the need for data on isotopically different molecules*.

$$I_{a_1} \text{ (high frequency)} \propto 3 \left(\frac{\partial \mu}{\partial \Delta R} \right)^2 \mu_{CO} \cos^2 \theta$$

$$I_e \text{ (low frequency)} \propto 3 \left(\frac{\partial \mu}{\partial \Delta R} \right)^2 \mu_{CO} \sin^2 \theta$$

* In what follows μ_{CO} is the inverse reduced mass of the CO group and μ is the dipole moment.

whence

$$\frac{I_e}{I_{a_1}} = \tan^2 \theta \tag{31}$$

The observed intensity ratio[42] for $Fe(CO)_3$ was $8:1$ which gives a value of $\theta = 70.5°$, corresponding to a bond angle of $109.4°$. The value of the bond angle is relatively insensitive to errors in the intensity measurement. If we take an error of ± 2 in the ratio (twice the observed error), the value of θ only changes from $106.6°$ $(6:1)$ to $111.4°(10:1)$. There is, of course, a second solution

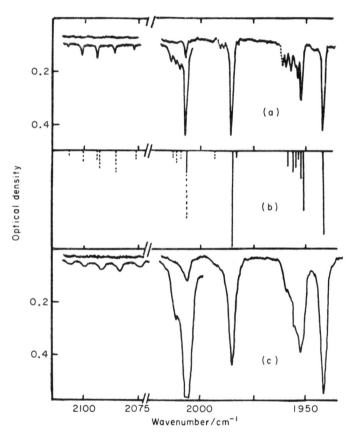

Fig. 7. (a) Spectrum of ^{13}CO-enriched $Cr(CO)_6$ in CH_4 at 20 K, after deposition of four pulses; 25 s photolysis with unfiltered Hg lamp, followed by 8 min photolysis with an Hg lamp and a $\lambda > 375$ nm filter. In the superimposed spectrum the quantity of $Cr(CO)_6$ has been increased approximately four times. Dotted bands at ≈ 1990 cm^{-1} are due to the small number of $Cr(CO)_6$ molecules still distorted; those at 1961 cm^{-1} are due to $Cr(CO)_5$. (b) Calculated spectrum for the O_h structure with $[^{13}CO]/[^{12}CO]$ $= 1$. The dotted spectrum represents a fourfold increase in the amount of $Cr(CO)_6$. (c) Spectrum of ^{13}CO-enriched $Cr(CO)_6$ in cyclohexane solution at 300 K; $[^{13}CO]/$ $[^{12}CO] = 1.14$. (Perutz and Turner, Ref. 37.)

corresponding to the negative value of the square root of Eqn (31), and this gives the same bond angle but with the molecule upside down!

Figure 6 shows the isotopic pattern for this fragment with the theoretical spectrum calculated for a C_{3v} pyramidal molecule with this bond angle. The overall intensity ratio of high frequency to low frequency bands is sensitive to the angle of depression from planar but within the low frequency region the pattern is almost insensitive to bond angle. Thus, in this case the *isotopic*

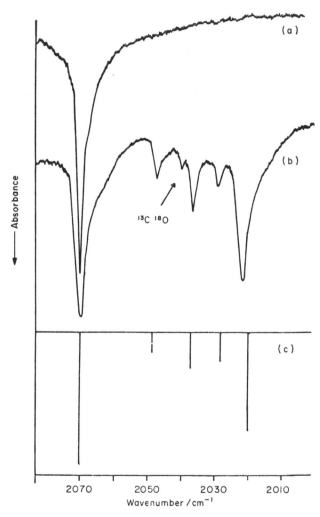

Fig. 8. (a) Infrared spectrum obtained from co-condensation of Pd atoms with Ar—$C^{16}O$ at 27 K. (b) Infrared spectrum obtained from co-condensation of Pd atoms with Ar—$C^{16}O$—$C^{18}O$ at 27 K. (c) Calculated spectrum for $Pd(C^{16}O)_n(C^{18}O)_{4-n}$ species. (Darling and Ogden, Ref. 9.)

intensity pattern really only confirms that the molecule has three equivalent CO's, and provides little further structural information.

Of course the use of carbonyl intensity ratios from isotopically pure molecules has been much used for estimating bond angles of stable substituted metal carbonyls.[51]

If the CO groups are not all equivalent a complication is introduced because $\partial\mu/\partial\Delta R$ will not then necessarily be the same for all groups. Consider a species such as $Mn(CO)_5Br$, $Cr(CO)_5NH_3$, or $Cr(CO)_5$ (matrix isolated), all having C_{4v} symmetry—four equatorial equivalent CO's and one axial CO. Suppose

$$\frac{\partial\mu}{\partial\Delta R}\text{(equatorial CO)} \equiv \mu'_{eq} \quad \text{and} \quad \frac{\partial\mu}{\partial\Delta R}\text{(axial CO)} \equiv \mu'_{ax}$$

A C_{4v} $M(CO)_5$ fragment has three infrared-active $(2a_1+e)$ and one infrared-inactive (b_1) CO stretching modes. If it is assumed that $\mu'_{ax} = \mu'_{eq}$, the equation corresponding to Eqn (32), is for this molecule

$$\frac{I_e}{I_{a_1\text{(total)}}} = \frac{4\sin^2\theta}{5-4\sin^2\theta} \tag{32}$$

i.e. the intensity ratio is independent of force field. This is simply a consequence of summing the intensities over all vibrations of the same symmetry type as in Eqn (14). The bond angle occurs in the equation because of the geometrical relationship between

$$\frac{\partial\mu_z}{\partial\Delta R}, \quad \frac{\partial\mu_x}{\partial\Delta R} \quad \text{and} \quad \frac{\partial\mu}{\partial\Delta R}$$

This ratio has a maximum value of 4 (when $\theta = 90°$), and a simple test of the

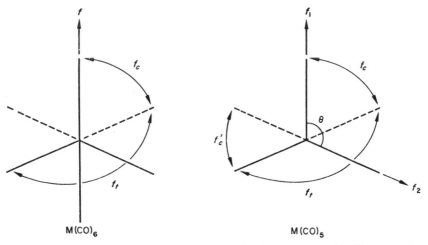

Fig. 9. Force constants for $M(CO)_6$ and an $M(CO)_5$ fragment with C_{4v} symmetry.

assumption is to see whether the observed ratios are greater than four. Although the ratios for $Mn(CO)_5Cl$ (2.08) and $Mn(CO)_5Br$ (1.74) in chloroform solution[52] lie well within the permitted range, the values for $Cr(CO)_5$ (5.3) and $W(CO)_5$ (4.9) in a CH_4 matrix[37] are considerably above the maximum. In matrix experiments one is fortunate in that the isotopic data provide 'accurate' frequency-factored force constants, and it is therefore relatively simple to calculate the L_{ik} values for the a_1 vibrations.

$$S_1 = aQ_1 (a_1 \text{ high}) + bQ_2(a_1 \text{ low})$$
$$S_2 = bQ_1 - aQ_2$$
$$S_1 = \Delta R_1 = \Delta R_{(\text{axial CO})}$$
$$S_2 = \tfrac{1}{2}(\Delta R_2 + \Delta R_3 + \Delta R_4 + \Delta R_5) = \Delta R_{(\text{equatorial CO})} \qquad (33)$$

Thus one can use the two intensity ratios $I_{a1 \text{ low}}/I_{a1 \text{ high}}$ (R_1) and $I_e/I_{a1 \text{ low}}$ (R_2) to calculate both θ and the ratio μ'_{ax}/μ'_{eq}. Since the eigenvectors are normalized, $a^2 + b^2 = 1$, (q.v.) it is convenient to write them in terms of an angle ϕ. (ϕ has no geometrical significance in the molecule.)

$$a = \cos \phi, \, b = \sin \phi, \, \tan 2\phi = 4f_c/(f_2 + 2f'_c + f_t - f_1)$$

(See Fig. 9 for definition of the force constants.)

$$\tan \theta = \left| \sqrt{R_2}/(\cos \phi \sqrt{R_1} - \sin \phi) \right|$$
$$\mu'_{ax}/\mu'_{eq} = 2 \sin \theta \, (\cos \phi + \sqrt{R_1} \sin \phi)/\sqrt{R_2} \qquad (34)$$

There are several solutions to these equations corresponding to the various combinations of positive and negative square roots of R_1 and R_2. Some solutions can be eliminated since it seems reasonable that μ'_{ax}/μ'_{eq} should be positive. This restriction leaves two possible solutions, the 'in-phase' solution ($\sqrt{R_1}$ and $\sqrt{R_2}$ both positive) and the 'out-of-phase' solution ($\sqrt{R_1}$ negative). Table 4 lists both solutions for a variety of molecules.

The question immediately arises as to which solution is correct. Braterman, Bau and Kaesz[53] compared the observed and calculated bond angles for a variety of $Mn(CO)_5X$ compounds and decided that the 'in-phase' solution gave bond angles much closer to the observed values (see Table 4). The spectra of ^{13}CO enriched $Cr(CO)_5$ provide a much better proof. Figure 10 compares (a) the observed spectrum of $Cr(CO)_5$ in a CH_4 matrix with (b) the spectrum predicted for a C_{4v} square pyramidal geometry using the 'in-phase' solution and (c) the spectrum predicted for a D_{3h}, trigonal bipyramidal structure.[37] It is clear from the figure that the molecule has a C_{4v} structure and that this method reproduces the observed spectra very well.

Surprisingly there is in general very little difference between the spectra predicted on the basis of the 'in-phase' and 'out-of-phase' solutions of Eqns (34), over the region illustrated in Fig. 10. There is, however, a substantial difference between the spectra predicted for the region of the high frequency, a_1, vibration[37] (Fig. 11). This figure confirms that the 'in-phase' solution is indeed the correct one. It should not be assumed that this is always the case. A similar calculation for $Mo(CO)_4$, which has a C_{2v} structure, shows that it is the 'out-of-phase' solution which corresponds to the observed spectrum.[40] Thus for

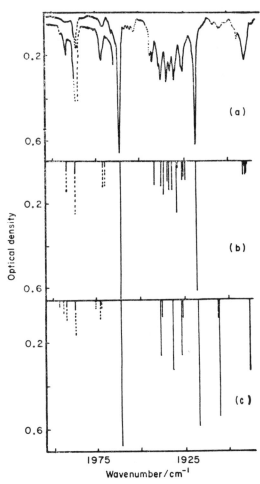

Fig. 10. (a) Spectrum of ^{13}CO-enriched $Cr(CO)_5$ in CH_4 at 20 K; 20 pulses deposited followed by 4.5 min photolysis with an unfiltered Hg lamp. In the superimposed spectrum the quantity of $Cr(CO)_5$ has been increased 4 times; $[^{12}CO]/[^{13}CO] = 1.0$. (b) Calculated spectrum of $Cr(CO)_5$ for the C_{4v} structure. Force constants $f_1 = 1531.45$, $f_2 = 1613.69$, $f_c = 36.99$, $f_c' = 30.37$, $f_t = 59.98$ N m^{-1}, bond angle $\theta = 92.3°$, $\mu'_{ax}/\mu'_{eq} = 0.877$. Arbitrary intensity units. The dotted spectrum represents a fourfold increase in the amount of $Cr(CO)_5$. (Ref. 37.) (c) Calculated spectrum for the D_{3h} structure: $f_e = 1599.1$, $f_a = 1599.4$, $f_{ee} = 46.35$, $f_{aa} = 92.31$, $f_{ae} = 28.00$ N m^{-1}. Labels a and e refer to axial and equatorial respectively.

$M(CO)_5$, the isotopic frequency pattern demonstrates qualitatively that the molecule belongs to the C_{4v} not the D_{3h} point group, and this allows an accurate estimate of the *five* frequency-factored force constants. (In the absence of the isotopically different molecules there are of course only three observables.) The intensity pattern in the high frequency region distinguishes 'in-phase' and 'out-of-phase' solutions.

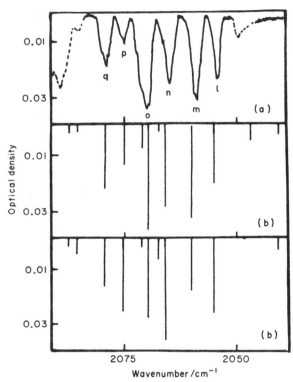

Fig. 11. (a) Spectrum of ^{13}CO-enriched $Cr(CO)_5$ in CH_4 at 20 K (approximately four times more $Cr(CO)_5$ than in Fig. 10); $[^{12}CO]/[^{13}CO] = 0.9$. The dotted part of the spectrum is not due to $Cr(CO)_5$. (b) Calculated spectrum for a C_{4v} structure with the in-phase solution. $\theta = 92.30°$, $\mu'_{ax}/\mu'_{eq} = 0.877$. The force constants are the same as for Fig. 10, but the intensity scale is four times greater. (c) Calculated spectrum for a C_{4v} structure with the out-of-phase solution. $\theta = 102.4°$, $\mu'_{ax}/\mu'_{eq} = 0.749$ (Perutz and Turner, Ref. 37).

We have recently demonstrated how the correct phase of the intensity problem is determined by the relative sizes of the two diagonal C—O stretching force constants describing the pairs of inequivalent CO groups.[20] The observed phases in $M(CO)_4$ (C_{2v}) and $M(CO)_5$ (C_{4v}) have also been rationalized.

Table 5 lists the bond angles calculated for some of the carbonyl fragments which have been produced in matrices. How reliable are these angles, particularly as with some stable substituted carbonyls nonsensical answers are obtained

TABLE 4
Observed intensity ratios, calculated bond angles, and dipole derivative ratios

Molecule	R_1	R_2	Obsvd	Calcd In phase	Out of phase	μ'_{ax}/μ'_{eq} In phase
HMn(CO)$_5$[a]	0.009 4	3.5	97	96.5	102	1.04
Mn(CO)$_5$Cl[a]	0.044	2.18	91.8	89.8	105	1.38
Mn(CO)$_5$Br[a]	0.068	1.86	92	91.6	111	1.51
Cr(CO)$_5$[b]	0.043	5.34	—	92.8	102.4	0.877
W(CO)$_5$[b]	0.031	4.95	—	93.7	102.1	0.902
Cr(CO)$_5$CS[c]	0.5	3	90?	82.8	117	1.4
Re$_2$(CO)$_{10}$[a, d]	0.593	3.05	94	79.3	122	1.37

[a] Cyclohexane solution. Ref. 65.
[b] CH$_4$ matrix 20 K. Ref. 53.
[c] Ar matrix 20 K. Ref. 45.
[d] Intensities taken from Ref. 62.

TABLE 5
Geometries of some carbonyls determined by relative infrared band intensities

Configuration	Carbonyl	Point group	Bond angles	Ref.
d^6	Cr(CO)$_6$	O_h		37
	Mo(CO)$_5$	C_{4v}	(ax−eq) 93°[a]	37
	Mo(CO)$_4$	C_{2v}	107°, 174°	40
	Cr(CO)$_3$	C_{3v}	105°	40
d^8	Fe(CO)$_5$	D_{3h}		33
	Fe(CO)$_4$	C_{2v}	≈120°, ≈140°	33
	Fe(CO)$_3$	C_{3v}	109.4°	42
d^9	Co(CO)$_4$	C_{3v}	≈100°	58
d^{10}	Ni(CO)$_4$	T_d		5
	Ni(CO)$_3$	D_{3h}		5
	Pd(CO)$_4$	T_d		9
d^{10}s^1	Ni(CO)$_3^-$	D_{3h}		48

[a] Dependent on matrix material (94.1° Ar, 92.8° CH$_4$).

if CO intensity ratios are used to calculate bond angles? Where do the errors in such cases creep in?

5.2.1 Double harmonic approximation

Brown and Darensbourg[54] have examined the intensities of the C—O stretching fundamentals of a range of substituted carbonyls. They conclude that the standard methods do not take into account electron flow via the π system during a vibration; for example, comparing $a_1(1)$ and $a_1(2)$

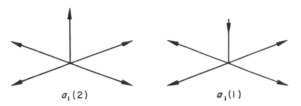

$a_1(2)$ $a_1(1)$

they suggest that

$$\frac{\partial \mu}{\partial Q_{a_1(1)}} \equiv \frac{\partial \mu}{\partial Q_1}$$

is very different from

$$\frac{\partial \mu}{\partial Q_{a_1(2)}} \equiv \frac{\partial \mu}{\partial Q_2}$$

for this reason. The present authors interpret this as a statement of electrical anharmonicity, i.e. in the above case, the value of $\partial \mu / \partial Q_1$ depends on whether (other than via the force field) $S_1 (= \Delta R_1)$ and $S_2 [= \frac{1}{2}(\Delta R_2 + \Delta R_3 + \Delta R_4 + \Delta R_5)]$ are mixed in or out of phase in the normal modes. This can be expressed in the dipole moment expansion by

$$\mu_z = \mu_z^0 + \left(\frac{\partial \mu_z}{\partial S_1}\right)_0 S_1 + \left(\frac{\partial \mu_z}{\partial S_2}\right)_0 S_2 + \frac{1}{2}\left(\frac{\partial^2 \mu_z}{\partial S_1 \partial S_2}\right)_0 \underline{S_1 S_2}$$

The term underlined is considered by Brown and Darensbourg to make a significant contribution to the intensity of the fundamental bands. However, the difficulty about this argument is that this term will *only* contribute to the intensity of ν_1 or ν_2 if the vibrations are mechanically *an*harmonic. This seems to be surprising in view of the weakness of carbonyl overtone bands (see above). This point is discussed at length elsewhere.[20]

5.2.2. MC—CO mixing

Bigorgne[55] has recently shown that whereas the 'M—C stretches' of carbonyl compounds contain heavy admixtures of other stretching and bending internal coordinates, the 'C—O stretch' is only mixed with the M—C stretching internal coordinate. The ratio L_{12}/L_{22} of Eqn (27) may be shown to be approximately equal to $- \mu_C/(\mu_C + \mu_O)$, which is between 0.55 and 0.60 for the three CO isotopes commonly used in structural studies. Bigorgne[55] has also calculated numerical values for the derivatives of the bond dipole moments, $\partial \mu_{MC}/\partial Q_{MC}$, μ'_{MC}, and $\partial \mu_{CO}/\partial Q_{CO}$, μ'_{CO}, for a series of carbonyls and carbonyl complexes. Thus the intensity of a 'C—O stretch' is given by the expression

$$I \propto (L_{12}\mu'_{MC} + L_{22}\mu'_{CO})^2$$
$$= L_{12}^2 \mu'_{MC}^2 + L_{22}^2 \mu'_{CO}^2 + 2L_{12}L_{22}\mu'_{CO}\mu'_{MC} \qquad (35)$$

Since all MCO groups of the same isotopic composition will have identical values of L_{12} and L_{22}, we may regard Eqn (35) as being the rigorous equivalent of the 'C—O' dipole moment derivative μ' above. Substituting numerical values in this equation we find that the intensity is determined to about 5% by the first, 65% by the second, and 30% by the third term. Thus, in contrast to the frequency, which is overwhelmingly determined by the CO part of the molecule (q.v.), the infrared intensity is strongly influenced by the MC contribution. Chemically equivalent CO groups will have identical values of μ'_{CO} and μ'_{MC}. Chemically inequivalent groups may have different values of these parameters giving rise to a different value of μ'. The different L_{12} and L_{22} values for the $^xC^yO$ isotopes give rise to intensities in the ratio $^{12}C^{16}O:^{13}C^{16}O:^{12}C^{18}O = 1:0.9415:0.9734$. Such differences are absorbed by the 'effective isotopic enrichment' $^{12}C^{16}O:$ $^xC^yO$ ratio, and are generally small compared to the errors involved in band intensity measurements. Inclusion of MC mixing therefore does not directly affect the determined bond angles.

Attwood and Brown[56] have claimed that the general quadratic valence force field gave better agreement with their observed intensity data for ^{13}CO-enriched $Mn(CO)_5Br$ than did the frequency-factored force field. In their calculations, they imposed the restriction that $\mu'_{ax} = \mu'_{eq}$ which removed a degree of freedom from the frequency-factored force field; this restriction may be responsible for their observations. They also used harmonic force constants which give a different description of the normal coordinate of an a_1 mode in the molecule than is given by anharmonic force constants. Since anharmonic frequencies and intensities are used in the calculations, anharmonic force constants should also be employed to calculate the force field.

5.2.3 Interactions with other ligands

All the fragments listed in Table 5 contain carbonyl groups and no other ligands. In the case of $HMn(CO)_5$ and $Mn(CO)_5Br$ the additional ligands seem to have little effect because the bond angles calculated from infrared band intensities agree closely with those measured by other means (Table 4). In $Cr(CO)_5CS$, however, the calculated value of θ is 83°.[39] Although the crystal structure of this molecule has not yet been solved, the similarity of $Cr(CO)_5CS$ to $Cr(CO)_6$ makes this angle seem highly unlikely. Nevertheless this angle can be used to predict the spectrum of isotopically different molecules with substantial success. Thus it seems that the ability to predict the spectrum and that to predict a bond angle are not necessarily related.

A possible origin of these 'false' bond angles is probably the neglect of the coupling between the a_1 C—O stretching modes and the a_1 modes of the ligand. (If the ligand is a polyatomic species it may contain modes of other symmetry which may couple with C—O stretches.) This is perhaps best illustrated by a calculation on the molecule $Cr(CO)_5(^{13}CO)$. Perutz and Turner[37] have calculated the frequency-factored force constants for $Cr(CO)_6$ in a CH_4 matrix, and, using these force constants we can predict the frequencies and intensities of the infrared-active bands of $Cr(CO)_5(^{13}CO)$.

Mode	Wavenumber/cm^{-1}	Relative intensity
a_1	2107.3	0.048
b_1	2017.5	0
a_1	2009.4	1
e	1985.6	13.45
a_1	1954.5	5.53

(Force constants $f_{CO} = 1644.27$, $f_{CO,CO}^c = 26.58$, $f_{CO,CO}^t = 52.35$ N m^{-1}.)

The first four frequencies involve principally the five ^{12}CO groups, while the band at 1954.5 cm^{-1} is primarily due to oscillation of the ^{13}CO group. If we now totally ignore coupling between the ^{12}CO and ^{13}CO entities and regard the five ^{12}CO groups as a pentacarbonyl fragment, we can use Eqns (34) to calculate θ and μ'_{ax}/μ'_{eq}. Although the expected values are $\theta = 90°$ and $\mu'_{ax}/\mu'_{eq} = 1$, we get $\theta = 92.8°$ and $\mu'_{ax}/\mu'_{eq} = 0.549$, purely due to neglect of this mixing. Similarly, the anomalous calculated bond angle in $Cr(CO)_5CS$ is the consequence of neglecting CO—CS coupling. In $HMn(CO)_5$ or $Mn(CO)_5Br$ this coupling is too small to have an appreciable effect on the calculated bond angles (primarily due to zero interaction force constants between M—X and C—O bonds), while in carbonyl fragments $M(CO)_x$ it is totally absent. It is the present authors' belief that these interactions, when ignored, are a major cause of the nonsensical answers obtained in some cases. Other errors also occur in substituted carbonyls where the μ'_{CO} may not lie along the MCO vector. This is more fully discussed elsewhere.[20]

5.2.4 Experimental errors

The bond angles appear to be relatively insensitive to errors in the measurement of the intensity ratios (cf. $Fe(CO)_3$). In cases such as $M(CO)_5$ or C_{2v} $M(CO)_4$,[33,37,40] where there are inequivalent carbonyl groups, the dipole derivative ratio is far more sensitive than the bond angles to errors in the intensity measurements and it appears to be acting as an 'error sink' (Table 4).

5.2.5 Non-linearity of MCO

If the M—C—O units are not linear the bond angles will be incorrect. In most X-ray studies terminal M—C—O units are linear or almost linear and deviations are usually ascribed to packing effects. It seems unlikely that totally the wrong shape could be assigned to a carbonyl fragment as a result of non-linear M—C—O groups.

5.2.6 Overlapping bands

Overlapping infrared bands of different carbonyl fragments can easily lead to the incorrect interpretation of results. This can occur particularly in metal atom/

CO co-condensation experiments where bands are usually much broader than in photolysis experiments. Such an overlap[57] resulted in Ozin mistakenly reporting the existence of D_{3h} $Cr(CO)_5$.

5.3   Recipe for Analysing an Isotopic Spectrum

In this section we summarize the method of analysing a spectrum and indicate one or two practical difficulties and their consequences.

1. The initial step is to use the frequencies and band intensities of the un-enriched metal carbonyl, $M(^{12}CO)_x$, to predict approximate frequencies of isotopically-different molecules and approximate band intensities. In addition, the strongest bands of $M(^{12}CO)_{x-1}(^{13}CO)$ may often be visible in the spectrum of the unenriched compound. For some fragments, e.g. $Fe(CO)_3$, the unenriched molecule provides enough data to calculate force constants and bond angles exactly, (q.v.), while others, e.g. $Cr(CO)_5$ or $Fe(CO)_4$ do not. In such cases an approximate force field must be used. A usable approximation can only be found by trial and error; (the Cotton–Kraihanzel approximation,[46] $f_{cis} = \frac{1}{2}f_{trans}$, for example, works well with $M(CO)_5$[37] but poorly with $Fe(CO)_4$.[33])

In general, it appears to be better to make approximations involving inter-action force constants than stretching force constants.

2. The approximate frequencies are used to assign the strongest bands in the spectrum. These are then used to refine the values of the force constants to obtain more accurate frequencies, intensities, and bond angles.

3. These new values allow weaker bands to be assigned and usually enable wrong assignments to be detected. When all the bands are assigned the refinement is carried out again.

There are several problems associated with the refinements. (a) The frequency-factored force constants are highly correlated and this can prevent some sophisticated computer programs from converging. It is often easier to use somewhat simpler programs which change force constants one at a time and which must necessarily converge.[37] (b) If part of the spectrum is for some reason obscured and no frequencies can be measured in that region it is possible to find more than one set of force constants that will reproduce the observed frequencies.* These force constants differ only in the positions predicted for the obscured bands. Thus $Co(CO)_4$ has been synthesized by photolysis of $Co(CO)_3NO$ in a pure CO matrix.[58] The ^{13}CO isotopic spectra indicate a C_{3v} structure but the region where the high frequency a_1 band should be observed is masked by absorptions of the CO matrix itself. Force constant refinements led to two minima, with similar errors, predicting a_1 bands at 2108 cm^{-1}, and 2130 cm^{-1}. Subsequent Raman spectra [41] (see below) confirmed that the correct value was

---

* For all molecules where there is more than one type of CO group there will always be a second set of frequency-factored force constants where the relative values of the stretching force constants are reversed and the interaction force constant is negative. This solution is always rejected, since it can be convincingly argued that, on molecular orbital grounds, carbonyl–carbonyl interaction force constants must be positive.[46]

2108 cm^{-1}. These multiple minima can be detected by starting the refinements from widely differing trial force constants. The problem is particularly acute in the case of radical carbonyl anions.[48,59] In all cases the region of the high frequency a_1 bands of these anions is totally obscured by the bands of the neutral parent carbonyl. In this case, the only criterion for choosing between the different solutions is comparison of the spectrum with that of the solution spectra of stable anions, e.g. $Co(CO)_4^-$.[60] (c) A more general problem is that of split bands. It is now well established that the bands of many carbonyls are split into a number of components in the matrix. Although there are instances where matrix splittings have been attributed to distortion of the molecule (e.g. $Ni(N_2)_4$,[49]) the majority of these splittings appear to be the result of multiple trapping sites in the matrix.[33,61] In some cases, these splittings can be removed by photolysis,[37] but in many they cannot.[33] In general, the band is split because its frequency is very sensitive to the small differences between the force constants of molecules trapped in the various matrix sites, while the frequencies of unsplit bands are not so sensitive to these changes. This sensitivity means that the exact value of the frequency of a split band will have very little effect on the calculated force constants. Thus for $Fe(CO)_4$, almost identical force constants were obtained for refinements[33] where the mean value of the split bands was used or where they were omitted altogether. Matrix splittings can also be caused by interaction between the metal carbonyl and the photo-ejected CO group and these splittings are discussed below.

5.4 Comparison of Infrared and Raman Spectra of Carbonyl Fragments

A few unstable carbonyls have been studied by both Raman[22,41] and i.r.[41,58] spectroscopy. $Co(CO)_4$ was generated by photolysis of $Co(CO)_3NO$ in a CO matrix (q.v.) and showed two infrared-active bands—2029 and 2011 cm^{-1} (Fig. 12a). The experiment was repeated using a series of isotopically different CO matrices (10%, 20%, 50%, 90% ^{13}CO) and bands were assigned to the various $Co(^{12}CO)_{4-x}(^{13}CO)_x$ species. The two bands of the unenriched molecule could have been the b_2 and e modes of a D_{2d} $Co(CO)_4$ fragment, or alternatively the e mode and one of the a_1 modes of a C_{3v} tetracarbonyl, the other a_1 being hidden by the absorption bands of the CO matrix. Calculations similar to those outlined above, showed the spectrum to be inconsistent with a D_{2d} structure but in complete agreement with the C_{3v} structure.[58]

Ozin and co-workers synthesized[22,41] $Co(CO)_4$ by co-condensation of Co atoms and pure CO. They obtained spectra identical to those produced by photolysis of $Co(CO)_3NO$. It is, in itself, very encouraging that two such different methods should give the same results. More importantly, the Raman spectra of these samples in the 2000 cm^{-1} region showed two depolarized bands, coincident with the infrared-active bands, and a polarized band at 2108 cm^{-1} (Fig. 12b). The polarization data appeared inconsistent with a C_{3v} structure, for which two

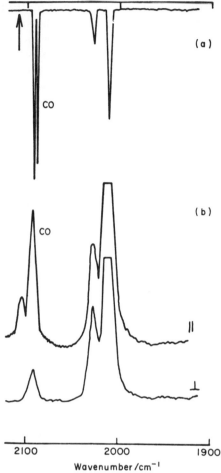

Fig. 12. (a) Infrared spectrum of Co(CO)$_4$ obtained by photolysis of Co(CO)$_3$NO in a CO matrix (Crichton *et al.*, Ref. 58). The arrow ↑ indicates the position of the very weak a_1 band calculated for a molecule with C_{3v} symmetry. (b) Raman spectrum ($I_{\parallel}$ and $I_{\perp}$) of Co(CO)$_4$. The molecule was prepared by co-condensation of Co atoms with CO (Turner, Ref. 38 and Ozin, Ref. 41).

polarized bands are predicted. The results suggested a D_{2d} geometry for the molecule with only one polarized band predicted, even though such a structure was inconsistent with the isotope shift data.* Thus there is a paradox here; either ^{13}CO isotopic enrichment data do not lead to the correct geometry or else

---

* More recently Ozin[41] has confirmed the C_{3v} structure in a CO matrix by repeating the ^{13}CO experiments, and analysing the e.s.r. spectrum of Co(^{13}CO)$_4$. There is e.s.r. evidence that, in an argon matrix, Co(CO)$_4$ may consist of a mixture of C_{3v} and D_{2d} molecules. The molecular orbital calculations of Refs 31 and 32 satisfyingly place the energies of these two structures very close together.

one or more of the a_1 bands of $Co(CO)_4$ has a depolarization ratio indistinguishably different from 3/4. It turns out that there are other carbonyl compounds where similar high depolarization ratios of a_1 Raman bands occur. These molecules include $Fe(CO)_5$, $Fe(CO)_4L$, and $Mn(CO)_5X$, the structures of which have been determined by X-ray or electron diffraction procedures. The molecules are all characterized by the fact that the a_1 mode with the high depolarization ratio lies close to a mode of different symmetry, in the case of $Co(CO)_4$, one of the species e. The phenomenon has been rationalized by Edgell[63] and Bigorgne.[62] Their explanations are based on the fact that the different types of CO group are in reality very similar. Thus if $Co(CO)_4$ had been tetrahedral, it would have had one infrared-active mode, t_2, and two Raman-active modes, one polarized a_1 and one depolarized t_2. The t_2 band can be considered as superimposed degenerate a_1 and e bands under C_{3v}, neither of which is polarized. Imagine that the molecule is now distorted very slightly, so that the degeneracy of the a_1 and e modes is lifted and two infrared-active and three Raman-active bands are observed. For such a case, Bigorgne has shown[62] that, by analysing the polarizability tensors and their relationship to the L matrix elements, the lower a_1 band will remain essentially depolarized in this molecule. Edgell's arguments show that the depolarization ratio changes only slowly as the symmetry of the molecule is reduced, whereas the frequency shifts of the bands are a much more sensitive guide to distortion.

The case of $Co(CO)_4$ therefore illustrates the point that, although Raman spectra can be very useful for detecting bands which cannot be seen in the infrared, a_1 bands are not always significantly polarized; thus polarization data do not necessarily assist in structural determinations.

5.5 Interaction with Photo-ejected CO Molecules

In the past, there has been considerable argument as to whether or not the structures of metal carbonyl fragments observed in matrices are dictated by the interaction of the photo-ejected CO groups with the vacant sites of the unsaturated carbonyls. There is now a very substantial body of evidence which shows that in normal circumstances (i.e. not in a pure CO matrix) such interactions with CO are not significant. For example, the spectrum of $W(CO)_5$ generated from photolysis of $W(CO)_5py$[64] is identical to that obtained by photolysis of $W(CO)_6$.[65]

Non-stereospecific interaction with the photo-ejected CO molecule is, however, a different matter. Ultraviolet photolysis of $Fe(CO)_5$ in an argon matrix produces $Fe(CO)_4$ and CO (Fig. 13a). Subsequent exposure of the matrix to the light from the Nernst glower of the infrared spectrometer rapidly destroys all the $Fe(CO)_4$ and regenerates the parent $Fe(CO)_5$.[33] If the u.v. photolysis is continued for several hours, it is found that the reaction can be only partially reversed. Furthermore, a detailed analysis of the infrared spectrum of the $Fe(CO)_4$ and ejected CO shows that the 'reversible' and 'irreversible' $Fe(CO)_4$ and CO actually absorb at *different frequencies* (Fig. 13). The 'reversible' CO absorbs close to bands assigned to CO dimers [66] and the 'irreversible' CO at the same frequency as monomeric CO.[38] Thus it appears that after brief photolysis the $Fe(CO)_4$ and CO are interacting weakly, while prolonged photolysis allows the CO to diffuse away through the matrix, preventing subsequent recombination.

Although this interaction affects the exact frequency of the bands it appears to have no effect on the overall structure of the carbonyl fragment, since the band patterns of the 'reversible' and 'irreversible' forms of $Fe(CO)_4$ are very similar. Similar effects have been observed for $Cr(CO)_5$.[67]

This non-stereospecific interaction with the photo-ejected CO molecule may, however, have a profound effect on the photochemistry of these carbonyls. The u.v. light used for the photolysis contains far more energy than is required to break the M—CO bond. Since no visible fluorescence is observed in these

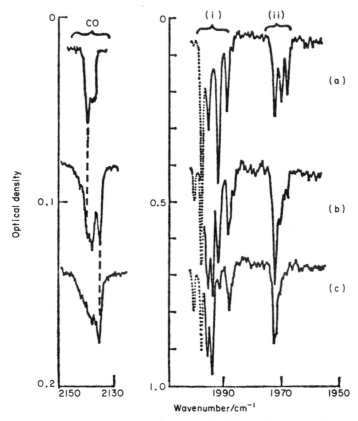

Fig. 13. Illustration of the differences between the infrared spectra of 'reversible' and 'irreversible' $Fe(CO)_4$ and CO, produced on ultraviolet photolysis of $Fe(CO)_5$ in an argon matrix (1 : 10 000) at 20 K. (The bands shown as broken lines are due to $Fe(CO)_5$. Higher frequency bands of $Fe(CO)_5$ have been omitted.) (a) after 7 min photolysis, (b) after 225 min photolysis, (c) after 5 min photolysis of (b) with a Nernst glower.

reactions, the excess of energy is presumably distributed as vibrational energy in the products. The interaction between carbonyl and CO would form an ideal mechanism for the rapid relaxation of these vibrationally excited states. The next section, therefore, describes experiments in which the vibrational relaxation of matrix-isolated CO is studied.

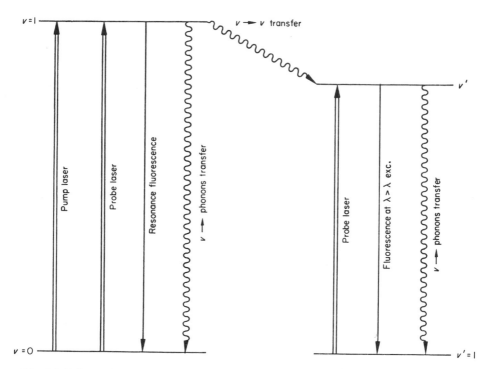

Fig. 14. Schematic energy diagram showing the principle of infrared fluorescence and double resonance experiments. The $v = 1$ level is excited by a laser pulse. The concentration of excited species is monitored either by fluorescence intensity measurements or by transient absorption of the probe laser.

6   I.R. ENERGY PROCESSES IN MATRICES

One of the least understood features of matrix isolation is the detailed nature of photochemical processes therein, including, for example, how the cage effect operates. Some aspects have been discussed elsewhere.[10] The use of photolysis and spectroscopy with plane polarized light has demonstrated that some species can be rotated during the photochemical act. For instance, the square pyramidal $Cr(CO)_5$ appears to be fluxional on irradiation with visible light, probably via a D_{3h} intermediate.[68] Several systems have now been studied by this technique.[69]

However, one unresolved question is whether such fluxional behaviour derives from a specific photochemical path or whether it is essentially a thermal process involving an instantaneous fluid hot spot; current thinking favours the former. The local thermal effect cannot of course be investigated by simply warming the whole sample. Nor is it expected that absorption into molecular vibrational bands from irradiation with conventional infrared sources (e.g. a Nernst glower) will supply sufficient energy to have any effect. However, infrared lasers are certainly powerful enough for such probing. The first problem is to understand something of the energy processes occurring when *stable* molecules are vibrationally excited; this is discussed in the next section. After this we consider some possible applications to the understanding of the mechanisms of photochemical reactions and, in addition, consider the potential of generating unusual species by infrared laser irradiation.

6.1   Vibrational Relaxation in Matrices

The vibrational relaxation dynamics of molecular substitutional impurities in solid matrices is of considerable interest, because the observed behaviour reflects details of molecule–lattice and molecule–molecule interactions which do not appear in experiments such as classical infrared absorption spectroscopy.

A molecule, excited into a high vibrational state, can relax to the ground state by three possible pathways:

1. Radiative relaxation, i.e. spontaneous emission resulting in infrared fluorescence
2. Radiationless relaxation by conversion of a vibrational energy quantum into several lattice vibrational quanta ($v \to$ phonons process)
3. Radiationless energy transfer to another vibrational level of the same molecule or another molecular species ($v \to v$ transfer process).

Time-resolved infrared spectroscopy is a powerful tool for evaluating the rate constants for these various processes.

In the solid-phase studies, time- and wavelength-resolved infrared fluorescence or double resonance techniques have been employed. These experimental methods have been considerably developed in gas phase studies.[70] In a fluorescence experiment populations of the vibrational levels are monitored through the infrared emission at the same wavelength as excitation (resonance fluorescence) or at a different wavelength (downward straight arrows on Fig. 14). In a double-resonance experiment, level populations are monitored through transient absorption of a probe c.w. laser (upward solid straight arrows on Fig. 14).

6.1.1   Laser-excited vibrational fluorescence of CO[71, 72]

A Q-switched frequency-doubled CO_2—N_2—He laser operating on the R(6) or R(8) rotational transition of the $00^01—02^00$ band of CO_2 allows the excitation of the $v = 1$ level of $^{12}C^{16}O$. A typical experimental apparatus is shown in Fig. 15. This enables about 1 % of the $^{12}C^{16}O$ molecules to be excited. The intensity of the CO fluorescence is found to have a single exponential decay, but the emission spectrum is fairly complicated. It includes fluorescence emission

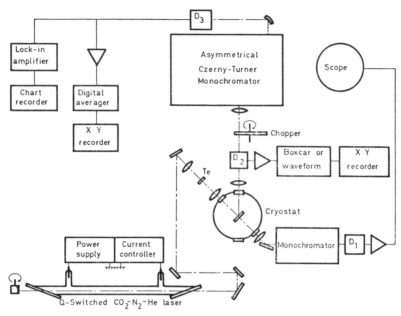

Fig. 15. CO fluorescence apparatus of Dubost and Charneau. The rotating-mirror Q-switched CO_2—N_2—He laser gives pulses of 1–10 kW peak power, 200 ns to 1 μs pulsewidth with a repetition rate from 10 to 400 s^{-1}. The optical cavity is ended by a grating, thus allowing operation on a single CO_2 vibration–rotation line. To obtain frequency matching with the matrix-isolated CO absorption line, the CO_2 laser is frequency-doubled using a tellurium crystal, with a low doubling efficiency (<1 %).
D_1, D_2 and D_3 are Ge—Au or PbSe (77 K) detectors (Dubost et al., Ref. 71).

not only from the upper levels of $^{12}C^{16}O$ but also from the isotopic species $^{13}C^{16}O$ and $^{12}C^{18}O$ present in natural abundance (Fig. 16). Time-resolved emission spectroscopy shows that the vibrational levels of $^{12}C^{16}O$ are rapidly quenched by efficient energy transfer to the isotopes. Since the isotopic concentration is low (1.1 % ^{13}CO and 0.2 % $C^{18}O$, respectively, in unenriched CO) a strong vibrational excitation of these molecules up to $v = 12$ is achieved.

The fluorescence decay time from which the $v = 1 \rightarrow v = 0$ rate in isotopic molecules can be estimated is 14.5 ms in an argon matrix and 20.6 ms in neon. The process is purely radiative. On the other hand, radiationless decay is very slow and may be in the region of one second. The transfer rate to a vibrational level v is deduced from the $v \to v - 1$ fluorescence rise-time. Although the decay time does not depend upon the concentration, the fluorescence rise-time is strongly dependent on the concentration of CO in the matrix. The rise-time increases from 25 to 800 μs as the concentration is reduced from 1:500 to 1:5000. This indicates that the energy transfer process is strongly dependent upon the distance between interacting molecules.

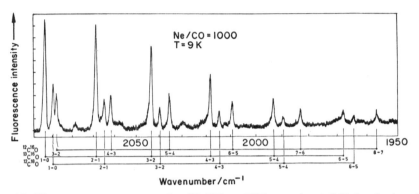

Fig. 16. Fluorescence spectrum of a Ne/CO = 1000 sample at 8 K (excitation frequency 2140.86 cm⁻¹). The fluorescence decay of the entire fluorescence, i.e. of the sum of the individual lines, is perfectly exponential with a decay time of 20.6 ms (Dubost et al., Ref. 71).

6.1.2 Infrared double resonance in NH₃[73]

Abouaf-Marguin et al.[73] have carried out an experiment using one laser source to excite NH_3 molecules to the $v = 1$ state of the ν_2 mode and a second laser to monitor excited state populations through transient absorption. A 10.3 μm pulsed CO_2—N_2—He laser is used as the pump and a second c.w. CO_2 laser operating at the same frequency probes the absorption of the sample. This method is much more sensitive than fluorescence because of the highly directional character and the high intensity of the c.w. laser beam. The two laser polarizations are crossed and a grid polarizer is placed in the c.w. laser beam to minimize interference from scattered light.

In an N_2 matrix, the transmission of the probe increases during the pump laser pulse because of the population of the $v = 1$ level. Immediately after the pulse, transmission of the probe decreases exponentially with a time constant of 2 μs; it then decreases rather more slowly, returning to its initial value in a few hundred μs. In rare gas matrices, the rapid increase and decrease are not observed, and there is only a slow change in transmittance following the excitation pulse.

The short exponential decay observed in N_2 is attributed to the vibrational relaxation of the $v = 1$ level of the ν_2 NH_3 mode. From the absence of this signal in rare gas matrices it is concluded that the vibrational relaxation time of NH_3

must be shorter than 500 ns, which is orders of magnitude faster than the radiative lifetime of NH_3 in the gas phase, ≈ 66 ms. The slow change in transmittance is attributed to the thermal relaxation of the sample. During the relaxation process, the vibrational energy is converted into heat. Since the linewidth of the ν_2 absorption band is temperature dependent, a change in temperature produces a change in absorption at a given wavelength. This experiment thus shows that with NH_3, radiationless relaxation processes are dominant, the opposite of the CO case.

6.1.3 Relaxation models
VIBRATION → VIBRATION ENERGY TRANSFER PROCESSES

The distribution of an assembly of molecules among the vibrational levels of a relaxing system which is vibrationally hot and translationally cold has been the subject of active experimental and theoretical investigation over the past few years.[70] Although this work is concerned with the gas phase, matrix-isolated molecules present a strong analogy to it. The molecular translational energy which constitutes the thermal bath in gases is replaced in solids by lattice vibrations. Isolated molecules are coupled together via long range dipole–dipole interactions.[74]

Processes such as the following

$$^{12}C^{16}O\ (v = 1) + {}^{12}C^{16}O\ (v = 0) \rightleftharpoons {}^{12}C^{16}O\ (v = 0) + {}^{12}C^{16}O\ (v = 1)$$
$$\Delta E = 0$$

are exactly resonant and produce an energy diffusion through the sample.[75]

Processes such as

$$^{12}C^{16}O\ (v = 1) + {}^{12}C^{16}O\ (v = 1) \rightleftharpoons {}^{12}C^{16}O\ (v = 0) + {}^{12}C^{16}O\ (v = 2) + \Delta E$$
$$\Delta E = 26.6\ \text{cm}^{-1}$$

or

$$^{12}C^{16}O\ (v = 1) + {}^{13}C^{16}O\ (v = 0) \rightleftharpoons {}^{13}C^{16}O\ (v = 1) + {}^{12}C^{16}O\ (v = 0) + \Delta E$$
$$\Delta E = 47.2\ \text{cm}^{-1}$$

are allowed since the energy difference falls in the frequency range of the matrix host. A phonon is then emitted or absorbed in order to compensate for this energy mismatch. The probability of a process occurring with $\Delta E < 0$ is smaller than that of the process with $\Delta E > 0$ by the Boltzmann factor. Due to the low temperature of the thermal bath ($T = 8$ K) a fast vibrational energy transfer to the heaviest isotopic species and 'up-the-ladder' excitation then occur. It must be noted that these transfer processes can only take place if they occur faster than vibrational deactivation, radiative or not. This condition is fulfilled for a large number of CO vibrational levels. However, the rate of radiative relaxation increases with v, and radiationless decay is also expected to become faster in high vibrational levels. This increase in relaxation rates prevents high levels from being appreciably populated. With NH_3, radiationless relaxation is several orders of magnitude faster than in CO and vibrational energy transfer never occurs.

VIBRATIONAL RELAXATION

Recent theories[76, 77] consider the coupling between an initially populated vibrational state and the manifold of nearly degenerate high multiphonon $v-1$ states, which leads to the creation of kinetic energy in the immediate neighbourhood of the molecule as a travelling wave in band lattice modes. There are two important conclusions. (1) The relaxation rate, K_v, depends exponentially upon the energy gap, $\Delta E = E_v - E_{v-1}$, i.e. upon the vibrational quantum energy, $K_{v \to v-1} \propto \delta^{-N}$, where $\delta \ll 1$ and $N = \nu_{v \to v-1}/\nu_{phonon}$ is the order of the process. (2) The relaxation rate of a high order process strongly depends upon the temperature.

$$K_{v \to v-1}(T) = K_{v \to v-1}(0) \left[1 - \exp\left(-\frac{h\nu_{ph}}{kT} \right) \right]^{-N}$$

The energy gap law is supported by the large difference in $v \to$ phonons rate between CO and NH_3. Nevertheless, the greatest care must be taken in making such comparisons. Brus and Bondybey[78] have recently studied the vibrational relaxation of matrix-isolated OH and OD in the $A^2\Sigma^+$ state. They found that the absolute value of the $1 \to 0$ rate was several orders of magnitude larger than for CO and N_2,[79] which have smaller energy gaps. Although the energy gap is larger in OH than in OD, the rate was faster for OH.

It is possible for an energy gap law to hold for a series of molecules having identical phonon structures, but light molecules having strongly anharmonic localized modes (e.g. the nearly free rotation of OH) should not be compared with others. Such modes strongly increase the relaxation rate and the energy gap law is not obeyed in this case. More theoretical work is needed in which the effect of localized modes is included. Unfortunately, the experiments described here cannot be used to test the second point since the measured decay times are temperature independent. The original reports of the strong temperature dependence of the CO fluorescence lifetime must be attributed to impurity effects.[72]

6.1.4 Conclusion

Infrared spectroscopy thus allows the direct study of vibrational relaxation and energy transfer in matrix-isolated molecules. The infrared data show that the internal vibrations of an isolated molecule is not only coupled to the lattice vibrations but also to the vibrations of other isolated molecules. The observed behaviour of such a system is strongly dependent on the relative magnitudes of these couplings. In the case of weak vibration–phonon coupling (i.e. slow $v \to$ phonon rate), dipole–dipole interaction between isolated molecules allows efficient $v \to v$ processes, energy transfer to the heaviest isotopes, and a highly non-equilibrium distribution of molecules among the vibrational levels. It should be pointed out that this occurs because the magnitude of the energy gaps is such that one-phonon processes take place and that the Boltzmann factor strongly favours the $\Delta E > 0$ processes.

Several applications of these phenomena can be considered. The strong infrared excitation of some isotopic species might make it possible to carry out an isotopic separation in the matrix by means of a selective chemical reaction or optical excitation. Also the strong excitation of the upper vibrational levels could be used to make a molecular solid state laser.

6.2 Infrared Laser-induced Matrix Reactions

It will be clear from what has just been said that no useful information will be derived from a trapped species irradiated with an infrared laser if the energy is rapidly degraded into matrix phonons and dissipated. The probability of this occurring will increase with molecular complexity and with the atomic weight of the constituent atoms since the energy separation of molecular vibrations and matrix phonons will decrease. However, there is a classic non-laser experiment which is very encouraging.

In 1963, Hall and Pimentel[80] showed that HONO trapped in argon could be isomerized *cis* ⇌ *trans* by irradiation with infrared light of appropriate frequency (3650–3200 cm^{-1}). The proposed mechanism is that energy, absorbed into ν_{OH}, is rapidly transferred to torsional motion above the barrier. The molecule then drops into a *cis* or *trans* ground state.

6.2.1 Mechanistic studies

An example will illustrate one of the possibilities. The C_{4v} fragment $Cr(CO)_5$ generated, as described earlier, by photolysis of $Cr(CO)_6$ in a matrix has a well defined visible absorption band.* Irradiation into this band causes reorientation of the fragment and recombination to $Cr(CO)_6$.[68] If this is a *thermal* process then irradiation with CO or frequency-doubled CO_2 laser light into one of the very strong CO stretching bands of the fragment should provide local energy sufficient to overcome the barrier to reorientation.

The photochemistry of diazocyclopentadiene can be effectively studied in matrices.[82]

The reverse reaction can be promoted by irradiation with 260 nm u.v. light. Does this reverse reaction involve only the ketene? If irradiation with infrared light absorbed at the ketene frequency results in reaction, then the mechanism is more likely to involve a bimolecular intermediate than loss of CO to form the carbene.

* The frequency of its maximum is, surprisingly, very sensitive to the matrix (Ref. 81), *probably* because of slight structural changes in the fragment.

6.2.2 Synthesis with i.r. lasers

The promotion of gas phase reactions using infrared lasers is a rapidly expanding field. There is surely the potential to do exciting reactions in matrices provided the conditions about relaxation properties mentioned earlier are met. There are a number of small molecules which absorb either CO_2, frequency-doubled CO_2, or CO laser light. Moreover, since the positions of vibrational bands are somewhat sensitive to the matrix, it should prove possible to 'fine tune' the absorption frequency of parent species to coincide with an appropriate laser frequency.

This is an appropriate optimistic note on which to end this review.

REFERENCES

(1) See e.g. G. C. Pimentel, in *Formation and Trapping of Free Radicals* (A. M. Bass and H. P. Broida, Eds.), p. 69. Academic Press, New York, 1960.

(2) J. S. Ogden and J. J. Turner, *Chem. in Br.* **7**, 186 (1971); A. J. Downs and S. C. Peake, in *Molecular Spectroscopy*, Vol. 1 (R. F. Barrow, D. A. Long and D. J. Millen, Eds.), p. 523 (Chem. Soc. Specialist Periodical Reports) (1973); (c) B. M. Chadwick, in *Molecular Spectroscopy*, Vol. 3 (R. F. Barrow, D. A. Long and D. J. Millen, Eds.), p. 281 (Chem. Soc. Specialist Periodical Reports) (1975); *Vibrational Spectroscopy of Trapped Species* (H. E. Hallam, Ed.), Wiley, London (1973).

(3) L. Y. Nelson and G. C. Pimentel, *Inorg. Chem.* **6**, 1758 (1967).

(4) S. D. Gabelnick, G. T. Reedy and M. G. Chasanov, *J. Chem. Phys.* **58**, 4468 (1973).

(5) R. L. DeKock, *Inorg. Chem.* **10**, 1205 (1971).

(6) L. Andrews, *J. Phys. Chem.* **71**, 2761 (1967); *J. Chem. Phys.* **48**, 972 (1968).

(7) A. Arkell, R. R. Reinhard and L. P. Larson, *J. Amer. Chem. Soc.* **87**, 1016 (1965).

(8) See e.g. several chapters in Ref. 2.

(9) J. H. Darling and J. S. Ogden, *Inorg. Chem.* **11**, 666 (1972).

(10) J. K. Burdett and J. J. Turner, in *Cryogenic Chemistry* (G. A. Ozin and M. Moskovits, Eds.), Wiley, London (1976).

(11) G. Herzberg, *Infrared and Raman Spectra*, Van Nostrand, Princeton, N.J. (1945).

(12) M. Allavena, R. Rysnik, D. White, V. Calder and D. E. Mann, *J. Chem. Phys.* **50**, 3399 (1969); D. Maillard, M. Allavena and J. P. Perchard, *Spectrochim. Acta* **31A**, 1523 (1975).

(13) J. Pacansky and G. V. Calder, *J. Phys. Chem.* **76**, 454 (1972); *J. Mol. Struct.* **14**, 363 (1972); S. D. Gabelnick, *J. Phys. Chem.* **76**, 2483 (1972).

(14) D. E. Milligan and M. E. Jacox, *J. Chem. Phys.* **55**, 1003 (1971).

(15) D. White, G. V. Calder, S. Hemple and D. E. Mann, *J. Chem. Phys.* **59**, 6645 (1973).

(16) J. W. Hastie, R. H. Hague and J. L. Margrave, *High Temp. Sci.* **3**, 56 (1971).

(17) J. S. Anderson, A. Bos and J. S. Ogden, *Chem. Commun.* 1381 (1971); A. Bos and J. S. Ogden, *J. Phys. Chem.* **77**, 1513 (1973).

(18) G. R. Smith and W. A. Guillory, *J. Chem. Phys.* **56**, 1423 (1972).

(19) See e.g. E. B. Wilson, Jr., J. C. Decius and P. C. Cross, *Molecular Vibrations*, McGraw-Hill, New York (1955); and J. Overend, in *Infra-Red Spectroscopy and Molecular Structures* (M. Davies, Ed.), Elsevier, Amsterdam (1963).

(20) J. K. Burdett, M. Poliakoff and J. J. Turner, in preparation.

(21) W. B. Person and D. Steele, in *Molecular Spectroscopy*, Vol. 2 (R. F. Barrow, D. A. Long and D. J. Millen, Eds.) (Chem. Soc. Specialist Periodical Reports) (1974).

(22) G. A. Ozin and A. Van der Voet, in *Progress in Inorganic Chemistry*, Vol. 19 (S. J. Lippard, Ed.), Wiley, New York (1975).
(23) J. H. Darling, M. B. Garton-Sprenger and J. S. Ogden, *Faraday Symp. Chem. Soc.* **8**, 75 (1974).
(24) L. Andrews, *J. Chem. Phys.* **50**, 4288 (1969).
(25) F. Königer and A. Müller, *J. Mol. Spectrosc.* **56**, 200 (1975); F. Königer, R. O. Carter and A. Müller, *Spectrochim. Acta* (in press).
(26) See e.g. G. A. Ozin and A. Van der Voet, *Can. J. Chem.* **51**, 3332 (1973).
(27) J. C. Decius, *J. Chem. Phys.* **20**, 1039 (1952).
(28) E. A. Koerner von Gustorf and F. W. Grevels, *Fortschr. Chem. Forsch.* **13**, 366 (1969).
(29) M. Wrighton, *Chem. Rev.* **74**, 401 (1974).
(30) S. F. A. Kettle, *J. Chem. Soc. A*, 420 (1966).
(31) J. K. Burdett, *J.C.S. Faraday II* **70**, 1599 (1974); *Inorg. Chem.* **14**, 931 (1975).
(32) M. Elian and R. Hoffmann, *Inorg. Chem.* **14**, 1058 (1975).
(33) M. Poliakoff and J. J. Turner, *J. Chem. Soc. Dalton*, 1351 (1973); 2276 (1974).
(34) For an excellent review of this field see P. S. Braterman, *Metal Carbonyl Spectra*, Academic Press, London (1975).
(35) H. Haas and R. K. Sheline, *J. Chem. Phys.* **47**, 2996 (1967).
(36) J. H. Darling and J. S. Ogden, *J. Chem. Soc. Dalton*, 1079 (1973).
(37) R. N. Perutz and J. J. Turner, *Inorg. Chem.* **14**, 262 (1975).
(38) J. J. Turner, *Angew. Chem. Int. Ed. Engl.* **14**, 304 (1975).
(39) M. Poliakoff, *Inorg. Chem.* (in press).
(40) R. N. Perutz and J. J. Turner, *J. Amer. Chem. Soc.* **97**, 4800 (1975).
(41) G. A. Ozin, personal communication.
(42) M. Poliakoff, *J. Chem. Soc. Dalton* 210 (1974).
(43) O. Crichton and A. J. Rest, *Inorg. Nucl. Chem. Lett.* **9**, 391 (1972).
(44) H. Hüber, E. P. Kündig, M. Moskovits and G. A. Ozin, *J. Amer. Chem. Soc.* **97**, 2097 (1975).
(45) L. H. Jones, R. S. McDowell and M. Goldblatt, *Inorg. Chem.* **8**, 2349 (1969).
(46) F. A. Cotton and C. S. Kraihanzel, *J. Amer. Chem. Soc.* **84**, 4432 (1962).
(47) J. K. Burdett, R. N. Perutz, M. Poliakoff and J. J. Turner, *Inorg. Chem.* (in press); J. K. Burdett and M. Poliakoff (in preparation).
(48) J. K. Burdett, *Chem. Commun.* 763 (1973).
(49) H. Hüber, E. P. Kündig, M. Moskovits and G. A. Ozin, *J. Amer. Chem. Soc.* **95**, 332 (1973).
(50) E. P. Kündig, M. Moskovits and G. A. Ozin, *Can. J. Chem.* **51**, 2737 (1973).
(51) See e.g. S. F. A. Kettle and I. Paul, in *Adv. Organomet. Chem.* (F. G. A. Stone and R. West, Eds.), **10**, 199 (1972).
(52) E. W. Abel and I. S. Butler, *Trans. Faraday Soc.* **63**, 45 (1967).
(53) P. S. Braterman, R. Bau and H. D. Kaesz, *Inorg. Chem.* **6**, 2097 (1967).
(54) See e.g. T. L. Brown and D. J. Darensbourg, *Inorg. Chem.* **6**, 971 (1967); **1**, 959 (1968); D. J. Darensbourg, H. H. Nelson and C. L. Hyde, *Inorg. Chem.* **13**, 2135 (1974).
(55) M. Bigorgne, *Spectrochim. Acta* **31A**, 1151 (1975); **32A**, 673 (1976).
(56) J. D. Attwood and T. L. Brown, *J. Amer. Chem. Soc.* **97**, 3380 (1975).
(57) E. P. Kündig and G. A. Ozin, *J. Amer. Chem. Soc.* **96**, 3820 (1974).
(58) O. Crichton, A. J. Rest, M. Poliakoff and J. J. Turner, *J. Chem. Soc. Dalton* 1321 (1973).
(59) P. A. Breeze and J. J. Turner, *J. Organomet. Chem.* **44**, C7 (1972); P. A. Breeze, Ph.D. Thesis, Cambridge University (1975).
(60) W. F. Edgell and J. Lyford, *J. Amer. Chem. Soc.* **93**, 6407 (1971).
(61) R. N. Perutz, Ph.D. Thesis, Cambridge University (1974).

(62) M. Bigorgne, personal communication.
(63) W. F. Edgell, *Spectrochim. Acta* **31A**, 1623 (1975),
(64) A. J. Rest and J. R. Sodeau, *Chem. Commun.* 696 (1975).
(65) M. A. Graham, M. Poliakoff and J. J. Turner, *J. Chem. Soc. A*, 2939 (1971).
(66) H. Dubost and L. Abouaf-Marguin, *Chem. Phys. Lett.* **17**, 269 (1972).
(67) J. K. Burdett, M. A. Graham, R. N. Perutz, M. Poliakoff, A. J. Rest, J. J. Turner and R. F. Turner, *J. Amer. Chem. Soc.* **97**, 4805 (1975).
(68) J. K. Burdett, R. N. Perutz, M. Poliakoff and J. J. Turner, *Chem. Commun.* 157 (1975).
(69) J. K. Burdett, I. R. Dunkin, J. Gryzbowski, M. Poliakoff and J. J. Turner (in preparation).
(70) C. B. Moore, *Adv. Chem. Phys.* **23**, 41 (1973).
(71) H. Dubost, L. Abouaf-Marguin and F. Legay, *Phys. Rev. Lett.* **29**, 145 (1972).
(72) H. Dubost and R. Charneau, *Chem. Phys.* **12**, 407 (1976); H. Dubost, Thesis, University of Paris XI, Centre d'Orsay, No. 1444 (1975).
(73) L. Abouaf-Marguin, H. Dubost and F. Legay, *Chem. Phys. Lett.* **22**, 603 (1973).
(74) D. L. Dexter, *J. Chem. Phys.* **21**, 836 (1953).
(75) M. J. Weber, *Phys. Rev. B4*, 2932 (1971).
(76) A. Nitzan, S. Mukamel and J. Jortner, *J. Chem. Phys.* **60**, 3929 (1974).
(77) D. J. Diestler, *J. Chem. Phys.* **60**, 2692 (1974).
(78) L. E. Brus and V. E. Bondybey, *J. Chem. Phys.* **63**, 786 (1975).
(79) D. S. Tinti and G. W. Robinson, *J. Chem. Phys.* **49**, 3229 (1968).
(80) R. T. Hall and G. C. Pimentel, *J. Chem. Phys.* **38**, 1889 (1963).
(81) M. A. Graham, R. N. Perutz, M. Poliakoff and J. J. Turner, *J. Organomet. Chem.* **34**, C34 (1972); R. N. Perutz and J. J. Turner, *J. Amer. Chem. Soc.* **97**, 4791 (1975).
(82) M. S. Baird, I. R. Dunkin and M. Poliakoff, *Chem. Commun.* 904 (1974).

Chapter 2

VIBRATIONAL INFORMATION FROM THE ELECTRONIC SPECTRA OF TRANSITION METAL COORDINATION COMPOUNDS

C. D. Flint

Department of Chemistry, Birkbeck College, University of London, Malet Street, London WC1E 7HX, U.K.

1 INTRODUCTION

This article differs from most in this series in that it does not deal specifically with infrared or Raman spectroscopy. Its purpose is to show that the study of the vibrational fine structure that is sometimes observed in the electronic absorption or emission spectra of transition metal complexes is a valuable source of vibrational information for these systems. This information complements the data obtained from the more usual vibrational techniques in much the same way that Raman data complement infrared data. The intensity mechanisms and selection rules for vibrational–electronic (or vibronic) spectroscopy are different from those involved in ground state spectroscopies and the technique has certain experimental advantages. In particular vibronic spectroscopy may enable the direct observation of infrared- and Raman-inactive fundamentals, the differentiation of internal vibrational modes from lattice vibrations, and the attribution of internal vibrational frequencies to specific symmetry coordinates. These last two applications are possible because the electronic excitation is essentially localized within a few hundred picometres of the metal atom whereas the vibrational excitations studied in the infrared and Raman spectroscopy of pure solids are delocalized over the whole crystal. In effect, one obtains a picture of the vibrational behaviour of a complex ion as viewed from the metal atom, an impression which parallels the way in which many coordination chemists regard the materials they handle. Thus it becomes possible to investigate the vibrational modes of the immediate environment of a metal atom without the contribution from the rest of the lattice or molecule becoming excessive. The great problem with the technique is that the number of compounds which are known to give electronic spectra displaying a useful amount of fine structure is limited, but this number is increasing rapidly as a result of the attention currently being given to dichroism spectroscopies and studies at very low temperatures. Moreover, in many vibrational studies, it may be possible to infer a solution to a problem from the results obtained using a related compound chosen for its suitability for the vibrational analysis of its electronic spectrum.

The largest terms contributing to the potential and kinetic energies of a molecule contain the nuclear and electronic coordinates in equivalent ways; from this viewpoint there is no essential difference between vibrational and electronic spectroscopies. The existence of these two divisions of chemical spectroscopy originates from the mass difference of the order of 10^4 between the electrons and nuclei. The electrons may then be regarded as moving in a static field due to stationary nuclei and described by functions which do not explicitly contain the nuclear coordinates. There will, however, be a different set of electronic functions for each set of nuclear coordinates. As the nuclei move, the electronic energy changes smoothly and behaves in a way similar to the energy stored in a spring. This separation of electronic and nuclear coordinates is known as the Born–Oppenheimer approximation.[1] Within this approximation it becomes possible to discuss electronic states, and transitions between states, by models which calculate electronic energy levels at constant internuclear distances. The models used most frequently in coordination compounds are the variants of ligand field theory. The features of those models that are important in the present context are mentioned below. Solution of the electronic Schrödinger equation at the ground state equilibrium nuclear geometry (or any other reference geometry) gives a series of electronic energy levels each characterized by the transformation properties of the associated wavefunction in the point group symmetry of the reference geometry. The variation of these electronic energy levels with the internuclear distances defines the potential surfaces of the electronic states, and the vibrational motion of the nuclei then occurs on these potential surfaces (see p. 57).

Transitions from one potential surface to another can then be caused by the external perturbation of an oscillating electromagnetic field of the appropriate frequency, polarization, and direction, or may occur spontaneously from a higher potential surface to a lower potential surface with emission of electromagnetic radiation. The quantization of the vibrational electronic energy levels may, in principle, result in an electronic spectrum having structure, although it may not always be possible to resolve this experimentally. The origin of the structure is discussed on pages 59–63. The above treatments neglect the translational symmetry of the crystal lattice. This proves to be a reasonable approximation for the larger complex ions but is inadequate to explain the details of the vibronic spectra of complexes of monatomic ligands. The effects of this translational symmetry are discussed on pages 63–66. The remaining sections deal with the experimental problems (p. 66) and the analysis and information content of the spectra (p. 70 and p. 73).

2   LIGAND FIELD THEORY

Almost all of the detailed interpretations of the d–d electronic spectra of coordination compounds have been based on one or more of the variants of ligand field theory.[2] The original form of this model was crystal field theory, on the basis of which the energy levels and wavefunctions of the crystal field states were calculated as the eigenvalues and eigenvectors of the perturbation matrix

$$|\langle \phi_i | \mathscr{H}' | \phi_j \rangle - E\delta_{ij}| \tag{1a}$$

Here ϕ_i and ϕ_j are the normalized antisymmetrized products of hydrogenic metal d-orbital functions and the perturbation operator

$$\mathscr{H}' = \mathscr{H}_C + \mathscr{H}_{CF} + \mathscr{H}_{SO} \ldots \tag{1b}$$

is the sum of the Coulombic repulsion of the d-electrons, $\mathscr{H}_C$, the external electrostatic field generated by the ligand electrons, $\mathscr{H}_{CF}$ (the crystal field), the spin-orbit interaction, $\mathscr{H}_{SO}$, and any other terms that may be deemed necessary. The first term, $\mathscr{H}_C$, is very much larger than the others and too large to be treated as a perturbation, but it may be partitioned into a large spherically symmetric part and a smaller non-spherical part. The spherical part may be regarded as screening the metal d-electrons from the metal nucleus and hence be combined with the nuclear attraction term, although the attraction of the d-electrons by the nucleus can no longer be described by the Coulomb Law. This 'central field approximation' does not affect the angular distribution of the metal electrons (which is determined by the spherical symmetry of the system), but grossly affects the radial part of the ϕ_i functions. These radial functions must then be derived by a procedure of the Hartree–Fock type. The crystal field may be treated in an analogous manner, being partitioned into a spherical part and a smaller part which has the site symmetry of the metal ion. The spherical part further modifies the radial part of the wavefunction, but this time the calculation of the correct form of this radial function is far more difficult and can only be carried out in idealized cases.

The usefulness of this crystal field model (and all other forms of ligand field theory) in spectroscopy depends on the collection of group theoretical ideas which surround the Wigner–Eckart theorem. This enables the matrix elements $\langle \phi_i | \mathscr{H}_C | \phi_j \rangle$, etc., to be decomposed into the product of a reduced matrix element (which depends on the radial functions and the explicit form of $\mathscr{H}_C$, etc.) and a numerical coefficient which may be calculated exactly from the symmetry properties of the perturbation and wavefunctions. Thus, in a cubic complex ion described by the simplest crystal field model, the interelectronic repulsion may be expressed in terms of two reduced matrix elements, and the crystal-field and spin-orbit perturbations in terms of one each. These matrix elements can be determined by experiment and the energies of all d-electron states can be expressed in terms of them. Moreover, since the radial functions are not going to be *very* different from those of the free ion, the approximate values of the Coulombic and spin-orbit parameters can be determined by experiments on the free ion.

The actual calculation of the numerical coefficients and subsequent diagonal-ization of the perturbation matrix is greatly simplified if, instead of using the antisymmetrized product functions ϕ in Eqn (1), linear combinations of these functions are used which transform correctly according to spherical symmetry or to the molecular point group. The former method is termed the weak field model because the crystal field terms appear off-diagonal and can be regarded as a perturbation of the free atom terms. The latter is referred to as the strong field model because the crystal field terms are on the diagonal. Of course the results of these two formalisms are identical but each has its own advantages. The weak field method often involves rather more calculation (although this is more easily automated), but its major advantage is that it is trivial to add a Racah–Trees correction to the free-ion terms. This correction, the origin of which is somewhat uncertain, is essential if large numbers of states are to be fitted accurately.[3] The strong-field method has the major advantage that the wavefunctions are expressed in terms of one-electron functions which transform in the same way as the molecular orbitals of the system. It is then possible to pass smoothly from the crystal-field formalism to a more realistic molecular-orbital model. This is of value in the prediction or rationalization of the relative shapes and positions of potential energy surfaces (see below and p. 59).

The impossibility of rationalizing the relative or absolute values of the crystal-field parameters obtained for different ligand–metal combinations using purely electrostatic methods has resulted in the development of empirical or semi-empirical molecular-orbital methods. The metal orbitals in the strong field version of crystal field theory are replaced, in the simplest form of m.o. theory, by linear combinations of metal and ligand orbitals having the correct transformation properties. For example, in an octahedral complex, the linear combinations transforming as the $x^2 - y^2$ row of the E_g representation and the xy row of the T_{2g} representation are

$$\Psi_{e_g}^{x^2-y^2} = \sin \theta \, d_{x^2-y^2} + \cos \theta \, \Sigma_{x^2-y^2} \tag{2a}$$

$$*\Psi_{e_g}^{x^2-y^2} = \cos \theta \, d_{x^2-y^2} - \sin \theta \, \Sigma_{x^2-y^2} \tag{2b}$$

$$\Psi_{t_{2g}}^{xy} = \sin \phi \, d_{xy} + \cos \phi \, \Pi_{xy} \tag{2c}$$

$$*\Psi_{t_{2g}}^{xy} = \cos \phi \, d_{xy} - \sin \phi \, \Pi_{xy} \tag{2d}$$

where $\Sigma_{x^2-y^2}$ (Π_{xy}) is the combination of ligand σ (π) orbitals that transform as the $x^2 - y^2$ (xy) row of the $E_g(T_{2g})$ representation. These linear combinations are tabulated in many places.[2,4] If θ and ϕ are zero, the $*\Psi_{e_g}^{x^2-y^2}$ and $*\Psi_{t_{2g}}^{xy}$ orbitals are the pure metal d-functions, and the molecular orbital model reduces to the crystal field model. The crystal field splitting is given, naively, in the m.o. model by $E(*\Psi_{e_g}) - E(*\Psi_{t_{2g}})$, although actual calculations require careful consideration of the nature of state, configuration, and orbital energies. Thus the magnitude of the ligand field splitting parameter, 10 Dq, reflects the difference between the amount the antibonding e_g-orbitals are raised in energy by σ-bonding and the amount the t_{2g}-orbitals are raised or lowered in energy by

π-bonding. In this way it is possible to rationalize the trend in the values of 10 Db for a range of ligands and a given metal. The substitution of linear combinations of ligand and metal orbitals for the spherical harmonics in Eqn (1a) invalidates the parameterization of the Coulombic and spin-orbit terms given above. In principle, nine Coulombic and two spin-orbit parameters are now required even in cubic symmetry but there is rarely, if ever, sufficient data to warrant the extraction of this number of quantities, and the d-orbital (spherical symmetry) approximation is employed. It is difficult to distinguish experimentally between the failure of this approximation and the failure of the original perturbation approximation.

The individual σ- and π- contributions to the crystal field cannot be separated in cubic symmetries, but in quadrate symmetries there are three crystal field parameters required by symmetry. In crystal field theory these are termed Ds, Dt and Dq. Simple molecular orbital arguments suggest that the crystal field parameters may be related to the empirical parameters $\delta\sigma$ and $\delta\pi$, where $\delta\sigma$ ($\delta\pi$) is the difference between the $\sigma(\pi)$ donor strengths of the ligands on the unique axis and those in the plane perpendicular to it. This alternative parameterization provides no additional information—it is merely an attempt to rationalize the observed Ds and Dt values. A significant advance on this m.o. procedure is the angular overlap model (AOM) of Jørgensen and Schäffer.[5,6] This model is primarily concerned with handling complexes of low symmetry, where the number of crystal field parameters required by symmetry may be too high to be determined by experiment. The central idea is that the σ- and π-antibonding effects of the ligands discussed above are proportional to the square of the angular overlap integrals between the metal and ligand orbitals, and these integrals may be decomposed into the product of a radial part (which depends only on the radial functions of the metal and ligand orbitals) and the bond length, and an angular part (which depends on the molecular geometry and the symmetries and orientations of the orbitals involved). For individual complexes of high symmetry, this model merely provides an alternative parameterization. The angular overlap parameters are e_σ and e_π, which separate the σ- and π-components of the metal–ligand interaction. For example, in a $trans$-MA_4B_2 complex of D_{4h} symmetry,

$$Dq = (1/10)[3e_\sigma(A) - 4e_\pi(A)] \tag{3a}$$

$$Ds = (2/7)[e_\sigma(B) - e_\sigma(A) + e_\pi(B) - e_\pi(A)] \tag{3b}$$

$$Dt = (2/3)[3e_\sigma(B) - 3e_\sigma(A) - 4e_\pi(B) + 4e_\pi(A)] \tag{3c}$$

The need to determine four parameters from three observables necessitates a further assumption. Usually this takes the form of assuming that either A or B does not have a π-bonding capability.

3 POTENTIAL SURFACES

Solution of the electronic Schrödinger equation (i.e. the total Schrödinger equation with the nuclear kinetic energy terms omitted) for all values of the nuclear coordinates to give a continuous set of functions $\Psi_i(q_\zeta, Q_\eta)$ and eigenvalues $\varepsilon_i(Q_\eta)$ may, in principle, be used to define a set of potential surfaces for a molecule. q_ζ and Q_η denote the complete sets of electronic and nuclear coordinates respectively. The subscripts are omitted where no confusion arises. The total electronic–nuclear wavefunction may then be approximated.[1]

$$\Psi_{ik}^{ev}(q, Q) = \Psi_i(q, Q)\chi_{ik}(Q) \tag{4a}$$

where the nuclear functions $\chi_{ik}(Q)$ are the solutions of the equation

$$[-\tfrac{1}{2}\sum_\eta \partial^2/\partial Q_\eta^2 + \varepsilon_i(Q)]\chi_{ik}(Q) = E_{ik}\chi_i(Q). \tag{4b}$$

Equations (4a) and (4b) constitute the Born–Oppenheimer approximation. For coordination complexes, the functions $\Psi_i(q, Q)$ cannot be calculated from first principles (p. 55), and the eigenvalues E_{ik} may then only be obtained by experiment. Experiment also shows that, excluding cases of degenerate or nearly degenerate electronic wavefunctions, the $\chi_{ik}(Q)$ functions describe harmonic oscillations to a good approximation.

It is usual to approximate the functions $\Psi_i(q, Q)$ by expanding them about some reference value of Q denoted by Q_0.

$$\Psi_i(q, Q) = \Psi_i^0(q) + \sum_{l \neq i}^\infty c_{il}\Psi_l^0(q)$$

where

$$c_{il} = [\varepsilon_i(Q_0) - \varepsilon_l(Q_0)]^{-1}\langle\Psi_l^0(q)|\sum_\eta (\partial V/\partial Q_\eta)_{Q_0}Q_\eta + \ldots|\Psi_i^0(q)\rangle \tag{5}$$

and V is the total potential energy term in the molecular Hamiltonian. Ligand field theory enables the *relative* $\varepsilon_i(Q_0)$ values and the angular functions in the d-electron part of $\Psi_i^0(q)$ to be expressed in terms of a small number of parameters. Equation 5 has been termed the Herzberg–Teller adiabatic approximation, while omission of the second term leaves the crude adiabatic approximation. In this latter case, a term

$$\langle\Psi_i^0(q)|\sum_\eta (\partial V/\partial Q_\eta)_{Q_0}Q_\eta|\Psi_i^0(q)\rangle$$

must be added to the potential energy term, $\varepsilon_i(Q_0)$, in Eqn (4b) to account for the variation of ε_i with Q. Ligand field theory does not provide a reliable means of calculating $(\partial V/\partial Q)_{Q_0}$.

The reference configuration, denoted by the subscript zero, is usually chosen to be the ground state equilibrium geometry and often has (or is considered as having) some symmetry. This results in the possibility of degeneracy in both the electronic and vibrational wavefunctions. For degenerate Ψ_i^0 the expansion (5) breaks down and the full perturbation matrix must be used. This has the form[7]

$$|\langle\Psi_i^{0r}|\sum_\eta (\partial V/\partial Q_\eta)_{Q_0}Q_\eta|\Psi_i^{0s}\rangle - \delta_{rs}\varepsilon_i^{'r}|$$

where the $\varepsilon_i^{\prime r}$ terms again contribute to the potential energy term $\varepsilon_i(Q)$ in (4b). The total potential energy term for a degenerate state then has a quasielastic part, which causes a conventional simple harmonic motion, and a vibronic part which distorts this elastic potential. The usual symmetry arguments[7] then show that for a single orbitally degenerate electronic state this vibronic part will be non-zero if there exists a vibrational mode of symmetry Γ_v such that Γ_v is contained in the symmetric direct product representation

$$[\Gamma(\Psi_i) \times \Gamma(\Psi_i)].$$

If the Γ_v is totally symmetric, the vibronic part will be diagonal and not cause any important effects, but if it is non-totally symmetric the vibronic interaction will split the vibronic degeneracy that is implied by the crude adiabatic approximation. Jahn and Teller showed that for non-linear molecules there is always a non-totally symmetric mode which will cause this splitting.[7] (It is necessary to exclude pure spin degeneracies where no external electrostatic perturbation can remove the degeneracy.) This Jahn–Teller effect has become a vast and complex topic; for the present purpose it is sufficient to emphasize that for a weak Jahn–Teller effect there will be a distortion of the potential surface in the directions of configuration coordinate space which transform as Γ_v, but for a strong Jahn–Teller effect the whole vibrational behaviour of the molecule is grossly affected.

Whilst quantitative potential surfaces are not easily derived from first principles, it is possible by using m.o. arguments to make a crude estimate of the differences between the shapes of the surfaces, and also of the differences between the positions of the minima of two states. It is reasonable to suppose that a molecule in an excited electronic state which is derived from a $(t_{2g})^{n-1}(e_g)^{m+1}$ configuration will have a longer metal–ligand bond length and a weaker metal–ligand stretching force constant than the same molecule in a state derived from the $(t_{2g})^n(e_g)^m$ configuration, because of the additional σ-antibonding electron in the excited state. The contribution of π-bonding to the force constant is expected to be less than that of the σ-bonding. Thus the potential surface of the excited state will be both flatter and displaced towards large metal–ligand distances compared with the ground state. Conversely, potential energy-surfaces of states belonging to the same strong-field configuration will have very similar shape and position but will be displaced vertically by the change in electron–electron repulsion. Using these simple arguments, qualitative Franck–Condon diagrams may be constructed from crystal field splitting diagrams (Fig. 1).

4 ELECTRONIC TRANSITIONS

Electromagnetic radiation may be regarded as being resolvable into an oscillating electric field and, perpendicular thereto, an oscillating magnetic field. The perturbation caused by these fields may cause a transition from one vibronic

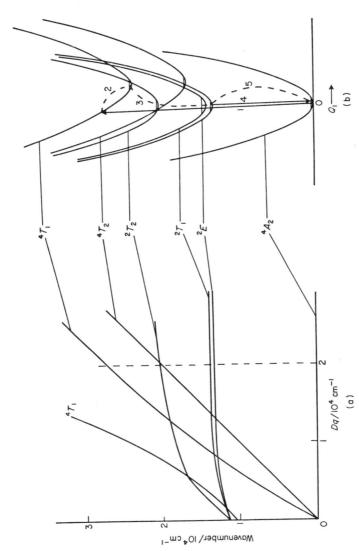

Fig. 1.(a) Ligand field splitting diagram showing the low-lying states of a d^3 ion in an octahedral environment ($B = 680$, $C = 2700$, $\xi = 0$ cm^{-1}).

(b) A section through the corresponding potential surfaces in the direction of the totally symmetric metal–ligand stretching coordinate, Q_1, when $Dq \approx 2000$ cm^{-1} (qualitative).

state, Ψ_{ik}^{ev}, to another, Ψ_{jl}^{ev}, provided that the frequency of the field corresponds to the energy difference between the vibronic states. The probability of this transition (i.e. the intensity of the observed spectrum) is proportional to the square of the matrix element,

$$D_{ik \to jl} = \langle \Psi_{ik}^{ev}(q, Q) | \mathbf{M} | \Psi_{jl}^{ev}(q, Q) \rangle \tag{6}$$

where $\mathbf{M}$ is the sum of the electric dipole operator, $e\Sigma \mathbf{r}_i$, and the magnetic dipole operator $(e/2mc) \Sigma \mathbf{r}_i \times \mathbf{p}_i$. Since $\mathbf{r}_i$ is of the order 10^{-10}m, $\mathbf{r}_i \times \mathbf{p}_i$ is of the order $h/2\pi \approx 10^{-34}$J s, the electric dipole contribution will dominate the magnetic dipole component except when the former is very small or zero for symmetry reasons.

To proceed, and especially to apply symmetry arguments to the above matrix element, it is necessary to approximate the $\Psi^{ev}(q, Q)$ functions by the Herzberg–Teller expansion, Eqn (5). Retaining just one other state, $\Psi_x^0(q)$, in the expansion we obtain[1]

$$\begin{aligned} D_{ik \to jl} \approx &\; \langle \Psi_i^0(q) | \mathbf{M}_e | \Psi_j^0(q) \rangle \langle \chi_{ik} | \chi_{jl} \rangle \\ &+ \langle \Psi_i^0(q) | \mathbf{M}_e | \Psi_x^0(q) \rangle \langle \chi_{ik} | c_{xj} | \chi_{jl} \rangle \\ &+ \langle \Psi_x^0(q) | \mathbf{M}_e | \Psi_j^0(q) \rangle \langle \chi_{ik} | c_{xi} | \chi_{jl} \rangle \end{aligned} \tag{7}$$

where c_{il} is given in equation (5) and $\mathbf{M}_e$ contains the sum over the electrons only.

The coefficients c_{il} (which are functions of the Q_n, because V depends on q and Q_n) are expected to be small, so that the first term will dominate the second and third terms unless the former is small or zero for symmetry reasons. Transitions which acquire their intensity because the first term is non-zero are said to be allowed, those which acquire their intensity from the second and third terms are said to be forbidden but vibronically allowed.

4.1 Allowed Electronic Transitions

An allowed electronic transition is one for which $\langle \Psi_i^0 | \mathbf{M}_e | \Psi_j^0 \rangle$ is non-zero. The electric and magnetic dipole operators transform as x, y, z and R_x, R_y, R_z in the reference geometry point group. Clearly for a centrosymmetric coordination complex, a d–d transition cannot be electric-dipole allowed since Ψ_i^0 and Ψ_j^0 both transform as g representations and $\Sigma \mathbf{r}_i$ transforms as a u representation; it may, however, be magnetic-dipole allowed. Even in non-centrosymmetric environments, the contribution from the electric-dipole allowed component is usually relatively small (compared with charge transfer and internal ligand transitions) because the wavefunctions are still predominantly composed of atomic d-functions. In practice the intensity of the electric-dipole component, the magnetic-dipole component, and the electric-dipole contribution to the forbidden component, are within a few orders of magnitude even in the absence of any strict selection rules, and any one may predominate. The matrix elements in Eqn (7) are signed quantities so the possibility of constructive and destructive interference arises.

Assuming that the allowed component predominates, the observed vibrational structure is governed by the vibrational overlap or Franck–Condon integral $\langle \chi_{ik} | \chi_{jl} \rangle$. This will be zero unless χ_{ik} and χ_{jl} have the same symmetry. Thus, for absorption or emission due to an allowed transition at low temperatures, only totally symmetric vibrational levels can be reached. One of the rare cases where this simple behaviour is observed is the $^4T_1(F) \leftarrow {}^4A_2$ transition of the $CoCl_4{}^{2-}$ ion.[8] Here, transitions are observed from the ground state to the vibrational levels of the excited state involving 0, 1 and 2 quanta of a mode of 278 cm^{-1}, which is probably the totally symmetric stretching vibration of the ion in the excited state. Where there is only one totally symmetric mode, the relative intensities of the members of this progression provide information on the relative displacement of the potential curves of the initial and terminal states. Inserting the appropriate form of the Hermite polynomials in the vibrational overlap integral, Ballhausen[9] has shown that the intensity of the nth member of a progression in a mode of frequency v is given approximately by:

$$I_n = [\tfrac{1}{2}\beta(\delta r)^2]^n I_0 / n! \tag{8}$$

where $\beta = 4\pi^2 v c M / h$, δr is the difference between the positions of the minima of the potential energy surfaces in the initial and terminal states along the totally symmetric stretching coordinate, and M is the mass of the monatomic ligand. The $^4T_1(F) \leftarrow {}^4A_2$ transition of the $CoCl_4{}^{2-}$ ion involves the transfer of electron density from the σ-nonbonding e-orbitals to the weakly σ-antibonding t_2-orbitals, and the resultant *small* change in the equilibrium metal–chlorine distance results in the observed progression in the metal–chlorine stretching mode. In this example, the pure electronic line is much stronger than the first member of the progression, showing that the change in equilibrium metal–chlorine distance is a few picometres. This small change is consistent with the similarity between the ground- and excited-state vibrational frequencies.[10] This formula is of value in assigning vibrational frequencies to symmetry coordinates since it is possible to associate an observed progression-forming mode with a totally symmetric coordinate which changes as a result of the electronic excitation (see p. 77). When there are several totally symmetric modes, differences between the admixtures of symmetry coordinates that constitute the normal modes of the ground and excited states invalidate the strict application of this formula for the intensities of progressions;[1] however, provided the difference is small, this does not invalidate its qualitative application.

The omnipresent Jahn–Teller effect will often mean that the potential surface of an excited state will have a different symmetry from that of the ground state. Under these circumstances the above considerations are modified so that the term totally symmetric applies to that largest subgroup that is common to the point groups of the molecule at vibrational equilibrium in the initial and terminal electronic states.

4.2 Forbidden Electronic Transitions

The second and third terms in Eqn (7) determine the vibrational structure of an electronically forbidden transition, or the contribution of the forbidden component of a transition which is both electronically and vibronically allowed. The second term will be non-zero if

$$\Gamma(\Psi_i^0) \times \Gamma(\mathbf{M}_e) \times \Gamma(\Psi_x^0)$$
$$\Gamma(\Psi_j^0) \times \Gamma(Q_\eta) \times \Gamma(\Psi_x^0)$$

and
$$\Gamma(\chi_{ik}) \times \Gamma(Q_\eta) \times \Gamma(\chi_{jk})$$

each contain Γ_1, and if χ_{ik} and χ_{jk} differ by a single quantum of the vibration along Q_η. A similar selection rule applies for the third term with i and j interchanged. Both these selection rules reduce to the requirement that, for the absorption or emission at low temperatures, the terminal vibrational level will correspond to one quantum of the vibration along coordinate Q together with any number of quanta of the totally symmetric vibrations, provided that $\Gamma(\Psi_i^0) \times \Gamma(\mathbf{M}_e) \times \Gamma(\Psi_j^0)$ contains $\Gamma(Q)$ (vibronic selection rule).

This is less restrictive than the selection rule for allowed transitions and quite different from infrared and Raman selection rules. The coefficients c_{il} in Eqn (5) are small and this vibronic mechanism is, therefore, important only for $\mathbf{M}_e$ as the electric dipole operator. The pure electronic transition is not allowed by this mechanism. The spectral feature corresponding to the transition to the state with one quantum of the vibration along Q and no other vibrational excitation is termed a vibronic origin. Based on these vibronic origins there will be progressions in totally symmetric modes, the intensities of which are governed by the appropriate Franck–Condon factors exactly as for an allowed transition.

The most important single factor which determines the *relative* intensities of the various vibronic origins in a single electronic state is the magnitude of $(\partial V/\partial Q_\eta)_{Q_0}$. This will be large only for those coordinates Q_η which involve motions which strongly influence the metal d-orbitals. The possibility of making at least order-of-magnitude estimates of the relative values of this term for different normal coordinates is a valuable source of vibrational information (see p. 73).

5 SOLID STATE EFFECTS

In the previous sections it has been assumed that the vibronic behaviour of coordination complexes, which is almost always studied by measurements on crystalline solids, can be interpreted using models that were developed for isolated molecules in the gas phase. The superficially similar assumption that the fundamental vibrations observed in the infrared and Raman spectra of complex solids may be interpreted by substituting the properties of the unit cell group for the molecular point group in the theory developed for isolated molecules has been very successful, but the failure of this approach[11] to account for the two- and multi-quantum excitations found in vibrational spectroscopy suggests that the assumption may be incorrect.

A continuous crystalline solid may be regarded as being divisible into translationally equivalent groups of atoms which constitute a unit cell. This division is arbitrary and a set of conventions is necessary to achieve consistency. These unit cells have dimensions of the order of 10^{-9} m for simple compounds. Exposure of such a crystal to infrared radiation of the appropriate frequency may cause the excitation of a vibrational quantum in the crystal, but, since the wavelength of the radiation will be some 10^4 times the lattice repeat unit, all vibrational motions thereby induced in neighbouring parts of the crystal will be nearly in phase. Similar considerations apply to Raman scattering. It is conventional to describe the phase relationship between adjacent cells by specifying a wave vector, $\mathbf{k} = 2\pi/\lambda$, where λ is the wavelength of the crystal wave-motion (i.e. the distance between molecules with the same phase). Clearly $\mathbf{k} = 0$ corresponds to in-phase motion, and there will be an upper limit to the physically meaningful value of $\mathbf{k}$ determined by the lattice repeat unit. The unit cell model and the extended crystal model with $\mathbf{k} = 0$ can be made equivalent, and, since infrared and Raman spectroscopies are limited to the observation of $\mathbf{k} = 0$ vibrations, the unit cell model is usually adequate to explain the results of these techniques.

In vibronic spectroscopy, two or more elementary excitations are created or destroyed. There is now no restriction in the wavevector values of these excitations other than the conservation of wavevectors:

i.e. $$\mathbf{k}_{photon} = \mathbf{k}_{electronic} + \mathbf{k}_{vibrational} = 0 \tag{9}$$

Non-zero values of $\mathbf{k}_{vibrational}$ (and of $\mathbf{k}_{electronic}$) are therefore observable, and an attempt at a complete interpretation of a vibronic spectrum must include consideration of these vibrational modes. For most coordination complexes, the metal ions are too far apart for the electronic energy levels to be significantly influenced by the value of $\mathbf{k}_{electronic}$ (this is not true for organic and simple inorganic solids), but the effect of non-zero $\mathbf{k}_{vibrational}$ along a specific direction will be to subject the unit cell to an external perturbation which will reduce the symmetry of the vibrational modes, change vibrational frequencies, and may split the components of a vibration which is degenerate at $\mathbf{k} = 0$. (Except where otherwise indicated $\mathbf{k}$ refers to the vibrational excitation.) It will also cause the mixing of vibrations which have different symmetry at $\mathbf{k} = 0$.

If the distance between the complex ions is large, the change in frequency of the internal vibrational modes with $\mathbf{k}$ (i.e. dispersion) will be small, but for complexes of monatomic ligands the dispersion of internal modes may be as much as a few tens of wavenumbers.[12, 13] The external vibrational modes will be more strongly dependent on $\mathbf{k}$. In the unit cell approximation, the motions corresponding to the translations of the unit cell will have zero frequency and are deleted. For non-zero $\mathbf{k}$ these acoustic modes have a finite frequency which, in the absence of interactions with other modes, increases as $\mathbf{k}$ moves away from zero and approaches a limiting value at the maximum value of $\mathbf{k}$ in any direction.[12,13,14] The maximum values of $\mathbf{k}$ (i.e. the end points of the $\mathbf{k}$ vectors) define the boundary of the (first) Brillouin zone. The zone-boundary acoustic phonons have a frequency which is comparable to the frequency of the optical phonons at $\mathbf{k} = 0$. These optical phonons also exhibit considerable dispersion and mix with the acoustic modes and the lower lying internal modes.

There is an additional difference between the unit-cell and extended crystal models which persists even at $\mathbf{k} = 0$. If the crystal is ionic or partially ionic in character, an electric field is set up which interacts with the oscillatory motion; in cubic crystals this results in a splitting of the motions which transform as x, y, or z into two components, a doubly degenerate transverse mode at $\mathbf{k} = 0$, and a singly degenerate longitudinal mode at higher energy. This transverse–longitudinal splitting may amount to a few tens of wavenumbers.

Calculations of vibrational frequencies for an extended crystal model are very much more difficult than for the corresponding unit cell model. The only published treatments refer to the antifluorite K_2PtCl_6 (*Fm3m*) structure.[12-15] A determination of the vibrational frequencies as a function of $\mathbf{k}$ on a compound of this structure by inelastic neutron scattering would be of the greatest interest. The calculation of theoretical vibronic spectra is even more difficult. The simplest and commonest assumption is that all vibrational modes of the correct symmetry or symmetries contribute equally to the vibronic spectrum. The graph of the normalized number of vibrational modes per unit wavenumber, against wavenumber, is known as a density of states curve. These curves may be calculated from the results of an extended crystal model. Comparison of these curves with the measured spectrum may enable the identification of turning points in the observed spectrum with specific vibrational modes.

An alternative way of looking at the lattice dynamics and intensity mechanism is the cluster model of Satten.[16] The metal ion is treated, in effect, as an impurity in its own lattice. Since the 'impurity' destroys the translational symmetry, the wavevector selection rules become irrelevant, and the isolated metal ions 'see' the vibrations of the complex and lattice as belonging to the irreducible representations of the site group. The division of the crystal into unit cells is neglected and the symmetries of the vibrations of the various shells of atoms around the metal are calculated as if the metal atom and its surroundings were an isolated cluster. The vibronic perturbation V_{ev} is then given by[17]

$$V_{ev} = \Sigma f_\beta^n Q_\beta^n \tag{10}$$

where Q_β^n is the amplitude of the normalized symmetry coordinate for the nth neighbour shell transforming to a particular row β of an irreducible representation. V_{ev} may also be expanded in spherical harmonics about the central atom.[17] For an O_h site, the T_{1u} field contains spherical harmonics of order $l = 1, 3, 5$, whilst a T_{2u} field contains $l = 3, 5$. If it is assumed that the lowest-order fields will dominate, the T_{1u} fields will be longer range than the T_{2u} fields.

The spectra that have been published to date seem to indicate that, for complexes of di- and polyatomic ligands, the unit cell approximation is adequate to explain the positions and intensities of the vibronic origins due to internal modes. The internal vibrations of complexes of monatomic ligands, however, usually show structure due to the transverse–longitudinal splitting [14] or to dispersion.[17] The unit-cell approximation is, however, inadequate to explain the appearance of vibronic spectra in the lattice-vibration region or to account for all the weaker features in the internal region.[14]

One way of checking whether a splitting of an internal mode is due to an extended crystal effect or not is to dilute the complex in a material of similar structure and remeasure the absorption or emission spectrum. This destroys the translational symmetry and hence eliminates $k = 0$ effects on internal modes and the transverse–longitudinal splitting. One must be careful, however, to avoid pair spectra and to ensure that the internal vibrational frequencies of the impurity do not overlap with allowed vibrational bands of the host. Rather complex behaviour can result if the latter condition is not fulfilled.[18]

6 SOME EXPERIMENTAL ASPECTS

The well-resolved electronic spectra that are necessary if vibrational information is to be obtained may be luminescence, absorption or excitation spectra. These three experimental techniques each have their own advantages and disadvantages. As in most fields of spectroscopy, a combination of techniques is often advantageous.

Irradiation of a complex[19] with an intense light source of wavelength corresponding to an absorption band causes excitation of some of the complex ions to an excited vibronic state (process 1, Fig. 1b). This is followed by rapid loss of vibrational excitation (process 2). Subsequently, the complex may relax to a lower excited state (process 3), and then return to the ground state either radiatively (process 4) or non-radiatively (process 5), it may undergo photo-chemical decomposition, or the excitation energy may be transferred to an adjacent molecule or ion. The kinetics of these relaxation processes may be complex, but in the majority of cases (and especially for first-row transition elements), the most intense luminescence is from the lowest excited electronic state to the ground state. The radiationless processes which reduce the intensity of the luminescence are slowed down by cooling the sample, so that most luminescence measurements are carried out at liquid nitrogen or liquid helium temperatures. The low temperature is also necessary to obtain sufficiently well-resolved spectra (see below). Luminescent coordination compounds are often photosensitive so that care must be taken to avoid an excessive intensity of the excitation source. The experimental arrangement is similar to that employed for Raman spectroscopy except that the intensity of the emission *may* be several orders of magnitude higher than even the strongest resonant Raman scattering and relatively low power sources are sufficient. The emission may be thousands of wavenumbers to low energy of the excitation frequency, which obviates the need for multiple monochromators.

Since luminescence measurements are usually performed at very low temperatures, and the lifetime of the emissive electronic state must be long compared with the period of molecular vibrations if significant luminescence is to be observed, emission occurs from the lowest internal vibrational level of the excited state (i.e. that possessing only zero-point vibrational energy—the contribution of acoustic modes of near zero frequency is mentioned below) to the vibrational levels of the ground state. The shortest wavelength emission line is termed the electronic origin, pure electronic line or zero–phonon line. The remaining transitions then represent transitions to excited vibrational levels of the ground electronic state and the intervals between the electronic origin and these vibronic lines correspond to ground-state vibrational frequencies; these may be directly compared with frequencies determined by infrared and Raman spectroscopy. If the temperature of measurement is not very low, vibrational levels of the excited electronic state become populated, and transitions from these vibronic levels to the vibrational levels of the ground state will occur. These 'hot bands' will be to the high energy side of the electronic origin if the excited-state vibrational frequency is greater than the ground-state vibrational frequency. Provided that the excited-state potential surface is not very different from that of the ground state, the positions of these hot bands will approximately mirror the spectrum to low energy of the electronic origin, but their intensity will be weighted by the appropriate Boltzmann factor. Under these circumstances, the identification of the electronic origin may not be obvious, but an unambiguous identification is usually possible by measuring the spectrum at several temperatures including the lowest available temperature, or by comparing the luminescence and absorption spectra at the same low temperature (when only the electronic origin has the same intensity, relative to the other bands, in both spectra). Less certain identifications can be made by identifying vibrational intervals observed by other spectroscopic techniques in the vibronic spectrum.

A second advantage of luminescence measurements is that the intensity of the emission from a given state is governed, amongst other factors, by the ratio of the rate constant for the emission process to the sum of the rate constants for all the relaxation processes. Since radiationless relaxation processes are usually slower for spin-forbidden transitions (other factors being equal) than for spin-allowed transitions, the spin selection rule which reduces the intensity of spin-forbidden electronic transitions when measured in absorption is of much less importance than in emission experiments, where it results in a longer lifetime for the excited state. This extended lifetime, coupled with the insensitivity of the energies of some spin-forbidden transitions to external electrostatic influences, means that the best-resolved vibronic spectra often arise from spin-forbidden transitions (see below). The low transition probabilities for spin-forbidden transitions may make the measurement of any structure difficult by absorption spectroscopy, but it is the competing non-radiative processes which control the observed intensity of emission.

A third advantage of luminescence measurements occurs where there are several electronic states of similar energy because the upper states invariably relax rapidly to the lowest state in the manifold. At low temperatures, emission occurs only from this lowest state. In absorption, the vibronic structure of the several states may overlap and so prevent unambiguous analysis.

Against these three advantages must be set the very considerable disadvantage that relatively few coordination complexes are known to show structured luminescence, but this is due in part to the limited number of searches that have been made for luminescence at very low temperatures. There is another important difference between emission and absorption processes. The half-life of the excited state from which emission occurs is typically in the range 10^{-7}–10^{-2} s. This time is sufficiently long for the excitation to be transferred to another nearby molecule with an excited state of identical or slightly lower energy.[20] This transfer is often referred to as the exchange of a quasiparticle—an exciton. In a compound containing only one type of complex ion, this exchange is of little importance. But real solids contain impurities and defects which, if they possess an excited state of energy just lower than the excited state of the majority species, may be excited to this state and the difference in energy be lost as nuclear motion. The impurity then cannot pass on the excitation to the majority species because, at low temperatures, it has insufficient energy and the exciton becomes trapped. Eventually this exciton decays either radiatively or non-radiatively, but any emission is characteristic of the impurity rather than of the host material. The energy transfer may be sufficiently fast for the exciton to visit thousands of lattice sites before it decays, so that a very small quantity of an impurity species may dominate the emission or quench it completely. The rate constant for the energy transfer is a strong function (at least r^{-3}) of the distance between the ions, and so it is much more important for salts of small- and medium-sized complex ions than for very large complexes. For species such as MnF_6^{2-} [21] and $Cr(en)_3^{3+}$,[22] the removal of the impurity may cause very great experimental problems. Fortunately the energy transfer may be prevented by diluting the complex ion of interest in a host material which does not have energy levels below the emissive state. A dilution to 1 mol $\%$ is sufficient to eliminate most pairs of the complex ions on adjacent lattice sites and hence greatly reduce the effects of energy transfer. If the host is colourless, and the complex ion has strong absorption bands, the excitation efficiency will not be greatly reduced by this process. The vibrational intervals observed in the emission will be those of the complex ion in its host, and by varying the host the effect of external influences on these vibrations may be studied and the contributions of dispersion effects and TO–LO splittings removed. Sensitivity and overlap problems make such studies by infrared, Raman or electronic absorption spectroscopy very difficult. The energy transfer from host to impurity may also be used to obtain the spectrum of a weak emitter or a complex available in very small amounts.[21]

The main advantage of the absorption technique is its generality, since many coordination complexes have at least one accessible transition which exhibits vibrational structure. The vibrational frequencies observed in this way are those of the excited state, but if the potential surfaces of the excited and the ground states are very similar, the excited-state frequencies may be similar to those of the ground state. Moreover, provided the nature of the excited state is well understood, any differences between the ground- and excited-state frequencies may yield information on the symmetry coordinates that contribute to the normal modes observed. The instrumental resolution required for detailed analysis of electronic spectra is similar to that needed in infrared- and Raman spectroscopy, i.e. not worse than a few wavenumbers. This is at the limit of performance of the best commercial double-beam recording spectrophotometers.

The measurement of excitation spectra (i.e. the intensity of emission at a constant wavelength as a function of excitation wavelength) is usually an attempt to combine the sensitivity of luminescence measurements with the flexibility of absorption measurements. Provided the efficiency of the luminescence is high, and an intense tunable source is available, the improvement in sensitivity may be several orders of magnitude. This improvement arises because the noise produced in a photodetector is almost proportional to the square root of the light intensity. A weak luminescence is therefore much more easily detected than the small absorption of an intense beam of light. A further advantage is that it may be possible to measure the vibronic spectrum of the different species in a complex mixture by using different observing frequencies, although energy transfer may complicate the interpretation of the results.[21]

The absorption or emission bands observed in the electronic spectra of coordination complexes have finite width and in many cases this width is sufficient to prevent the resolution of individual vibrational components. The origin of this broadness is not completely understood but a number of contributory factors have been identified. Firstly, the bands have a natural line width determined by the lifetime of the excited state. Since $h/2\pi \approx 1 \times 10^{-34}$ J s which corresponds to 5×10^{-12} cm^{-1} s, significant broadening can occur if the initial or terminal state has a lifetime of less than 10^{-12} s. This is often the major source of broadening of the higher lying vibronic transitions.[1] Secondly, the spectra are measured with the complex ion embedded in a solid medium. This medium cannot be perfect and the complex will be subjected to random electric and magnetic fields due to crystal strain, imperfection, and disorder. The degree of broadening produced by this mechanism will depend on the sensitivity of the electronic energy levels to external influences, but even for the much-studied $^2E_g \leftrightarrow {}^4A_{2g}$ transition of octahedral chromium(III) complexes, the energy of which is almost independent of the environment, this mechanism contributes from a few tenths to some tens of wavenumbers to the measured spectral width.[23] This is often the main broadening mechanism for relatively sharp transitions at liquid helium temperatures. At higher temperatures, the lattice in its initial electronic state occupies a range of acoustic and internal vibrational levels. Even if there is no change in the vibrational quantum numbers during the electronic transition, any differences between the vibrational frequencies, anharmonicities, or non-adiabaticities of the states will cause a broadening. These are often the main broadening mechanisms for relatively sharp bands at liquid nitrogen temperatures and above, but their effects may be apparent at lower temperatures.[24] In addition to these broadening mechanisms, there is a problem of congestion of lines. For example, even for the relatively simple case of the $^4T_{2g} \leftarrow {}^4A_{2g}$ transition of the $Cr(NH_3)_6{}^{3+}$ ion at low temperatures, and neglecting the Jahn–Teller effect, several hundred strong vibronic bands are expected within two or three thousand wavenumbers. The Jahn–Teller effect may increase this number substantially. A relatively small broadening of the lines themselves soon washes out any structure. This problem may be reduced by measuring the magnetic circular dichroism spectrum of the compound. The circular dichroism is a signed quantity and this may help the identification of indistinct spectral features. It also provides an aid to the identification of vibrational modes.[25]

In order to observe vibrational structure, it is desirable to study electronic transitions whose energies are nearly independent of external perturbations, and where both the initial and terminal states are well separated from other electronic states. The sensitivity to external perturbations is particularly important, since this governs the magnitude of the effects due to strain, changes in vibrational frequencies, and the Jahn–Teller effect. It also reduces the congestion due to progression-forming modes. Because crystal-field spin-allowed transitions to, or from, the ground state are of necessity sensitive to their environment, the most detailed analysis of vibronic structure has been carried out for spin-forbidden transitions between the ground state and low lying excited states. The ^2E_g, $^2T_{1g}$, $^2T_{2g} \leftrightarrow {}^4A_{2g}$ transitions of d^3 ions in cubic or nearly cubic environments are particularly favourable for study because of the ease of synthesis of suitable complexes, and because these transitions occur in or near the visible region (which is convenient for electronic spectroscopy). However, metal ions of other electron configurations could in principle give rise to complexes whose spectra show considerable vibrational structure; there are, however, only a few reports of such detailed experimental studies.

7   DETERMINATION OF INFRARED- AND RAMAN-INACTIVE VIBRATIONAL FREQUENCIES

The vibronic selection rule (p. 63) differs from the infrared- and Raman-selection rules and depends on the symmetry of the initial and terminal electronic states. Table 1 gives the symmetries of the vibrational modes that may act as vibronic origins for a transition between electronic (ligand field) states of symmetries Γ and Γ' for an octahedral molecule. If the electronic transition is spin-allowed, and the spin-orbit coupling constant is small compared with the separation of the initial and terminal states from other states, it is usually

TABLE 1
Symmetries of vibronic origins for the $\Gamma_g \to \Gamma_g$ electronic transition of octahedral molecules

		A_1 Γ_1	A_2 Γ_2	E Γ_3	T_1 Γ_4	T_2 Γ_5
	Γ_g					
A_1 Γ_1		t_{1u}	t_{2u}	$t_{1u}+t_{2u}$	$a_{1u}+e_u+t_{1u}+t_{2u}$	$a_{2u}+e_u+t_{1u}+t_{2u}$
A_2 Γ_2			t_{1u}	$t_{1u}+t_{2u}$	$a_{2u}+e_u+t_{1u}+t_{2u}$	$a_{1u}+e_u+t_{1u}+t_{2u}$
E Γ_3				$t_{1u}+t_{2u}$	all u	all u
T_1 Γ_4					all u	all u
T_2 Γ_5						all u

	Γ_6	Γ_7	Γ_8
Γ_6	$a_{1u}+e_u+t_{1u}+t_{2u}$	$a_{2u}+e_u+t_{1u}+t_{2u}$	all u
Γ_7		$a_{1u}+e_u+t_{1u}+t_{2u}$	all u
Γ_8			all u

sufficient to consider only the orbital symmetry of the electronic states; in other cases the double-group symmetry must be utilized. Of these u vibrations in Table 1, the t_{2u} modes are the most interesting for isolated complexes, since they are both infrared- and Raman-inactive but may appear strongly in vibronic spectra. For pure (i.e. undiluted) complexes which crystallize in cubic space groups, the vibronic spectra may show the transverse-optic/longitudinal-optic splitting of the t_{1u} fundamental vibrations. These splittings are not usually accessible from ground state vibrational studies.

Figure 2 shows the $^2E_g \to {}^4A_{2g}$ luminescence of Cs_2MnF_6 measured at 5 K. In this substance, the $MnF_6{}^{2-}$ ion occupies a perfect octahedral site.[26] The weak band at 16031 cm^{-1} is identified as the electronic origin by its coincidence with a similar band in the 5 K absorption and excitation spectra. Moreover, at higher temperatures a series of hot bands is observed to high energy of the 16031 cm^{-1} band which mirrors the band observed to low energy but which is reduced in intensity by a factor $\exp(\Delta E/kT)$ where ΔE is the vibrational interval involved. The low intensity of the electronic origin is in agreement with the magnetic dipole nature of this line, and this has been confirmed by polarization studies on $MnF_6{}^{2-}$ ions in non-cubic but centrosymmetric environments.[30] For this electronic transition, both the initial and terminal states transform as Γ_{8g} in the $O_h{}^*$ double group, so vibrations of all odd symmetries are vibronically active. The 332 and 616 cm^{-1} bands are immediately assignable as the t_{1u} F—Mn—F bending and t_{1u} Mn—F stretching vibrations respectively, because modes of these wavenumbers are observed clearly in the infrared spectrum. The 230 cm^{-1} band is not observed in the infrared and must be assigned as the t_{2u} bending mode. The weaker bands just to the low energy side (i.e. higher vibrational frequency) of the 332 and 616 cm^{-1} bands are assigned as the infrared- and Raman-inactive longitudinal–optic component of the t_{1u} modes, because they are absent in the luminescence spectra of the $MnF_6{}^{2-}$ ion when it is diluted

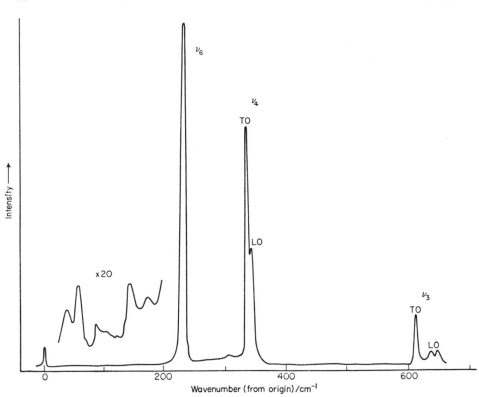

Fig. 2. $^2E_g \rightarrow {}^4A_{2g}$ luminescence spectrum of Cs₂MnF₆ at 5 K. The inset showing the lattice vibration region was measured at 80 K to reduce the intensity of emission from traps.

into host lattices which do not have vibrations near these frequencies. The motions of the caesium ions which surround the MnF_6^{2-} entity form the basis of a_{1g}, e_g, t_{1g}, $2t_{2g}$, a_{2u}, e_u, $2t_{1u}$, and t_{2u} representations. Contributions from the odd modes (which are, of course, not vibrations of the primitive unit cell) occur in the region between 30 and 110 cm⁻¹. The low intensities of these modes are as expected, since the vibronic perturbation [$(\partial V/\partial Q_n)_{Q_0}$ in Eqn (5)] produced by the motion of the caesium ions is expected to be much weaker than that caused by that of the fluorine ions. Alternatively, and equivalently, these bands may be assigned to maxima in the lattice-vibration density of states. Studies of the low frequency vibronic spectra of metal ions in inorganic lattices may provide extensive data against which lattice dynamical models may be tested.[12-16]

Even when a complex ion has less than octahedral symmetry, the intensities of some of the internal vibrations in the infrared or Raman spectra may be too low to permit the identification of the vibrations. These internal vibrations may, however, appear strongly in the vibronic spectra. Examples of this are the $Cr(CN)_6^{3-}$ ion in $K_3Co(CN)_6$ (which is discussed in the next section), and the

$Cr(OD_2)_6^{3+}$ ion. In the latter case, all five t_u O—Cr—O and Cr—O—D bending modes are immediately identifiable from the emission or absorption spectrum. References to other complexes for which t_{2u} modes have been identified by vibronic spectroscopy are given in Table 2.

TABLE 2
Assignments of ground state t_{2u} vibrations of octahedral transition metal coordination complexes from electronic spectroscopy

Complex	Compound	Wavenumber/cm⁻¹	Reference
CrF_6^{3-}	$K_2NaGaF_6:Cr$	$\nu_6 = 200$	27
	$K_2NaAlF_6:Cr$	$\nu_6 = 203$	28
MnF_6^{2-}	Cs_2MnF_6	$\nu_6 = 229$	14, 26
	K_2MnF_6(hexagonal)	$\nu_6 = 230$	21
	K_2MnF_6(trigonal)	$\nu_6 = 216$	21
	$K_2SiF_6:Mn$	$\nu_6 = 230$	18
	$Cs_2SiF_6:Mn$	$\nu_6 = 227$	18
	$Cs_2GeF_6:Mn$	$\nu_6 = 229$	18
IrF_6	IrF_6	$\nu_6 = 206$	29
$ReCl_6^{2-}$	$K_2PtCl_6:Re$	$\nu_6 = 120$	30
	$Cs_2ZrCl_6:Re$	$\nu_6 = 135$	31
	$Cs_2SnCl_6:Re$	$\nu_6 = 136$	30
$ReBr_6^{2-}$	$Cs_2ZrBr_6:Re$	$\nu_6 = 87$	32
	$Cs_2SnBr_6:Re$	$\nu_6 = 85$	30
	$Rb_2SnCl_6:ReBr_6^{2-}$	$\nu_6 = 87$	30
	$Rb_2SnBr_6:Re$	$\nu_6 = 83$	30
$OsBr_6^{2-}$	$Cs_2ZrBr_6:OsBr_6^{2-}$	$\nu_6 = 86$	33
$Cr(CN)_6^{3-}$	$K_3Co(CN)_6:Cr^{3+}$	δ(C—Cr—C) = 86–119	34
		δ(Cr—C—N) = 354–364	
$Cr(NCS)_6^{3-}$	$K_3Cr(NCS)_6$	δ(N—Cr—N) = 40	
		δ(Cr—N—C) = 269	35
		δ(N—C—S) = 478	
$Cr(OD_2)_6^{3+}$	$TlCr(SO_4).12D_2O$	δ(O—Cr—O) = 190	36
		OD_2 wag = 540	
$Cr(NH_3)_6^{3+}$	several	δ(N—Cr—N) = 194–230	37, 38
		NH_3 rock = 670–724	
$Cr(ND_3)_6^{3+}$	several	δ(N—Cr—N) = 172–202	37, 38
		ND_3 rock = 509–546	

8 THE ALLOCATION OF VIBRATIONAL FREQUENCIES TO SYMMETRY COORDINATES

The central problem in the analysis of vibrational spectra is to allocate the observed vibrational frequencies to motions involving specific combinations of the molecular symmetry coordinates. There is no way by which this can be done with certainty and the spectroscopic literature contains many examples of disagreement over the assignment of observed frequencies. The method of isotopic substitution, together with a reliable model for the molecular dynamics, provides the best technique, but the synthesis of the isotopically substituted compounds may present problems and, for the heavier elements, the frequency changes may be too small to measure with ease. Moreover, in order to interpret the results of an isotopic substitution experiment, the observed isotopic shift must be compared with that calculated on the basis of a dynamical model and a trial allocation of the fundamentals. For complex molecules reliable models are not available. Frequently vibrational spectra are assigned by a combination of experience and guesswork. The measurement of vibronic structure may assist in this assignment problem in two ways. Firstly, the intensities of vibronic origins depend on the magnitudes of $(\partial V/\partial Q_n)_{Q_0}$ in Eqn (5). An accurate calculation of these quantities is not possible, but it is reasonable to assume that a vibrational motion which involves mainly atoms more than, say, 4Å (0.4 nm) from the metal atom, and which does not change the metal–ligand bonding, will cause a much weaker vibronic perturbation than the motions of the ligating atoms. No such discrimination is afforded by infrared or conventional (i.e. non-resonance) Raman spectroscopy. Secondly, the electronic energy levels of the lighter transition metals are well understood, and it is often possible to predict which equilibrium bond distances are likely to be changed as a result of an electronic transition. This change in bond length will result in progressions in the terminal state vibrational mode(s) associated with that bond distance. It therefore becomes possible to associate a terminal-state frequency with a specific molecular coordinate. The change in equilibrium bond lengths will also result in a change in the vibrational frequency associated with that coordinate. This may also assist in the assignment of the frequencies.

8.1 The Differentiation of Metal–Ligand Vibrations from Lattice- and Internal-Ligand Vibrations

Metal–ligand vibrations often occur in the same spectral region as lattice vibrations. Both of these types of modes may appear strongly in infrared and Raman spectra and their disentanglement in these spectra is not always a simple matter. The perturbation of the metal d-orbitals by the ligands depends primarily on the nature of the atoms involved and the group overlap integral. The variation of this perturbation with the nuclear normal coordinates will be large for those normal coordinates which involve motions of the ligating atoms, or of the ligand donor atom's σ-bonding 'lone pair', but small for lattice vibrations and internal ligand motions which cause little change in the group overlap integrals. Vibronic origins involving skeletal vibrations of the complex are expected, therefore, to be considerably stronger than bonds due to lattice vibrations in vibronic spectra, and this may be sufficient to permit the identification of the internal vibrational modes. It is not usually possible to differentiate $\mathbf{k} = 0$ lattice vibrations from the vibronic spectra because of the presence of zone boundary frequencies, but comparison of infrared and vibronic spectra may enable an identification to be made.

This method of distinction has been used many times in the literature; indeed, it is implicit in almost all interpretations of vibronic spectra. The simplest examples are found for compounds with the antifluorite K_2PtCl_6 structure (Table 2 and Fig. 1). Frequently the lattice and internal modes are mixed together so that there are several bands with appreciable intensity. The relative intensities of the various modes may then be a very approximate indication of the extent of this mixing, but it is essential to remember that the vibronic spectrum reflects this mixing at all $\mathbf{k}$ values, not just the $\mathbf{k} = 0$ situation studied in infrared and Raman spectroscopy and unit-cell group analysis. An example where this mixing is strong is the much-studied $^2E_g \rightarrow {}^4A_{2g}$ transition[34] of $Cr(CN)_6^{3-}$ in $K_3Co(CN)_6$ (Fig. 3). The use of a diluted crystal is necessary to obtain a sufficiently well resolved spectrum, but the lattice vibrations are likely to be of similar frequency in $K_3Cr(CN)_6$ and $K_3Co(CN)_6$. In this lattice, the Cr^{3+} ion occupies a site with inversion symmetry only. It is reasonable to associate the maxima near 90 and 150 cm^{-1} with the split components of the t_{2u} and t_{1u} C—Cr—C bending modes, respectively, but the complexity of the spectrum demonstrates the extent of the mixing of internal and external coordinates. The assignments of the internal modes have been supported by studies on a range of salts containing the $Cr(CN)_6^{3-}$ ion. The 150 cm^{-1} group of bands appears strongly in the infrared spectrum, but the 90 cm^{-1} group appears only weakly, as expected for the above assignments. The mixing of internal and external modes appears stronger in the vibronic spectrum than in the infrared spectrum, indicating that mixing of these modes when $\mathbf{k} \neq 0$ is important.

A related application is illustrated by the $^2E \rightarrow {}^4A_2$ luminescence and $^2E, {}^2T_1 \leftarrow {}^4A_2$ absorption spectra of $2Cr(en)_3Cl_3 \cdot KCl \cdot 6H_2O$.[22] The absorption bands in the infrared spectrum of this compound caused by the low frequency vibrations of the $Cr(en)_3^{3+}$ entity are weak and partly obscured by a water librational mode. The corresponding low frequency modes appear strongly in the luminescence and absorption spectra, but the water mode is not observed.

In principle it should be possible to distinguish metal–ligand vibrations from internal ligand vibrations by a similar argument. However, when there are internal ligand vibrations of frequency sufficiently close to the metal–ligand vibrations for confusion to arise, the coupling between the motions is likely to be strong and the designations of the modes become less meaningful. Some attempt to use this criterion has been made for the $Cr(en)_3^{3+}$ ion.[22]

8.2 The Identification of Ligand Rocking and Wagging Modes

The discussion in the previous section might be taken to indicate that only those vibrations which involve substantial motion of the ligating atoms will produce strong vibronic origins in electronic spectra. The amino- and aquo-complexes of chromium(III) provide a marked exception to this view, because in the spectra of these compounds the vibronic origins due to the NH_3 rocking, OH_2 rocking and OH_2 wagging modes are among the strongest bands in the

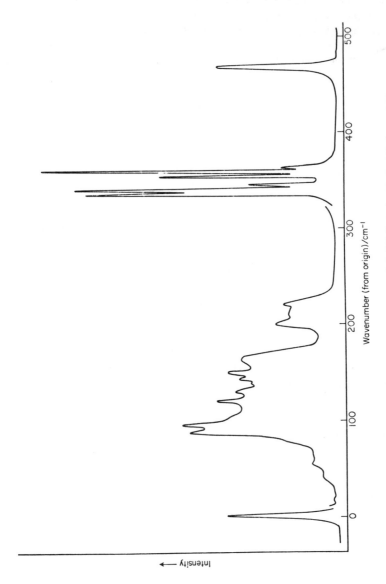

Fig. 3. $^2E_g \rightarrow {}^4A_{2g}$ luminescence spectrum of $Cr(CN)_6^{3-}$ in $K_3Co(CN)_6$ at 5 K.

$^4E_g \leftrightarrow {}^4A_{2g}$ luminescence spectra and absorption spectra.[36-39] These motions do not involve substantial motion of the ligating atom, but the σ-bonding lone pair is moved out of the metal–ligand axis during the motion. The resultant perturbation of the metal d-electrons may then be understood, either by an extension of the crystal field approach which considers the interaction of the d-electrons with the electron density of the ligand lone-pair electron density, or by the angular overlap model in which the orbital motion changes the magnitude of the (d, σ) group overlap integral. If this interpretation of the high intensity of vibronic origins involving ligand rocking/wagging modes is correct, it should be possible to use the spectra as an aid in the identification of these modes, and in their differentiation from ligand twisting modes. An attempt to do this for the $Cr(en)_3^{3+}$ ion has been described.[22]

8.3 The Identification of Metal–Ligand Stretching Vibrations from the Intensity of Progressions in Electronic Spectra

The observation of progressions in an electronic spectrum indicates that the potential surfaces of the two states connected by the transition differ along the normal coordinate corresponding to the progression-forming mode. If the nature of the electronic states is well understood, it is often a trivial matter to predict the symmetry coordinates along which a difference is likely to occur, and comparison with the measured spectrum may make it possible to associate an observed vibrational interval with one or more symmetry coordinates. Only totally symmetric vibrations may appear, but the equilibrium nuclear geometries of the two states may not have the same symmetry and in these cases the appropriate point group is the largest subgroup common to the equilibrium point groups of the ion in the two states. Whilst this complication increases the variety of the motions that may be observed, it also renders the assignments less certain.

The lowest $^2E_g \rightarrow {}^4B_{1g}(D_{4h})$ luminescence transition of $trans$-$Cr(en)_2F_2^+$ shows weak progressions in modes of 512 and 230 cm^{-1} based on electronic and vibronic origins.[40] The same intervals occur strongly in the Raman spectrum. The emission is from the lower spin-orbit component of the ^2E state, and the splitting of the $^4B_{1g}$ state is too small to resolve optically. Neither the initial nor the terminal states are subjected to a significant Jahn–Teller or pseudo-Jahn–Teller effect. The progression-forming modes must then be of a_{1g} symmetry in D_{4h}. A simple m.o. argument[40] shows that the Cr—F bond will be longer, and the Cr—N bond shorter, in the $^4B_{1g}$ state as compared with the ^2E_g state, and it is reasonable to associate the 512 cm^{-1} mode with the a_{1g} Cr—F, and the 230 cm^{-1} mode with the Cr—N stretching coordinates. A similar study of $trans$-$Cr(py)_4F_2^+$ gives a wavenumber of 521 cm^{-1} for the Cr—F stretching mode.[41] In this case, the a_{1g} Cr—N stretch does not appear strongly in the luminescence spectrum, but it may be that the Cr—N distance is not very different in the ^2E_g and $^4B_{1g}$ states because increased metal–pyridine π-bonding in the ground state counters the expected increase.

The ground state a_{1g} Cr—N stretching fundamental has been assigned to a band at $230\ cm^{-1}$ in *trans*-Cr(en)$_2$F$_2{}^+$, which is much lower than the range usually attributed to these modes in ethylenediamine complexes; the assignment is, however, supported by the observation of progressions in a mode of 255 cm^{-1} in the $^1T_1 \rightarrow {}^1A_1$ absorption spectrum of 2Co(en)$_3$Cl$_3$.NaCl.6H$_2$O.[42] This transition corresponds to the transfer of an electron from a non-bonding t_2 orbital to an antibonding e orbital, and should involve a substantial increase in the Co—N bond distance. The difficulty with this interpretation is that the $^1T_1$ state is probably subject to a strong Jahn–Teller effect. The vibronic origins observed are, however, remarkably similar to those in the $^2E \rightarrow {}^4A_2$ luminescence spectrum of the Cr(en)$_3{}^{3+}$ ion, which cannot be strongly influenced by a Jahn–Teller effect. This suggests that this Jahn–Teller effect does not greatly disturb the vibrational behaviour of the excited state. The $^1T_1 \leftarrow {}^1A_1$ absorption of the Co(NH$_3$)$_6{}^{3+}$ ion in [Co(NH$_3$)$_6$][Co(CN)$_6$] is also of great interest.[43] The Co(NH$_3$)$_6{}^{3+}$ ion occupies a site of C_3 or S_6 symmetry, but is little distorted from O_h symmetry. The spectrum shows a long progression in a mode of $420\ cm^{-1}$ which shifts on deuteration to $380\ cm^{-1}$. This vibration must involve mainly Cr—N stretching, although it is not possible to differentiate between the a_{1g} or e_g modes of the CrN$_6$ entity. The observation of e_g modes would be good evidence for a Jahn–Teller induced tetragonal distortion of the excited state. The 80 K $^2E \rightarrow {}^4A$ luminescence spectrum of the Cr(NCS)$_6{}^{3-}$ ion shows[35] progressions in two modes of $825\ cm^{-1}$ and 220 cm^{-1}. The Raman spectrum shows two strong bands at 840 and $240\ cm^{-1}$. The differences between the wavenumbers of these pairs of bands could be attributed to the different temperatures of the measurements, but the differences are much larger than is observed in most systems; moreover, none of the infrared-active vibrations show comparable shifts. The ^2E_g state is fairly close to the Jahn–Teller distorted $^4T_{2g}$ state, since the two states are mixed via $\mathcal{H}_{SO}$ and would be expected to show signs of Jahn–Teller distortions. It is probable, therefore, that the 820 and $220\ cm^{-1}$ modes correspond to the e_g C—S and Cr—N stretches, and that the corresponding a_{1g} modes dominate the Raman spectrum and largely obscure the e_g modes.

9 CONCLUSION

The theoretical basis for the interpretation of the major features of the vibronic spectra of coordination compounds is well established. Experimental studies on complexes of d^3 ions have provided a substantial amount of new vibrational data for these species although much remains to be done especially with the complexes of $4d^3$ and $5d^3$ ions. The data on other systems are sparse. The criteria outlined in Section 7 suggest that the spin-forbidden transitions of octahedral d^2, octahedral d^4, octahedral and tetrahedral d^5, tetrahedral d^7, and octahedral and tetrahedral d^8 complex ions as well as those of several five-coordinate species may show detailed vibrational structure. In addition many spin-allowed transitions may give well resolved spectra at very low temperatures. In particular, the observation of vibrational structure in the low temperature absorption spectra of salts of the $Co(en)_3^{3+(22)}$ and $Co(NH_3)_6^{3+(43)}$ ions suggests that the enormous number of well characterized low-spin d^6 ions could be a fruitful field for experimental spectroscopy. Rare-earth and actinide complexes have been excluded from this article but the electronic spectra of these systems also offer considerable scope for vibrational analysis. Moreover, vibronic spectroscopy is not limited to compounds of metal ions with partly filled d- or f-configurations because some electron-transfer transitions show vibrational structure. Many more high-resolution, low-temperature experimental studies are needed to determine the range of application of this technique.

REFERENCES

(1) C. J. Ballhausen and Aa. E. Hanson, *Annu. Rev. Phys. Chem.* **23**, 15 (1972).
(2) M. Gerloch and R. C. Slade, *Ligand Field Parameters*, Cambridge University Press, Cambridge, England (1973).
(3) J. Ferguson, *Prog. Inorg. Chem.* **12**, 159 (1970).
(4) C. J. Ballhausen, *Introduction to Ligand Field Theory*, McGraw-Hill, New York (1962).
(5) C. K. Jørgensen, *Modern Aspects of Ligand Field Theory*, North Holland, Amsterdam (1971).
(6) C. E. Schäffer, *Struct. Bonding (Berlin)* **5**, 68 (1968).
(7) M. D. Sturge, *Solid State Phys.* **20**, 91 (1967).
(8) J. Ferguson, *J. Chem. Phys.* **39**, 116 (1963).
(9) C. J. Ballhausen, in *Spectroscopy in Inorganic Chemistry* (C. N. R. Rao and J. R. Ferraro, Eds), Academic Press, New York (1970).
(10) J. S. Avery, C. D. Burbridge and D. M. L. Goodgame, *Spectrochim. Acta* **24A**, 1721 (1968).
(11) S. S. Mitra, in *Optical Properties of Solids* (S. Nudelman and S. S. Mitra, Eds), Plenum Press, New York (1969).
(12) G. P. O'Leary and R. G. Wheeler, *Phys. Rev.* **131**, 4409 (1970).
(13) S. L. Chodos, *J. Chem. Phys.* **57**, 2712 (1972).
(14) S. L. Chodos, A. M. Black and C. D. Flint, *Chem. Phys. Letts.* **33**, 344 (1975).
(15) D. Durocher and P. B. Dorain, *J. Chem. Phys.* **61**, 1364 (1974).
(16) R. A. Satten, *J. Chem. Phys.* **40**, 1200 (1964).
(17) S. L. Chodos and R. A. Satten, *J. Chem. Phys.* **62**, 2411 (1975).
(18) S. L. Chodos, A. M. Black and C. D. Flint, *J.C.S. Faraday II* **72**, 579 (1976).
(19) L. S. Forster, *Transition Met. Chem.* **5**, 1 (1969).
(20) D. L. Dexter, *J. Chem. Phys.* **21**, 836 (1953).
(21) A. M. Black and C. D. Flint, *J.C.S. Dalton*, 977 (1974).
(22) C. D. Flint and A. P. Matthews, *J.C.S. Faraday II*, in press.
(23) D. E. McCumber and M. D. Sturge, *J. Appl. Phys.* **34**, 1682 (1963).
(24) H. Silsbee, in *Optical Properties of Solids* (S. Nudelman and S. S. Mitra, Eds), Plenum, New York (1969).
(25) P. J. Stephens, *Annu. Rev. Phys. Chem.* **25**, 201 (1974).
(26) C. D. Flint, *J. Mol. Spectrosc.* **37**, 414 (1971).

(27) J. Ferguson, H. J. Guggenheim and D. L. Wood, *J. Chem. Phys.* **54**, 504 (1971).
(28) P. Greenough, *Proceedings of the* 14*th International Conference on Coordination Chemistry*, Dublin, 1974.
(29) J. C. D. Brand, G. L. Goodman and B. Weinstock, *J. Mol. Spectrosc.* **37**, 464 (1971).
(30) A. M. Black, Thesis, University of London (1974).
(31) A. R. Reinberg and S. G. Parker, *Phys. Rev.* **131**, 2085 (1970).
(32) H. H. Patterson, J. L. Nims and C. M. Valencia, *J. Mol. Spectrosc.* **42**, 567 (1972).
(33) J. L. Nims, H. H. Patterson, S. M. Khan and C. M. Valencia, *Inorg. Chem.* **12**, 1602 (1973).
(34) C. D. Flint and P. Greenough, *J.C.S. Faraday II* **70**, 815 (1974).
(35) C. D. Flint and A. P. Matthews, *J.C.S. Faraday II* **70**, 1301 (1974).
(36) C. D. Flint, *Coord. Chem. Rev.* **14**, 47 (1974).
(37) C. D. Flint and P. Greenough, *J.C.S. Faraday II* **68**, 897 (1972).
(38) C. D. Flint, P. Greenough and A. P. Matthews, *J.C.S. Faraday II* **69**, 23 (1973).
(39) F. D. Camassei and L. S. Forster, *J. Mol. Spectrosc.* **31**, 129 (1969).
(40) C. D. Flint and A. P. Matthews, *J.C.S. Faraday II* **70**, 1307 (1974).
(41) C. D. Flint and A. P. Matthews, *Inorg. Chem.* **14**, 1008 (1975).
(42) R. Dingle and C. J. Ballhausen, *Kgl. Dan. Vidensk. Selsk., Mat. Fys. Medd.* **35**, 12 (1967).
(43) R. A. D. Wentworth, *Chem. Commun.* 532 (1965).

Chapter 3

INDUSTRIAL PLANT APPLICATIONS OF INFRARED AND RAMAN SPECTROSCOPY

H. A. Willis

Plastics Division, I.C.I. Limited, P.O. Box 6, Bessemer Road, Welwyn Garden City, Hertfordshire, U.K.

1 INTRODUCTION

On-line analysis is becoming an essential part of chemical plant processes. Activity in this field has been stimulated by the availability and falling cost of small computers. Data acquired from instruments throughout a plant, such as raw material and finished product composition, temperatures, pressures and flow rates, may be processed by the computer and applied either directly, or by the intervention of an operator, to give the degree of control which is necessary for efficient operation. The success of these complex operations depends upon the precision, response-time, and long term reliability of the instruments used.

Experience shows that the least reliable features of on-line analysers are mechanical sampling devices such as scoops, syphons, valves and pumps. Any analytical instrument which can function either without or with the minimum of such auxiliary devices is strongly preferred. Furthermore, analytical probes which come into direct contact with the product stream are to be avoided, as they may break away, so contaminating the product and ruining the analyser. Thus, ideally, the analytical equipment makes no direct contact with the material to be analysed. This is possible in principle (though not always in practice) with analysers utilizing radiant energy. The energy emitted by a remote source falls on the sample, and the required characteristics of the sample are determined by analysing the radiant energy which is transmitted, reflected, or scattered. High energy radiation (e.g. X-rays, β-rays and γ-rays) are used in some analysers, but this radiation may be injurious to health, and formidable safety precautions may be needed which are both inconvenient and expensive. Very long wavelength radiation (e.g. radio waves) is used in some cases, but this is of limited value in analytical applications. This directs attention to the ultraviolet, visible and infrared regions of the radiant energy spectrum. Analysers based on the absorption of ultraviolet radiation are well known[1] and have been used with great success. Highly efficient detectors for this region of the spectrum have been known for many years. There is a choice of sources which produce an energy continuum (e.g. the hydrogen lamp) or sources emitting a series of discrete lines (e.g. the mercury vapour lamp). With comparatively cheap filters single lines may be selected to construct a multiwavelength analyser. Furthermore, lenses and windows for this radiation are cheap and durable.

Ultraviolet (u.v.) analysers are ideal for determining the concentration of one component of a mixture when this component is the only one having significant absorption in a specific u.v. region. A simple example would be the determination of an aromatic additive such as a stabilizer or antioxidant in a non-u.v. absorbing substrate such as polyethylene or polypropylene. Other well-known examples are the determination of the thickness of polyester films[1] or the thickness of a u.v.-absorbing coating on polyolefin films.

The situation is much less satisfactory if more than one u.v. absorber (in the specific region examined) is present in the sample, since generally u.v. spectra are broad and featureless.

There is little doubt that the greatest potential for analysis in terms of radiant energy methods exists in the infrared region of the spectrum. Even so, it has taken a long time to develop satisfactory 'plantworthy' analysers operating in this region. While it may well be the most favoured region analytically, it is technically a difficult one in which to operate. Detectors are generally slow, inefficient and fragile. In almost all other regions of the spectrum monochromatic sources or at least multiline sources of high intensity are available. This makes wavelength selection and detection much simpler. Only within the last few years have selective infrared emitters been available in the form of lasers[2, 3] and so far these are expensive and of unproven performance. It is necessary to rely on black body emitters which, being both multiwavelength and multidirectional, are extremely inefficient. Indeed the waste energy from these sources is usually an embarrassment because it serves to heat other parts of the analyser, which themselves become emitters and produce interfering signals. Of all the problems besetting the designer of infrared analysers, this has proved to be one of the most intractable, leading to a slow drift of output signal as the different parts of the apparatus slowly change in temperature. Surprisingly, it is the introduction of computers which has reduced this problem to manageable proportions.

It is true of most analytical apparatus, and especially true of infrared analysers, that they have extremely high analytical precision, but very poor absolute accuracy. Under computer control, it is possible to standardize the apparatus at very frequent intervals—say every 15 min—and apply a correction within the computer. If the signal from the instrument is very noisy, it is possible to 'edit' the instrument output, for example by averaging over extended periods or cutting out transient spikes. Thus, while the computer is essential to collect the data and to present it, it is also essential as a means of controlling the analytical instruments.

We have so far considered only infrared equipment. By the criteria we have considered for satisfactory plant control instruments, Raman spectroscopy would seem also to be well suited to this application. Considering that the first infrared instruments for plant control are now about thirty years old[4] and that the field is only now beginning to develop beyond simple gas analysis, it is perhaps not surprising that the much newer technique of laser Raman spectroscopy must be considered primarily in terms of its potential rather than as a proven method.

Apart from plant control, infrared spectroscopy has been applied extensively to the control of plant effluents (mainly gaseous, but also solid and liquid). There have also been a number of claims concerning Raman spectroscopy in this kind of work.

The following sections of this review are arranged according to applications, taking in descriptions of instruments as appropriate.

2   GAS STREAM ANALYSIS

This is the oldest, and until fairly recently almost the only, plant application of infrared absorption measurements. The reason for this is that sampling is much simpler with gases. The infrared absorption of liquids and solids is so high that for most practical purposes it is not possible to operate in the usual transmission mode with samples above a few millimetres in thickness, and usually 0.1–0.5 mm will be the optimum. For useful transmission measurements the sample must be presented as a layer of uniform thickness. This immediately excludes the direct measurement of powders or granules and has in the past severely restricted the application of infrared plant stream analysis of solids. However, there has recently been considerable interest in this method for gauging plastic films.

Likewise, liquid samples present practical problems because the thin cells necessary to contain them in the analyser are subject to blocking by suspended solid particles in the plant stream, and scouring and erosion of the cells (which may cause leakage or severe deterioration in the optical properties of the cell). Gases, on the other hand, being of much lower density, can be handled in cells upwards of a few centimetres in length, they can be filtered to remove suspended matter, and, especially if dry, are rarely corrosive.

Apart from the noble gases, and the simple diatomic gases (e.g. hydrogen, nitrogen, oxygen and chlorine), all gases and vapours have characteristic and, in principle, distinguishable absorption spectra. Since the major constituents of air are not detected, this form of analysis is applicable to the measurement of gases and vapours in air without the use of costly separation equipment.

The non-dispersive infrared gas analyser is devised in such a way that one type of analyser is applicable with only minor modification to the determination of almost any gas or vapour. These factors have made the manufacture of infrared gas analysers potentially profitable. On the other hand, dispersive infrared instruments, with their delicate sources, optics and detectors, are less attractive in the unfriendly environment of the production plant.

Thus, the first successful plant gas analysers were of the non-dispersive type. Not only does this dispose immediately of the complex optics, but it also means that energy of all wavelengths is available simultaneously for the analysis, enabling a less sensitive, and thus far more robust detector to be used. Further, a less intense energy source is adequate and the delicate Nernst filament or Globar beloved of the spectroscopist, can make way for a Nichrome spiral.

2.1   Infrared Gas Analysers

It is perfectly possible to build an analyser consisting merely of a source, an analysis cell and a detector with a chopper as beam modulator. The addition of a few more optical components makes a more practical instrument, giving some compensation for source intensity changes. Some straightforward analyses, e.g. single components in air, may be dealt with adequately by this method.[5, 6] The total absorption analyser has, however, a very serious deficiency. The source emits over a wide wavelength range, and the detector responds to all these wavelengths. However, the gas to be measured absorbs only a limited range of wavelengths and the attenuation of the signal which is achieved is therefore inevitably small and the analyser is relatively insensitive. A much more satisfactory device may be made by restricting the system so that it will respond only to analytically useful wavelengths.

This important principle was recognized as long ago as 1938 when Veingerov described an analyser[4] with a selective detector. This is shown diagrammatically in Fig. 1.

A detecting chamber, containing the gas to be analysed, consists of an internally polished tube which is closed at one end with a calcium fluoride window and at the other with a telephone earpiece. Radiation from a Nernst

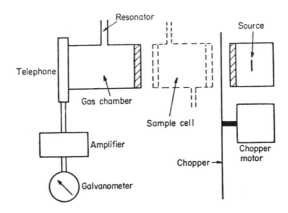

Fig. 1. Early Veingerov analyser using microphone detector (courtesy of Adam Hilger Limited, Ref. 18).

filament enters through the window. The gas in the chamber, being an infrared absorber, becomes heated and expands. A chopper, mounted between source and detector, obstructs the radiation beam for half the period of each rotation of the chopper motor, thus inducing a pressure fluctuation in the detector. This in turn vibrates the membrane of the telephone earpiece and generates an electrical signal which is amplified and taken to a galvanometer.

The device is a selective detector, since only radiation absorbed by the wanted gas causes heating of the gas. Radiation of other wavelengths, falling on, for example, the telephone earpiece, if absorbed may heat the gas by conduction and thus cause a rise of pressure in the detector. However, this pressure change is not modulated by the chopper and so should not be detected.

A cell containing the gas to be analysed, and having a window at either end, is interposed between source and detector. The gas in this cell absorbs part of the energy which would otherwise heat the detector, hence reducing the output signal. The strength of the output signal can be related, by calibration, to the pressure of the wanted gas in the sample cell.

There are two important features embodied in this apparatus. Firstly, the detector is sensitized to all the absorption wavelengths of the gas simultaneously. This gives a high signal gain and is called the 'multiplex' advantage. Secondly, other gases, because they have a different absorption pattern, have either no effect, or only a minor effect, on the signal. This is known as the 'correlation' advantage.

The principle of a sealed container in which pressure changes are generated through absorption of radiant energy has recently been revived under the new name of photoacoustic spectrometry.[7] Current reports suggest that the method is applicable to liquids and solids as well as gases, and there are indications that it may be a technique of significance in plant control applications.

A similar analyser was developed by Pfund.[8] This was intended for the determination of carbon dioxide in air, and also used a gas-filled detector, but in this case the pressure change was detected with a stethoscope. Not only did this instrument have a selective detector, it also had a selective source, namely a jet of heated carbon dioxide. Since the emission wavelengths of a hot gas coincide with the absorption wavelengths, the device in principle is highly selective. Unfortunately, the amount of energy emitted by the gas at any wavelength cannot exceed (and is usually much less than) the amount emitted by a black body at the same temperature. Further, it would not appear practical to raise a gas to the same temperature as, for example, a Nernst filament (which is capable of operation up to 2000°C).

Selective detector analysers

The general principle of the Veingerov selective detector analyser has been developed over the years and is now widely used in practical instruments. A good deal of this development was due to Luft,[9] and the detector is now universally known as the Luft cell.

Figure 2 shows schematically the selective detector analyser. The detector consists of two chambers, each having a window to admit radiation. The chambers are separated by two diaphragms, one of which is perforated, which form the plates of a condenser. Both chambers are filled with the gas to be detected. The chopper consists of a disc from which two 90° sectors are removed so that both halves of the cell are either illuminated or dark (Fig. 2). Assuming that the various cells are empty, equal absorption of energy emitted by the Nichrome spiral source occurs on each side of the cell on the 'hot' cycle. The gas to be analysed is now admitted to the sample cell. The gas absorbs some of the radiation so that the beam reaching chamber D_1 is deficient in energy at those wavelengths which would otherwise be absorbed by the gas in D_1. The gas in D_2 expands more than that in D_1, on the 'hot' cycle and contracts again on the 'cold' cycle. The capacity of the condenser formed by the two diaphragms thus changes in an alternating manner, and the electronic equipment is devised so as to measure this alternating signal.

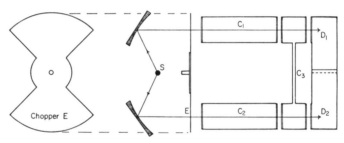

Fig. 2. Selective detector gas analyser. S = source; C_1 = sample cell; C_2 = compensating cell; C_3 = filter cell; D_1, D_2 = detector cells.

The main object of the compensating cell is to provide an optical balance. This is necessary because generally these analysers do not have a conventional optical imaging system. The various cells consist of lengths of tubes internally polished so that the radiation from the sources is conveyed by light piping into the detector.

The sensitive element of the Luft detector, namely the gas with which it is filled, presents a large cross-section to the radiation beam. Usually the entrance windows of the detector are circular, and of the same diameter as the gas cells. Because of the considerable depth of the detector, there is no need to focus the beam—in fact focusing the beam is likely to reduce the detector sensitivity. For these reasons, it is particularly appropriate to use non-focusing light-pipe optics with the Luft detector. This may well be one reason why this kind of analyser has achieved considerable popularity, because the optical system can be built from large rigid pieces which will withstand rough treatment.

The filter cell, apart from acting as transfer optics between the source and measuring cells, can be used as a negative (subtractive) filter. Some gas may be present in the sample which has, fortuitously, absorption at some of the wave-lengths at which the required gas absorbs. By putting a sufficiently high con-centration of this interfering gas in the filter cell, the energy at the coincident wavelengths is completely removed, thus desensitizing the apparatus. It is obvious that this subterfuge must be used with discretion, because the analyser is necessarily made less sensitive to the wanted gas.

Rather than using a gas filter, it is sometimes simpler to use a subtractive[10] transmission filter. It may be possible to put the filter into one of the cells in place of a window, thus saving cost and space. A vast number of permutations of this apparatus are possible, offering combinations of desirable and undesirable features.[1,11]

In particular cases it is impossible or inappropriate to sensitize the cell with the gas to be detected, bearing in mind that the gas filling must remain stable and constant for several months. The gas may condense if it has insufficient vapour pressure at the operating temperature. It may polymerize or react with the walls of the container. It may also slowly decompose. In all these cases, it is necessary to seek some more neutral gas which has at least some of its absorption bands in common with those of the gas to be measured, although the detector is now no longer a true positive filter and it may be appropriate to restrict the wavelength response of the analyser by incorporating negative filters either as gases in the filter cell, or as transmission filters.

Negative (subtractive) filter analysers

Although the positive filter (Luft type) analyser has a great deal to commend it, it suffers from the unfortunate disadvantage that the Luft detector, being based on a vibrating membrane, can give trouble when the analyser is subjected to mechanical vibration. This is by no means uncommon in a plant environment, and while the trouble may be ameliorated by making an analysis of the problem and fitting appropriate antivibration devices, this may prove costly or ineffective. In such a situation, it may be better to use an instrument based on a bolometer detector, or some other non-selective detector, which is much less sensitive to vibration. Selectivity is achieved with a negative filter as shown in Fig. 3. The 'negative filter' is in practice the sensitizing cell. This is filled, to an appropriate pressure, with the gas to be detected, so that radiant energy which would be

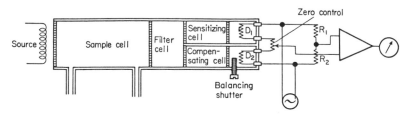

Fig. 3. Typical negative filter analyser.

absorbed by this gas cannot fall on detector D_1. It will be evident that, if the sample cell is now filled with a mixture containing the required gas, this will attenuate the signal falling on detector D_2, but will leave detector D_1 unaffected, and the output signal from the two back-to-back detectors will clearly depend upon the concentration in the sample cell of the component sought.

As in the positive filter analyser previously described, sensitivity to gases in the plant stream whose spectra overlap that of the required component can be reduced by introducing these unwanted gaseous components into the filter cell. Indeed, where the overlap of absorption bands is severe, unwanted gaseous components may be admitted to the compensating cell, although this 'negative sensitization' is a somewhat dubious procedure which requires some skill for its satisfactory use.[12]

The price paid for abandoning the selective detector may be severe. For example, instruments of this kind are particularly prone to differential temperature effects. As always, the particular problem must be considered in detail before a choice is made.

Negative filter gas analysers with multilayer interference filters

It is possible to abandon entirely the idea of negative filtering with the gas which is to be determined, and to build a gas analyser in which wavelength selection is achieved with a multilayer interference filter [13-15] which transmits only a narrow wavelength band corresponding to a peak absorption of the wanted gas. It is preferred in practice to use a pair of filters, one corresponding to a band peak, and the other to a wavelength at which the wanted component does not absorb. This arrangement of filters is used with a single broad band detector (e.g. thermocouple, bolometer or photocell) in an arrangement such as is shown in Fig. 4. The action of the instrument is that the filters are interposed

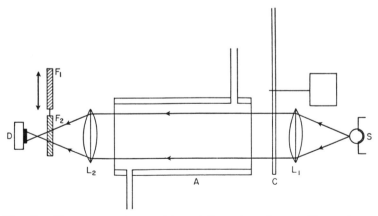

Fig. 4. Negative filter gas analyser with multilayer interference filters. A = sample cell; C = chopper; D = detector; F_1, F_2 = filters; L_1, L_2 = lenses; S = source (courtesy of Feedback Limited).

alternately in the same radiation beam, with an intermediate blank shutter. In this way two separable signals are detected along the same optical path with the same detector, and this disposes of a number of possible sources of error.

The two signals are given the notation I (=signal at band peak) and I_0 (=comparison signal), and by Beer's law

$$\log (I_0/I) = kcl$$

where k is a proportionality constant, l is the cell path length, and c is the concentration of the gas to be determined. If the output is in the form $\log(I_0/I)$, this will be directly proportional to the concentration of the component sought, since in an analyser, k and l are constant. The value of k will depend, in practice, on the filter characteristics, so it will be expected to change if the filters are changed. The logarithm of each signal is taken separately and one is subtracted from the other.

This form of output signal is different from that in the analysers previously described, as in those the output was a measure of the difference between the energies in the two beams. The method of signal separation is to be preferred. It gives superior compensation for fluctuations in the intensity of the source and for loss of light from suspended matter in the samples; this is because the percentage change in I_0 and I is practically the same, leaving (I_0/I) virtually unchanged. This is clearly not true of $(I_0 - I)$.

The price which is paid is that the instrument now depends only upon the absorption of the gas at one wavelength, rather than upon the complete spectrum, and this must result in loss of signal. On the other hand, the single wavelength method may have distinct advantages if the gas is to be determined in a mixture, as there is much a greater chance that a wavelength can be chosen which is free of overlap by other constituents.

Some other features of these analysers are discussed later, as they are very similar to those of the analysers used for near infrared liquid analysis.

Selective source analysers

It is evident that selectivity could be achieved by use of a source which emitted only the wavelength of interest. However, only strong emitters are likely candidates[16] (in practice, only carbon dioxide, cf. the original Pfund analyser).

A more promising idea is to use an infrared laser as a power source. For example, the helium–neon laser will emit at 3.39 μm, and this is of obvious interest as all substances containing CH_2 or CH_3 groups will absorb this radiation. Thus, Gerritsen[17] has described a methane detector based on this principle, and Hill et al.[18] have given details of an ethanol detector.

As other infrared lasers become available their application as sources in non-dispersive analysers may well prove important. There is currently no instrument of this type commercially available, but interest is being shown in this idea for pollution studies.

2.2 Some Applications of Non-Dispersive Gas Analysers in Production Control

Although non-dispersive analysers have a wide range of application, in practice by far the largest use is in the determination of carbon dioxide and carbon monoxide. The infrared absorption bands of carbon dioxide and carbon monoxide are of substantial intensity, and the most prominent bands occur in the 4–5 μm region, where most other gases have very low absorption. This means that selective detection of carbon monoxide and carbon dioxide with an infrared analyser is comparatively easy.

One reason for great interest in this area is that measurement of the amounts of oxides of carbon in flue gases represents a simple and effective method of determining the efficiency of fuel combustion in furnaces. This clearly comes into greater prominence not only because of the purely economic consideration of containing fuel costs at a time of rapidly rising prices, but also on conservation grounds to reduce the demand for fossil fuels, and to ensure correct combustion to reduce atmospheric contamination.

Generally, a furnace converts a mixture of oxygen and a hydrocarbon to carbon dioxide and water. The most efficient combustion is achieved when the carbon dioxide in the flue gas is at a maximum, hence the analysis system for a furnace will often contain an infrared carbon dioxide analyser. On the other hand it is evident that this one measurement will not be sufficient for control purposes, since a fall in carbon dioxide content may arise from either too much fuel or too much air. Since inadequate air supply will evidently lead to incomplete oxidation of carbon, it will be accompanied by a rise in the carbon monoxide content of the flue gas. Hence an infrared carbon monoxide analyser is often incorporated as well, and these two analysers will form the basis of a control system.

With the current concern about atmospheric pollution, gaseous combustion by-products, including unburned gaseous hydrocarbons, oxides of nitrogen and sulphur dioxide are all of importance in flue gas. Nitrous oxide, sulphur dioxide and gaseous hydrocarbons all may be monitored by infrared gas analysers, and many companies offer instruments operating in the 0–500 parts per million (ppm) range for these materials.

Flue gas is sooty, hot, wet, and often corrosive because it contains some sulphur trioxide, and it is evident that the analysers would soon rot away unless considerable care were taken to clean up the sample. Thus filtering to remove solids, water washing to remove sulphur trioxide, followed by drying and temperature regulation are required before the gas is admitted to the analysers.

The infrared gas analyser in steel production

The controlled combustion of fuel is of particular importance in the steel industry. On the one hand, this industry consumes vast amounts of fossil fuels because of the high processing temperatures. On the other hand, the precise carbon content of the product is outstandingly important, and this changes by interaction between the steel and the atmosphere in which it is heated. Thus an essential element of the control of steel production is a knowledge of the composition of the reactor atmosphere.

In a blast furnace the atmosphere, known as 'top gas', contains 20–40% carbon monoxide and 10–20% carbon dioxide. For production control, high precision (≈ 0.1%) is required in the measurement of the concentration of these gases. This calls for good precision in the analysis, and both the temperatures and pressure of the gas sample in the analyser must be controlled to close limits. It is found, in practice, that this is best achieved by siting the analysers in remote, clean, temperature-controlled cubicles. The gas to be analysed is drawn into the sample cell through a large manifold which permits cyclic sampling from a series of points with one analyser assembly. The manifold contains filters to remove suspended solids and liquids and, within this part of the sampling system, the temperature and pressure of the gas are adjusted to predetermined values. Since an elaborate mechanism is necessary to control sampling, it is usual to have the system computer-controlled, and the computer can perform the additional task of standardizing the analyser at preset time intervals. It is common also to use other types of analysers for the determination of oxygen and hydrogen, etc., for which infrared methods are not applicable. The description given will serve to underline a common feature of infrared analysis in a plant context. The complete assembly is so large and complex that the infrared analyser is a small and, in cost terms, even an insignificant part of the analytical equipment.

In basic oxygen steel furnaces the carbon content of the steel is controlled by blowing oxygen through the molten product with a lance. The end of the 'blow' must be timed to give a steel with the correct carbon content, and this is determined by an analysis of the carbon monoxide and carbon dioxide content of the atmosphere. A non-dispersive infrared analyser is particularly valuable here, as it is both specific and rapid. Sulphur dioxide analysers may also be incorporated in systems producing high quality steels.

The use of infrared gas analysers in metal production is not confined to iron and steel. Some non-ferrous metals (e.g. aluminium) must be prepared in an atmosphere free of water vapour, and thus an infrared gas analyser can be employed to good effect. As water vapour is condensable, this analyser is usually operated at elevated temperatures.

The infrared gas analyser in steel processing

There is considerable interest in infrared analytical control methods for steel fabricators, particularly in the mass production of small machine and automobile components. A low carbon content is needed for ease of machining, but subsequently, to harden the surface, the components are heated in a carbon-rich atmosphere. Initial heating is conducted in a substantially oxygen-free atmosphere so as not to burn out the carbon already present. This is formed by passing air and a hydrocarbon gas over a catalyst to produce a mixture of carbon monoxide, hydrogen and nitrogen, with minor amounts of carbon dioxide and water. An efficient control of this part of the process is achieved from a measurement of the carbon dioxide content of the oven with an infrared analyser, since minor changes in the air:fuel ratio show up most quickly in the carbon dioxide content. The analyser signal may be used directly to control the rate of fuel input.

The second stage of the process involves the deliberate addition of hydrocarbon (e.g. methane or propane) to the furnace atmosphere to boost the carbon content of the surface layer of the fabrication, and the same infrared analyser can be used to follow this process by observing the carbon dioxide content of the atmosphere. The air/hydrocarbon feed is controlled to ensure that the carbon dioxide content changes to a predetermined pattern. Control may also be achieved by following the hydrocarbon content of the feed gas with an infrared analyser.

Since the changes in gas composition occur rather slowly, a multipoint sampling system will permit efficient control of a number of process streams with one analyser.

Nuclear power station reactor gas

Carbon dioxide is used as a heat exchange gas in some nuclear power plants and high purity of this gas is essential. Reaction between the carbon dioxide and graphite in the reactor core can lead to carbon monoxide formation; the carbon dioxide may become contaminated by water vapour if there are leaks between the carbon dioxide and the steam coils. Both carbon monoxide and water vapour levels may be continuously monitored with infrared analysers.

Another problem is that of hydrocarbon impurities in the carbon dioxide. Simple hydrocarbons such as methane may be determined directly with an infrared analyser. Lubricant oils present more difficulty, but Grubb Parsons Limited have produced an analyser in which the heavy oils are cracked to ethylene, which is then measured in a conventional analyser.[11] The possibility of leakage of the carbon dioxide into the steam must be considered, and Bartley and Moult[19] have suggested the use of an infrared analyser for its detection. Leakage into the air is another possibility. This is a serious problem as the carbon dioxide is radioactive. A multipoint carbon dioxide analyser is used in an alarm system against this hazard.

Chemical manufacturing processes

There are innumerable applications for infrared gas analysers in chemical plant streams. Interesting examples occur in hydrocarbon reforming processes. Here a hydrocarbon (e.g. natural gas) is treated with steam over a catalyst to form hydrogen, carbon monoxide and carbon dioxide. The most common feed stock is natural gas and in this case the composition of the inlet gas may be determined with an infrared methane analyser, and the composition of the 'reformed' gas with infrared carbon monoxide and carbon dioxide analysers.

The mixed reformed gases may be used directly in the preparation of methanol, viz.

$$2H_2 + CO \rightarrow CH_3OH$$
$$\text{and } 3H_2 + CO_2 \rightarrow CH_3OH + H_2O$$

Particular proportions of $H_2 : CO : CO_2$ are needed according to the catalyst used and these proportions can be changed by altering the hydrocarbon : water ratio at the beginning of the process.

Another important application of the reforming process is in the manufacture of ammonia. In this case the carbon monoxide is oxidized to carbon dioxide, which is removed, leaving hydrogen which is mixed with air to give a 3:1 hydrogen : nitrogen ratio. The catalyst used to convert the hydrogen and nitrogen to ammonia is extremely sensitive to carbon monoxide. This is an ideal application for an infrared gas analyser since the major constituents, hydrogen and nitrogen, do not absorb infrared radiation. Thus, it is possible to detect 0–50 ppm carbon monoxide. If necessary the carbon dioxide, water and methane, all of which are present in ppm amounts, may be determined with infrared analysers. An infrared ammonia analyser may be used to determine the catalyst efficiency.

Many other examples could be quoted of the application of infrared gas analysers in chemical process streams, but it will generally be found that infrared gas analysers are applied either for the determination of non-hydrocarbon gases (especially carbon dioxide, carbon monoxide, or water) or to the determination of individual simple hydrocarbons (especially methane, ethane, ethylene and acetylene) where these are present in a plant stream in which no other hydrocarbons occur at any significant concentration. Originally, in an excess of optimism, infrared gas analysers were installed widely in refineries and the like, where complex hydrocarbon mixtures are encountered. Unfortunately, as pointed out earlier, attempts to reduce interferences in these analysers are frequently self defeating. Infrared gas analysers have been largely displaced from this field, and rightly so, by process gas chromatographs.

Fermentation processes

Processes involving the action of microorganisms on organic substances are now becoming more common. Some processes are concerned with drug manufacture, others with the production of proteins from hydrocarbons. Infrared gas analysers are widely used to monitor these processes by measuring the carbon dioxide evolution.

Gas analysers for atmospheric pollution studies

In atmospheric pollution studies it is necessary to determine small concentrations of gases and vapours, usually in the range 0–10 ppm. The non-focusing optics and light pipe gas cells of the conventional infrared gas analyser make the instrument quite unsuitable for this work, and more specialized apparatus has been developed (see Section 8).

3 INFRARED TRANSMISSION ANALYSERS FOR LIQUIDS

Relative to gases, liquids show extremely strong absorption of infrared energy. The familiar infrared absorption spectra which are universally employed for identification of organic liquids, are determined from layers about 20 μm thick.

This has significant implications for liquid analysers working on the principle of infrared absorption. In quantitative terms, an error in thickness of the cell produces the same percentage error in the analytical result. Unfortunately, changes of this magnitude can be brought about very easily. For example, the cell plates may be eroded by corrosive matter in the sample. If the sample is being pumped through the cell, pressure fluctuations from the pump may cause the cell to pulsate, or it may be slowly distorted under pressure. An equally difficult practical problem is that the cell inlet point is likely to be clogged with particulate matter in the liquid stream.

In the near-infrared region, where only weakly absorbing overtone and combination modes occur, useful absorption spectra can be measured on layers of liquids (or homogeneous solids) up to 30 mm thick. This immediately disposes of the thin cell problem, and has, surprisingly, some further advantages. Measurements can now be made in a region of the spectrum where glass and fused silica are reasonably transparent. Complete cells can be made from these materials by fusion, thus disposing of the problem of cells which leak through cemented joints. These cells are, furthermore, more robust and less subject to erosion by water and acids than those made from the usual infrared cell materials. There is also a convenient and cheap radiation source for this region—the tungsten filament lamp. In practice some attention must be paid to mounting the lamp correctly, so that the glass envelope does not blacken along the line of sight in the instrument and the filament does not sag. Moreover, the tungsten lamp has a low heat capacity and is subject to rapid intensity fluctuations unless a stable power supply is used. Finally, some excellent photodetectors are available for this region which have high sensitivity at ambient temperature. The best known, most reliable, and cheapest is lead sulphide, with a useful range of between 1.0 and 3.2 μm, peaking at about 2.2 μm.[20] The working range can be extended to about 4 μm with lead selenide,[21] and this is adequate to cover the most accessible overtone and combination band region.

4 ANALYTICAL POTENTIAL OF THE NEAR-INFRARED REGION

The near-infrared region contains absorption bands which relate almost exclusively to XH groups and may well be applicable therefore to any analysis which requires the discrimination of one XH group from another. Thus, for example, the OH group (as in alcohol, organic acid, glycol, or water) may be monitored in the presence of the CH group (in an aliphatic or aromatic hydrocarbon). The same is true of the NH group of amines and amides.

A further useful feature is that CH groups of different kinds can be distinguished. Thus the unsaturated groups =CH— and =CH$_2$ may be determined in a saturated hydrocarbon environment, and the aromatic CH group may be observed and measured in the presence of either saturated or unsaturated hydrocarbons. Beyond the bands of XH groups, the only commonly occurring group having significant absorption bands in this region is the carbonyl group of esters (bands at 2.2 and 2.9 μm). Details of these absorption bands are collected in Table 1.[22]

TABLE 1

Short wave correlation table

		First overtone	Combination	Fundamental
Saturated	—CH$_2$—	H	⊢—⊣	⊢—⊣
Aliphatic	—CH$_3$	H	H	H
Unsaturated	=CH— and =CH$_2$	H	H	H
Aromatic	CH	H	H ⊢H	H
Unsaturated	≡C–H	H		H
Alcoholic and Phenolic	—OH	H	H	⊢—⊣
Acidic Bonded	—OH	H	H	⊢——⊣
Water	H–O–H	H ⊢—⊣		⊢—⊣
Esters	C=O		H	⊢⊣ First overtone
Amines and Amides	N–H	H	⊢—⊣	⊢———⊣

1.5   2.0   2.5   3.0
Wavelength/μ m

It will be seen that each of the groups to which reference has been made show a series of bands in the near-infrared region. Generally, the lowest frequency band (in the 3 μm region) is the fundamental X—H stretching mode. Between about 1.8 μm and 2.6 μm are the first combination bands, $\nu(X—H) + \delta(X—H)$, and, near 1.6 μm, the first overtone, $2\nu(X—H)$. More detail is given by Kaye[23] (Table 2). Band intensities commonly decrease progressively from fundamental to combination, to first overtone, and this can be useful because it may well be possible to select a band of suitable intensity for a particular analysis. Differentiation between different groups may be possible at one wavelength but not at another. For example, OH bands of water and alcohols overlap near 3.0 μm, but are well separated in the combination bands near 2.0 μm.

4.1 General Optical Design of Near-Infrared Transmission Analysers

The sensitive area of the lead sulphide and other infrared photocells is comparatively small (1–2 mm^2), hence it is necessary to use at least a rudimentary

TABLE 2
Near-infrared analytical applications

System	Wavelength/μm	Sensitivity[a]/%
Water in hydrocarbons	2.70	0.004–0.02
	1.9	0.02 –0.06
	1.4	0.2 –0.6
Water in alcohols	2.70	0.05 –0.2
	1.9	0.035–0.08
Water in carboxylic acids	1.4	0.04
Alcohols in hydrocarbons	2.76	0.03 –0.10
(diluted in CCl_4)	1.4	0.1 –0.3
Alcohols in acids	2.76	0.2 –0.5
(diluted in CCl_4)	1.4	0.5 –1.0
Acids in hydrocarbons	3.0	0.005–0.03
	2.0	0.2 –0.3
Acids in anhydrides	2.0	0.5 –1.0
Amines in hydrocarbons	1.5	0.04 –0.10
Benzene in hydrocarbons	2.45	0.1 –0.3
	1.2	0.3 –0.5
Olefins in hydrocarbons	1.62	0.04 –0.2

[a] These figures represent minimum concentrations determinable (Kaye, Ref. 23).

focusing optical system, rather than light-pipe optics, especially if the source is a tungsten filament lamp which will also have only a small area. For analysers, there is no point in using a conventional optical dispersing system, because multilayer interference filters (by which narrow wavelength ranges may be isolated) can be obtained relatively cheaply for this short wavelength region. Filters with 2, 5 or 11% half-band widths are available with peak transmissions of up to 80%. There may be practical difficulties if the analysis requires sharply tuned filters, as the manufacturers' tolerance on peak transmission wavelength may not be better than ± 0.1 μm. However, some tuning is possible, as tilting a filter in relation to the beam direction will reduce the peak wavelength by as much as 2%. Instrument design should, therefore, allow filters to be tilted, and when purchasing spare filters a maximum transmission of between 0 and +0.5% of the wavelength required should be specified to allow for tuning.

There are several possible optical configurations for near-infrared analysers, but the essentials are that beams of two different wavelengths are generated, one known as the measuring beam, and the other the comparison beam. Generally, the measurement wavelength will coincide with the peak of the absorption band to be measured. For example, in the determination of terminal hydroxy groups in a polyether,[22] $HO—CH_2—CH_2—O—CH_2—CH_2—O—$, the measurement wavelength would be approximately 2.1 μm (Fig. 5). This might vary by a small amount in different compounds, and the correct wavelength in a particular case would be decided by measuring the transmission characteristics of the sample in a spectrometer. Having decided on the measurement wavelength, the comparison wavelength is selected as one at which there is little change in transmission as the concentration of the hydroxyl group varies. This would be, in the case of Fig. 5, near 2.0 μm. This second reference wavelength is necessary to account for fluctuations in source or detector sensitivity, or change in the overall transmission of the sample such as would occur if scattering particles were suspended in the sample. It is important for the best possible compensation to have the measurement and comparison wavelengths as close as possible to each other, although the two filter transmission bands should not overlap significantly otherwise there will be a loss of sensitivity. As in the case of the gas analyser with interference filters, the signals from the two filters are detected separately with one detector, and the form of calculation is the same.

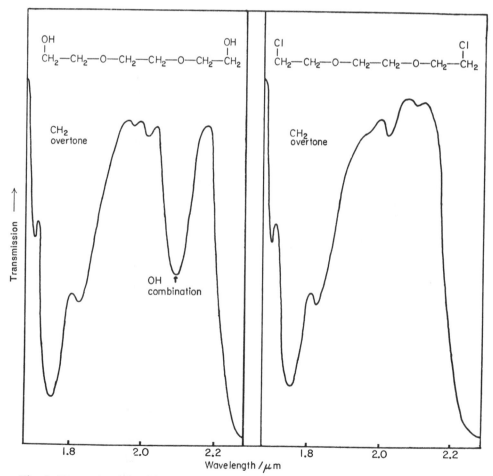

Fig. 5. Determination of hydroxyl groups in a polyether (Miller and Willis, Ref. 22).

Strictly speaking, the two filter transmissions, I_0 (comparison) and I (measurement), should be separately measured, and the logarithm of the ratio determined at some stage in the electronic amplifier. Approximate mathematical solutions which avoid logarithms, e.g.

$$\log \left(\frac{I_0}{I}\right) \approx k_1 \left(\frac{I_0 - I}{I_0 + I}\right) \approx k_2 \left(\frac{I_0 - I}{I_0}\right)$$

where k_1 and k_2 are constants, sometimes cause difficulty, depending upon the measuring method, and when purchasing an analyser it is as well both to look carefully at the circuitry, and to subject the analyser to tests to ensure that the calibration holds tolerably well against voltage fluctuations and any expected variation in transparency of the sample. Other problems include the effect of change of temperature of the apparatus which may well cause a slow drift in the output signal. This can arise from radiation emission from components in the analyser, or from drift in the peak wavelengths of the filters with temperature change.

Popular forms of this type of infrared analyser are shown in Figs. 6 (a) and (b). In Fig. 6 (a), the light beam is moved from one filter to the other by rotating the pair of mirrors fixed in the axial tube. In Fig. 6 (b), the two wavelengths are generated by rotating a wheel containing a pair of filters. There is probably no significant difference in performance between these two designs.

4.2 Some Applications of Near-Infrared Transmission Analysers

The general field of application of these analysers, and their advantages in control applications, have already been discussed. Table 2 shows the wavelengths of the absorption bands which may be used for particular analyses, together with an indication of the sensitivity which may be expected. The determination of the molecular weight of polyethers has been referred to above and more detail is given by Miller and Willis.[22] Clearly, this form of analysis is applicable to other polymers with terminal hydroxyl groups, e.g. polyesters. Vinyl polymerization may be followed in a different way by determining the concentration of residual monomer during the polymerization. For example, Miller and Willis[22] have demonstrated the change in intensity of the 1.7 μm band of methyl methacrylate, as polymerization proceeds. Although there are many applications for the near-infrared analyser, probably the most important, technically, is the determination of water. This determination can be extremely sensitive, it being possible to determine amounts down to 50 ppm in some circumstances. The determination is comparatively straightforward for water in a polar compound such as acetone.[24] Willis and Miller[24] have measured the water bands at approximately 2.9 and 1.9 μm and determined the calibration curves shown in Fig. 7. The situation is less straightforward in non-polar compounds (e.g. hydrocarbons) as there is no significant bonding between the water and the hydrocarbon, and self-association of the water is likely to an increasing extent as the

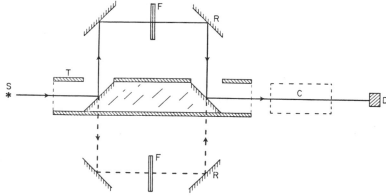

Fig. 6 (a). Filter analyser with rotating mirror (courtesy of Cambridge Consultants Limited, Cambridge). S = source; D = detector; R = ring mirrors; T = rotating mirror tube; F = filters; C = sample cell.

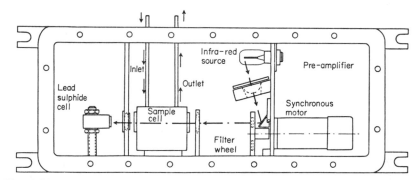

Fig. 6 (b). Rotating filter wheel analyser (courtesy of Anacon (U.K.) Limited).

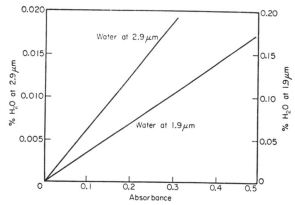

Fig. 7. Calibration for the estimation of water in acetone (Willis and Miller, Ref. 24).

water content rises. Unfortunately, self-association leads to a change (increase) in both the wavelength and intensity of the hydroxyl absorption band. A useful way out of the difficulty is to add a known excess of (say) acetone to the non-polar substance. This will stabilize the position and intensity of the water band.

5 ANALYSERS FOR LIQUIDS IN THE MID-INFRARED REGION

Many of the quantitative analyses performed in the laboratory with a conventional infrared spectrometer operating on the mid-infrared region may equally well be performed in a process control environment and with a two wavelength analyser, such as those illustrated in Figs 4 and 6.

As discussed above, normal transmission measurements on liquids are frequently unsatisfactory with process analysers, because of the problems of maintaining thin cells in good condition. For this reason, analysers based on the attenuated total reflection (a.t.r.) principle have clear advantages for plant analysers.

So much has been written on the subject of attenuated total reflection (a.t.r.) in infrared measurements[25, 26] that it would be inappropriate to discuss the subject here, except in general terms. The simplest apparatus used is similar to that in Fig. 8. The a.t.r. element, which is a transparent prism of relatively high refractive index, has the liquid to be analysed in contact with one of its surfaces. The beam which emerges from the prism is attenuated by the sample to a different extent at different wavelengths. For practical purposes it may be assumed that the radiation beam has penetrated into the sample for a short

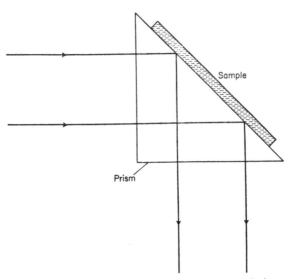

Fig. 8. The attenuated total reflection (a.t.r.) technique.

distance, so that the attenuation gives rise to what is in effect an absorption spectrum. However, the apparent thickness of the sample is proportional to the wavelength of the radiation. The apparent thickness depends upon the refractive index of the liquid and that of the prism. It also depends upon the angle between the radiation beam and the normal to the prism surface which is in contact with the liquid. Since it is usual to send the beam in and out of the prism along the normal to the prism surface, an isosceles prism is used, and the angle referred to above is equal to the base angle of the isosceles prism.

With these and other variables, it is not possible to give precise values for the equivalent thickness of an a.t.r. cell, but Table 3 gives approximate working

TABLE 3
'Apparent' sample thickness in a.t.r. and
m.i.r. spectroscopy

Angle of incidence[a]	30°	45°	60°
Ge ($n = 4.0$)[b]	0.13	0.06	0.03
KRS-5 ($n = 2.4$)	∞	0.42	0.31

[a] The 'angle of incidence' is the angle between the axis of propagation of the radiation beam and the normal to the prism surface which is in contact with the sample. The calculation is made for the case in which the radiation enters and leaves the prism along the normal to the entrance and exit faces. Thus the angle quoted is also the angle between the entrance face and the prism surface in contact with the sample.

[b] It is assumed that the refractive index, n, of the sample is 1.5. This is a good representative value for common organic substances.

How to use the table:

1. Multiply the number in the table by the wavelength of the radiation in μm to give the apparent thickness in μm in an ATR experiment.

2. Multiply also by the 'number of reflections' in the case of a multi-a.t.r. (m.i.r.) plate. This is only a nominal value, but is adequate for scouting experiments.

values. It will be seen from the table that the equivalent thickness of the liquid layer is very small at short wavelengths, and generally there is little point in attempting to use a.t.r. at wavelengths below 3 μm. Fortunately, it is possible in most cases to encompass measurements in this short wave region by transmission spectroscopy, as has previously been described, so in practice these two methods prove to be complementary in their application.

Table 3 gives values for the two prisms most commonly used in a.t.r. spectroscopy, namely thallium bromoiodide (usually known as KRS-5) and germanium. KRS-5 is a soft crystal which is rather easily deformed. Germanium, on the other hand, is a very hard crystal which easily snaps if too much pressure is applied to it. KRS-5 has a transmission range between the visible region and at least 20 μm. Unfortunately, it has some solubility in water and if the plant stream is likely to be wet, it may be better to use germanium which is practically insoluble in water. However, germanium has a transmission range which extends only to about 12 μm. The data in Table 3 apply irrespective of the thickness of the liquid layer, provided that the thickness exceeds the depth of penetration; hence it is possible to use very large thick cells for liquids. This is just what is required in plant applications because the problem is rarely that of shortage of sample—it is more the problem of the clogging and erosion of the cells. Hence the particular value of a.t.r. methods in infrared analysers for liquids.

Reference to Table 3 shows that the effective thickness of an a.t.r. cell is small, and indeed it will prove in many cases inadequate for a satisfactory analysis. Fortunately, this problem can be surmounted by the use of a multiple a.t.r. usually known as an m.i.r. (multiple internal reflection) prism, and in this case the triangular prism is replaced with a trapezoid as in the various cells shown in Fig. 9. In these designs, liquid may be placed in contact with both surfaces of the m.i.r. prism, and a large number of reflections (say up to 25) can be accommodated. This considerably enhances the intensity of the spectrum. Even so, the much weaker spectrum obtained with a germanium prism may mean that it is unsatisfactory in some applications.

Figure 9 (a) shows an apparatus suitable for a low viscosity liquid plant stream. The internal reflector plate is metallized opposite the gasket to prevent attenuation of the beam by the gasket material. Fig. 9 (b) shows a plate mounted across a pipe of substantial diameter (50 mm or more). In another arrangement the plate is mounted in the side of a pipe (Fig. 9 (c)). Many other arrangements have been suggested[26] but those described above appear to be the most practical for flow-through liquid cells in plant applications. It is important that the liquid should flow past the plate, but without allowing a static layer of liquid to remain in contact with the plate or allowing deposits to build up on the surface. Deliberately introduced turbulance may be necessary.

If an m.i.r. cell is to be used in an analyser, some optical focusing system is necessary to condense the light on to the input side of the m.i.r. plate. The analyser shown in Fig. 10 has been used satisfactorily. The filter arrangement may be either the usual two-wavelength filter pair, interposed alternately in the beam, or it may be a circular variable filter, in which case a spectrum may be recorded which is somewhat similar to that from a normal spectrometer. The instrument in this latter form is useful for general survey purposes. The kind of spectrum which is obtained in this operating mode is seen in Fig. 11. Being single beam, the background is not flat, but the spectrum is quite adequate for qualitative or quantitative analysis.

The instrument in this form is useful for scouting work in order to decide which filters to purchase for a two filter analyser.

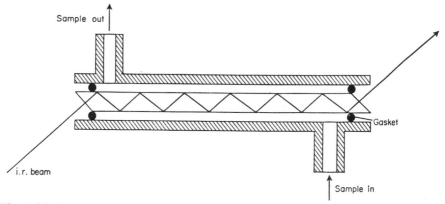

Fig. 9 (a). Sample system for low viscosity liquids (courtesy of Wilks Scientific Corp. Inc.).

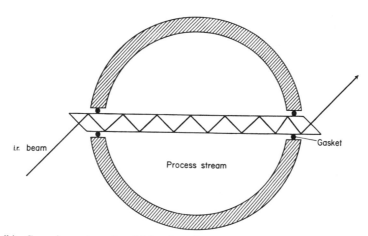

Fig. 9 (b). Sample system for high viscosity stream (courtesy of Wilks Scientific Corp. Inc.).

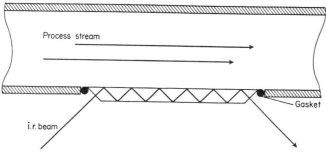

Fig. 9 (c). m.i.r. 'window' sampling system (courtesy of Wilks Scientific Corp. Inc.).

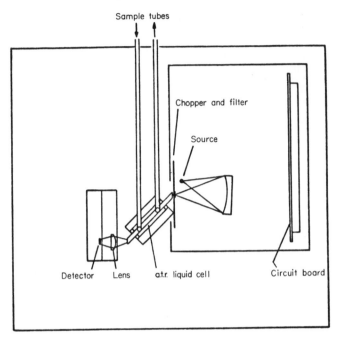

Sample tubes

Chopper and filter

Source

Detector   Lens   a.t.r. liquid cell   Circuit board

Fig. 10. Infrared analyser with m.i.r. plate (Wilks MIRAN analyser—courtesy of Wilks Scientific Corp. Inc.).

5.1   Some Applications of Internal Reflection Analysers

Because of the comparatively short effective path length which may be obtained in an m.i.r. cell, the possibility exists for working with aqueous solutions. This is generally considered to be impossible in infrared spectroscopic measurements. As an example of what can be achieved, the infrared spectra of water and an aqueous solution of ethanol are shown in Fig. 12. These were recorded in a spectrometer with a germanium m.i.r. plate, and they show that a two-filter analyser, with filters tuned to 9.6 and 10.3 μm would be suitable for the quantitative determination of ethanol in water. It is evident that many other analyses of aqueous solutions are made possible by the use of the m.i.r. method, although it must be emphasized that only when the solutions are concentrated (i.e. $>20\%$ second component) is the method likely to succeed. Another and somewhat surprising application is in monitoring the dissolved carbon dioxide in wine and soft drinks. In spite of the absorption of water it is very simple to measure dissolved carbon dioxide by means of the absorption band at 4.3 μm.

These examples demonstrate the versatility and power of the multiple internal reflection method for the continuous analyses of liquid systems. In terms of viscous liquids, the m.i.r. method has been applied to the analysis of mixed plasticizers for PVC; for example, mixtures of phthalates and phosphates. Where

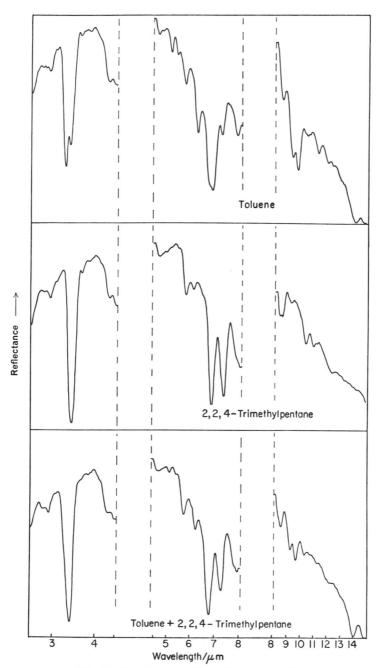

Fig. 11. Spectra recorded with m.i.r. analyser.

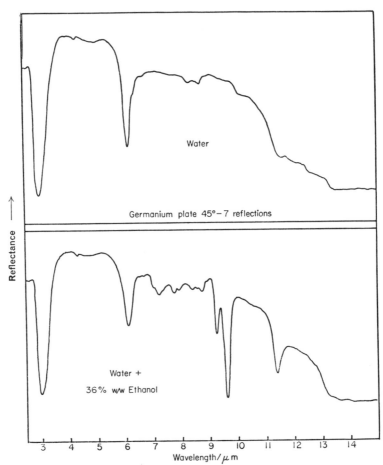

Fig. 12. m.i.r. spectra of water and a water–ethanol mixture (courtesy of Wilks Scientific Corp. Inc.).

the liquid is particularly viscous, the m.i.r. cell can be heated. Thus Dutton[27] has reported the use of a continuous total internal reflection analyser in following the hydrogenation of liquid oils and margarine. In addition to the relative simplicity of sampling in a flow-through a.t.r. cell, he points out that when measuring by a.t.r. (as opposed to infrared transmission) it is not necessary to remove suspended catalyst (nickel) particles from the oil.

The infrared spectrum of soya bean oil after hydrogenation is shown in Fig. 13. The significant feature is the band at 10.3 μm (965 cm^{-1}). Natural oils such as that from soya beans contain *cis* unsaturated groups. The hydrogenation catalyst removes some of these groups completely, but at the same time converts a proportion of the *cis* groups to *trans* groups, causing the appearance of the well known out-of-plane C—H deformation of the *trans* unsaturated group at 10.3 μm

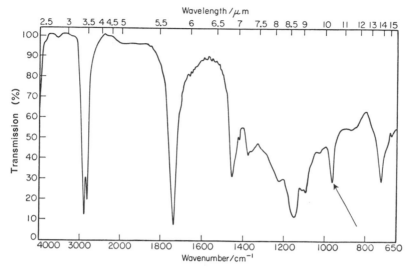

Fig. 13. Infrared spectrum of hydrogenated vegetable oil. Arrow indicates adsorption band (indicative of degree of hydrogenation) used in MIRAN II analyser (courtesy of Wilks Scientific Corp. Limited).

(965 cm^{-1}). Hence by measuring the strength of this band it is possible to monitor the progress of the hydrogenation. Satisfactory spectra were obtained with a nominal 11 reflection plate which, together with the sample, was kept at 150°C. The cell contents were stirred with a magnetic stirrer. The liquid fat was circulated by means of a diaphragm pump at $12.5 \text{ cm}^3 \text{ min}^{-1}$ through the cell and back to the reaction vessel. Results obtained with this measuring apparatus agreed well with those obtained by the more conventional methods previously used (Fig. 14).

6 INFRARED DIFFUSE REFLECTANCE ANALYSERS FOR SOLIDS

Films such as polyethylene, polypropylene and polyester are solid samples in a continuous and substantially homogeneous form and are, in principle, well suited to infrared transmission measurements. The gauging of films, and coatings on films by infrared analysers will be considered later. It is much more generally the case, however, that the solids encountered in manufacturing processes in the chemical, ceramic and food industries are powders, small crystals or granules. These materials represent extremely unfavourable samples for analysis with transmission analysers because in ordinary circumstances the amount of radiation lost by scatter, or diffuse reflectance, is so high that meaningful transmission measurements are impossible.

When a radiation beam strikes the surface of a non-absorbing solid, the proportion of light reflected, R, from a beam normally incident on the surface is given by $R = [(n-1)/(n+1)]^2$, where n is the refractive index. This is, for the

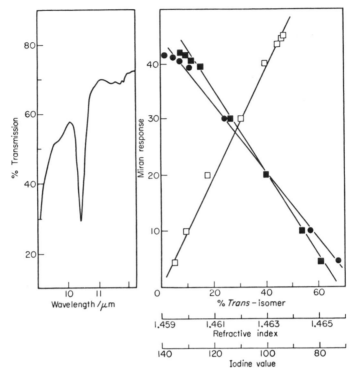

Fig. 14. *Trans*-isomer band at 10.3 μm (left) indicates degree of hydrogenation while 11 μm band is used as reference. MIRAN analyser response (right) is plotted *v.* % *trans*-isomer (□), refractive index (●), and iodine value (■), (courtesy of Wilks Scientific Corp. Limited).

vast majority of solids, about 1.5, so that $R = 0.04$. For a continuous solid (e.g. a sheet of glass or a piece of plastic film) which presents two surfaces to the radiation beam, the radiation loss by reflection is therefore about 8%, which presents no particular problem. In powders and granules, however, there is a multiplicity of surfaces, hence the transmission is very low. The usual way of overcoming this problem in laboratory experiments is to immerse the solid in a transparent liquid having approximately the same refractive index. In infrared work this would be liquid paraffin or fluorolube. Alternatively, the interstices of the sample can be filled by compressing it with a transparent powder of approximately the same refractive index—that is the potassium bromide disc method. Clearly neither of these methods are applicable to solids in a production stream. Spectra can be measured by pressing a powder into contact with a total internal reflection prism, but such spectra are weak because the contact area is small, and in any case this would again not represent a process which could easily be applied to a plant stream. The reason for the poor transmission is that the diffuse reflectance is high, and this raises the question as to whether a measurement of diffuse reflectance would be analytically useful. In diffuse reflectance, radiation leaves the sample in all directions. Thus only a portion of the diffusely reflected radiation can be captured, and generally the measurement of diffuse reflectance has been confined to the near-infrared region where experimental conditions are particularly favourable, as was discussed earlier in relation to infrared transmission measurements on liquid samples.

The reflectance from a solid is usually considered to be made up of two separate components.[28] One component is the normal specular surface reflectance which, for an absorbing substance, is given by

$$R = [(n-1)^2 + k^2]/[(n+1)^2 + k^2]$$

for normally incident radiation, where n is the refractive index and k is the so-called 'absorption index', defined as $k = K\lambda/4\pi$, where λ is the wavelength in microns. K is the Lambert's Law coefficient, given by

$$K = (1/l) \log_e (I_0/I)$$

where I_0 is the intensity of incident radiation, I is the intensity of transmitted radiation, and l is the sample thickness.

Note that, when applying this equation, λ and l must be expressed in the same units. Thus k can be determined from the normal transmission spectrum. Calculations based on experimental values of band intensities show that k is usually <0.1 at wavelengths between 3 μm and the visible, even for the strongest bands in this region. Since n is also effectively constant in this region, it follows that no analytically useful spectrum results purely from the specularly reflected radiation in the near infrared. The other contribution to the reflectance spectrum is from radiation which has penetrated some of the particles and has thus been attenuated by absorption. This radiation is subsequently reflected (by specular reflectance) into the detecting system and gives, in effect, a kind of absorption spectrum. Thus, the intensity of the spectrum depends upon the thickness of sample traversed by the radiation. This means that a powder of larger particle size shows a stronger spectrum, except that the absorption reaches a maximum when the particles are so large as to be effectively opaque at a particular wavelength. The effect is that the absorption can no longer be simply related to thickness or concentration; it is somewhat similar to measuring the transmission of a layer of material which is non-uniform in thickness. For this reason also, it is not possible to measure useful diffuse reflectance spectra on heavily absorbing samples, such as black metallic oxides, or materials which are loaded with carbon black.

In spite of the somewhat dubious state of the theory of diffuse reflectance, the ability to perform analysis on powders with no sample preparation has meant that a good deal of effort has been put into devising instruments for measuring these spectra. One form of commercial apparatus is shown in Fig. 15 (a). Being a near-infrared instrument, it has the familiar tungsten filament lamp source and lead sulphide detector; the filters are mounted in a wheel which is rotated by means of a synchronous motor. Radiation is directed on to the sample and the diffusely

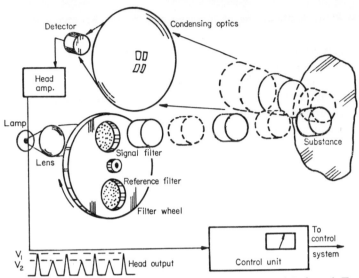

Fig. 15 (a). Near-infrared reflectance analyser (courtesy of Infrared Engineering Limited).

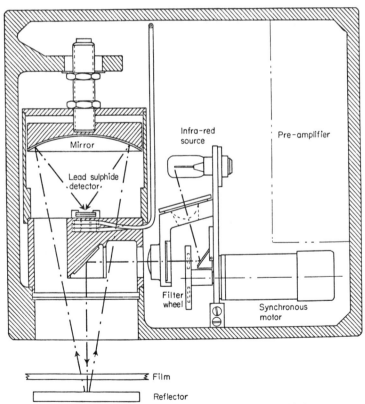

Fig. 15 (b). Infrared reflectance gauge modified for film thickness measurements (courtesy of Anacon (U.K.) Limited).

reflected light is collected on the large mirror and directed into the detector. This form of analyser is clearly very attractive for use when a solid product is being carried on a conveyor belt. The analyser is suspended over the belt a few inches away from the product to be analysed. This is an excellent example of the best kind of radiant energy analyser, where there is no contact between the analyser and the product.

6.1   Some Applications of Diffuse Reflectance Analysers

Near-infrared diffuse reflectance analysers have found a major application in the measurement of the water content of a very wide range of substances, both organic and inorganic. In many industries this measurement is of outstanding importance. In the food industry, for example, excess of water can reduce shelf life and impair flavour while overdrying can degrade the product. Other substances, such as tobacco, are sold with an agreed water content, while in materials such as sand and clay the consistent quality of the product depends upon holding the water content within narrow limits. There has, in any event, been a much greater emphasis on measuring water content since the recent large increases in the cost of fuel.

By way of example, Fig. 16 shows the near-infrared diffuse reflectance spectrum of tobacco with different water contents. The bands at 1.45 and 1.94 μm are due to water, and the intensity of both these bands increases with increasing water content. These spectra were measured on a spectrometer with an integrating sphere.[28]

The water absorption bands in the near-infrared region vary considerably in intensity, and so, by using the band of most appropriate intensity, it is possible

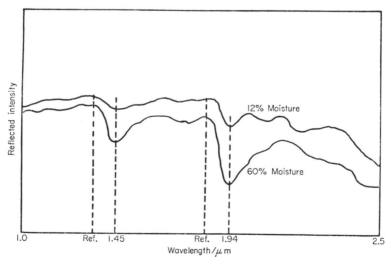

Fig. 16. Diffuse reflectance spectra of tobacco (courtesy of Infrared Engineering Limited).

to measure water contents from ppm up to 50% w/w. Some examples of applications are given in Table 4. When considering the application of diffuse reflectance for the measurement of water content, it is as well to avoid relatively large granular materials such as whole grain or coffee beans, because, as mentioned earlier, complete absorption may occur of radiation which traverses a large particle. Thus the measurement will be biased towards water on the surface of the particles and may thus prove to be unrepresentative of the whole. On the other hand, the method works well with rolled oats, instant coffee, and spray-dried milk. There is often a positive advantage in working with a moving rather than a stationary sample, especially when the area of individual particles is large compared with the viewing area, as a more representative value is then achieved.

One of the biggest practical problems in the installation of an infrared reflectance gauge to measure water content is in establishing a satisfactory calibration curve. It is often best, at least initially, to calibrate the gauge reading against the water content of the sample as determined by some agreed standard method, e.g. Carl Fischer water content, or loss of weight in a particular oven drying cycle. Even if these water contents are not correct, they usually represent an agreed and satisfactory control procedure for the product.

TABLE 4
Examples of water content as determined by near-infrared diffuse reflectance spectroscopy (based on data supplied by Infrared Engineering Limited)

Substance	Range, %	Accuracy, %	Wavelength/μm
Industrial sand	0–20	±0.1	1.94
Clay dust (spray drier)	0–15	±0.05	1.94
Building clay mix	0–30	±0.5	1.94
Salt (NaCl)	0–5	±0.02	1.94
Magnesium oxide	0–10	±0.05	1.94
	0–3	±0.01	2.95
Ground barley	0–12	±0.1	1.94
Synthetic protein	0–10	±0.1	1.94
	0–40	±0.5	1.94
Concrete	0–10	±0.25	1.94
Cement	0–1	±0.03	2.95
Asbestos	0–15	±0.1	1.94
	0–70	±0.5	1.45
Tea	0–12	±0.1	1.94
Wood shavings	0–16	±0.25	1.94
Tobacco leaf and stem	0–25	±0.2	1.94
	25–50	±0.4	1.45
Soap powder	0–14	±0.2	1.94
Instant potato	0–12	±0.2	1.94
Paper	2–12	±0.2	1.94
Sand	0–10	±0.1	1.94
Sugar beet pulp	0–20	±0.3	1.94

7 MEASUREMENT OF THE THICKNESS OF PLASTIC FILMS

With the increasing use of plastic films, especially in the packaging trade, considerable effort has been devoted to methods of measuring film thickness. This is partly for economic reasons since selling film which is thicker than needed wastes raw materials. There is also the more immediate practical reason that film of uneven thickness will not reel smoothly.

The traditional method of measuring film thickness is with a β-ray gauge. However, special safety precautions are necessary for such gauges, and they are not very satisfactory for thin films, where the mass of film is comparable with the mass of air in the gauge gap and the latter varies with the air temperature. For these reasons there has been considerable interest in alternative gauging methods (e.g. air jets, ultrasonics) and, in particular, gauges based on absorption in the ultraviolet and infrared regions of the spectrum. The simplest form of gauge is more or less identical with the two wavelength transmission analyser previously described. For some time there has been a u.v. absorption gauge available for measuring the thickness of polyester (polyethylene terephthalate) film,[1] but this is not applicable to the two major packaging films, polyethylene and polypropylene, since neither of these aliphatic hydrocarbon polymers have absorption in the ultraviolet region.

The series of absorption bands in the near-infrared region which are due to the CH_2 group already have been noted (Table 1). These are of particular interest in film gauging as the band intensity falls progressively through the series towards shorter wavelength. Thus it should be possible to cope with a very wide range of film thickness (from a few μm upwards) by choosing the appropriate absorption band in this series. Figure 17 shows the spectra of polypropylene at 14 and 500 μm thickness. In principle, the 3.43 μm band would be suitable for measuring thin film, and that at 1.7 or 2.4 μm for the thicker film.

The equipment previously described for near-infrared transmission measurements is in principle suitable for this kind of infrared film thickness gauge. Such a gauge may be operated in transmission, with the source assembly on one side, and the detector on the other side of the film. If it is required to measure the film in the longitudinal direction (usually known as machine direction or M.D.) the two halves are mounted in a fixed C frame. To measure in the transverse direction (across the film web or T.D.) the source unit and detector must both be moved across the film. This introduces considerable complication, but very satisfactory, if very expensive, equipment is available which will hold the two halves of the measuring equipment in precise register while traversing.

Some of the complication can be avoided by operating in either a specular or diffuse reflection mode. The source and detector are mounted in one unit on one side of the film. The diffuse reflectance arrangement already described (Fig. 15a) may well prove suitable, but the arrangement used in practice is as shown in Fig. 15b. Of the possible diffuse reflectors that described by Stay,[29] being based on polytetrafluorethylene, is particularly useful because the surface is highly

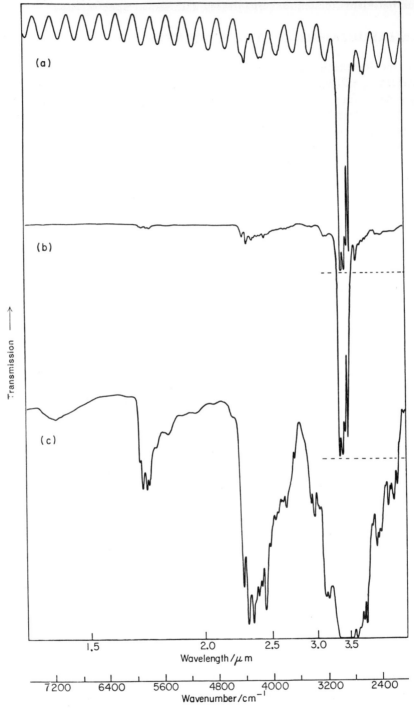

Fig. 17. Transmission spectra of polypropylene. (a) = 14 μm film; (b) = as (a), with fringes suppressed; (c) = 500 μm sheet.

resistant to contamination and staining. The choice of diffuse or specular reflector is best left to experiment. The specular reflector will return more light and so will be used if energy is at a premium; on the other hand, the apparatus with a diffuse reflector will be much more tolerant of optical misalignment. This assembly is usually placed above the film so that when the web breaks it does not foul the sensitive parts of the gauge. It may foul the reflector which is usually in the form of a continuous strip under the film. Although in principle the two-filter instrument is able to compensate for obscuration of the reflector because both beams are obstructed, in practice the precision required of these gauges is so high that second- or even third-order effects are likely to be important. This is the stage at which standardization and computer control comes to the fore, since, provided there is no gross contamination or loose material on the reflector, it is possible, in the absence of the film, to traverse the gauge across the reflector and record a new 'background' in the computer memory. In all these arrangements it is possible to have a gap of several inches between the heads, reflectors, and film, and this makes rethreading relatively easy. Thus the risk of damage to the gauge equipment is considerably reduced. These gauges are also reasonably tolerant of film flutter, i.e. an up-and-down oscillation of the web, but it is necessary for the film to be flat rather than wrinkled; otherwise the effective thickness of the film is increased (i.e. there is more film per unit area as viewed from the gauge).

In a different arrangement the film is used as its own diffuse reflector, and this is particularly appropriate to polyethylene, or to other films which show significant radiation scattering.[30] Here again, source and detector are on the same side of the film. The amount of radiation backscattered by the film is usually considerably less than that from an independent reflector, consequently the whole arrangement is optically more critical, and it is necessary to steer the film to ensure that it remains always at a constant distance from the detector head. The particular advantage of this kind of film thickness gauge is that it may be used to determine the thickness of the film in the 'bubble' process. In this method of film manufacture, which is almost universally used to make polyethylene film and lay flat tube, a relatively thick polyethylene tube is extruded, the size of which is increased (and its thickness correspondingly reduced) by inflating and stretching by air pressure. Since there is no obvious method by which a reflector could be conveniently placed inside the bubble, the self-scattering approach is particularly appropriate, especially as the pressure inside the bubble may be used to maintain the side of the bubble in contact with the measuring head of the thickness gauge. The alternative is to wait until the film has been slit, and then use a conventional β-ray gauge or an infrared gauge of the transmission or reflection type as previously described. Since this must be done much later in the process it is possible that a good deal of useless film may have been made before the thickness is known. Furthermore, it is very convenient to have the film profile available close in time and space to the extruder. Change of profile means adjusting the extruder die and, if the results of adjustments are seen quickly by the operator, the whole process of setting up a film line is speeded up with a corresponding improvement in plant efficiency. This method requires some caution in its application. Since the radiation is returned by scattering centres within the film (rather than beyond it) only a portion of the radiation returned has penetrated to the full depth of the film, and clearly it is only this latter radiation which is truly indicative of the film thickness. If the film has high internal scattering power as, for example, from added inorganic fillers, there may be very little of the back scattered radiation which has entirely penetrated the film, and although the signal stability may be good, in fact the measurement will be relatively insensitive.

There is a further point of interest in film thickness measurement by infrared methods. Because these films are substantially flat, having plane parallel surfaces, and are of a thickness of the same order as the wavelength of the infrared radiation, interference fringes may be seen in the infrared spectrum. The way in which the fringes develop may be seen by reference to Fig. 18. As explained previously, at any air/substance interface a proportion of the radiation striking a surface is reflected. Thus some radiation is reflected at the film/air interface where the radiation beam emerges from the film. The radiation so reflected now strikes the first film surface, where a proportion is again reflected, this time in the same direction as that of the original radiation beam. The possibility now exists of additive or subtractive interference between these two beams. In principle, further reflected beams should be taken into account, but in practice this is not

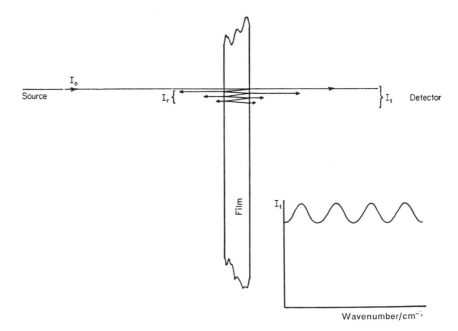

Fig. 18. Fringe development in a thin cell.

important because the intensity, beyond the second beam, is too small to be significant.

When the thickness of the film is such that the path length of the second beam within the film is an exact integral number of wavelengths, the first and second beams emerge exactly in phase and reinforce one another. It is as if no loss by internal reflection had occurred, hence the transmission reaches a maximum. As the wavelength is changed, the beams slowly move out of phase and the transmission falls until the exact out-of-phase condition occurs at which the transmission is a minimum. The practical effect is seen in Fig. 17 (a), and takes the form of a series of bands in the background of the spectrum approximating to a sinusoidal change. It would clearly be very difficult to measure the intensity of the band in this spectrum without removing this 'fringe' pattern.

The phenomenon[31,32] is well known when measuring the infrared spectra of thin films, and it is usually coped with in the laboratory by mounting the film between a pair of infrared-transparent plates and filling the gaps between the plates and the film with a transparent immersion liquid. Thus there is effectively no reflection loss at either film surface, and the outer surfaces of the plate are so far apart that the fringe effect is negligible. While this is a good laboratory method when only a few samples are involved, it is clearly out of the question in a production plant.

Of the methods devised to overcome this problem, that of Willis and Boyes[31] relies on the properties of polarized radiation. It is well known that if radiation strikes a surface other than normally it is reflected partially plane polarized and, in particular, if the angle between the beam axis and the normal to the surface is the Brewster angle, the reflected light is fully plane polarized. It may now be argued that if the film is set up so that the radiation beam strikes it at the Brewster angle and the beam itself is polarized so as to remove completely that radiation vector which could be reflected, then no reflection will occur and the fringe pattern will be suppressed. This is indeed proven to be so in practice.

The application of this principle in a laboratory instrument is demonstrated[33] in Fig. 19. It will be evident that the same system may be readily incorporated into a plant analyser. The film strip is arranged so that the normal to the film surface is at the Brewster angle to the axis of the radiation beam. The diagram shows a parallel plate polarizer, but in plant application we now use grid polarizers[34] as these are mechanically easier to incorporate in analysers, are very efficient polarizers, and have relatively very good transmission for the wanted vector.

7.1   Measurement of Coatings on Films with an Infrared Gauge

The application of the film gauge with fringe suppression by means of a polarizer will be illustrated in the measurement of a film coating. While, when measuring base film thickness, infrared gauges may be shown to have some advantages over β-ray gauges, in the direct measurement of coating thickness,

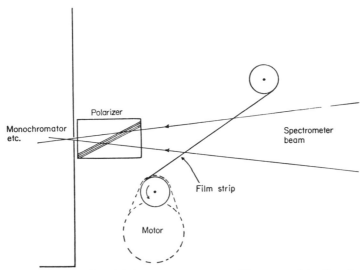

Fig. 19. Apparatus for film thickness measurement. The normal to the plane of the film is at the Brewster angle to the incident beam.

gauges based on infrared or u.v. absorption are most frequently used because only in this way is it possible to discriminate between coating and base. Subtractive methods (i.e. base + coating − base) are generally highly unsatisfactory as the coating is much thinner than the base.

Figure 20 (a) is the spectrum of polypropylene film in the thickness often used for wrapping. For many purposes, the water vapour transmission of such a film is undesirably high; hence it is coated with a vinylidene chloride copolymer. Figure 20 (b) is the spectrum of the coated film, and it is required to measure the coating thickness. The band chosen for the determination is that at 9.3 μm, the comparison wavelength being 8.9 μm. Figure 21 shows the effect obtained by measuring the coating thickness in a longitudinal (M.D.) film strip 2 m long. The measurement is made with a spectrometer, operated at the two fixed wavelengths. As expected, the transmission at the comparison wavelength is substantially constant, but by means of the 'measurement' wavelength an interesting pattern of thickness change is seen.

Taking into account the running speed of the film it is possible to relate this profile to mechanical operations on the plant, e.g. frequency of rotation of rollers conveying the film, indicating that minor eccentricity of the rollers is responsible for some profile variation in the machine direction.

8 EFFLUENTS, POLLUTION AND TOXICITY PROBLEMS

The chemical industry is becoming increasingly concerned with effluents and with potential toxic hazards associated with handling chemicals. **Raman**

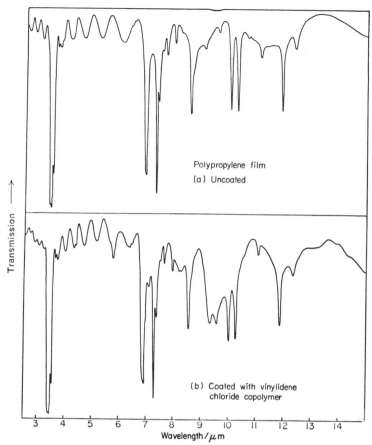

Fig. 20. Infrared spectra of polypropylene film, (a) uncoated, and (b) coated with vinylidene chloride copolymer.

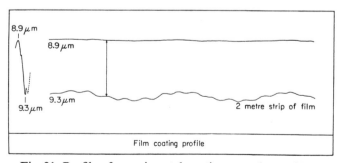

Fig. 21. Profile of experimental coating on polymer film.

spectroscopy has so far been little used in this context as an analytical method but it does appear that it may have important applications in pollution control. Infrared spectroscopy is a technique which is often better used for distinguishing between materials, rather than for attempting to determine the very low concentrations of components typically found in effluents and waste. Nevertheless, infrared analysers must now be thought of as practical and reliable instruments in this field.[35–37]

8.1   Closed and Open Path Methods of Gas Detection and Determination

These methods might be described in broad terms as either taking the gas to the instrument or taking the instrument to the gas. If it is required to monitor local gas concentrations, say at agreed points on a production plant, it will be usual to set up a multipoint sampling system by which air samples from many different locations are piped successively into a static analyser. In the case of a spectroscopic analyser, this means pumping the gas into a cell inside the analyser. In addition to these 'closed path' methods, a need has arisen for *in situ* sampling, where the required gas is determined in the atmsophere by either active methods (passage of a radiation beam into the atmosphere and detecting transmitted or scattered radiation) or by passive methods (e.g. measuring the self-emission of the required constituent). These are known as 'open path' methods.

8.2   Closed Path Gas Analysers with Multipass Absorption Cells

A number of the gas analysers discussed earlier in this chapter are in principle suitable for the detection of gaseous pollutants by closed path methods. In practice almost every one must be rejected, in the form so far described, because of lack of sensitivity at the levels necessary in pollution work. One important advance in this field was the recognition that a large sensitivity gain can be achieved by an arrangement whereby the radiation beam passes many times through the same volume of gas. This principle was first demonstrated in practical form by White[38] who devised a cell similar to that shown in Fig. 22.

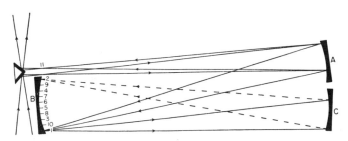

Fig. 22. A multi-reflection gas cell (J. W. White type) (courtesy of Heywood and Company Limited).

The gas is contained in the space between the three mirrors A, B and C, all of which have the same radius of curvature, and the distances AB and BC are themselves also equal to the radius of curvature. The radiation beam is brought to a focus first inside the cell. It then diverges on to mirror A, which throws a sharp image on to mirror B. From B the light diverges on to mirror C, to be returned once more to mirror A. In this way a large number of passes are achieved through the same volume of gas, until a final reflection from mirror A sends the beam out of the cell on to a collecting mirror. In the original White design, the number of passes through the cell was governed by separately moving mirrors A and C. In practice this was an extremely tedious operation, but recently Wilks has shown that if mirrors A and C are fixed to a common back plate, and the whole plate is rotated about a pivot at right angles to the ABC plane, the number of passes can be altered from one to twenty by a simple rotation of a micrometer head at the end of the cell. Thus a cell approximately 500 mm in length, and with a volume of about 5 dm^3, can have an effective path length, in metre steps, between 1 and 20 m. With such a large number of reflections involved, the three mirrors must have very high reflectivity; in practice the transmission after 20 passes can be as high as 70%. To maintain this performance it is necessary to prevent fouling, by filtering the gases to be examined. Another potentially serious problem is adsorption of the sample on the walls of the cell. This can reduce the concentration of the required gas in the cell, and can also result in a cell memory, because the adsorbed gas is slowly released over many hours or days, thus contaminating samples subsequently placed in the cell.

In addition to the 20 m cell, several longer cells are available, but these are intended more for special requirements than for routine plant applications (Plate I). With this pattern of cell, determinations can be made on a large number of gases in the ppm range. Table 5 is condensed from Wilks' compilation,[15] and shows the detection limits for some common gases in using the multipass cell described above, compared with the presently accepted toxic limits.

In the previous discussion of infrared gas analysers, it was pointed out that generally these employ non-focused radiation; hence they cannot be used with multipass cells. While in principle there would seem to be no reason why an instrument with a linear 20 m light-pipe cell could not be built, it does not seem a very practical proposition. Furthermore, since the radiation is propagated through the cell by reflection from the cell walls, a very high standard of optical finish would be required. This means that if the required sensitivity in a closed-path analyser can be achieved only by multipassing, the analyser must have focusing optics, and this restricts the method to conventional dispersive or Fourier transform spectrometers, or analysers of the Miran type. The latter may have a fixed or variable filter. Figure 23 is a diagram of a variable filter instrument with the multipass gas cell attached. Figure 24 shows the instrument (air) background, and a spectrum of methyl methacrylate vapour as an indication of its performance with a variable filter. The instrument may be permanently connected into a multipoint sampling system; it is, on the other hand, not too

TABLE 5
Table of toxic and detection limits for common gases (reproduced by permission of Techmation Limited)

Compound	Maximum allowable exposure (8 hour weighted average)/ ppm	Analytical wavelength/ μm	Minimum detectable concentration (MIRAN analyser, 20 m cell/ ppm
Acetic acid	10	8.5	0.1
Acetonitrile	40	6.5	4
Acrolein	0.1	8.8	0.1
Ammonia	50	10.3	0.2
Benzene	10	3.3	0.15
Benzyl chloride	1	7.9	0.7
2-butanone (MEK)	200	8.5	0.08
Carbon disulfide	20	4.54	0.5
Carbon monoxide	50	4.7	0.2
Carbon tetrachloride	10	12.6	0.06
Chloroform (trichloromethane)	50	13.0	0.06
Cresol (all isomers)	5	8.6	0.3
Dimethylformamide	10	9.2	0.1
Dioxan (diethylene dioxide)	100	8.9	0.05
2-ethoxyethyl acetate (cellulose acetate)	100	8.8	0.03
Ethylamine	10	3.4	0.2
Ethyl ether	400	8.8	0.06
Formaldehyde	3		
Formic acid	5	8.2	0.2
Hydrogen chloride	5	3.37	0.5
Hydrogen cyanide	10	3.04	0.4
Methyl alcohol (methanol)	200	9.5	0.2
Methylamine	10	3.4	0.1
Methyl cellosolve	25	8.8	0.05
Methyl chloride	100	13.4	1.5
Methyl iodide	5	7.9	0.4
Methyl mercaptan	10	3.38	0.4
Methyl methacrylate	100	8.5	0.03
Nitrobenzene	1	11.8	0.4
Nitromethane	100	9.3	1.5
Perchloroethylene	100	10.9	0.05
Phenol	5	8.4	0.1
Phosphine	0.3		0.3
Pyridine	5	14.2	0.2
Styrene	100	11.0	0.4
Sulfur dioxide	5	8.6	0.5
1,1,2,2-tetrachloroethane	5	8.3	0.3
Tetrahydrofuran	200	9.3	0.6
Toluene	200	13.7	0.5
Vinyl chloride	1	10.9	0.3
Xylene (xylol)	100	12.6	0.6

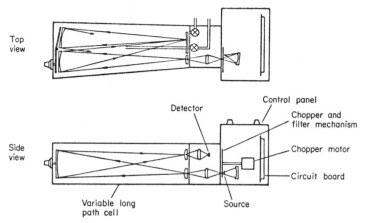

Top
view

Side
view

Control panel

Chopper and
filter mechanism

Detector

Chopper motor

Circuit board

Variable long
path cell

Source

Fig. 23. Schematic of MIRAN II gas analyser with 20 m cell (courtesy of Wilks Scientific
Corp. Limited).

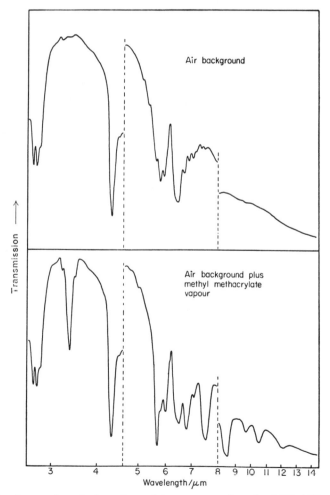

Air background

Air background plus
methyl methacrylate
vapour

Transmission ⟶

Wavelength/μm

Fig. 24. Spectrum of methyl methacrylate vapour using the MIRAN analyser with
multipass gas cell.

heavy to be transported manually. This is a very useful feature when it is required to map out 'toxic' gas concentrations on a production plant prior to the installation of a permanent multipoint monitoring system.

In the form shown, the analyser needs to be powered by mains electricity. An alternative form is available which, by means of a built-in rechargeable battery, may be used for some hours remote from a mains supply. In none of these forms, however, is the instrument intrinsically safe. It cannot, therefore, be used in atmospheres containing inflammable or potentially explosive gases. Where the analyser forms part of a fixed installation this usually presents no problem, as it will ordinarily be housed in a specially built cubicle. The instrument in intrinsically safe form is likely to be so heavy as to be no longer portable, and therefore for scouting experiments some compromise must be made. One method is to remove the gas cell from the analyser, evacuate it, carry it to the analysis area, and there obtain a sample of the atmosphere to be tested in the cell. This somewhat laborious procedure may be avoided by using a long sampling line on the input to the gas cell (e.g. 100 m PVC garden hose may be used). It may then be some minutes before a representative sample of the required atmosphere is pumped to the cell. The preferred method is to set the analyser to the wavelength of maximum absorption of the required gas and continue pumping until the radiation absorption (as indicated by the output meter) settles out at a maximum value. In spite of the time delay, a survey of a plant can be conducted by this method much more rapidly, and with far less labour, than by traditional methods.

When scouting work is complete, and the best sampling sites have been chosen, it may well be preferred to use some quite different analytical principle for a fixed multipoint analysis system. However, if one gas is to be determined in the presence of others, or if several gases are to be determined, the infrared analyser may have advantages. The circular variable filter analyser may be used, taking absorbance readings at a series of predetermined wavelengths, and determining the composition of the gas mixture by a computer calculation.

8.3 Closed Path Gas Analysers with Special Sources or Detectors

Unless the sensitivity necessary for the determination of gaseous pollutants is to be achieved by the application of a multipass cell, it is necessary to improve the efficiency of the radiation source or the efficiency of detecting the radiation. The obvious improvement in the source is to abandon the black body emitter and substitute a laser. There has been a good deal of work done here but it is a solution which is more appropriate to open-path analysers, and the developments will be discussed in that context.

With regard to efficiency of detection, the greatest choice appears to be in the use of multiplex methods; that is, methods in which a number of the absorption bands of the wanted gas are measured simultaneously by the detector. This principle is already invoked in the Luft detector cell, but here it merely compensates for the inefficiency of the Luft cell compared with the more usual detectors (thermocouples, bolometers and pyroelectric detectors).

In the closed path applications, attention has been directed at the Fourier transform spectrometer[39] because in addition to its multiplex advantage[40] it may be operated at extremely high spectral resolving power. This is particularly valuable when detecting light gases with rotational fine structure, since the intensity of the narrow rotational lines apparently increases as the spectral resolving power is increased (Fig. 25) and at the same time increased discrimina-

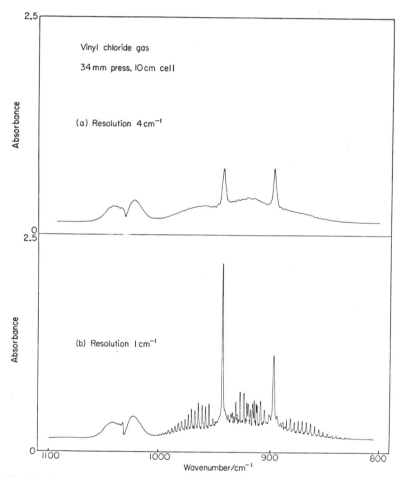

Fig. 25. Apparent increase in absorbance of a gas at high resolving power.

tion is achieved. The major argument against this application of the Fourier transform spectrometer is its complexity and high cost, but much of this lies in the necessity for a dedicated computer. However, when a computer is available, it may be used to improve the sensitivity of the spectrometer by spectrum accumulation, and 'correlation' between the observed spectrum and that of the required component (or components) may be performed with the computer. It may therefore be considered to be among the more powerful types of apparatus available for the detection of gases at low concentrations in air.

8.4 Correlation Instruments

The correlation principle may be used in a dispersion spectrometer. In the usual design of infrared dispersion instrument, the dispersed and focused spectrum is produced in a plane containing the exit slit. If the exit slit is replaced by a series of detectors, each one of which is placed in the image plane, at the absorption maximum of a rotational line of the gas to be detected, a signal which is at once strong (by the multiplex advantage), and highly selective, is achieved (Fig. 26). In a related design, in the plane of the focused spectrum is placed an

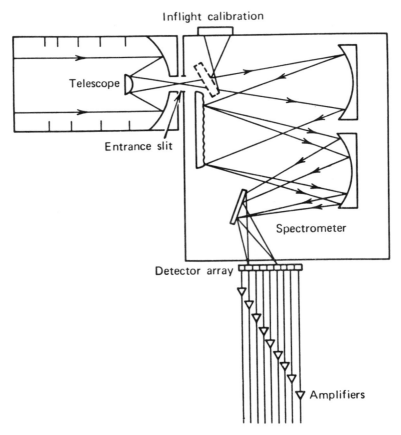

Fig. 26. Correlation spectrometer with multiple detectors (Pitts and Metcalf, Ref. 36).

opaque mask in which are cut slots corresponding to the absorption lines of the gas to be detected.[41,42] Radiation transmitted by the mask is condensed to fall upon a single detector (Fig. 27). The mask is oscillated in the focal plane in

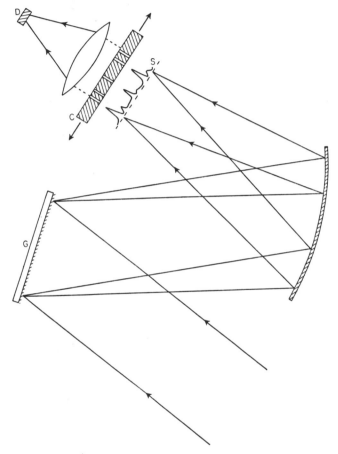

Fig. 27. Spectrometer with correlation mask. D = detector; C = correlation mask; S = spectrum; G = grating.

the dispersion direction to modulate the signal; alternatively, the mask is held stationary while the dispersing element (prism, or more usually grating) is moved in a cyclic fashion so as to oscillate the focused spectrum in the plane of a stationary mask. In either form, both the multiplex advantage and high selectivity for the required gas are maintained.

The multiplex advantage, with a normal (i.e. non-selective) detector, may also be secured in a non-dispersive instrument by pressure modulation (Fig. 28). In a conventional source–absorption cell–sensitizing cell arrangement, the sensitizing cell contains the gas to be detected. By pulsating the gas pressure in the

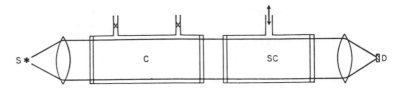

Fig. 28. Non-dispersive system with pressure modulation. S = source; C = sample
cell; SC = sensitizing cell; D = detector.

sensitizing cell, the beam is modulated preferentially at those frequencies at
which the absorption bands of the required gas occur. This method is evidently
most powerful when the gas has significant fine structure in its spectrum at
atmospheric pressure, since under these conditions the extent of modulation
depends not only upon the change in intensity of the individual bands within the
'rotational fine structure' with pressure pulsation, but also upon the increase in
half-band width of the rotational lines as the pressure is increased. Pressure
modulation is evidently an under-exploited effect and some further thought along
these lines in tackling problems of gaseous pollutants may well be rewarding.

8.5   Detection and Determination of Pollutants by Open Path
Methods

Closed path methods of determination of pollutants in air are particularly
appropriate to monitoring plant atmospheres for the protection of operators on
chemical plants. It will be evident, however, that there is a requirement for
measuring pollutants in the atmosphere around industrial plants. Here multi-
station sampling is no longer appropriate and open path methods appear to be
most desirable.

In open path methods of determination of pollutants, there are two distinct
approaches; either 'active' or 'passive' methods are possible. In 'active' methods,
an artificial radiation source is necessary for the determination. In 'passive'
methods a natural radiation source is used.

Detection of pollutants by 'passive' methods

In these methods, the source is either the sun or the self-emission of the wanted
gas. If the sun is to be used as an energy source, the 'closed path' methods
previously described are generally applicable, except that the emphasis must
generally be placed on those regions of the electromagnetic spectrum which are
clear of the absorption of water vapour and carbon dioxide. The kind of apparatus needed for such measurements is shown diagrammatically in Fig. 29. For
practical purposes the sun is at infinity, and the larger the diameter of the
Cassegrainian collector the greater the signal strength. Some idea of the pollutants which may be determined with this apparatus is indicated in Fig. 30 which
shows atmospheric transmission across a 1000 feet (c. 300 m) path at sea level,

Plate I. Multi-pass gas cells. The longest stands about 2.5 m high (courtesy of Wilks Scientific Corp. Limited)

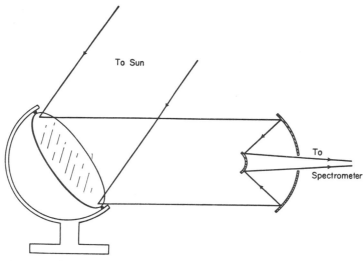

Fig. 29. Solar source open path detecting system.

and the absorption patterns to be expected for some pollutants of interest. In relation to the 'pure' atmospheric background it should be possible to ascertain whether it is feasible to determine various pollutants in an open air path. There are, of course, many sources of atmospheric pollution which arise from causes quite unconnected with the chemical industry. These are listed in Table 6.

Obviously these measurements are only possible in sunlight; hence some efforts have been made to use the Earth's emission as a radiation source, since it would seem to be an attractive proposition for a fixed installation giving measurements continuously. Unfortunately, there is a major problem. Transfer of radiant energy will only occur between two bodies if they are at different temperatures, and then net transfer will occur from the hotter to the colder body. As far as the detector is concerned, this presents no problem, as it can be operated at any desired temperature, although it will be usual to cool it (with, for example, liquid nitrogen or helium) in order to increase its sensitivity.

However, energy transfer between the Earth and the gas may occur in either direction, or not at all. If the gas is cooler than the Earth, an absorption spectrum will be measured; it if is at the same temperature there is no energy transfer and no spectrum will be measured. If the gas is warmer, an emission spectrum will be recorded. Rather than becoming involved in this complication, it seems better to eliminate the Earth's radiation and concentrate on the self-emission of the gas measured with an instrument with a cooled detector so that an emission spectrum is always presented. The Earth's radiation (or radiation which may enter the system from buildings, trees, etc.) is excluded either by sighting the instrument at the sky or limiting the range with a reflector at the end of the sight line, sufficiently large to fill the field of view of the instrument.

The emission spectrum of a substance is of the same nature as its absorption

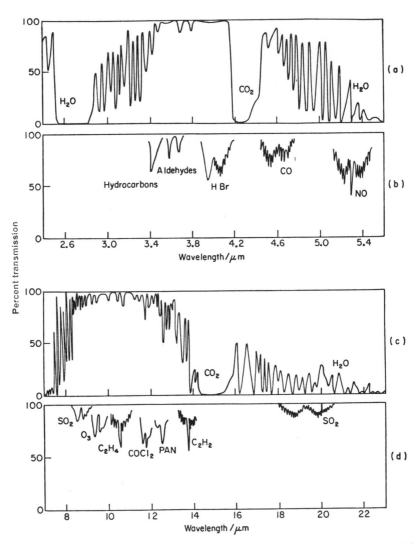

Fig. 30. Atmospheric and pollutant absorption bands. (a) and (c): atmospheric absorption over a 300 m path at sea level. (b) and (d): absorption band positions for common atmospheric pollutants (Pitts and Metcalf, Ref. 36).

spectrum, energy maxima occurring at effectively the same frequencies as those in the absorption spectrum, and the methods of detection are the same. However, the amount of radiation emitted by a gas at a temperature near ambient is small compared with that from the Sun, and it is important to collect as much energy as possible and to use it efficiently. The radiation is coming effectively from infinity, hence a very large parabolic mirror can be used as collector. Multiplex and correlation methods are particularly appropriate since not only does this

TABLE 6
Estimated pollutant concentrations in the atmosphere

Pollutant	Principal sources	Typical city concentration/ ppm	Typical rural concentration/ ppm
Carbon monoxide	Auto exhaust	5.0	0.1
Sulphur dioxide	Oil burners	0.2	0.002
Nitric oxide	Combustion	0.2	0.002
Nitrogen dioxide	Combustion	0.1	0.001
Ozone	Atmospheric photochemical reactions	0.3	0.010
Methane	Natural gas, decaying organic matter	3.0	1.4
Ethylene	Auto exhaust	0.05	0.001
Acetylene	Auto exhaust	0.07	0.001
Peroxyacetyl nitrate	Atmospheric photo-oxidation of olefins	0.03	0.001
Olefins with three or more carbons	Auto exhaust	0.02	0.001
Total hydrocarbons excluding methane	Auto exhaust	2.0	0.005
Ammonia	Decaying organic matter	0.010	0.010
Hydrogen sulphide	Decaying organic matter	0.004	0.002
Formaldehyde	Incomplete combustion, atmospheric reactions	0.05	0.001

Pitts and Metcalf, Ref. 36.

increase efficiency, it also reduces the interference to be expected from any radiation fortuitously collected from extraneous sources.

A further problem in these emission measurements is that the amount of energy emitted by the gas depends upon the number of gas molecules in the instrumental line of sight, and also upon the gas temperature. Corrections may be made either by measuring the gas temperature or by measuring the relative amount of energy received in two emission bands which are well separated in wavelength, enabling the effective temperature of the gas to be computed by a two-colour pyrometer method. Hence the concentration of the gas may be calculated.

Detection of pollutants in air by 'active' radiation methods

Where an artificial source is to be used, the detected energy is that from the source, modified by interaction with the gas to be detected. Purely in terms of the strength of the signal at the detector it is evident that the energy from the source must be confined within the volume of atmosphere to be monitored, and here a laser source, which emits radiation in a definite direction, is clearly strongly favoured. The interaction between the laser and the atmosphere which is exploited in the measurement may involve either absorption or scattering. In practical terms this will mean either an infrared absorption or a Raman scattering measurement, and both have been shown to be effective, so we shall describe these two principles here.

In terms of infrared absorption methods it is usual to have the laser and detector in one unit, and to couple them with a reflector to give a path of several miles. The 3.39 μm line of the helium–neon laser is of obvious interest since the majority of compounds containing the CH group absorb at this wavelength[17, 18] Practical equipment for measurements with a neon laser is described by Kucerovsky et al.[37] In order to ease the problem of locating the reflector to return the laser beam to the detector, a helium–neon laser emitting the usual red line is arranged so that its beam follows the same path as that of the (invisible) infrared line.

This apparatus is particularly powerful for methane because there is an almost exact match of frequency between this neon line and the absorption maximum of methane gas. In favourable cases, high sensitivities have been claimed for this method.[36] In general, however, because of mismatch between emission and absorption wavelengths, and the very small widths of both the laser line and the rotational line of a light gas, the sensitivity may be disappointingly low. There may be possibilities for improving this situation by magnetically shifting the maximum of the laser line.[43] Another problem with mismatch is that the line profiles of the rotational fine structure of gases are pressure- and temperature-sensitive, the peak height falling and the half-band width increasing with temperature and pressure. If the laser line falls in the steep edge of a band, there can be a complicated relationship which will need to be determined experimentally.

In spite of these problems, a remarkably large number of gases of interest in pollution studies may be measured at very low concentrations by this method; detection limits clearly depend on many factors, but generally a limit of a few parts per billion (ppb, parts in 10^9) may be expected. Some common gases and the laser lines which may be used to detect them are collected in Reference 36.

In the infrared absorption method just described, the field of application of the equipment is limited by the necessity to catch the laser beam at the end of the measurement path so as to return it to the detector. Furthermore, the technique is largely 'one gas, one laser'. It would clearly be very valuable to overcome both these problems, and this has led to considerable interest in the possible application of Raman spectroscopy to the remote analysis of, for example, stack gases. The general idea is to project the beam from a powerful laser into the atmosphere to be measured, and to collect the radiation back-scattered along the line of sight. This scattered light is analysed with a conventional Raman spectrometer. A considerable amount of unshifted radiation (i.e. radiation of the original wavelength) is returned because of scatter from particulate matter in the atmosphere, but in addition Raman-scattered radiation from the normal constituents of air (nitrogen, oxygen, carbon dioxide and water) and from gaseous pollutants can be detected. Raman scattering is a very weak effect; hence large optics and a very powerful laser are necessary. Thus, Leonard[44] describes a practical system in which the source is a 10 kW peak output pulsed nitrogen laser, of 337.1 nm wavelength, amplified by a second pulsed nitrogen laser to give a peak power of 50 kW. The back-scattered radiation is collected on a 25 cm diameter Newtonian telescope and directed into the monochromator. Some degree of multiplexing is achieved by using an array of ten detectors. The system is modulated so that the receiving gates are open only when a pulse has been transmitted.

The detection limit varies widely between different pollutants, as there is considerable overlap between the lines of different gases. Typically, however, 100 ppm of NO and SO_2 should be detected at a range of 300 m. While it appears that sensitivities below 1 ppm are unlikely to be achieved without considerable apparatus development, the virtues of remote detection make this method particularly interesting, and considerable thought is being given to methods of increasing its sensitivity.[45,46]

Another useful aspect of the Raman scattering method is that the time delay between sending and receiving the returned pulse may be used to determine the distance of the pollutant from the detector. This has led to the acronym for this technique, LIDAR—*light detection and ranging.*[47]

8.6 Measurements of Solid and Liquid Pollutants in Water

The previous section was devoted to measuring pollutants in air; it is equally important to determine pollutants in water. As with gaseous pollutants, there have been developments in laboratory techniques of high sensitivity (the analogue of closed-path methods), and *in situ* determinations (the analogue of open-path methods).

There would appear to be no application of infrared methods to the remote sensing of liquid and solid pollutants. However, Schwiesow[46] has suggested that Raman measurements may permit, for example, the detection of oil on a water surface and there may be some possibilities in this approach.

The detection and determination of pollutants, particularly in water, has been the subject of considerable effort. It must be confessed that presently Raman techniques are generally less sensitive than infrared ones and the latter have therefore gained favour. To apply infrared methods to trace constituents in water, it is necessary to transfer these constituents to another medium which is more compatible with the technique. Generally, the highest sensitivity for any CH-containing compound is achieved by measuring it in carbon tetrachloride solution. Many pollutants are easily extracted merely by shaking the water sample with carbon tetrachloride. The method is extremely sensitive, but it is important to prevent contamination from, for example, stopcock grease. Thus it is as well to do a blank determination, by the procedure used, with 'pure' water.

Some frequently encountered pollutants are not readily extracted from water into carbon tetrachloride, but Simard et al.[48] show that in the case of phenols, chemical modification to the bromo compound enables this difficulty to be overcome. These workers have concentrated on measurements taken in the field, and they have used the Miran analyser, as previously described, powered by batteries. Figure 31 shows the measurements of oil and phenol, the latter having been converted to tribromophenol. The authors claim a sensitivity of 0.1 ppm for oil in water, and 3 ppb for phenol. It is clear that this method can be applied to a wide range of organic contaminants in water.

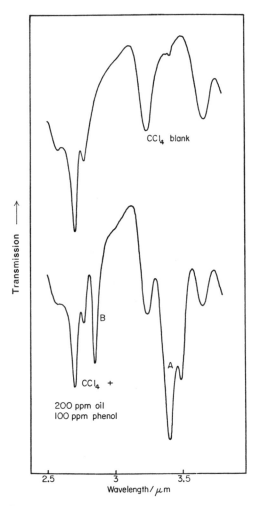

Fig. 31. Spectra of extracted oil and phenol in carbon tetrachloride. A = oil; B = phenol (courtesy of Wilks Scientific Corp. Inc).

9 PYROMETRY

An important application of infrared spectroscopy in industrial processes is in temperature measurement by remote methods, that is, methods in which the temperature of a material is measured with no physical contact between the measuring equipment and the material. The only objects whose radiation properties can be fully and simply described are black body radiators which are perfect emitters. The total amount of energy emitted per unit area of such an object is given by the Stefan–Boltzmann Law: $W = \sigma T^4$ where W is the radiant energy emitted per unit area, T is the absolute temperature, and σ is the Stefan-Boltzmann constant. The wavelength distribution of this energy is expressed by Planck's Law:

$$ J_\lambda = \frac{Ac_1\lambda^{-5}}{\exp\left[(c_2/\lambda T)-1\right]} $$

where J_λ is the amount of energy emitted at wavelength λ, A is the area of the black body, and c_1 and c_2 are constants. If it is required to measure the temperature of a black body, it is merely necessary to measure the total energy emitted by means of a thermocouple, bolometer, or some other thermal energy detector. Such a device is called a total radiation pyrometer. In practical cases, very few objects are black body radiators, and the emission of a 'non-black' body at a particular wavelength λ is a fraction of that emitted by a black body. The spectral emissivity, ε_λ, is given by

$$ \varepsilon_\lambda = 1-t_\lambda-\rho_\lambda, $$

where t_λ is the proportion of radiation of wavelength λ incident on a body which is transmitted (i.e. the infrared transmission spectrum) and ρ_λ is the proportion of radiation of wavelength λ incident on a body which is reflected (i.e. the infrared specular reflection spectrum). A particularly interesting case is when $t_\lambda \neq 0$; that is, when the body whose temperature is to be measured is partially transparent, and this is the case with organic films, e.g. polyethylene, polypropylene, cellulose and polyester films.

The spectral emission of some partially transparent films is shown in Fig. 32. In this experiment, the emission from a series of polyester films, at 100°C, of the thicknesses indicated, was measured in a single-beam spectrometer and compared with the emission of a black metal plate at the same temperature. The contour of this plate emission is modified from that of a black body radiator by atmospheric water vapour and carbon dioxide absorption in the spectrometer beam, and by the use of a constant mechanical slit width rather than a constant spectral slit width. The emission spectrum shows a remarkable similarity to the absorption spectrum, as may be seen from the Figure.

From Fig. 32 a conclusion of particular significance may be drawn relating to the measurement of the temperature of organic films. If a total radiation pyrometer were used, the amount of energy measured from a film at a particular

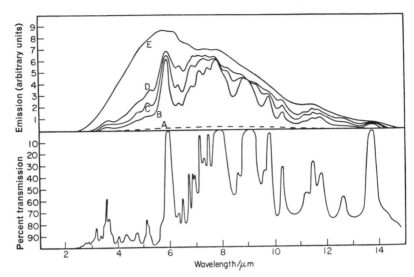

Fig. 32. Emission and transmission spectra of polyethylene terephthalate (P.E.T.) films. Top: emission curves at 100°C. A = instrument background; B = 12 μm thick P.E.T.; C = 25 μm thick P.E.T.; D = 50 μm thick P.E.T.; E = black metal plate. Bottom: transmission spectrum of 12 μm thick P.E.T.

temperature is not constant, but depends upon the film thickness. On the other hand, if the sensitivity of the pyrometer is restricted to those spectral regions where $t_\lambda = 0$, i.e. at 7.9 and 9.0 μm in the case of polyethylene terephthalate, there is no thickness effect. The emissivity is reduced only by reflectance, and this is a constant at a particular wavelength which may be determined experimentally. If it is required to measure film temperatures, the first experiment will be to measure the infrared transmission spectra of a series of films of different thicknesses and find those wavelengths at which the transmission is effectively zero. The pyrometer will then consist of a lens (or mirror) to collect radiation from the film, a detector, and a filter to restrict the wavelength range to the limits decided by the transmission experiment.

Referring to Fig. 32, it is evident that, where there is a choice, it is advantageous to use that filter which coincides as nearly as possible with the emission maximum at the expected film temperature. Thus, if the expected film temperature is 275°C, a 7.9 μm filter is preferred to a 9.0 μm filter. There are many other practical features to be considered in pyrometer design, and these are described in the numerous patents in this field.[49]

Another application of interest in this general area is the measurement of the temperatures of organic fibres (e.g. polyester and nylon fibre). Even if the instrument contains a filter which restricts the wavelength range to that in which complete absorption occurs, the area of the fibres emerging from a spinneret is too small to fill the field of view of a pyrometer. An ingenious method has been devised for overcoming this problem.[50]

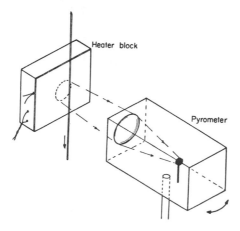

Fig. 33. Oscillating head fibre pyrometer.

The pyrometer looks at the fibres in front of a background heater and provision is made so that the field of view of the pyrometer may be filled with the background and the fibres, or the background alone (Fig. 33). If the fibres are hotter than the background, more energy is measured when the fibres are present, than when absent. As the background temperature is increased, a point is reached at which there is no difference in signal whether the fibres are present or not, and then the background becomes hotter than the fibres, so the instrument output is less when the fibres are present. The output of the instrument in this mode of operation, with a slowly increasing background temperature, is shown in Fig. 34. The fibre temperature is readily determined from this experiment. This is a variety of 'disappearing filament' pyrometer.

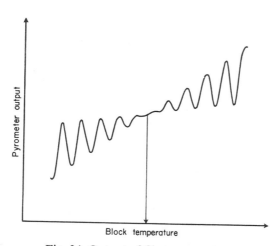

Fig. 34. Output of fibre pyrometer.

ACKNOWLEDGEMENT

I would like to acknowledge the considerable assistance I have received from Mr B. J. Stay, who has drawn a number of the Figures, and assisted with checking the manuscript and references.

REFERENCES

(1) A. Verdin, *Gas Analysis Instrumentation*, Macmillan, London (1973).
(2) A. K. Levine (Ed.), *Lasers* (Vols I and II), Marcel Dekker, New York (1968).
(3) S. L. Marshall (Ed.), *Laser Technology and Applications*, McGraw-Hill, New York (1968).
(4) M. L. Veingerov, *Dokl. Akad. Nauk, SSSR* **19**, 687 (1938).
(5) G. Kivenson, R. T. Steinbeck and M. Rider, *J. Opt. Soc. Amer.* **38**, 1086 (1948).
(6) N. C. Jamison, T. R. Kohler and O. G. Koppius, *Anal. Chem.* **23**, 554 (1951).
(7) A. Rosencwaig, *Anal. Chem.* **47**, 592A (1975).
(8) A. H. Pfund, *Science* **90**, 366 (1939).
(9) K. F. Luft, *Angew. Chem.* **19B**, 2 (1947); *Z. Anal. Chem.* **164**, 100 (1956).
(10) W. V. Dailey, *Proc. 11th National I.S.A. Analysis Instrumentation Symp.*, Montreal, Plenum, New York, p. 189 (1965).
(11) D. W. Hill and T. Powell, *Non-dispersive Infrared Gas Analysis*, Adam Hilger, London (1968).
(12) A. E. Martin, A. M. Reid and J. Smart, *Research (London)* **11**, 3 (1958).
(13) O. S. Heavens, *Optical Properties of Thin Solid Films*, Butterworths, London (1955).
(14) Feedback Instruments Ltd., England. PSA 401 Analyser.
(15) Wilks Scientific Corporation, Norwalk, U.S.A. Miran II Analyser.
(16) A. O. Sall and S. B. Stanevich, *Opt. Spectrosc.* **7**, 162 (1959).
(17) H. J. Gerritsen, *Trans. Soc. Mining Eng.*, AIME, **428** (1966).
(18) D. W. Hill, T. Powell and H. A. H. Boot, *Proc. XII Coll. Spectrosc. Int. Exeter*, Adam Hilger, London, p. 361 (1966).
(19) W. B. Bartley and E. Moult, *Engineer (London)* **206**, 484 (1958).
(20) H. Levenstein, *Anal. Chem.* **41**, 81A (1969).
(21) E. H. Putley, *J. Sci. Instr.* **43**, 857 (1966).
(22) R. G. J. Miller and H. A. Willis, *J. Appl. Chem.* **6**, 385 (1956).
(23) W. Kaye, *Spectrochim. Acta* **4**, 257 (1954).
(24) H. A. Willis and R. G. J. Miller, *Molecular Spectroscopy* (E. Thornton and H. W. Thompson, Eds), Pergamon, London, p. 133 (1959).
(25) J. Fahrenfort, *Spectrochim. Acta* **17**, 698 (1961).
(26) N. J. Harrick, *Internal Reflection Spectroscopy*, Interscience, New York (1967).
(27) H. J. Dutton, *J. Amer. Oil Chemists' Soc.* **51**, 407 (1974).
(28) W. W. Wendlandt and H. G. Hecht, *Reflectance Spectroscopy*, Interscience, New York (1966).
(29) B. J. Stay, *Research Disclosure* **11** (March 1975).
(30) 'Accuray' Infrasystem Model BF100D. Infra Systems Inc., Columbus, Ohio, 43202, U.S.A.
(31) Brun Sensor Systems Inc. Brit. pat. 1 348 978; Infra Systems Inc. Brit. pat. 1 348 979; and Brit. pat. 1 348 980.
(32) H. A. Willis and W. A. Boyes, Brit. pat. 1 137 144.
(33) H. A. Willis and M. E. A. Cudby, *Z. Anal. Chem.* **263**, 291 (1973).

(34) J. P. Auton and M. C. Hultey, *Infrared Physics* **12**, 95 (1972).
Grid Polarizers are marketed by Cambridge Consultants Ltd, Cambridge, England, and Perkin-Elmer Inc., Norwalk, U.S.A.
(35) J. A. Hodgeson, W. A. McClenny and P. L. Hanst, *Science* **182**, 248 (1973).
(36) J. N. Pitts and R. L. Metcalf, Eds, *Advances in Environmental Science and Technology*, Vol. 2, Wiley-Interscience, New York (1971). Articles by P. L. Hanst, p. 91, and H. Sievering, p. 263.
(37) Z. Kucerovsky, E. Brannen, K. C. Paulekat and D. G. Rumbold, *J. Appl. Meteorol.* **12**, 1387 (1973).
(38) J. U. White, *J. Opt. Soc. Amer.* **32**, 285 (1942).
(39) P. L. Hanst, A. S. Lefohn and B. W. Gay, *Appl. Spectrosc.* **27**, 188 (1973).
(40) P. B. Fellgett, *J. Phys. Radium* **19**, 149 (1958).
(41) D. T. Williams and B. L. Kolitz, *Appl. Opt.* **7**, 607 (1968).
(42) Barringer Research Ltd, Rexdale, Ontario, Canada.
(43) R. Paananen, C. L. Tang and H. Statz, *Proc. I.E.E.E.* **51**, 63 (1963).
(44) D. A. Leonard, *Instruments and Control Systems* 73 (August 1972).
(45) W. H. Smith and J. J. Barrett, *A.I.A.A. Journal* **11**, 589 (1973).
(46) R. L. Schwiesow, *A.I.A.A. Journal* **11**, 87 (1973).
(47) S. H. Melfi, *Proc. 2nd Joint Conference on Sensing Environmental Pollutants*, 1973, p. 73 (1974).
(48) R. G. Simard, I. Hasegawa, W. Bandaruk and C. E. Headington, *Anal. Chem.* **23**, 1384 (1951).
(49) For example, R. H. Buteaux and H. A. Willis, Brit. pat. 960 173.
(50) H. Beaven and R. E. Ricketts, *J. Sci. Instr.* **44**, 1048 (1967).

Chapter 4

TIME-RESOLVED AND SPACE-RESOLVED RAMAN SPECTROSCOPY

M. Bridoux and M. Delhaye

Service de Spectrochimie Infrarouge et Raman C.N.R.S. Université des Sciences et Techniques de Lille, B.P.36 59650 Villeneuve d'Ascq, France

1 INTRODUCTION

The use of laser excitation has greatly stimulated interest in Raman spectroscopy, particularly for the study of molecular or crystal vibrations. This paper will not deal with well-known conventional methods, because these have been treated adequately in a number of excellent texts, but will describe and illustrate the latest techniques that have been developed for the study of a variety of problems in physical chemistry which require time-resolved and space-resolved Raman spectra. Examples of these are: fast chemical reactions (in gas, liquid, or solid phases); photochemical processes; transient species; electronically, vibrationally, or rotationally excited states; phase transitions in solids; heterogeneous samples; defects in solids; biological samples.

For these types of application two interesting features of lasers can be pointed out:

1. The ability to focus the energy of the laser beam on a very small spot on the sample, whose dimensions need be limited only by the wavelength.
2. The ability to deliver a large number of photons in a pulse of very short duration.

However, careful attention must be paid to the following restrictions: (a) the energy density must not exceed those values above which the sample would be modified or even destroyed by heating or photo-decomposition; (b) the peak power density must be limited if the 'spontaneous' Raman effect only is to be studied. Non-linear phenomena, such as intense stimulated Raman emission, appear when a given threshold is exceeded and make impossible the detection of the weak spontaneous Raman lines.

As an illustration of the very substantial improvement in performance that has been achieved during the last twenty-five years, the evolution of the time neces-sary to record a Raman spectrum is shown in Fig. 1. When mercury lamps and simple spectrometers were used, it could take several hours. The use of improved grating monochromators and photomultipliers reduced the recording time to a fraction of a second. Then the development of lasers, as well as sophisticated

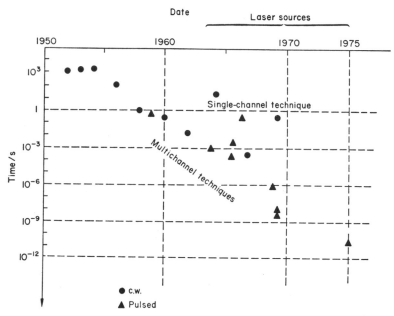

Fig. 1. Diagram showing how the time necessary for the recording of a Raman spectrum has been reduced over the period 1950–75.

techniques allowing the simultaneous recording of a great number of elements of the spectrum, enabled the time range to be shortened down to a microsecond in 1969, to a nanosecond shortly thereafter, and recently to the picosecond range. This figure shows that, since 1960, we have developed the so-called 'multichannel' techniques, as well as improved 'single-channel' instruments.[1-3]

2 CAPABILITIES AND LIMITATIONS OF SINGLE-CHANNEL SPECTROSCOPY

The term 'monochannel' or 'single-channel' is used to cover all the techniques in which only one radiation detector (photomultiplier) is used to analyse an optical spectrum by means of a *scanning* monochromator. Conventional Raman spectrophotometers, and also most of the laboratory-built instruments, make use of continuous wave lasers for excitation, and a photomultiplier for detection of the weak scattered light, coupled with either d.c. amplification or the so-called 'photon-counting' technique. The 'spectral elements' are successively explored and analysed by a 'scanning' process, which is performed by rotating the gratings of the monochromator continuously or stepwise. The result is then presented as a two-dimensional diagram in which the y-axis is used to represent the intensity of a Raman band, and the x-axis to represent either the wavenumber (frequency) (related to the scanning of the spectrum by the monochromator), or the time-scale (when the temporal changes of intensity are plotted at a fixed wavenumber for kinetic measurements).

The scanning speed is limited by the time constant of the electronic detector/amplifier system. It is well known that, for a desired value of the signal-to-noise ratio, the time constant can only be reduced if the level of the signal is increased. However, the so-called 'rapid scanning' Raman spectrometers are very useful for studying chemical reactions (in gas, liquid or solid samples) with a time resolution from minutes down to seconds.[4, 5]

Even if we consider an ideal instrument, the intensity of a given Raman line is measured with a finite precision given by the following equation, where P_r is the number of Raman light photons detected by the photomultiplier during the time of measurement, P_s is due to quanta arising from stray light in the optics, and Q is due to the fluorescence of the sample, the background from the emission of hot samples and the electrons thermally emitted by the photocathode. S/N is the signal-to-noise ratio.

$$\frac{S}{N} \approx \frac{P_r}{(P_r + P_s + Q)^{\frac{1}{2}}}$$

When using c.w. excitation, P_r, P_s and Q are linearly dependent on the recording time.

In a rather unusual manner, we shall now consider the case where the same number, P_r, of Raman photons are observed in a very short time, i.e. by exciting the sample by a pulsed laser. The number, Q, of 'spurious' events can be considered negligible compared to P_r. Nevertheless, pulsed lasers are not useful because single-channel techniques need a great number of repetitively reproducible impulses.

If only one spectral element is observed, the time resolution can go down to picoseconds by using pulsed mode-locked lasers. But it is often necessary to know how the different species evolve during a chemical or physical phenomenon. In this case recording of complete Raman spectra in a convenient spectral region is needed. Spectrum analysis by *successive* scanning of the spectral lines becomes a very poor process, because during the scanning of all the spectral elements a large amount of information is wasted.

The basic layout of a single-channel spectrometer is shown in Fig. 2, and an example of a Raman spectrum recorded by means of this technique (scanning rate of the Raman spectrum $= 100 \, \text{cm}^{-1} \, \text{s}^{-1}$) is shown in Fig. 3.

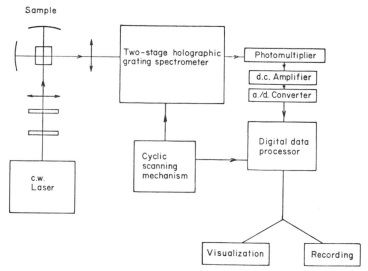

Fig. 2. Basic layout of a single-channel spectrometer.

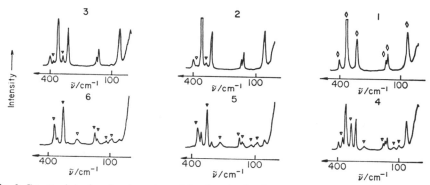

Fig. 3. Spectral study of a phase transition by single-channel rapid Raman spectroscopy. $SbCl_5$ (solid) $\rightleftharpoons Sb_2Cl_{10}$ (solid). Recording time per spectrum $= 4\,s$; $\diamondsuit$ = Raman bands of the monomer; $\triangledown$ = Raman bands of the dimer. Raman spectra 1–6 were recorded successively at 10 s intervals during the phase transition at 212 K (R. Heimberger and M. J. F. Leroy, *Spectrochim. Acta*, **31A**, 653, 1975; F. Wallart, Thesis, University of Lille, 1970).

3   MULTICHANNEL SPECTROSCOPY

3.1   Multichannel Analysis of a Raman Spectrum

The techniques of multichannel Raman spectroscopy have been extensively studied and developed in our laboratory in order to overcome the difficulties associated with obtaining a Raman spectrum in a very short scanning time with a single-channel spectrometer. This technique allows the ultra-rapid analysis of the whole spectral image by means of a photoelectric detector having a large number of independent channels collecting information simultaneously.[6] The result of such an analysis can be represented, as in Fig. 4, by a three-dimensional diagram in which the z-axis is used as the intensity coordinate, and the y-axis is used as the wavenumber coordinate. The N independent channels analysed along the y-axis by the detector define the spectral resolution in the spectral range under consideration. The x-axis may be used as a space or a time coordinate axis.

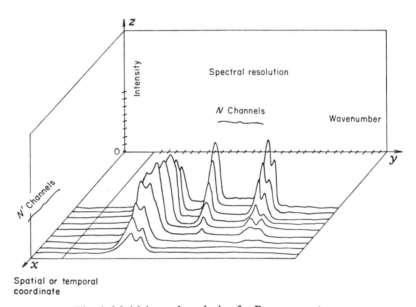

Fig. 4. Multichannel analysis of a Raman spectrum.

The N' independent channels along the x-axis can be used in several ways. Most often the x-axis is parallel to the entrance slit, that is to say is parallel with the spectral lines, and then the N' channels can be used to obtain the 'space resolution' of the different geometric elements of the sample. In another way the N' channels can be used to obtain 'time-resolved spectra' by means of a deflection of the images at a known speed along the x-axis.

The fundamental concept of the multichannel spectrometer involves the following elements of operation:

1. All the information included in a spectral image must be stored in a 'three-dimensional' memory during the exposure time.
2. The information put into the memory must subsequently be analysed by a scanning device which performs data processing such as reading out and display of the intensities at each point of the spectral image.

It is well known that Raman scattering is a low light-level phenomenon. The

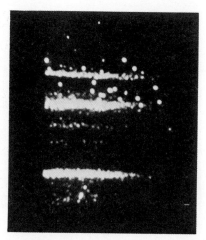

Plate I. TV monitor photograph of the Raman spectrum of acetone excited by a single laser pulse of 25 ps duration ($\lambda_0 = 530$ nm, spectral range 1000–1800 cm^{-1}).

300 μm

Plate II. Photograph of small crystals of PBr$_5$ taken through the Raman microscope. The spectrometer was set so as to detect the crystals by way of their scattering, characteristic of the constituent PBr$_4^+$ ion, of a Raman band at $\Delta \tilde{\nu} = 72$ cm^{-1}, $\lambda_0 = 514.5$ nm.

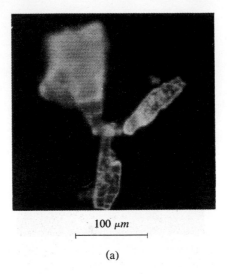

100 μm

(a)

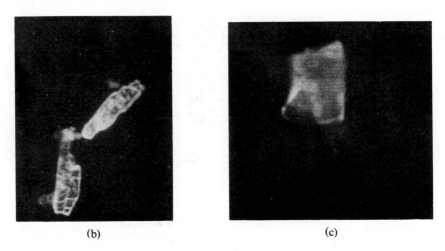

(b)   (c)

Plate III. Photograph, through the Raman microscope, of a mixture of K_2CrO_4 and MoO_3 (a) detected with white light (b) detected by way of a Raman band at 818 cm^{-1} characteristic of MoO_3 and (c) detected by way of a Raman band at 850 cm^{-1} characteristic of the chromate ion. ($\lambda_0 = 514.5$ nm.)

effect at each point of the image can be, in the particular case of the spectral analysis of evolving systems, as low as a few photons. Photographic emulsion, which was the first photodetector used in multichannel spectrometry, is not useful for rapid multichannel spectrometry. The characteristic time associated with the build-up of the latent image would be very long, of the order of seconds, minutes, or even hours, due to the very low quantum efficiency of the photographic material. It should also be remembered that, in the nanosecond or picosecond time range, the sensitivity of photographic plates becomes lower for longer exposure times.

For multichannel Raman spectrophotometry, highly sensitive photoelectric image devices can collect the Raman information in a much shorter time than can photographic material. Figure 5 shows the block diagram of the particular

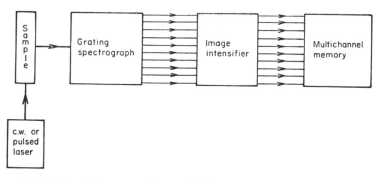

Fig. 5. Block diagram of the multichannel Raman spectrometer.

multichannel instrument that we have developed in our laboratory during the last 12 years. A c.w. or pulsed-laser excites the Raman spectrum of the sample in the same way as with conventional equipment. The scattered light is focused on to the entrance slit of a spectrometer having one or several stages. The instrument is built in such a way as to reduce the stray light to the lowest possible level. Concave stigmatic holographic gratings (Jobin–Yvon) have recently been shown to provide an attractive solution to this problem.

In the last stage of the spectrometer, the spectral image is focused on to the photocathode of an image-intensifier tube. Photoelectrons emitted by each element of the photocathode surface build an electronic image of the Raman spectrum. An electron–optical lens system, either magnetic or electric, or a microchannel plate, are included in the image-intensifier tube for focusing the electron image on a fluorescent screen. Connection of several intensifier tubes (cascade image-intensifier) gives a high photon gain (10^4–10^6). This means that, on average, for each photon acting on the photocathode, 10^4–10^6 photons are emitted at the corresponding surface of the fluorescent screen output. The spectral image, thus intensified, is transferred on to a secondary detector to be stored.

A large light-collection efficiency is achieved by coupling the intensifier tube to the secondary detector by a fibre optic. Several kinds of secondary detectors have been experimented with, from photographic or cinematographic film, to the latest low light-level television camera tubes having an electrical storage target with integration capability and storage capacity (SEC or SIT tube).[7-9]

These television camera tubes have the main advantages of direct beam read-out of the image elements and 'real time' information transfer onto a magnetic tape, a magnetic disc, or the memory of a computer.

3.2 Capabilities of the Multichannel Raman Spectrometer

The following points summarize the advantages of such a multichannel spectrometer:

1. Simultaneous analysis of a great amount of information; classical intensifier tubes and television camera tubes allow the analysis of $(N \times N') = 10^5$ channels of information.
2. High sensitivity; the sensitivity of the photocathodes is similar to that of a good photomultiplier. Thus it is theoretically possible to record information into the memory of the television tube target for only a few photons acting on the photocathode.
3. Photometric reproducibility.
4. No reciprocity effect.
5. Storage capacity; this is of the same order of magnitude as that of sensitive photographic material.
6. Short response time; this allows the storage of all the spectral elements in a 'single exposure' of duration as short of a few picoseconds.

This last property is turned to good account in Raman spectroscopy with pulsed lasers. Some intensifier tubes have a gated stage and can be switched off and on electronically. Then the image-intensifier tube operates in the single-frame mode and is able to record the spectral information during a single laser pulse. This technique allows the recording of Raman spectra in a very short exposure time with a good signal-to-noise ratio because, during this short time, the noise due to the thermionic emission of the photocathode is negligible. Where Raman lines of low intensity must be recorded, integration of multi-exposures of very short duration is possible and a large gain in the signal-to-noise ratio is achieved.[10-13]

Some other image-intensifier tubes (e.g. streak cameras) involving deflecting plates allow the high-speed continuous deflection of the Raman lines in a defined direction (streak mode) and are very promising for time-resolved Raman spectroscopy. Figure 6 is a schematic diagram of the multichannel spectrometer used for time-resolved Raman spectroscopy.

Whatever the method of excitation of a Raman spectrum (c.w. or pulsed) the energy necessary to record the whole Raman spectrum by means of these techniques is from about 10 μJ to 1 J. When using a pulsed laser (ruby, YAG, or dye) only a small part of the energy drawn from a single pulse of 1 ms–1 ps duration is sufficient to record the Raman spectrum.

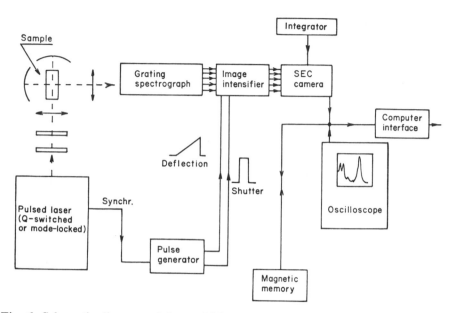

Fig. 6. Schematic diagram of the multichannel spectrometer used for time-resolved Raman spectroscopy.

3.3 Time-resolved Raman Spectroscopy with a Multichannel Spectrometer

Figure 7 and Plate I show a few examples of the results obtained in our laboratory by multichannel techniques. The latest experiments carried out have shown the possibility of recording spontaneous Raman spectra in as short a time as 25 ps.[14,15] The energy available from a mode-locked laser is greater than that necessary. Great care must be taken to prevent the occurrence of phenomena far more intense than the spontaneous Raman effect, that is to say, the stimulated Raman effect or breakdown.

Even with such short times, the spatial resolution along the x-axis enables one to locate, with a fair precision, the different regions of the sample focused along the slit of the spectrometer and irradiated by the laser beam. If it is not of interest to take advantage of that spatial resolution, a fast deflection of the images along the x-axis can be achieved. Therefore the duration of the pulse is not the only parameter to define the temporal resolution of the instrument. Streak cameras permit ultra-fast electrostatic deflection of the images during the pulse and allow, theoretically, temporal resolution as high as 1 ps. In practice our experiments show that for Raman spectroscopy it is necessary to use the most sensitive streak camera. That is why the use of an optical deflection of the images has been preferred. When very short time resolutions are necessary it is

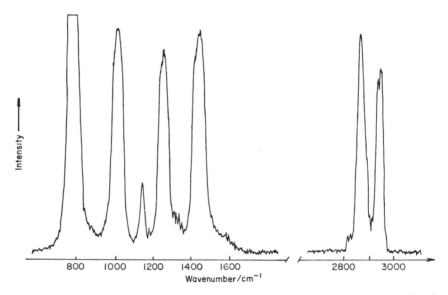

Fig. 7. Raman spectrum of cyclohexane excited by a single laser pulse of 25 ps duration.

easy to realize optical delay-lines by means of multiple reflections of the laser beam. This optical design allows, from a single laser pulse, the sample to be excited by a train of successive pulses. These time-shifted pulses can either excite the same part or a different part of the sample. Figure 8 is a diagram of one of the optical devices in use.

Figure 9 shows an example of an application of these techniques in which a mode-locked YAG laser with a frequency multiplier gives two pulses of 25 ps (265 and 530 nm). The first one, in the ultraviolet region, produces a photo-chemical excitation of the sample; the second one, with a fixed delay time, excites the Raman spectrum.

4   SPACE RESOLUTION. RAMAN MICROANALYSIS AND MICROSCOPY

It is well known that a Raman spectrum can be observed from a very small amount of sample excited by a laser beam. We consider that interesting applica-

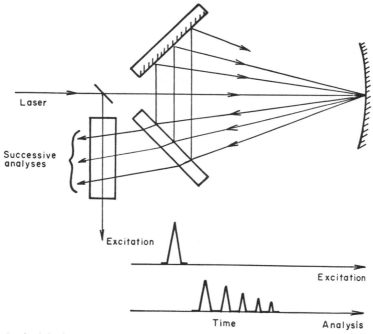

Fig. 8. Optical device which allows, following a single laser pulse, a sample to be excited by a train of successive pulses.

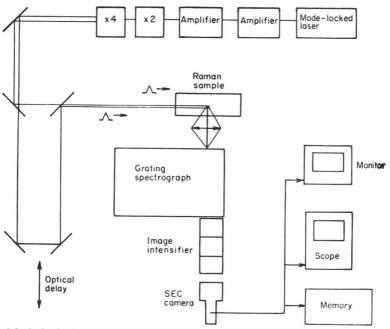

Fig. 9. Mode-locked YAG laser, incorporating a frequency multiplier, being used to give two pulses of 25 ps duration (265 and 530 nm), the first to give a photochemical excitation of the sample and the second, with a fixed delay time, to excite the Raman spectrum of the sample.

tions are made possible by using the Raman light characteristic of a given polyatomic species for 'mapping' or 'imaging' heterogeneous samples.[16-18] Either single-channel or multichannel techniques can be used.

The first technique consists of illuminating a microsample by a laser beam focused through a lens onto a small spot which is theoretically limited by diffraction only. The maximum power must then be reduced to under a milliwatt to avoid overheating and decomposition of the sample. By using the conventional single-channel technique, the low intensity of the Raman spectrum necessitates a very slow recording or the use of data accumulation devices. Multichannel systems provide the following advantages that are most important in microanalysis:

(*a*) When recording the Raman spectrum of a very small sample, the simultaneous measurements of the intensities of N spectral elements improve the signal-to-noise ratio by $\sqrt{N}$ as compared with a scan of the same duration.

(b) When it is required to identify and to locate one of the polyatomic constituents of the sample, very many 'elements' of the surface can be simultaneously examined at the same wavelength. This allows 'mapping' the distribution of a given substance in a heterogeneous sample, with a resolving power limited only by the wavelength of the scattered light beam, specifically a fraction of a micrometre.

The power density is reduced because the laser beam illuminates the whole area of the sample under observation. This allows the use of lasers of up to 100 mW in power without damaging the material.

Figure 10 represents the basic layout of the Raman microscope.[18] The image of the surface, enlarged by a conventional microscope lens, is projected on to the photocathode of an image-intensifier phototube, through an 'optical filter' tuned to select a Raman line characteristic of one of the compounds existing in the sample. The 'optical filter' must be carefully designed so as to

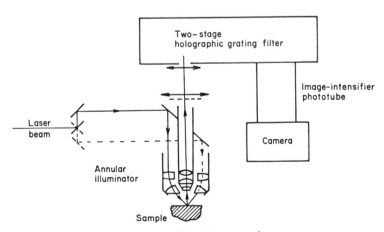

Fig. 10. Layout of the Raman microscope.

reduce the stray light to a very low level. In usual instruments, the stray light rejection capability is of the order of 10^{-10}–10^{-12}, which allows Raman micrographic studies even of low frequency crystal modes. This technique has been improved recently by the introduction of holographic concave gratings (Jobin–Yvon).

Plate II shows, as an example, some microcrystals placed under vacuum in a cylindrical sealed glass tube. A second example is given in Plate III, which presents three micrographs of the same heterogeneous sample obtained with the Raman microscope. The sample is a mixture of molybdenum oxide and potassium chromate microcrystals, placed *without any preparation* on a glass plate. The image obtained by illumination with white light does not distinguish between the two components. But the images recorded by laser excitation setting the gratings of the filter so as to isolate the scattered radiation corresponding to a Raman band characteristic of either MoO_3 or CrO_4^{2-}, allow a separate identification of each crystal unambiguously. It is worth noting that such images are recorded on the time scale of a second, which allows the observation of, for instance, samples evolving in chemical or photochemical reactions, or of the propagation of phase transitions in solids. The space resolution achieved in these experiments is only limited by the resolving power of the optical microscope, that is, less than one micrometre.

5 CONCLUSION

Recent developments of Raman spectroscopic techniques have taken advantage of the special qualities of laser light sources. It seems clear from our results that multichannel spectroscopy is able to extract more information from a Raman spectrum than can be expected with conventional photographic or scanning techniques. However, this is only true under the conditions such that the overall gain of the image detector is sufficient to permit the storage of the information associated with a single photo-electron emitted by the photocathode. Space- or time-resolved spectral information, whether analogue or digital, is quantitative in nature, and is simultaneously and immediately available for all the Raman lines.

The spectral data obtained from very short laster pulses are useful in the study of species with very short lifetimes. The Raman microanalysis of a sample offers to the chemist a powerful method for the investigation of heterogeneous systems.

The spectral response of multichannel spectrometers can now range from the ultraviolet (200 nm) to the infrared (1200 nm) and we think that the application of this technique to resonance Raman spectroscopy and coherent anti-Stokes Raman scattering would be fertile.

REFERENCES

(1) M. Delhaye and M. Bridoux, *C.R. Acad. Sci. Paris* **261**, 2079 (1965).
(2) M. Delhaye, *Appl. Opt.* **7**, 2195 (1968).

(3) M. Delhaye, in *Fourth Conference on Molecular Spectroscopy*, The Institute of Petroleum, England (1968), p. 275.
(4) F. Wallart and J. C. Merlin, *C.R. Acad. Sci. Paris* **271**, 894 (1970).
(5) M. Delhaye, P. Dhamelincourt, J. C. Merlin and F. Wallart, *C.R. Acad. Sci. Paris* **272 B**, 1003 (1971).
(6) M. Bridoux and M. Delhaye, *Nouv. Rev. Opt. Appl.* **1**, 23 (1970).
(7) G. W. Goetze, in *Advances in Electronics and Electron Physics*, Vol. 22 A (J. D. McGee, Ed.), Academic Press, London, p. 219 (1966).
(8) G. W. Goetze and H. Boerio, in *Advances in Electronics and Electron Physics*, Vol. 28 A (J. D. McGee, Ed.), Academic Press, London, p. 159 (1969).
(9) B. Singer, *E.I.E.E. Trans. Electron. Devices*, Vol. ED 18, No. 11, 1016 (1971).
(10) C. M. Savage and P. D. Maker, *Appl. Opt.* **10**, 965 (1971).
(11) D. A. Long, in *Advances in Raman Spectroscopy* (Proc. 3rd Int. Conf. on Raman Spectrosc.), Heyden and Son, p. 1 (1973).
(12) J. R. Smith, *Sandia Lab. Report* (SAND 75.8224), March 1975.
(13) W. H. Woodruff and G. H. Akkison, *Anal. Chem.* **48**, 186 (1976).
(14) M. Delhaye, in *Lasers in Physical Chemistry and Biophysics*, Elsevier, Amsterdam, p. 213 (1975).
(15) M. Bridoux, A. Deffontaine and C. Reiss, *C.R. Acad. Sci. Paris*, in press.
(16) G. J. Rosasco and J. H. Simmons, *Amer. Ceram. Soc. Bull.* **53**, 626 (1974).
(17) G. J. Rosasco and J. H. Simmons, *Amer. Ceram. Soc. Bull.* **54**, 590 (1975).
(18) M. Delhaye and P. Dhamelincourt, *J. Raman Spectrosc.* **3**, 33 (1975).

Chapter 5

THE VIBRATIONAL SPECTRA OF IONIC VAPOURS, LIQUIDS AND GLASSES

J. Paul Devlin

Department of Chemistry, Oklahoma State University, Stillwater, Oklahoma 74074, U.S.A.

1 INTRODUCTION

The central objective of this chapter is to review the advances in the understanding of the structures of molten salts that have resulted from infrared and Raman spectroscopic studies. Most of the chapter is devoted to a presentation and analysis of published spectra, and interpretations thereof, for ionic liquids. However, partly because of possible insights gained for condensed phases from data for the simpler vapour phases, and partly because the vapour phase is an integral part of a total high-temperature salt system, it seemed appropriate to include a review of recent developments in the vibrational study of salt vapours. These vapours are composed primarily of ion pairs and, since the question of the presence of ion pairs in molten salts and concentrated liquid salt solutions is a common one, the relevance of the vapour phase data to the question of melt structure is obvious. Further, the vapours can readily be condensed at temperatures well below T_g, the glass transition temperature, to give glassy salts presumably having structures quite similar to those of the corresponding melt. The spectra of such glasses, as well as those obtained by supercooling the liquid, are simplified by the low temperatures. Hence, where practicable, spectroscopic measurements on glassy salts are useful in structural studies on molten salts. Results for such systems are included here where they add to the understanding of the melt structures.

In this review the broader subject of the vibrational spectroscopy of molten salts has initially been sectioned by considering the two major classes of salts, those involving oxyanion and polyhalide anions, separately. Since the author's background includes experience with the oxyanion but not the polyhalide melts, the oxyanion section has a more personal and critical character. The division into these two areas of study is natural since the research objectives have, in general, been quite different. Studies of these two classes of melts have differed in emphasis primarily because the identity of the anion unit is easily established in the oxyanion melts so that attention has been directed to displaying the nature and magnitude of the perturbations experienced by the stable anion unit, as well as the degree to which collective motions, based on either internal or external modes, influence the vibrational spectra. By contrast, the basic structure, and possibly even the existence, of a polyhalide anion (MX_n^{m-}) within a melt is in general not known *a priori* and may not be obvious from the vibrational spectrum. As a result, most studies of these melts have concentrated on establishing the character of the more stable anionic units. Partly for this reason, and partly because of the crowding of the vibrational modes in the low frequency range $(0–600 \text{ cm}^{-1})$, the spectra have rarely been sufficiently detailed to encourage speculation on either anion perturbations or the relative importance of co-operative modes.

This review serves as an overview of the work done in measurement and interpretation of the vibrational spectra of molten salts and the vapours of molten salts during the period 1965 to 1975. However, the section on oxyanion melts stresses structural ideas rather than attempting to quote frequencies for all systems that have been studied. Also, the section on ion pairs in the vapours above ionic melts is deliberately restricted primarily to polyatomic anionic systems, since vapour phase data for simpler salts, such as LiF and MgF_2, have only a limited utility in structural studies of ionic melts. The latter comment derives from the fact that, for an ion to serve as an effective structural probe, it must have either sufficient symmetry to possess degenerate modes or vibrational modes which are unusually responsive, in intensity or frequency, to structural perturbations. The common oxyanions each possess vibrational modes having these properties.

Much of the published research for the oxyanion systems, whether vapour or condensed phase, is open to the criticism that the emphasis has been on nitrate ions and the behaviour of the $\nu_3(e')$ mode and, more particularly, the magnitude of the splitting of this degenerate mode. However, such criticism can be likened to a criticism of proton n.m.r. spectroscopy for deriving data from the resonance of a single nucleus. The idea, first advanced by Janz,[1] that the $\nu_3(e')$ splitting would be a useful probe of the structures of molten salts and concentrated aqueous solutions is a sound one, and has been used regularly throughout Section 1 of this review.

2 OXYANION SALTS

It has been recognized for many years that the vapours in equilibrium with simple alkali halide salts near their melting points include the monomer ion pairs, (M^+X^-), as well as dimers, $(M^+X^-)_2$, as the principal components.[2, 3] Several studies of the matrix isolation variety have yielded extensive vibrational data for these species as well as for the Group IA pseudohalides,[11, 12] and the fundamental frequencies for the M^+X^- monomers are summarized in Table 1. As expected, the smaller and lighter ions, through a mass effect combined with the effect of stronger coulombic interaction (by virtue of closer approach), form ion pairs having the higher stretching frequencies, the range being from 249 cm^{-1} for KCl to 867 cm^{-1} for LiF.

Since no weak covalent bonds are involved it is not surprising that the alkali halides vaporize as ion pairs or aggregates of ion pairs. The situation is much different, however, if either the cation or anion is a polyatomic unit, as is the case for ammonium salts or alkali metal salts with oxyanions. It is generally recognized, for example, that NH_4Cl volatilizes as NH_3 and HCl while, similarly, NH_4NO_3 dissociates in the vapour phase to give primarily HNO_3 and NH_3. The infrared spectrum of NH_4NO_3 vapours isolated in an argon matrix confirm the presence of NH_3 and HNO_3[13] but, particularly at low volatilization temperatures ($T < 50\ °C$), complexation as hydrogen-bonded NH_3HNO_3 cannot be ignored. Ault and Pimentel have shown that NH_3 and HCl form an extremely strongly H-bonded complex upon reaction in an inert matrix

TABLE 1
Vibrational frequencies for matrix-isolated Group IA halide monomers

Species[a]	Matrix	Observed frequencies/ cm^{-1}	References
LiF	Ne	867	4–10
LiCl	Kr	569	4, 6
LiBr	Kr	512	6
LiI	Kr	433	6
NaF	Ne	515	4, 6
NaCl	Ar	335	11
KCl	Ar	249	11

[a] Frequencies refer to the ^7Li isotopic species.

medium,[14] suggesting that the complex is probably more stable than the $NH_4{}^+Cl^-$ ion pair in the vapour phase as well. Thus, any association of NH_3 with either HCl or HNO_3 in the vapour phase of the corresponding salt is expected to produce an NH_3HX complex.

From the viewpoint of the chemistry of condensed phase ionic systems, the unique characteristic of the volatilization of the ammonium salt might appear to be the ability reversibly to reform the salt by condensation of the vapours. Thus, although condensation of the NH_4NO_3 vapours at 10 K yields a glassy mixture of $NH_4{}^+$, $NO_3{}^-$, HNO_3 and NH_3, warming of the condensate to temperatures above 200 K yields crystalline NH_4NO_3.[13] However, it is now clear that condensation of the vapours of the melts of numerous Group I oxyanion salts gives back the parent salt. The comparison with the ammonium salts ends there, however, as both mass spectroscopic[15] and matrix isolation vibrational spectroscopic studies[16,17] have shown that alkali metal nitrate and chlorate salts, like the halides, vaporize primarily as the monomer ion-pairs $(M^+XO_3^-)$, with a significant dimer concentration as well. Infrared matrix isolation data confirm that this is also the case for Group IA perchlorates.[18]

The vibrational spectra of the simple oxyanions such as NO_3^-, ClO_3^-, ClO_4^-, CO_3^{2-} and SO_4^{2-} have become the principal structural probe for numerous chemical systems including solutions of salts in water and ammonia, molten salts and ionic glasses. In all such disordered systems the oxyanion experiences asymmetric structural perturbations of varying magnitudes because, in contrast to the forces experienced by a nitrate ion on a trigonal site in a rhombohedral lattice (such as D_{3d}^6 NaNO_3 and LiNO_3 crystals), the symmetry of the force field operating on the oxyanion is lower than the D_{3h} symmetry of the isolated anion. Thus the ordered crystal spectra for oxyanions situated on symmetric sites within a cation cage provide a useful reference point for discussion of the spectra of disordered condensed-phase salts. For example, the nitrate ion on the trigonal site in LiNO_3 or NaNO_3(II) has two double degenerate modes, ν_3 and ν_4, each of which will split into two modes of different frequency if the anion site loses its three-fold symmetry axis, as it invariably will for disordered systems such as molten salts. Thus, in considering the spectra of disordered salt systems, the question is not whether the degenerate modes of the oxyanions are split—they must be—but rather (a) what is the magnitude of the splitting and (b) what does this magnitude imply structurally in the light of what is known for more completely characterized systems?

It is in terms of this latter question that the spectra of the simple metal–oxyanion ion pairs isolated in inert gas matrices have a particular significance. The $M^+NO_3^-$ ion pairs isolated in argon at 10 K represent a simple well-defined structure when contrasted with the structural complexities of ionic melts and solutions. Further, it is reasonable to expect that the structural distortion of an oxyanion by a particular cation is a maximum for the ion pairs. In this context the splittings, such as measured for the $\nu_3(e')$ asymmetric stretching of the nitrate ion in $M^+NO_3^-$ ion-pairs, provide a good empirical basis for judging the physical implications of smaller splittings obtained from structurally more complex systems.

2.1   Vapours of Molten Salts Isolated in Inert Matrices

There has been a very thorough recent review of the techniques of matrix isolation vibrational spectroscopy,[19] so these techniques, as adapted to high-temperature vapour species and to the vapours of molten oxyanion salts in particular, will not be described here. Rather, the emphasis is on the spectroscopic data obtained for the various oxyanions paired with cations, as well as the magnitude of the anion distortions implied by these data.

2.1.1. Group IA nitrates

At sufficiently high melt temperatures nitrate salts decompose to produce vapours of NO_2 and NO with an oxide residue. However, an early publication on Group IA nitrate vapours reported the electronic spectrum of gaseous KNO_3.[20] Subsequently, mass spectroscopic[15] and electron diffraction[21] studies confirmed that the vapours of molten $LiNO_3$ and $NaNO_3$, well above the salt melting points, contain a significant fraction of MNO_3 units. James and Leong made use of this salt volatility in a vibrational spectroscopic study of the intense infrared bands of the crystalline Group IA nitrates.[22] Using vapour deposition, it was possible to obtain salt films of a desired thickness. By depositing the nitrates from the molten salts at ~ 650 K in inert matrices at low temperature, Smith, James and Devlin showed that the dominant species in the vapour phase is the monomer ion-pair $(M^+NO_3^-)$ and that, for adequately dried salts, decomposition to NO and NO_2 is unimportant.[16]

The fundamental vibrational frequencies for the Group IA nitrate ion pairs isolated in various inert matrices are summarized in Table 2, and a typical spectrum, that of $Li^+NO_3^-$ in argon, is presented in Fig. 1. The data are

TABLE 2
Infrared frequencies/cm^{-1} of alkali–metal nitrate monomers for various matrix media

Mode^a	LiNO$_3$			NaNO$_3$		KNO$_3$			RbNO$_3$	
	Ar	CO$_2$	CCl$_4$	Ar	CO$_2$	Ar	CO$_2$	CCl$_4$	Ar	CCl$_4$
1	1011	1017	1015	1023	1023	1031	1035	1028	1033	1029
2	817	823		825	826	830	829		830	
3a	1264	1275	1266	1283	1284	1291	1295	1282	1293	1284
3b	1524	1515	1509	1484	1480	1462	1462	1437	1456	1430
4a	736									
4b	765									
M—O	528									

^{a} The mode numbering scheme is as follows: $\nu_1(a_1')$, $\nu_2(a_2'')$, $\nu_3(e')$ and $\nu_4(e')$ in D_{3h} nomenclature. M—O refers to the M—ONO$_2$ stretching frequency.

incomplete as the M—O stretching mode has been reported only for $Li^+NO_3^-$, while the $\nu_4(e')$ components were too weak to be identified in most cases. The most remarkable feature of the ion-pair spectra are the large $\nu_3(e')$ mode splittings which vary from 163 cm^{-1} for $Rb^+NO_3^-$ to 260 cm^{-1} for $Li^+NO_3^-$, apparently depending on the polarizing power of the cation. These $\Delta\nu_3$ values are two and a half to four times as great as those observed for the melts and aqueous solutions of the same salts and are a qualitative measure of the limiting distortion of the nitrate anion by a particular cation.

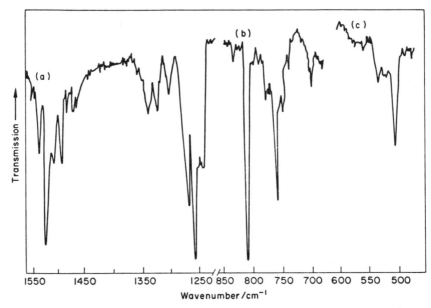

Fig. 1. Infrared spectrum of LiNO₃ vapour matrix-isolated in argon at 12 K. Curve (b) is for a sample five times as thick as the one used to obtain curves (a) and (c) (Smyrl and Devlin, Ref. 40).

The anion distortion by the various cations has been made more quantitative by conversion of the frequency data of Table 1 into force constant values, assuming a unidentate structure of C_{2v} symmetry for the ion. Except for use of a Urey-Bradley force field, the approach resembled that used by Brintzinger and Hester in their study of the vibrational effects to be expected from cation polarization of oxyanions.[23] That is, a force field was found that reproduced the 'free ion' (D_{3h}) frequencies. This field was then modified by increasing K_1 and decreasing K_2, with the force constants as defined in Fig. 2(b). This polarization effect, obtained while holding the remaining force constants at their original values, is shown by the solid lines of Fig. 2(a). The ν_{3a} and ν_{3b} curves of Fig. 2(a) were then matched against the observed $\Delta\nu_3$ values to obtain the ΔK (i.e. K_1-K_2) values listed in Table 3. The force constants of Table 3 confirm that the anion distortion is a maximum for the $Li^+NO_3^-$ case, in line with cation polarizing powers, with the N—O bond, the oxygen atom of which is coordinated to a lithium ion, being reduced to less than half the strength of the other two bonds. Brooker and Bredig have placed the dependence of the ion-pair $\Delta\nu_3$ values on P, the cation polarizing power, on a sound quantitative basis.[24] Defining $P = (z/r)/S_{eff}$, where S_{eff} is the screening efficiency factor of an electronic shell, they have obtained the plots in Fig. 3 for which even the $Cu(NO_3)_2$ and $Tl^+NO_3^-$ $\Delta\nu_3$ values seem to fall in line, despite previous arguments that covalency is as important as polarization for these two cases.[16]

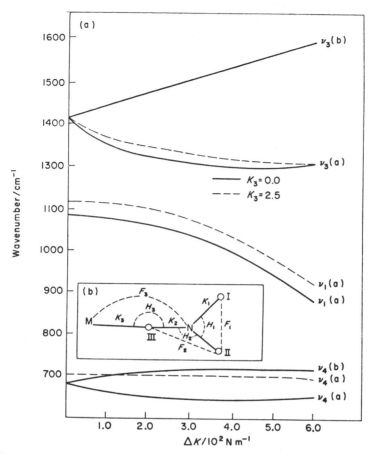

Fig. 2. (a) Dependence of calculated ν_1, ν_3 and ν_4 frequencies of the nitrate ion on ΔK (i.e. $K_1 - K_2$) and K_3. (b) C_{2v} structure and Urey–Bradley force constants (Smith *et al.*, Ref. 16).

TABLE 3
Spectroscopic and force constant data for the alkali–metal nitrate monomers

M^+	$\Delta\nu_3{}^a$	$K_1{}^b$	$K_2{}^b$	ΔK^c
Li	240^d	7.57	2.87	4.70
Na	201	7.12	3.77	3.35
K	171	6.87	4.27	2.60
Rb	163	6.82	4.37	2.45

[a] $\Delta\nu_3$ is the observed splitting (in cm^{-1}) of the $\nu_3(e')$ fundamental of the nitrate ion associated with the designated cation.

[b] Force constants in 10^2 N m^{-1}.

[c] $\Delta K = K_1 - K_2$.

[d] The LiNO$_3$ values used were for a CO$_2$ matrix; all others are for argon matrices.

In a more recent experimental study, Jacox and Milligan used matrix reactions to prepare CO_3^-, CO_3^{2-} and NO_3^- ions paired with K^+ in argon matrices.[25] The $K^+NO_3^-$ species, prepared by the reaction of NO, O_2 and K atoms, gave ν_3 frequencies identical to those obtained by vapour deposition (Table 2). Further, the CO_3^- ion, polarized by K^+, after being formed from CO, O_2 and atomic K, resembled the NO_3^- ion in the $Li^+NO_3^-$ pair in that a valence force field calculation indicated that the C—O bond, the oxygen atom of which is coordinated to the K^+ ion, is less than half the strength of the other C—O bonds.

It is not surprising, considering the magnitude of the distortion of the anion in the $M^+NO_3^-$ ion pairs, that the 'inactive' symmetric stretching mode, ν_1, is infrared allowed and, although it is not shown in Fig. 1, it has an intensity comparable to that of the ν_2 out-of-plane bending mode. The ratio of the ν_1 to ν_2 intensities, as for the melts, decreases through the series lithium to potassium. However, the frequency of ν_1 increases with increasing cation size, a trend that

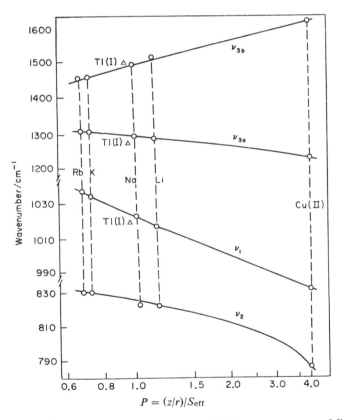

Fig. 3. Vibrational frequencies of matrix-isolated nitrate monomers, MNO₃, as a function of cation polarizing power v. log P, with $P = (z/r)/S_{\text{eff}}$ (Brooker and Bredig, Ref. 24).

is the reverse of that observed for molten and crystalline nitrates. Brooker and Bredig have explained this behaviour in terms of the increased importance of the cation polarizability, α, in the condensed phases, because of the enhanced polarization of a given cation by the several neighbouring anions.[24] Thus, for the melt they discovered a strong linear correlation between the frequency of ν_1 and the logarithm of the product of the cation polarizability and the cation polarizing power. If the decreasing frequency of ν_1 for the MNO_3 monomers is attributable to the increasing polarizing power (Fig. 3), as it seems to be, some such explanation of the reverse trend for the condensed phases is needed.

The position of the $Li^+NO_3^-$ cation–anion stretching mode in Fig. 1 is consistent with the monomer-crystal frequency shifts for this mode that have been noted for the alkali halides. Thus, the value for Li^+F^- monomer (867 cm^{-1}, Table 1) bears a similar relation to the value in the crystal (491 cm^{-1})[26] as the value for $Li^+NO_3^-$ monomer (528 cm^{-1}) bears to the value in the crystal (310 cm^{-1}).[27] However, the low intensity of this band relative to the ν_3 band components is surprising, since the translational lattice mode is extremely intense for alkali halides. Wilmshurst's reflection spectra for molten $LiNO_3$ also suggest that the lattice band of the melt has an intensity comparable with that of the ν_3 infrared band of the complex.[28]

Since molten $AgNO_3$ has been a popular subject for spectroscopic studies, and since the vibrational spectra of its melt and aqueous solution rival those of $LiNO_3$ in the richness of their interesting features (which are a subject of Section 2.4), it is disappointing that, of the univalent nitrates studied, only $AgNO_3$ behaves in the classical manner; that is, it dissociates to NO_2 and AgO rather than volatilizes intact. Since $AgNO_3$ and $TlNO_3$ behave similarly in many respects, and $TlNO_3$ is more easily volatilized than the Group IA nitrates, the failure of $AgNO_3$ to volatilize is, at this stage, surprising.

2.1.2 Group IA chlorates

With the exception of $LiClO_3$, the Group IA chlorates may be readily volatilized at temperatures in the 700 K range. Even $LiClO_3$, when thoroughly dried, vaporizes associatively as well as dissociatively so that a study of the vibrational spectra of matrix isolated Group IA chlorates has been possible.[29] The fundamental frequencies of lithium, sodium and potassium chlorate ion pairs in an argon matrix are listed in Table 4, and a typical spectrum, that of $Na^+ClO_3^-$ in xenon, can be seen in Fig. 4. There are three major differences between these data and those of the corresponding nitrates. Most noticeable is the much smaller size of $\Delta\nu_3$, which is less by a factor of three to four. Further, the magnitude of this splitting of the components of ν_3 is nearly cation-independent, ranging only from 42 to 51 cm^{-1} for xenon matrices. On the other hand, both components of the $\nu_4(e)$ chlorate mode were observed in each case, and the data of Table 4 indicate that the large $\Delta\nu_4$ value increases with the polarizing power of the cation, though the mixing of ν_{4a} with ν_{M-O} complicates the analysis in the case of $Li^+ClO_3^-$.

TABLE 4
Observed and calculated vibrational frequencies/cm⁻¹ for the alkali–metal chlorate monomers

C_{3v}	C_s	Free ion	LiClO₃ Obs[a]	LiClO₃ Calc[b]	NaClO₃ Obs[a]	NaClO₃ Calc[c]	KClO₃ Obs[a]	KClO₃ Calc[d]
ν_{3a}	ν_1a'	982	966	971	972	970	968	972
ν_1	ν_2a'	930	900	905	914	915	922	921
ν_2	ν_3a'	610	630	645	622	615	627	612
ν_{4a}	ν_4a'	479	557	561	478	479	479	479
ν_{M-O}	ν_5a'		481	453		305		256
ν_{Cl-O-M}	ν_6a'			87		63		57
ν_{3b}	ν_7a''	982	1020	1015	1017	1018	1017	1015
ν_{4b}	ν_8a''	479	533	529	518	521	508	516
ν_{Cl-O-M}	ν_9a''			77		52		46

[a] Chlorate frequencies in argon matrices, with averaging of matrix site splittings where necessary.

[b] Average error is 1.64%; five force constants fitted to seven frequencies.

[c] Average error is 0.32%; four force constants fitted to six frequencies.

[d] Average error is 0.78%; four force constants fitted to six frequencies.

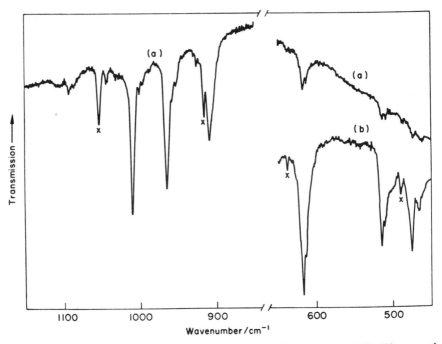

Fig. 4. Infrared spectrum of NaClO₃ vapours isolated in xenon at 12 K. The sample for curve (b) was approximately 4 times the thickness of that for curve (a). The bands labelled with an X are believed to be produced by a Na⁺ClO₃⁻ species of C_{3v} symmetry (Smyrl and Devlin, Ref. 17).

The small $\Delta\nu_3$ values, although surprising by comparison with the nitrate results, were to be expected on the basis of a force constant analysis reported earlier by Gardiner, Girling and Hester.[30] From a unidentate model it was shown that, following a sharp initial increase in $\Delta\nu_3$ with increasing polarization of the anion, as measured by the difference in force constant, ΔF, for the coordinated and free Cl—O bonds, the $\Delta\nu_3$ value becomes insensitive to further distortion of the anion. This behaviour is depicted in Fig. 5, from which it is

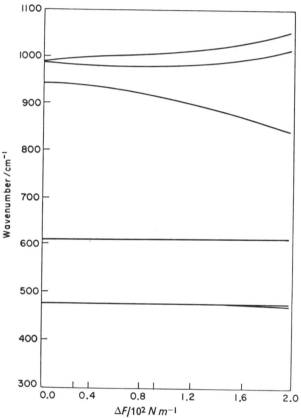

Fig. 5. A plot of calculated frequencies against polarization distortion, F, for the ClO_3^- ion (Gardiner *et al.*, Ref. 30).

clear that the $\Delta\nu_3$ values for the $M^+ClO_3^-$ ion-pairs (≈ 50 cm^{-1}) are in the range where $\Delta\nu_3$ is insensitive to variation in ΔF. By contrast, the decrease in ν_1 is predicted to accelerate with increasing anion polarization and the data in Table 4 confirm that ν_1 is dropping rapidly in the range bounded by the polarization effects of sodium and lithium ions (914–900 cm^{-1}).

Beginning with an initial force constant set proposed by Gardiner *et al.*,[31] the observed frequencies for chlorate ions were converted to a set of modified valence force-field force constants for each ion pair. By constraining the off-diagonal interaction terms to the initial values and adjusting the M—O stretching constant, K_s, only in the case of $Li^+ClO_3^-$, the force constants in Table 5 were obtained by fitting four force constants to six observed frequencies. The complete set of calculated frequencies are included in Table 4. The force constants reflect the effects of polarization of the anion by the cation on each of the anion frequencies. They show that the cation polarization of the anion does increase through the series from potassium to lithium, but that the ΔK values are smaller by a factor of two than for the nitrates. Also, the ΔK value comes entirely from the reduced strength of the coordinated Cl—O bond with no contribution from increasing strength of the free Cl—O bond.

In other respects the vibrational data on the chlorate ion resemble the results for the nitrate ion. The relative infrared intensity of the ν_1 band increases with increasing polarizing power of the cation while the concurrent decrease in the frequency of ν_1 also mirrors the behaviour of the nitrate ion. The mixing of ν_{4a} with ν_{M-O} complicates the interpretation of the difference between the ν_{M-O} values of $Li^+ClO_3^-$ and $Li^+NO_3^-$ (528 cm^{-1}). However, the average of the $Li^+ClO_3^-$ ν_{4a} and ν_{M-O} values (519 cm^{-1}) is certainly comparable with that of ν_{M-O} for $Li^+NO_3^-$.

2.1.3 Group IA perchlorates

Though the perchlorates are a known source of O_2 at elevated temperatures,

TABLE 5
Force constants for the alkali–metal chlorate monomers

Force constant[a]	Coordinate involved[b]	Force constant value[c]			
		'Free ion'	$LiClO_3$	$NaClO_3$	$KClO_3$
K_r	Cl—O	5.715	6.03	6.08	6.04
K_R	Cl—O*	5.715	4.17	4.60	4.76
K_S	M—O*		1.21	1.21	1.21
H_α	O—Cl—O	2.236	2.49	1.98	2.01
H_β	O—Cl—O*	2.236	2.54	2.47	2.44
H_θ, H_ϕ	M—O*—Cl		0.035	0.035	0.035
F_{rr}		0.311	0.311	0.311	0.311
F_{rR}		0.311	0.311	0.311	0.311
$F_{\alpha\beta}$		0.659	0.659	0.659	0.659
$F_{\beta\beta}$		0.659	0.659	0.659	0.659

[a] Force constants subscripted with r, R or S are for bond stretching; those with α, β, θ or ϕ are for inter-bond angle deformations. F_{rr}, F_{rR}, $F_{\alpha\beta}$ and $F_{\beta\beta}$ are off-diagonal elements in the force constant matrix, corresponding to interaction constants.

[b] The asterisk denotes the oxygen atom coordinated to the metal atom.

[c] Stretching force constants are given in 10^2 N m^{-1} and angle deformation constants in a J rad^{-2}.

a spectroscopic study has shown that the Group IA perchlorates volatilize at about 700 K with even less decomposition than is noted for the chlorates.[32] This volatility has made possible a vibrational study of the tetrahedral ClO_4^- anion polarized by contact with alkali metal cations. The vibrational frequencies for the $M^+ClO_4^-$ ion pairs, with M being lithium, sodium or potassium, are presented in Table 6 and the infrared spectra for these species in the 600–1250 cm^{-1} range appear in Figure 6. The spectra show that the triply degenerate perchlorate modes, $\nu_3(t_2)$ and $\nu_4(t_2)$, are split in each case. The large $\nu_3(t_2)$ splittings are more like those of the nitrate ion than those of chlorate and, in fact, the separation of the ν_{3a} and ν_{3c} components, given in Table 6, agree to within a few percent with the corresponding nitrate values. As for the nitrates, $\Delta\nu_3$ is sensitive to the polarizing power of the cation.

The presence of three components for both $\nu_3(t_2)$ and $\nu_4(t_2)$ is conclusive evidence that the cation coordination is bidentate or bidentate-like. Strong cation interaction through a single oxygen atom, as for a unidentate structure, would reduce the perchlorate symmetry to C_{3v} with only two separate ν_3 component bands possible. The observed frequency pattern requires a significant metal interaction with two oxygen atoms of the perchlorate ion, an observation which suggests that early electron diffraction results for $M^+NO_3^-$ units, which were interpreted in terms of a unidentate model but with the M^+ ion positioned off the N—O axis, may be valid.[21]

Throughout the spectra reported for the oxyanion salt vapours isolated in inert matrices, there are features which have been assigned to dimers of the ion pairs. These features are of interest because they represent a reasonably simple

TABLE 6
Vibrational frequencies/cm⁻¹ for the fundamentals of the alkali–metal perchlorate monomeric ion pairs and the spacings $\Delta\nu_3$ between the components of the ν_3 triplet

Mode	$LiClO_4$	$NaClO_4$	$KClO_4$
ν_1	895	906	917
ν_4	612 ⎫ 636 ⎬ 34 646 ⎭	616 ⎫ 621 ⎬ 27 643 ⎭	622 ⎫ ⎬ 13 635 ⎭
ν_{3a}	994	1011	1028
ν_{3b}	1143	1127	1122
ν_{3c}	1220	1192	1184
ν_{MO}	538 544		
$\Delta\nu_{3a,b}$	149	116	94
$\Delta\nu_{3a,c}$	227	181	156
$\Delta\nu_{3b,c}$	78	65	62

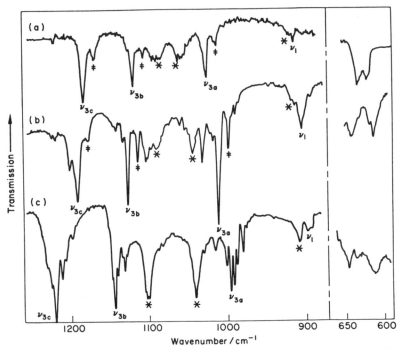

Fig. 6. Infrared spectra of $M^+ClO_4^-$ ion pairs isolated in an argon matrix. (a) $K^+ClO_4^-$, (b) $Na^+ClO_4^-$, (c) $Li^+ClO_4^-$. Dimer features are labelled with an asterisk (*) while ^{37}Cl monomer bands are indicated by a dagger (‡) (Ritzhaupt and Devlin, Ref. 32).

structure that clearly lies somewhere between the monomeric ion pair and the crystalline state in terms of the magnitude of the asymmetric forces operating on the anion. The behaviour of the ν_1 and ν_3 modes is particularly interesting and features (marked with an asterisk) assigned to the dimer $(Li^+ClO_4^-)_2$ are apparent in Figure 6. The ν_1 frequency of the perchlorate ion is 965 cm^{-1},[33] so the dimer value of 908 cm^{-1} lies between this frequency and that of the monomer mode (895 cm^{-1}). The $(\nu_{3a}-\nu_{3b})$ difference for the dimer (61 cm^{-1}) is approximately half that of the monomer (149 cm^{-1}). These results are typical of the differences between monomer and dimer modes for all the oxyanion salts, as can be seen from the listing of dimer frequencies in Table 7 and the monomer frequencies in Tables 2, 4 and 6.

In general it is apparent that oxyanions paired with a single cation in monomeric ion pairs are strongly distorted from the free ion structures. This is reflected in the large splitting of degenerate vibrational modes of the oxyanion and the red shifting of the frequency of the symmetric stretching mode. The magnitude of the splittings, particularly for ν_3 of nitrates and perchlorates, is much greater than that observed for the corresponding molten salts or aqueous solutions and suggests that cation polarization of specific anions is strongly attenuated in such

TABLE 7
Vibrational frequencies/cm⁻¹ for the dimers (MXO$_n$)$_2$

Mode	(NaNO₃)₂^a	(KNO₃)₂^a	(RbNO₃)₂^a	(KClO₃)₂^b	(LiClO₄)₂^c	(NaClO₄)₂^c	(KClO₄)₂^c
ν_1	1035	1047	1040	935	908	917	923
ν_2	835	835	835	611			
ν_{3a}	1336	1337	1331		1040	1044	1058
ν_{3b}	1440	1420	1415	1000	1101	1090	1085
ν_{3c}					≈1200	≈1185	≈1175

^{a} Ref. 16.
^{b} Ref. 29.
^{c} Ref. 32.

media. The nature of this attenuation, particularly for aqueous solutions, is discussed in Section 2.2.

2.1.4   Other polyatomic anion salts

There have been two extensive vibrational studies of ionic vapours involving polyatomic anions other than oxyanions. The systems involved, MAlF$_4$ and MBeF$_3$, where M is Li or Na, resemble each other in that the formation of ion pairs in the vapour phase accompanies addition of MF to a molecular liquid, AlF$_3$ or BeF$_2$.

(a) MAlF$_4$—the vapours of equimolar mixtures of NaF or LiF with AlF$_3$ in the 1200 K range contain primarily the M$^+$AlF$_4^-$ ion pairs.[34,35] Infrared band frequencies assigned to the monomeric ion-pairs isolated in a neon matrix[35] are presented in Table 8. These data have been transformed into symmetry

TABLE 8
Vibrational frequencies/cm⁻¹ for
^{7}LiAlF$_4$, NaAlF$_4$ and ^{7}LiBeF$_3$ monomers
in neon matrices

Species	LiAlF₄^a	NaAlF₄^a	LiBeF₃^b
a_1	900	884	1245
	649	674	586
	541	379	491
	313	302	
b_1	900	884	861
	266	323	213?
b_2	817	811	
	433	372	
	221		

^{a} Ref. 35.
^{b} Ref. 37.

force constants through a normal coordinate analysis which also contributed to the assignments. Since the electron diffraction data indicate that the tetrahedral AlF_4^- ion is associated with Na^+ in a bidentate complex of C_{2v} symmetry,[36] the effects of cation polarization on the spectrum of the AlF_4^- ion should resemble the effects for the case of $Li^+ClO_4^-$ involving the bidentate ClO_4^- ion.[32] However, by contrast and somewhat surprisingly, the $\nu_3(t_2)$ asymmetric stretching mode is split into only two components spaced by 83 cm^{-1} and 73 cm^{-1} for $Li^+AlF_4^-$ and $Na^+AlF_4^-$, respectively. The small magnitude of this splitting relative to the 230 cm^{-1} spread reported for the three components of $\nu_3(t_2)$ for the perchlorate ion in $Li^+ClO_4^-$ is also interesting.[152] The splitting is more nearly comparable with the ca. 50 cm^{-1} values found for $\Delta\nu_3$ of the monomeric ion pairs involving the chlorate ion.[29]

The $M^+AlF_4^-$ data resemble the oxyanion results in at least three respects: (i) the frequency of the symmetric stretching mode, $\nu_1(a_1)$, of the AlF_4^- tetrahedral anion increases with decreasing cation polarizing power (649 cm^{-1} for $Li^+AlF_4^-$ and 647 cm^{-1} for $Na^+AlF_4^-$), (ii) absorption bands, apparently produced by dimeric species, $(M^+AlF_4^-)_2$, have been observed and (iii) the metal–anion bond stretching frequencies are similar to those found for $M^+ClO_4^-$ species (Table 4), viz. 541 cm^{-1} for Li—F and 302 cm^{-1} for Na—F.

(b) $LiBeF_3$—matrix-isolation spectra indicate that the dominant species in the vapour of an equimolar mixture of LiF and BeF_2 at 780 °C is BeF_2 rather than $Li^+BeF_3^-$.[37] However, when a BeF_2 vapour stream passes over LiF at 930 °C, the resulting vapour, when matrix isolated, gives an infrared spectrum that has been attributed to $Li^+BeF_3^-$ together with comparable amounts of LiF and BeF_2 and with smaller amounts of more complex species.

The $Li^+BeF_3^-$ ion pair has been tentatively assigned (on the basis of a force constant calculation) to a C_{2v} structure involving the bidentate BeF_3^- ion. The results, given in Table 8, suggest that bands at 1245 and 888 cm^{-1} originate from the doubly degenerate asymmetric stretching mode of the unperturbed ion. It seems possible that either the small distortion splitting for $LiAlF_4$ (83 cm^{-1}) or the very large splitting for $LiBeF_3$ (357 cm^{-1}) is in error, although the difference resembles that between $LiClO_4$ (227 cm^{-1}) and $LiClO_3$ (54 cm^{-1}), but in the opposite sense in terms of a tetrahedral–pyramidal comparison.

2.2 Vapours of Molten Salts in Associating Matrices

In the previous section simple ion pairs isolated in inert matrix media such as argon, xenon, krypton and nitrogen have been considered. For such media the assumption is that the vibrational spectrum of a particular ion pair is a close facsimile, in terms of band positions, to that for the corresponding vapour phase, the spectrum of which may be very difficult to observe directly.[19] Empirically it is known that this assumption is valid for molecular species, but the interionic mode of Li^+F^- in inert matrices is strongly shifted (ca. 60 cm^{-1}) relative to its value in the gas phase.[38] Thus, the frequencies for the internal modes of the polyatomic anion are probably very close to the yet-to-be-observed vapour phase frequencies for the $M^+XO_n^-$ species, whereas the external mode frequencies may be low by as much as 10% relative to those observed for gas phase species.

For the foregoing reasons, unless a chemical reaction in a matrix is to be studied, pure inert gases have been the choice for the matrix media. However, the ability to volatilize the $M^+XO_n^-$ species has also presented a unique opportunity to observe the details of the solvation of the ion pairs by solvent molecules such as H_2O and NH_3. That is, the addition of such solvent molecules to the inert matrix gas in increasing amounts has permitted observation of the ion pairs with progressively more of the inert gas molecules surrounding a given $M^+XO_n^-$ unit replaced by the associating solvent species.[39] The influence of the M^+ ions on the XO_n^- units has been observed while varying the amount of H_2O (and NH_3) in the M^+ coordination shell, in a stepwise fashion, from 0 to $n-1$ where n is the coordination number of the M^+ ion.

2.2.1 Group IA nitrates in H_2O and NH_3

The spectra for the ν_3 frequency range in Fig. 7 indicate the effect on the nitrate ion of increasing the number of H_2O molecules in the Li^+ coordination shell from zero to $n-1$ for the $Li^+NO_3^-$ ion pair (the $\% H_2O$ is given in the Figure). The first substantial change, as the H_2O level was increased to 6%, was the reduction of $\Delta\nu_3$ to 168 cm^{-1}. This reduction was thus identified as the effect of single H_2O coordination. The further enrichment of argon with H_2O caused a continuing decrease in $\Delta\nu_3$ to 115 ($12\% H_2O$), then 90 ($25\% H_2O$) and finally 65 cm^{-1} (pure H_2O). Because of some fluidity at a matrix surface as it forms, plus the attraction of the cation for the H_2O molecules, it was not possible to be certain to what extent H_2O substitution for argon occurred around an average Li^+ ion for a particular concentration of water (with the exception of the first H_2O to enter the coordination shell). Nevertheless, the decrease in $\Delta\nu_3$ was related to an effective stepwise reduction in the polarizing power of the Li^+ ion accompanying a transfer of negative charge from the H_2O molecules coordinated to Li^+.

Similar results have been obtained for the ammonia solvation of the ion pairs in an argon matrix.[39] The result of progressively more complete ammonia solvation of $K^+NO_3^-$ in an argon matrix is also revealed by the gradual reduction of $\Delta\nu_3$, as can be seen from Figure 8. It is remarkable that the polarizing power of the K^+ ion is so effectively cancelled by solvation that the $\Delta\nu_3$ value for K^+ solvated by $n-1$ NH_3 molecules (20 cm^{-1}) is less than 15% of that produced by the bare K^+ ion (171 cm^{-1}). It is also notable that a large cation effect is retained in the pure NH_3 glassy matrices, as $\Delta\nu_3$ is 47 cm^{-1} for $Li^+NO_3^-$ compared with the 20 cm^{-1} value for $K^+NO_3^-$.[40]

The data obtained for the limiting cases of pure water and pure ammonia matrices are particularly interesting. It has been documented that a vapour deposit of water prepared at ca. 15 K has an amorphous structure[41,42] which has been characterized as glassy since its structure resembles that of liquid water.

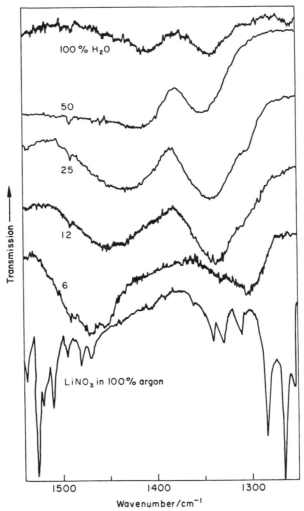

Fig. 7. Infrared bands of the nitrate ion in the ν_3 region for $Li^+NO_3^-$ ion pairs isolated in matrices with compositions varying from pure argon to pure H_2O. The numbers indicate the percentage H_2O in the mixed H_2O–argon matrices (Ritzhaupt and Devlin, Ref. 39).

For depositions at temperatures well below the glass transition temperature the situation can be presumed to be similar for NH_3. Thus, the ion pairs deposited in these media at 10–15 K experience an environment resembling that of an ion pair in aqueous or liquid NH_3 solutions. The vibrational spectra for $Li^+NO_3^-$ and $K^+NO_3^-$, as summarized in Table 9 for glassy H_2O and glassy NH_3 matrices, should thus be useful in the interpretation of the spectra of concentrated solutions.

Since the regular decrease in $\Delta\nu_3$ with increasing H_2O (or NH_3) concentration

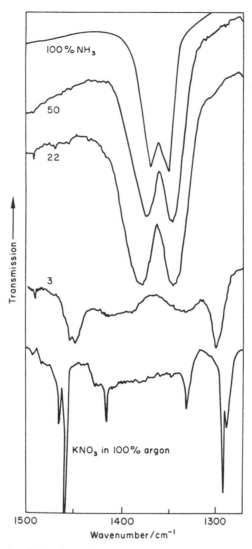

Fig. 8. Infrared bands of the nitrate ion in the ν_3 region for $K^+NO_3^-$ ion pairs isolated in matrices with composition varying from pure argon to pure ammonia. The numbers indicate the percentage ammonia in the mixed ammonia–argon matrices (Ritzhaupt and Devlin, Ref. 39).

in the argon matrices, plus the residual cation effect for pure H_2O (or NH_3) media, indicates that the cations and anions remain contact-paired for all matrix compositions, it is not surprising that the 47 cm^{-1} value for $\Delta\nu_3$ for $Li^+NO_3^-$ in pure NH_3 agrees closely with the value reported for a 1:4 solution of $LiNO_3$ in liquid NH_3.[43,44] At such a solution concentration most of the NO_3^- ions must be in direct contact with a Li^+ cation and the comparison of solution and

TABLE 9
Infrared band frequencies/cm^{-1} for
monomeric LiNO$_3$ and KNO$_3$, matrix isolated
in water and ammonia

Mode	LiNO$_3$		KNO$_3$	
	H$_2$O	NH$_3$	H$_2$O	NH$_3$
ν_2	827	828		830
ν_{3a}	1347	1345	1348	1348
ν_{3b}	1412	1392	1398	1368

matrix ν_3 frequencies shows that the solution spectra are affected by this contact. Naturally, the resolution for the low temperature matrix studies is superior to that for spectra of solutions at room temperature because of thermal broadening in the latter. This difference is apparent in the case of KNO$_3$ in NH$_3$ as the distinct ν_3 doublet in the matrix spectrum (Fig. 8) has been revealed in the liquid solution by a curve resolution technique.[45]

The application of the glassy H$_2$O matrix data to the interpretation of aqueous solution spectra is complicated somewhat by the strong association of H$_2$O with the NO$_3^-$ ions,[46] whether the latter are ion-paired or otherwise. The magnitude of the $\Delta\nu_3$ splitting for K$^+$NO$_3^-$ in pure glassy H$_2$O (50 cm^{-1}) results from distortion of the NO$_3^-$ ion through interaction with the water matrix rather than with the contacting hydrated K$^+$ ion.[39] As a result, the vibrational spectra for solvent-separated and K$^+$ contact-paired NO$_3^-$ are expected to be indistinguishable. On the other hand, the large $\Delta\nu_3$ value for Li$^+$NO$_3^-$ in glassy H$_2$O (65 cm^{-1}) does reflect the ion-pairing and has led to the suggestion[39,40] that considerably larger splittings reported for concentrated LiNO$_3$ solution[47] may include a contribution from dipole–dipole coupling.

The influence of coordination with H$_2$O or NH$_3$ on the polarizing power of the cation is similar for these two molecules.[39] The reduction in the ν_3 splitting arising from coordination of one H$_2$O molecule is very similar to that arising from association with one NH$_3$ molecule. Along this same line, the $\Delta\nu_3$ values in Table 7 for the dimers (M$^+$NO$_3^-$)$_2$ in an argon matrix, for which each M$^+$ ion is thought to be two-coordinated to NO$_3^-$ ions, are similar to those for the singly solvated units, (H$_2$OM$^+$NO$_3^-$) and (NH$_3$M$^+$NO$_3^-$). The implication is that coordination with an NO$_3^-$ ion reduces the effective M$^+$ polarizing power by a comparable amount. For the particular case where M$^+$ is Li$^+$, $\Delta\nu_3$ for the three cases is 168 cm^{-1} (H$_2$O), 178 cm^{-1} (NH$_3$) and ca. 150 cm^{-1} (NO$_3^-$), while when M$^+$ is K$^+$ the corresponding splittings are 79, 77 and 85 cm^{-1}, respectively.

2.2.2. Other MXO$_n$ vapours in H$_2$O and NH$_3$

There are no published data for M$^+$ClO$_3^-$ or M$^+$ClO$_4^-$ ion-pairs in mixed matrices of argon with either H_2O or NH_3. However, infrared spectra are available for these species in pure glassy H_2O and NH_3.[32,48] The effect of H_2O and NH_3 cation-solvation on the magnitude of the splittings of the $\nu_3(e)(ClO_3^-)$ and $\nu_3(t_2)(ClO_4^-)$ bands is consistent with the $M^+NO_3^-$ results. For example, in an NH_3 medium the ν_3 band splittings decrease (from the large argon matrix values) to the extent that band overlap makes it difficult to judge the residual splittings. This is demonstrated in curve (a) of Fig. 9 (B) for $K^+ClO_3^-$. Figure 10 also shows the strong decrease in the $\Delta\nu_3$ $Li^+ClO_4^-$ value for H_2O and NH_3, but from Fig. 9 (A) it is clear that $\Delta\nu_3$ of the $M^+ClO_3^-$ ion-pair remains substantial in a water matrix. By analogy with the nitrate results, and recalling that the chlorate ion ν_3 splitting is most responsive for small perturbations,[30] the magnitude

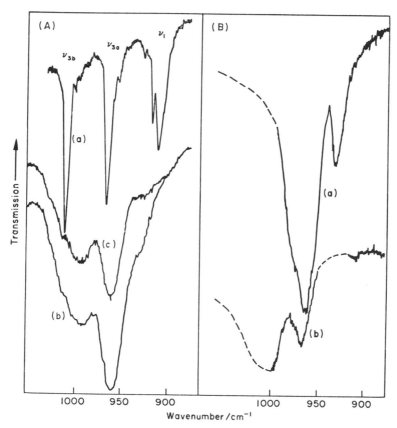

Fig. 9. Infrared spectra in the (ν_1, ν_3) region of $M^+ClO_3^-$ ion-pairs in various matrices. (A) $Na^+ClO_3^-$ (a) in xenon and (b) in H_2O; (c) $K^+ClO_3^-$ in H_2O. (B) (a) $K^+ClO_3^-$ and (b) $Li^+ClO_3^-$ in ammonia. The latter curves are composites obtained by overlapping data for NH_3 and ND_3 matrices to minimize the influence of the matrix ν_1 band. The ν_2 band of $Li^+ClO_3^-$ was obscured by a ClO_2 band that has been removed in the diagram (Smyrl and Devlin, Ref. 48).

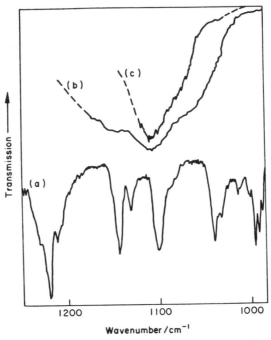

Fig. 10. Infrared spectra of the Li⁺ClO₄⁻ ion pair in (a) argon, (b) H₂O, and (c) NH₃ matrices. Dashed lines indicate the region of overlap with matrix bands (Ritzhaupt and Devlin, Ref. 32).

of the residual splitting in Fig. 9 (A), curves (b) and (c), can be attributed to water–chlorate interaction. This view differs from that expressed in reference (48) but is consistent with the observations described above for the $M^+NO_3^-$ ion-pairs in mixed water–argon matrices. Thus, for the $M^+XO_n^-$ ion-pairs it seems to be generally true that H_2O associates much more strongly with the anion than does the NH_3 molecule.

2.3   Aggregates of Molten Salt Vapour Species in Inert Matrices

The matrix isolation studies of MXO_n melt vapours described in Section 2.1 have confirmed that the dominant vapour species are the simple monomer ion-pairs, at least in the 400–500 °C temperature range. There is also some evidence in most cases for the presence of dimers $(MXO_n)_2$, apparently at a concentration of less than 10%, though the dimer–monomer ratio is expected to be temperature dependent. However, when the ion pair to matrix gas ratio is increased sufficiently, the ion pairs aggregate in a manner similar to that reported for $H_2O^{(49)}$ and $CH_3OH^{(50, 51)}$ in nitrogen and argon matrices. Thus, the infrared spectrum for samples with a low matrix ratio contain features that have been assigned to trimers and higher aggregates.[52] As was hinted at in the previous section, this permits observation of the variation in the polarizing power of the cation with the increasing number of XO_n^- ions coordinated with the M^+ ions. As the aggregate size increases at higher concentrations of the salt vapour species, the spectra have been observed to converge on those characteristic of the corresponding molten salts.[52] Since the aggregates thus constitute a low-temperature form of the salt having a structure similar to the melt, the aggregate phase has been referred to as glassy.

The value of glassy aggregate spectra to the resolution of structural arguments has been limited, but one application will be examined here and a particular insight gained from the glassy aggregate spectra will be described in the section on molten salts. The application of the aggregate spectra stems from the inability to measure the infrared v_3 band without serious band distortion when working with pure oxyanion melts or glassy thin films. For the oxyanion salt the v_3 band has an unusually great intensity, so that anomalous behaviour of the refractive index and consequent large fluctuations in sample reflectivity in the v_3 frequency region complicates absorption measurements on samples more than a few thousand ångströms in thickness. This problem is avoided by using matrix aggregates since the aggregates are sufficiently small that a true absorption spectrum is obtained.[52]

2.4 Molten Oxyanion Salts

Since the earliest days of structural studies of molten salts a seemingly disproportionate share of attention has been devoted to the oxyanion salts, and, in particular, the Group I nitrates. More recently, much of the interest has switched to the polyhalide anion systems, the subject of Section 3 of this Chapter, but it remains true that the quantity of vibrational data for the molten nitrates surpasses that for any other group of melts. These data have been the source of considerable conjecture and discussion but it seems, at this time, that a relatively complete and largely non-controversial interpretation can be given to the existing data. The resulting description for the oxyanion melts will be developed in this section but it should be noted that the description in some instances will also reflect guidance from other areas of physical–chemical research such as classical dynamical calculations for many-particle systems.

2.4.1 Molten nitrate internal modes

There are a number of excellent reasons why structural studies of molten salts have been concentrated on the Group I metal nitrates and thallium nitrate. These salts have relatively low melting points (200–450 °C) and large temperature ranges over which the melts are stable. The Raman spectra can be obtained using a simple oven assembly with standard pyrex glass or quartz capillary cells in the axial–transverse sampling geometry.[53-55] Further, the nitrate melts do not attack either diamond, silicon or Irtran-6, so infrared spectra can be obtained by either attenuated total reflection[56] (a.t.r.) or transmission methods.[57] The nitrates tend to crystallize with simple unit cells of high symmetry, such as the two-molecule unit cells of the trigonal (D_{3d}^6) forms of $NaNO_3$ and $LiNO_3$, so that the solid state serves as a convenient reference state. Further, as emphasized in Section 2.1, the alkali metal nitrates vaporize readily so that the ion pairs, $M^+NO_3{}^-$, are available as a second structurally simple reference state, while low temperature condensation of the vapours produces the glassy phase and thus structural studies of the 'melts' in the absence of thermal effects are possible. Finally, the nitrates are water soluble to the extent that, by working with a range of temperatures, all compositions of salt–water mixtures from dilute solution to anhydrous molten salt can be studied.

In brief, the nitrate ion can be studied in an exceptional variety of configurations. Of even more importance to the spectroscopic studies, however, are certain favourable properties of the vibrational spectrum of the nitrate ion. The nitrate ion's internal modes have frequencies in a range (700–1500 cm^{-1}) easily accessible to infrared and Raman studies. More vitally, the nitrate ion possesses degenerate modes, $\nu_3(e')$ (asymmetric stretch) and $\nu_4(e')$ (in-plane bend) which split in a manner indicative of the extent of anion distortion, as well as a mode, $\nu_1(a_1')$ (symmetric stretch), for which the frequency and infrared intensity are sensitive to the environment of cations. Also adding to the interest, while complicating the spectroscopic measurements and interpretations, is the unusually great infrared intensity arising from the large magnitude of the oscillating dipole, (dp/dQ_3), associated with ν_3. Finally, the mass of the nitrate ion is sufficiently low that the external modes, based on both translational and rotational displacements, occur in spectral regions accessible to modern spectrometers.

The particular observations for the internal-mode region of the spectra of molten nitrate salts which appear to have the most structural significance are as follows.

1. The $\nu_3(e')$ band is split into two or more components, as originally observed for $LiNO_3$ by Wilmshurst and Senderoff[28] and by Janz and James.[58] The magnitudes of the ν_3 splittings, as deduced in more recent studies, are apparent from Table 10, which summarizes the measured infrared and Raman frequencies for Group I molten salts.

2. As is clear from Table 10, and as has been noted by several authors[56,59,67,69] there are mismatches, outside the expected experimental errors, between infrared and Raman frequencies, in particular for the ν_1 modes of $LiNO_3$ and $AgNO_3$. Discrepancies for ν_2 and ν_3 band positions have also been cited.[56,59,67] Further, it is noteworthy that the ν_1 Raman band has a shoulder near the peak frequency of the ν_1 infrared band,[60] while the ν_2 infrared band for $LiNO_3$ has a shoulder near the peak of the ν_2 Raman band.[56]

3. The ν_1 mode is weakly infrared-active while the ν_2 mode is similarly Raman-active. This activity, indicative of some perturbation of the D_{3h} structure of the

TABLE 10
Frequencies/cm^{-1} and assignments of bands observed from Raman, infrared emission (Ref. 59) and other spectroscopic studies of molten alkali–metal nitrates. Unless otherwise indicated 'Other' refers to a.t.r. or single plate absorption measurements (Ref. 56)

LiNO₃ Raman[a]	LiNO₃ Emis-sion	LiNO₃ Other	NaNO₃ Raman[c]	NaNO₃ Emis-sion	NaNO₃ Other	KNO₃ Raman[e]	KNO₃ Emis-sion	KNO₃ Other	RbNO₃ Raman[f]	RbNO₃ Emis-sion	RbNO₃ Other	CsNO₃ Raman[g]	CsNO₃ Emis-sion[b]	CsNO₃ Other	AgNO₃ Raman[h]	AgNO₃ Emis-sion	AgNO₃ Other	TlNO₃ Raman[i]	TlNO₃ Other[j]	Assignment
2940, 2820		2830		2770	2790		2750	2750		2745	2703		2720	2597						$2\nu_3$
2440		2440		2415	2420		2400	2390		2390	2353		2380	2439						$\nu_1 + \nu_3$
2160		2170																		
2070		2090		2070	2075		2070	2050		2060	2041		2050	2041						$\nu_3 + \nu_4, 2\nu_1$
1770		1780		1765	1765		1755	1757		1750	1754		1745	1754			1745			$\nu_1 + \nu_4$
1641		1656				1662									1605					$2\nu_2$
1465	1445	1424	1420	1435	1410≈1395	1410≈1395	1388≈1405		1400		≈1400		1390			1420	≈1390	1390	1390	ν_3
1360	1328	1345	1365	1330	1345≈1335	1325≈1335	1338≈1340		1320		≈1330		1318			1275	1260	1300	1285	
1064	1050	1053	1057	1048	1047	1045	1045	1046	1041		1042	1042	1039	1036		1037	1025	1036	1032	ν_1
823	820	818	828	826	825	830	829	831	830		823	829	830	833		804	800	817	815	ν_2
746, 718	735	742	732	730	≈730	720	≈720	714	710		712	709	710	704		729≈740	712≈720	707		ν_4
350		343[b]		215	217[d]	170			≈110				≈100			120		145		ν_{trans}
145(154)[k]			115(115)[k]			95(90)[k]			85					≈100[d]				85		ν_{rot}

[a] Ref. 60. [b] Ref. 61. [c] Ref. 62. [d] Ref. 57. [e] Ref. 55. [f] Ref. 64. [g] Ref. 65. [h] Ref. 66. [i] Ref. 67. [j] Ref. 68. [k] Ref. 63.

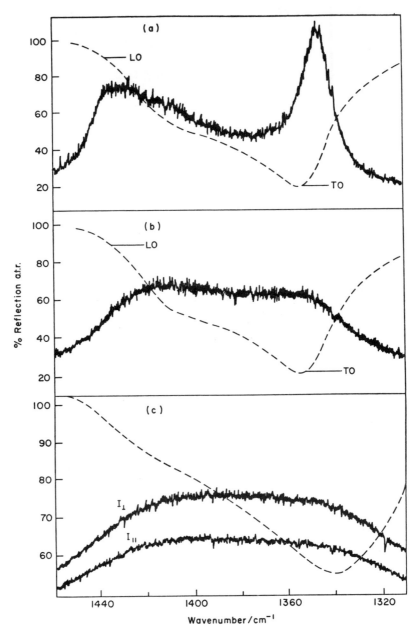

Fig. 11. Raman (–) and TM wave a.t.r. (– – –) curves for (a) ordered KNO₃(III), 122 °C, (b) disordered KNO₃(I), 200 °C and (c) molten KNO₃, 350 °C. The a.t.r. solid-state spectra are for crystals with the C_3 axis perpendicular to the prism–sample interface. The a.t.r. liquid curve shows a predictable distortion and ≈ 10 cm⁻¹ peak displacement for the low frequency portion (Devlin *et al.*, Ref. 78).

nitrate ion, decreases through the series $LiNO_3$ to $CsNO_3$ for both v_1[56] and v_2.[55]

4. The splitting of the $v_4(e')$ band is clearly observable for melts of $AgNO_3$,[66,71] $LiNO_3$[70] and $NaNO_3$.[55,62]

5. In mixtures of KNO_3 with either $Mg(NO_3)_2$ or $Ca(NO_3)_2$ the v_1 and the $2v_2$ nitrate bands each split into a doublet.[72-74] On the other hand, the v_2 infrared band shifts in steps from the value in pure KNO_3 (829 cm^{-1}) to the value in pure $AgNO_3$ (801 cm^{-1}) as the mole fraction of potassium in a mixed $KNO_3/AgNO_3$ melt is varied from 1.0 to zero.[75] This variation in melt composition is also accompanied by a regular increase in the intensity of the v_1 Raman band.[76]

The splitting, Δv_3, of the v_3 band into components spaced by as much as 145 cm^{-1} for $AgNO_3$ and 110 cm^{-1} for $LiNO_3$, with progressively smaller spacings through the Group IA series, has been the subject of careful measurement and considerable debate. The obvious but apparently somewhat naive explanation for the magnitude of these splittings is that the nitrate anion is distorted by the asymmetrically positioned counter-ions with the extent of the distortion determined primarily by the polarizing power of the cation. However, the Δv_3 values are markedly greater than the site splittings familiar from crystalline Group I nitrates, such as the ca. 18 cm^{-1} site splitting for $KNO_3(II)$,[77] so alternative explanations have been sought, particularly by proponents of a distorted crystal description of the melts. In this respect, Devlin, James and Frech pointed out that the v_3 splittings resemble in magnitude the v_3 transverse–longitudinal (T/L) splittings for trigonal nitrate crystals and that orientationally disordered nitrate crystals, such as $KNO_3(I)$ and $RbNO_3(I)$ and (II), have v_3 Raman bands that are nearly indistinguishable from the bands of the corresponding molten salt.[64,78] Figure 11 shows the comparison between the spectra of $KNO_3(I)$, molten KNO_3, and $KNO_3(III)$, the ordered trigonal form. Since the broad doublet for $KNO_3(I)$ reflects the dispersion for the T and the L branches because of the breakdown of the $k \approx 0$ selection rule,[79] the implication is that the broad doublets observed with melts of the various Group I nitrates have a similar origin, although Chisler had previously related these broad crystal and melt features to a Jahn–Teller distortion of the nitrate ion.[80]

The possibility that co-operative modes having transverse and longitudinal characteristics are responsible for the breadth and structure of the v_3 band is subject to test via dilution of the nitrate ion while holding the cation unchanged.[78] With this in mind, Brooker et al. diluted $LiNO_3$ with $LiClO_4$ to the 5 mole percent nitrate range, a concentration for which the dipole–dipole coupling of nitrate v_3 modes that is the source of the large crystalline state v_3 splittings is expected to be considerably reduced, but found no significant reduction in Δv_3.[60] On the other hand, dilution of $LiNO_3$ with $LiClO_3$ was found to reduce the Δv_3 Raman value by 35% and the overall v_3 band width by a similar amount, as can be seen in Figure 12.[81] Similarly, infrared emission spectra (Fig. 13) confirm that the v_3 splitting for $NaNO_3$ is strongly reduced by dilution with

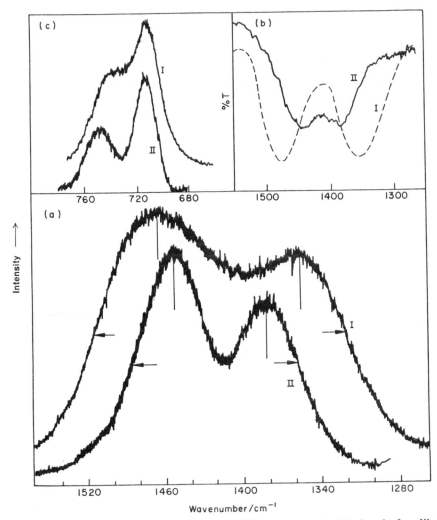

Fig. 12. Vibrational bands for pure liquid LiNO₃ compared with bands for dilute solutions of LiNO₃ in LiClO₃. (a) ν_3 Raman band for (I) pure LiNO₃ (533 K) and (II) 2% LiNO₃ in LiClO₃ (413 K), (b) ν_3 infrared band for (I) pure LiNO₃ aggregates in a CO₂ matrix (≈100 K) and (II) 5% LiNO₃ in LiClO₃ (413 K) and (c) ν_4 Raman band for (I) pure LiNO₃ (533 K) and (II) 8% LiNO₃ in LiClO₃ (413 K) (Devlin *et al.*, Ref. 81).

NaClO₃,[59] and vapour co-deposition of small quantities of LiNO₃ with either LiClO₃ or LiClO₄ has produced glassy films for which the infrared $\Delta\nu_3$ value is <70 cm⁻¹.[82]

At least two additional explanations of the ν_3 splitting have been proposed. Bates *et al.* suggested that coupling of the ν_3 mode with large amplitude rotational motions characteristic of the high temperature melts may account for the splitting.[83] Although this was proposed for carbonate melts, the source of the

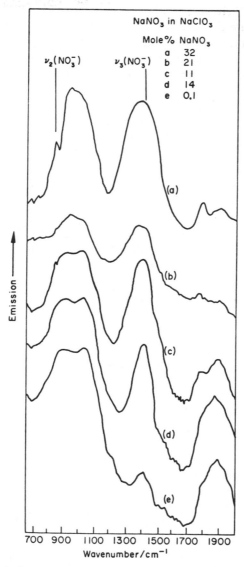

Fig. 13. Infrared emission of NaNO₃ dissolved in molten NaClO₃ and measured at about 340 °C (Bates and Boyd, Ref. 59).

splitting of ν_3 is likely to be the same for nitrate melts. However, this explanation would seem to require a radical change in the ν_3 band at low temperatures, which is not observed either in bulk glasses [81] or in thin film glass deposits.[52] In an alternative explanation of the magnitude of $\Delta\nu_3$, Irish *et al.* have proposed that melts contain nitrate ions in two distinct types of site: one, with the nitrate ion in a cation cage; and a second, with the NO_3^- ion associated primarily with a particular cation.[84] However, to be consistent with the data for the bulk of the melts, which indicate that the two ν_3 components are of comparable intensity for the various nitrate salts over wide temperature ranges, this model imposes the unlikely requirement that these two sites be nearly equally probable and that the relative probabilities be insensitive to change of either cation or temperature.

The interpretation that seems most consistent with the available data is that the ν_3 mode is split by the asymmetric cation field, but, as established by the anion dilution studies,[59, 81, 82] this distortion splitting is less than the $\Delta\nu_3$ values measured for the pure melts. The distortion-split doublet is further split by a resonance interaction that is activated through dipole coupling of the ν_3 modes of neighbouring nitrate ions.[81] This is one manner by which the intense dipole oscillation of the ν_3 mode, which was referred to earlier, complicates the interpretation of the vibrational spectrum. Transfer of excitation energy via dipole–dipole coupling[85] also quite probably limits the lifetimes of anion excited states and thereby gives rise to the considerable breadth of the ν_3 band components for the pure molten nitrates. An equivalent explanation can be given in terms of short-lived phonons with dispersion.

The infrared–Raman mismatch of the ν_1 frequencies has also been attributed to different factors, including correlation field splitting[56] and the existence of two anion sites.[60] Though such infrared–Raman frequency differences for a single fundamental mode are common in crystal spectra because of correlation field effects, a good argument can be made that there is no adequate mechanism for coupling the ν_1 modes of neighbouring nitrate ions to produce differences as large as have been measured for certain pure melts (≈ 10 cm^{-1}). Brooker has shown experimentally that factor group splitting for ν_1 in crystalline Group IA nitrates is less than 4 cm^{-1} in all cases.[86] The two-site model has been criticized above, but a variation on that model, namely one permitting a range of nitrate environments varying continuously from symmetric and crystal-like to strongly asymmetric, with the latter resembling the anion environment in small clusters, $(MNO_3)_n$, seems to explain the ν_1 data.[52]

In addition to the non-coincidence of infrared and Raman ν_1 values, it is necessary to keep in mind the fact that the ν_1 frequency is lowered on melting the solid by about 10 cm^{-1},[22, 70] and is sharply reduced for the monomeric pairs relative to the melt values.[16] For the $Li^+NO_3^-$ case the ν_1 values increase in a series from the monomer value of 1017 cm^{-1} in a CO_2 matrix, to the dimer value of 1032 cm^{-1}, through the trimer frequency of 1042 cm^{-1}, to the aggregate value of 1050 cm^{-1}.[52] This last value is, within experimental error, equal to the infrared ν_1 frequency for the molten salt (see Table 10). This sequence is displayed in Fig. 14, curve b, with the 1073 cm^{-1} crystal value indicated by a vertical dashed line. Clearly, the more strongly Li^+ is associated with a nitrate ion, the lower is the ν_1 frequency but the greater is the induced infrared activity.[16, 56] Thus, the infrared–Raman frequency mismatch for the melts can be attributed to the presence of a large anion population at positions resembling the crystal sites. These anions are responsible for the intense Raman band (at

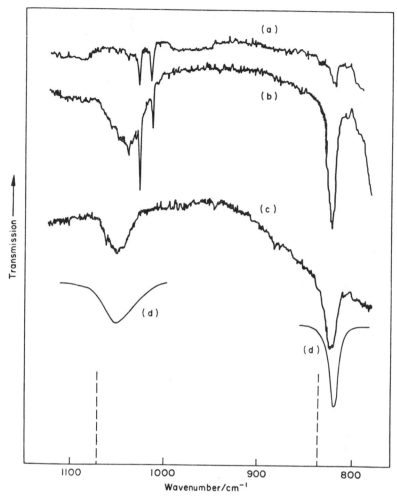

Fig. 14. The infrared spectra for LiNO₃ (ν_1 and ν_2 modes) in different environments. (a) matrix-isolated in CO_2, (b) isolated-aggregated mixture in CO_2, (c) pure film deposited at $-180\ ^\circ C$ and (d) the molten salt at $275\ ^\circ C$. The vertical dashed lines represent the solid-state LiNO₃ ν_1 and ν_2 transverse mode frequencies ($25\ ^\circ C$) (Pollard et al., Ref. 52).

$1060\ cm^{-1}$) but contribute only very weakly to the infrared absorption. The crystal-like population drops off with increasing cation–anion interaction, so the Raman band intensity tails off to lower frequencies, resulting in band asymmetry.[60] The infrared absorptivity (and emissivity) increases with the degree of anion distortion, which also is responsible for the lowering of the ν_1 frequency. Thus the infrared band intensity maximizes at ca. $10\ cm^{-1}$ below the peak of the Raman band before tailing off somewhat asymmetrically as in curve (d), Fig. 13. The intensity of the ν_1 band in the melt spectrum is seen to reach zero at the frequency characteristic of the ion-pair, as it must, since this corresponds to the maximum anion distortion.[16]

Since this model for interpreting the non-coincidence of infrared and Raman ν_1 peak intensities relies on the existence of a range of anion distortions, and since this range (from the crystal to the monomeric ion pair) is greatest for cations with the largest polarizing power, it is consistent that the effect is most pronounced for lithium and decreases through the Group IA series (note the ν_1 mismatch magnitudes in Table 10). The ν_1 peak positions are quite well determined, so that there must exist some significant physical explanation for the mismatch. The ν_2 peak frequencies are equally well-determined, so that the smaller infrared–Raman mismatch for this mode may have a similar explanation to that for ν_1. However, the role played by absorption and scattering would be reversed, since for D_{3h} symmetry ν_2 is Raman- rather than infrared-inactive. The situation is likely to be much different with respect to non-coincidences that have been noted for ν_3 band components (Table 10), since no completely reliable infrared band peak frequencies have been published for ν_3. The great infrared intensity of this mode makes it difficult to separate the influence of anomalous dispersion in the refractive index from absorption effects by either transmission or a.t.r. measurements[56] and, further, causes re-adsorption to be a complicating factor in emission studies.[59] A complete analysis of the optical constants by a.t.r. is possible,[87] in principle, but calls for more careful control of the angle of incidence than has been used for molten salts. A simpler approach to fixing the positions of the ν_3 infrared components is to alternate ultra-thin films of glassy salts with somewhat thicker layers of argon. As long as the individual salt layers are much thinner than the wavelength of light, reflectivity problems which arise because of the dispersion in the refractive index should be eliminated.[88] Preliminary efforts have shown that the infrared frequencies of the ν_3 band components converge on the Raman frequencies of the melt as the thickness of the individual glass layers is reduced.[89] This is consistent with the observation that the infrared-active components of ν_3 for glassy nitrate aggregates are coincident with the corresponding Raman features,[52] but does not necessarily imply that the non-coincidences, such as reported by Bates et al. for molten carbonates and concentrated aqueous carbonate solutions, are not significant.

Unlike ν_3, the ν_4 nitrate bending mode is only weakly infrared-active, which implies that this mode has a small associated oscillating dipole. Therefore, dipole coupling is eliminated as a mechanism for the production of strong co-operative effects involving this mode, and the splitting of ν_4 which has been observed for lithium, sodium and silver nitrate melts should reflect a simple splitting of the $\nu_4(e')$ degeneracy via cation-cage distortion of the anion. Thus, for example, the slight increase in the ν_4 splitting when $LiNO_3$ is diluted with $LiClO_3$ (Fig. 12), has been cited as evidence that the asymmetry of the nitrate environment is not reduced by this dilution and, therefore, the concomitant 35% reduction in $\Delta\nu_3$ must result from the reduction in a co-operative effect.[81] However, the assignment of this splitting of the ν_4 band to the loss of the mode degeneracy is not universally accepted. Apparently because a band of frequency close to that of the higher component of ν_4 for pure Group I melts (≈ 740 cm^{-1}) exists with increased intensity in melts containing bivalent cations, where the existence of many types of anion sites is well established,[72–74] some authors have been led to attribute the ν_4 doublet to the existence of two types of anion sites in the Group I melts as well.[60]

For melt mixtures containing M^{2+} ions, the ca. 740 cm^{-1} ν_4 component seems to denote the presence of nitrate ions in close association with an M^{2+} cation. This consideration has led to the fairly commonly applied view that the splitting of ν_4 constitutes an appropriate test for ion-pair formation, particularly in aqueous solutions. However, Gardiner et al.[43] and more recently Lundeen and Tobias[90] have encountered ion pairs for which the splitting of ν_4 is not observable. It seems likely that the splitting in the Group I nitrate melts is also in contradiction to the 'rule' and merely reflects the asymmetry of the cation cage.

As mentioned, there remains no doubt that the nitrate anion has two or more significantly different sites in Group IIA mixtures with Group IA melts. The characteristic spectroscopic effects in these mixtures, the splitting of both the ν_1 and $2\nu_2$ bands, can be understood simply by recognizing the existence of different types of anion cavities, depending on whether the cation cage consists of only alkali metal cations or also contains one or more M^{2+} cations.[72,74,91] The presence of the M^{2+} ion should also introduce a large asymmetry in the cage potential, capable of activating forbidden modes (ν_2 in the Raman) and of lifting vibrational degeneracies, as well as shifting non-degenerate active modes, such as ν_1, relative to the value for the alkali–metal cation cage.[74] Other than the weak asymmetry of the ν_1 band, which has already been discussed, the pure Group IA melts do not show the doubling of ν_1 or $2\nu_2$ which characterizes the melts with known multiple sites, so it is not consistent to evaluate the ν_4 band complex in terms of these mixtures.

The concept of a number of distinct cation configurations about the anion in molten mixtures was originally applied by Devlin and Li to mixtures of KNO_3 and $AgNO_3$.[75] A model which envisaged the nitrate ion coordinated with four (or more) cations, with the identity of the cations determined statistically, successfully reproduced the variation in the ν_2 peak position and general band structure for a range of compositions from pure $AgNO_3$ (ν_2, 800 cm^{-1}) to pure KNO_3 (ν_2, 829 cm^{-1}). As a result, it was suggested that each anion is associated with the several cations of a given cage. However, Clarke and Hartley have interpreted the low frequency Raman data for such mixtures on the basis of pairwise interactions alone,[92] but Janz and co-workers[66,76] have found the variations in the ν_1 Raman band intensities for similar mixtures to be consistent with the statistical model for the cation cage.

The Raman studies of the internal modes of oxyanion melts have been concentrated on the measurements of band positions and qualitative band shapes rather than band intensities. However, in a few instances attention has shifted to the integrated band intensities and the manner in which these intensities vary with salt composition. Perhaps the most complete results are available for mixtures of $AgNO_3$ with $TlNO_3$, for which a plot of ν_1 molar intensities, I_m, (defined as $I_m \propto IM/1000\rho$ where I, M and ρ are, respectively, integrated intensity, molecular weight and density) against mole percent $AgNO_3$, has a definite minimum.[66] On the other hand, a nearly linear decrease in I_m of ν_1 accompanies dilution of $AgNO_3$ with Group IA nitrates.[76] However, this decrease in I_m, which is quite different from that for dilution with $TlNO_3$, has in both cases been related to a reduction in the extent of back-donation of π-electron density to the nitrate ion. The decrease in back-donation would result in a reduction in the polarizability of the anion and, consequently, a drop in I_m for ν_1. Views based on the importance of 'covalent' bonding, such as π-electron back-donation, in molten silver salts have recently gained support from surface tension studies on $AgNO_3$–alkali metal nitrate mixtures.[93]

There have also been occasional attempts to deduce quantitative information from polarizability correlation functions obtained from the Fourier transform of the Raman band shapes. Clarke and Miller[94] have emphasized that information on rotational relaxations must be derived from the anisotropic scattering as originally shown by Gordon,[95] and that other bandwidth contributions must be removed. This separation is facilitated in ionic melts by the large liquid temperature range and, in particular, by the ability to sample the glass phase where molecular reorientation effects will normally disappear. Thus, they found that ca. $20\ cm^{-1}$ of the ν_1 bandwidth for $Ca(NO_3)_2 \cdot 1.5\ KNO_3$ glass-forming mixtures is preserved in the glass phase and, therefore, is probably a result of structure distribution.[94] Raman ν_1 bandshapes of thin glassy films of $LiNO_3$, KNO_3 and $TlNO_3$ have similarly been shown to compare closely with those of the molten salts, confirming the importance of the distribution of the anions over a range of sites.[52] From this viewpoint it is not surprising that the ν_1 Raman band of glassy $LiNO_3$ is double the width of the KNO_3 band, since the greater the polarizing power of the cation the greater is the range of the site asymmetries. The validity of the latter statement can be seen by comparing monomer ν_1 (and $\Delta\nu_3$) frequencies given in Table 10 with solid state values.

2.4.2   Other oxyanion melt internal modes

There are more limited vibrational data available for molten chlorates, perchlorates, carbonates, sulfates and thiocyanates. However, the chlorate and perchlorate melts, which are as easily studied as the nitrates, have not proved to contain a molecular structural probe as effective as the nitrate ion, while the higher melting points of the carbonates and sulfates complicates both the measurement and interpretation of the spectra.

CHLORATE MELTS

As for the nitrates, the early infrared studies of chlorate melts indicated that the $\nu_3(e)$ band for the lithium salt is split into two components[96] while more recent Raman and emission infrared data suggest that the splitting is general for the Group I chlorates.[97-99] However, the matrix isolation studies for the chlorate ion-pairs were marked by the small magnitude of the $\nu_3(e)$ splitting (Table 4) and the chlorate melt frequencies given in Table 11 show that the ν_3

TABLE 11
Frequencies/cm⁻¹ and assignments of fundamental and lattice vibrational bands observed for Group IA chlorates and AgClO₃ melts

Frequencies/cm^{-1} and assignments of fundamental and lattice vibrational bands observed for Group IA chlorates and $AgClO_3$ melts

LiClO₃		NaClO₃		KClO₃		AgClO₃	Assignment[e]
Infrared[a]	Raman[b]	Infrared[c]	Raman[d]	Infrared[c]	Raman[d]	Infrared[a]	
1018	1043	1000		1000		969	ν_3
977	978		973	970[f]	963	≈931	ν_3
≈938	948	935	937	$\begin{cases} 932^f \\ 933 \end{cases}$	932	≈895	ν_1
620	625	614	617	610	612	595	ν_2
	510		495	491		477	ν_4
≈478	483		481	485	484	≈440	ν_4
≈338		200		160			ν_{trans}
	140		≈120		≈120		ν_{rot}

[a] Reflection spectra, Ref. 96.
[b] Ref. 98.
[c] Emission spectra, Ref. 99.
[d] Ref. 99.
[e] Based on C_{3v} nomenclature.
[f] Glass transmission spectra, Ref. 29.

splittings for the melts are also significantly smaller than for the corresponding nitrates. On the other hand, the matrix studies indicated that the $\nu_4(e)$ mode of the chlorates is more sensitive to distortion than for the nitrates and, again, this is reflected in the melt spectra as even the KClO₃ ν_4 Raman bands show some structure[99] that is not apparent for KNO₃. Also, the ν_1 chlorate peak shifts to lower frequencies through the series LiClO₃ to KClO₃ but, in general, both the melt and matrix isolation results confirm the view that the internal mode spectrum of the chlorate ion is not as sensitive a probe of the anion environment as is the case for the nitrate ion.

PERCHLORATE MELTS

The matrix spectra for the alkali metal perchlorates indicate that the triply degenerate $\nu_3(t_2)$ mode splits by an amount which is dependent on the distortion of the perchlorate ion;[32] the presence of three components complicates the determination of peak positions (see Fig. 10). However, the published vibrational data for the pure perchlorate melts are limited to Raman and low resolution infrared reflection spectra for LiClO₄.[33, 60, 96] The Raman spectrum suggests a large splitting of ν_3, and this has been confirmed by the observation of three components in the infrared spectrum of thin glassy $LiClO_4$ deposits.[32] In this case, however, the corresponding splitting observed for ν_4 for the isolated ion-pairs is not detected in the melt spectra. The melt and glass phase data for $LiClO_4$ are compiled in Table 12 and a comparison of the infrared and

TABLE 12
Infrared and Raman band frequencies/cm^{-1} for the fundamental modes of molten $LiClO_4$

Infrared^a		1139		948	627	≈ 470	260
							≈ 315
	$\approx 1160^c$	1110^c	1070^c				
Raman^b	1180	1118		954	633	462	
Assignment	ν_{3c}	ν_{3b}	ν_{3a}	ν_1	ν_4	ν_2	

^{a} Reflection spectrum, Ref. 96.
^{b} Ref. 60.
^{c} Estimated from glass transmission curve, Ref. 32.

Raman frequencies for ν_1 reveals a significant mismatch similar in magnitude to that for $LiNO_3$.

CARBONATE MELTS

There are no infrared data for carbonate melts and the Raman study of the pure melts has been restricted to Li_2CO_3[83] though there are additional Raman results for the lithium–potassium–sodium eutectic,[100] mixtures of Group IA carbonates with the corresponding halide,[83] an Li_2CO_3–$CaCO_3$ mixture,[83] and Na_2CO_3 in a ternary molten fluoride mixture.[101] Though lack of infrared data makes a complete comparison impossible, the carbonate spectra, summarized in Table 13 and illustrated in Fig. 15, appear to be closely analogous to the spectra of the corresponding nitrates. The $\nu_3(e')$ mode is split in each case, though slightly less than for the nitrates; the ν_1 mode shows the same qualitative dependence on cation size; the ν_2 mode is activated in the Raman and, as for the nitrates, increases in frequency when Li^+ is replaced by Na^+ ions. No distinct splitting of $\nu_4(e')$ was observed, but a comparison of the curves in Fig. 15 reveals that the ν_4 band of the lithium salt is much broader than that of Na_2CO_3. An interesting experimental aspect of the most extensive Raman study of the reactive carbonate melts[83] has been the successful use of a windowless high-temperature cell developed by Quist.[102]

SULFATE MELTS

Infrared[103] and Raman[103, 104] studies of the melts of certain alkali–metal sulfates have been reported but have provided no direct information on the $\nu_3(t_2)$ mode and, in general, were incomplete because of the limitations on sampling methods and instruments available at that time. The infrared results

TABLE 13
Band positions^{a,b}/cm^{-1} observed in the Raman spectra of molten carbonates

Assignment	Li$_2$CO$_3$			NaCl–Na$_2$CO$_3$^{c} (745 °C)	KCl–K$_2$CO$_3$^{c} (670 °C)
	Pure (765 °C)	LiCl^c (625 °C)	CaCO$_3$^{c} (775 °C)		
$\nu_1(a_1')$	1072 s, p	1074 s, p	1072 s, p	1050 s, p	1040 s, p
$\nu_2(a_2'')$	878 vw	872 vw	874 vw	880 vw	n.o.
$\nu_3(e')$	1496 m	1496 m	1510 m	1440 m	1407 m
	1418 m	1422 m	1418 m	1400 m	1380 m
$\nu_4(e')$	702 w	704 w	712 w	695 w	687 w
$2\nu_2$	1752 w	1748 w	1742 w	1758 w	1764 w

^{a} Frequency accuracy: $\nu_1 \pm 2$, $\nu_2 \pm 5$, $\nu_3 \pm 10$, $\nu_4 \pm 5$, $2\nu_2 \pm 5$ cm^{-1}.

^{b} s = strong; m = medium; w = weak; v = very; p = polarized; n.o. = band not observed.

^{c} Eutectic compositions: Li$_2$CO$_3$–LiCl (60 mole percent LiCl, m.p. 506 °C); Li$_2$CO$_3$–CaCO$_3$ (33 mole percent CaCO$_3$, m.p. 662 °C); Na$_2$CO$_3$–NaCl (57 mole percent NaCl, m.p. 640 °C); K$_2$CO$_3$–KCl (65 mole percent KCl, m.p. 630 °C).

did reflect some distortion of the sulfate ion in the pure Group IA melts because the $\nu_2(e)$ band is weakly activated. As with the other oxyanions, the frequency of ν_1 decreases with increasing atomic number of the Group IA cation. The infrared data also include considerable information on the effect of added divalent metal cations, as well as of Ag$^+$, on the sulfate ion structure since the spectra clearly reflect the presence of a strong association of SO$_4$$^{2-}$ with these M^{2+} cations within the Group IA sulfate melts.[103] Fundamental frequencies for sulfate–cation configurations containing the divalent cations have been assigned and are indicated in Table 14 for zinc, copper, cobalt and nickel. The labelling of the modes in Table 14 is based on an assumed C_{3v} symmetry for the distorted SO$_4$$^{2-}$ ion and presumes a rather specific pairing of the M^{2+} and SO$_4$$^{2-}$ ions. The structures within these melt mixtures could also be described in the same terms used for the alkali metal nitrate melts containing Mg(NO$_3$)$_2$ and Ca(NO$_3$)$_2$ (Section 2.4.1), but increased covalency may result in an increase in the specific nature of the interaction where transition metal ions are involved.

2.4.3 Oxyanion melt external modes

Most published data for the low frequency external mode region of oxyanion salt melts are for the Group I metal nitrates and mixtures thereof. Although pre-laser Raman studies produced no data for the external mode region (0–400 cm^{-1}), numerous papers have since been devoted, at least in part, to the analysis of this portion of the Raman spectrum. By contrast, the original infrared reflection studies by Wilmshurst[48, 96] did produce useful low-frequency spectra, particularly for the lithium salts, and modern instrumentation has since per-

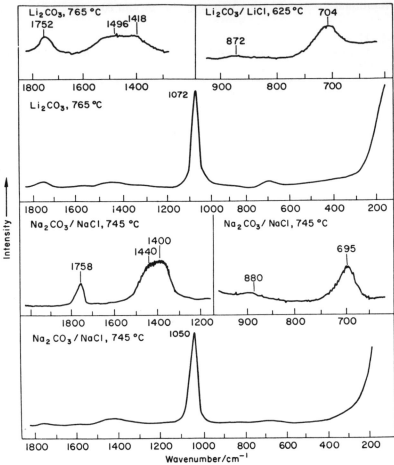

Fig. 15. Raman spectra of molten Li₂CO₃ at 765 °C and molten Li₂CO₃–LiCl eutectic mixture (60 mole per cent LiCl) at 625 °C. Raman spectra of molten Na₂CO₃–NaCl eutectic mixture (57 mole per cent NaCl) at 745 °C (Bates *et al.*, Ref. 83).

TABLE 14
Infrared-active fundamental frequencies/ cm⁻¹ for the SO₄²⁻ ion with C_{3v} symmetry in ZnSO₄, CuSO₄, CoSO₄, and NiSO₄ solutions

ZnSO₄	CuSO₄	CoSO₄	NiSO₄	Assignments
1155[a]	1145[a]	1155[a]	1145[a]	$\nu_4(e)$
1030	1025	1030	1030[a]	$\nu_1(a_1)$
970	945	950	945[a]	$\nu_2(a_1)$
630	640	625	630	$\nu_5(e)$
615	610	615	615	$\nu_3(a_1)$
475	495	475	490	$\nu_6(e)$

[a] Frequencies determined from overtone and combination bands. All the others were determined directly.

[b] Ref. 103.

mitted more complete studies via thin film transmission[57,72] and emission studies.[59,99]

The lattice region Raman spectra of pure nitrate melts are all similar. In each case a shoulder is present in the 50–200 cm^{-1} range on a rapidly changing background often referred to as the 'liquid wing' (see the top curve of Fig. 16 (a)).

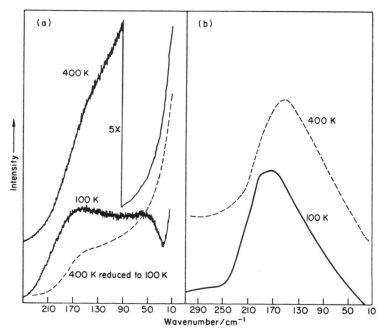

Fig. 16. (a) Low-frequency Raman spectra of LiClO$_3$ + 18% LiNO$_3$ at 100 K and 400 K. Dashed curve is the 400 K spectrum reduced to 100 K. (b) 100 K and 400 K spectra completely reduced for thermal effects (Ritzhaupt and Devlin, Ref. 109).

Several techniques have been devised to remove the liquid wing[63,64,105] and thus display an intense broad Raman band positioned according to the values listed as ν_{rot} in Table 10. There are two strong reasons for assigning this band to the librational motion of the nitrate ion about an axis in the plane of the anion. It has been established that the intense Raman band in this region of the spectrum of crystalline LiNO$_3$ and NaNO$_3$ has such an origin[106] and that this crystal band moves rapidly towards the liquid state value as the temperature of the crystal approaches the melting point.[55,63] Perhaps more conclusive, however, is the observation that salts containing more nearly spherical anions, such as ClO$_4^-$, have no such Raman feature and scatter only weakly in this spectral region,[60,68] possibly via a charge-induced anisotropy mechanism.[107] The most intense Raman band in the melt 'lattice' region is therefore assigned to the out-of-plane libration of the nitrate ion, a motion which produces a change in the anisotropic part of the polarizability.

The original devices for removing the liquid wing in order to expose the librational Raman band were more or less artificial. However, Shuker and Gammon[108] have emphasized that the wing can be treated as an outgrowth of (a) the breakdown of optical selection rules and (b) the thermal population of states associated with the mode of dominant scattering strength, in this case the librational mode. They have successfully applied this concept to the analysis of the lattice region of the Raman spectra of oxide liquids and glasses.[108] Among other interesting implications, this model prescribes how the thermal contribution to the Raman scattering can be removed at a given temperature and predicts that the liquid wing will vanish as the temperature approaches 0 K. Ritzhaupt and Devlin have found that this expectation is fulfilled for the glass-forming ionic liquids (a) 18% $LiNO_3$ in $LiClO_3$ and (b) $Ca(NO_3)_2KNO_3$.[109] The spectra of Fig. 16(a) show that at ca. 100 K the liquid wing is strongly reduced relative to that near 400 K. Further, this study confirmed that reduction of high-temperature spectra by a frequency- and temperature-dependent factor[108] reproduced the observed low temperature curves accurately, provided the higher temperature is not significantly greater than T_g, the glass transition temperature.

It is possible that the Shuker–Gammon approach is also applicable to orientationally disordered crystals such as $CsNO_3(I)$[65] and $RbNO_3(I)$.[64] These systems, which display a liquid wing, also illustrate the breakdown of the $k \approx 0$ optical selection rule[79] and have one dominant low-frequency Raman mode.

Though the low-frequency Raman band for the nitrates and chlorates is generally acknowledged to have a librational origin, it is not so clear how much any co-operative motion contributes to the band shape. The method of Shuker and Gammon is arrived at by a crystal-like analysis but it assumes modes of reduced correlation lengths (<40 nm) and it relates the scattering intensity to a first-order scattering from a single type of mode. The band breadth is attributed to breakdown of the $k \approx 0$ selection rule and the frequency dispersion in k-space. The impressive success of this approach in predicting the temperature-dependent behaviour of both oxide and ionic glasses and liquids lends credence to the assumptions of the model. On the other hand, similar bands have been observed for relatively dilute solutions of nitrate salts for which collective aspects of the librational mode should be largely eliminated.[94, 110] The question seems to be not whether co-operative motion is required for the band to exist—it is not—but rather whether or not the breadth and shape of the band reflects a co-operative character for the librational mode.

The collective character of the infrared-active translationally based modes in the far-infrared region for the pure alkali nitrates (Table 10) has been displayed through a dipole-correlation study based on the Fourier transform of the far-infrared curves.[57] The absorption spectra of the melt, obtained by transmission measurements using a diamond cell, are dominated by structured bands having component positions and intensities similar to those of high-temperature crystal spectra, as can be seen for $NaNO_3$ in Figure 17. Band broadening is the most

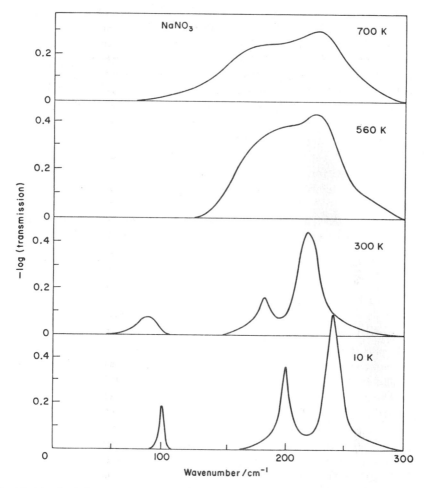

Fig. 17. The far-infrared absorption spectra of sodium nitrate (m.p. 580 K) at different temperatures (Wegdam *et al.*, Ref. 57b).

apparent effect of increased temperature and this occurs without a significant discontinuity at the melting point. This added breadth is revealed, through the Fourier transform, in terms of reduced phonon lifetimes. The investigators have thus deduced that collective modes, resembling ordered crystal-state phonons, but having a reduced spatial and temporal range, are characteristic of the ionic melts, with the phonons progressively less well developed at increasingly higher temperatures.

A similar interpretation was given previously for the 'lattice' modes of both ionic and covalent network glasses[72] and Wilmshurst recognized the lattice-like qualities of the far infrared bands that were apparent in his melt reflection measurements.[28, 96] More recently, Exarhos, Miller and Risen have identified pseudo–phonon states from the far infrared spectra of ionic metal metaphosphate glasses. They find that the observed spectra can be treated in terms of a single damped harmonic oscillator[111] with frequency dispersion reflecting the collective nature of the vitreous state vibrations. This view is analogous to the one that Shuker and Gammon[108] have applied to the Raman lattice spectra. Wong and Angell have added to the arguments for such a viewpoint by demonstrating that the pressure response of the far infrared bands for mixed $TlNO_3$–$Mg(NO_3)_2$ glasses resembles the known response of the TO modes of alkali–halide lattices.[112]

Far infrared data for chlorate melts as well as Group IA nitrate melts have recently been obtained by infrared emission techniques using a Fourier transform spectrometer (FTS).[59, 99] The results, which have been listed in Tables 10 and 11 and which are depicted in Fig. 18, indicate a somewhat lower frequency for the chlorates than the nitrates, as expected for a translationally based mode considering the greater mass of the chlorate ion.

2.4.4 Summary for oxyanion melts

The description of the molten Group I oxyanion salts based on vibrational spectroscopic data involves the oxyanion in a cage of counter-ions, with the most probable sites those in which the anion interacts more or less equivalently with four or more cations, much as in the crystalline state. However, there is an appreciable range of configurations even for these more probable 'sites', as indicated by the inherent breadth of the ν_1 band, and also a significant asymmetry as indicated by large values for $\Delta\nu_3$ and $\Delta\nu_4$ (degeneracy splittings). In addition, there exist sites of increasingly greater asymmetry but of progressively lower probability, sites which are 'frozen in' for the glass phase[52] but which may result primarily from extremely large mean amplitudes of the lattice vibrations of the melts.[57b] These more asymmetric sites are probably responsible for the lack of coincidences between the infrared and Raman frequencies of ν_1 in pure melts.

A great portion of the vibrational spectra can be understood in these terms with no need to invoke other elements of crystalline state spectra, such as phonon branches and correlation field and T/L splittings. Where these splittings are small and not obvious in the crystal phase, it is reasonable to ignore them in the amorphous phase. However, these effects are not always small in the spectra of crystalline oxyanion salts, even for internal modes. It is well known that the T/L splittings are in the 50–150 cm^{-1} range for the ν_3 modes of nitrates, sulfates, perchlorates and carbonates and greater than 10 cm^{-1} for ν_2 of certain nitrates and carbonates.[113] Although it is not as generally recognized, factor group splittings can be just as large, as has been discovered for orthorhombic $KNO_3(II)$,[77] for which the a_g–b_{3g} splitting is 88 cm^{-1}. For the internal vibrations, such large T/L and factor-group solid-state splittings are invariably a result

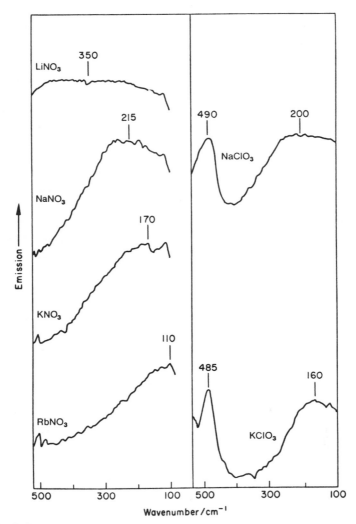

Fig. 18. Far-infrared emission spectra of molten alkali metal nitrates and chlorates. Nitrate spectra recorded at 340 °C; chlorate spectra recorded at approx. 380 °C (Bates and Boyd, Ref. 59).

of large dipole oscillations associated with the internal mode in question. This coupling mechanism is also available in the melts.

With the recognition of these large dipole forces, and considering calculations on disordered linear chains which indicate only a minor influence of disorder on the frequency distribution of the chain collective modes,[114] it is reasonable to seek phonon-like contributions to the internal mode spectra with the understanding that these do not imply the existence of long-range order. As Shuker and Gammon have expressed it,[115] the long wavelength collective modes, of which the crystal optical modes are an example, would not be affected by the disorder due to an averaging of the spatial disorder, so that the correlation range may be long. Some such explanation must underly the recent observation that the disordering of trigonal KNO_3(III) by extensive ^{15}N substitution ($> 50\%$) does not break up the TO–LO ν_3 phonons of the system, nor appreciably alter the $k \approx 0$ selection rule.[116] All phonon branches, whether based on internal or external vibrations, have long wavelength ($k \approx 0$) components, so the view applies to all modes for disordered systems. As for crystals, the phonon character of the modes will only be important in spectroscopic interpretations if there exists a strong coupling force. Only when such forces exist will the frequency dispersions and/or the correlation field splittings have a significant magnitude. The coupling forces appear to be sufficiently great for the ν_3 modes of molten nitrates (and probably other oxyanion melts) for the collective character of the modes to have a significant influence on the ν_3 mode infrared and Raman bands.

The spectroscopic significance of the phonon-like qualities of amorphous phase vibrations that are based on external modes is more generally acknowledged. Wegdam *et al.* assert that the time correlation study of such modes indicates that a description in terms of phonons with a finite lifetime is meaningful.[57b] The band for such a mode thus yields accurate structural information only if the collective nature of the mode is recognized, so that the analysis provides for the density of states as well as the variation of spectral intensity with k-vector value. It has also been stressed[57b] that the amplitudes of the ion motions in the translational lattice modes are so great at the high temperatures of the ionic melts that local ion symmetries change continuously, on a time scale somewhat greater than that of the ion internal vibrations, and in a manner that renders the internal modes an ineffective probe of local lattice symmetries or forces. However, the internal mode spectra of glasses have been found to match the molten salt spectra quite closely in appearance.[52, 94] This suggests that either the large amplitudes in the melt are not a significant spectroscopic factor, or that the types of transient 'sites' experienced in the melt because of large amplitude lattice vibrations are frozen into the glass structures.

3 POLYHALIDE ANION SALT MELTS

Ionic polyhalide melts typically result from the addition of alkali metal halides (MX) to the more covalent metal halides MX_n. More often than not, for the systems that have been studied spectroscopically, the metal in the MX_n species is either from the transition metal or Group VA series, although substantial information is also available for BF_3, BeF_2 and MgF_2. The liquid may sometimes be considered ionic prior to the addition of any alkali halide but, for this review, the emphasis is on the molten mixtures with the pure MX_n melt spectra discussed only as they relate to the ionic mixtures.

3.1   AlX₃—MX

The AlX$_3$—MX melts have been studied more extensively than any other polyhalide systems. Reasons for this interest have included a need for structural information on molten cryolite (Na$_3$AlF$_6$), the electrolyte used in the commercial production of aluminium and, more recently, the apparent value of AlX$_3$-rich mixtures in the processing of hydrocarbon fuels. These mixtures are also noted for an ability to stabilize low oxidation states in the acidic (high AlX$_3$ content) region.

The vibrational spectroscopic data for these melts have been limited to Raman spectra. Because of the high melting temperatures and corrosive character of these melts, definitive Raman measurements, particularly for fluorides, have been possible only after significant advances in cell design. The most successful cell design which gives strong Raman signals with only minor background effects, even at 1000 °C, is apparently a modified version of the windowless cell originally described for Raman applications by Quist.[117] Such cells, which depend on liquid surface tension to minimize leakage from the slots cut for light transmission, have been fabricated from nickel, copper,[117] and graphite,[118] and are normally enclosed in a quartz sleeve for mounting in a suitable oven. Gilbert, Mamantov and Begun showed that the interference from light emitted from the cell walls, which can be prohibitive at 1000 °C, is made insignificant by cutting a hole in the cell wall opposite the port for exit of the Raman scattered radiation.[118] Thus, the spectrometer does not see any strongly emissive hot surfaces; the basic cell is illustrated in Figure 19.

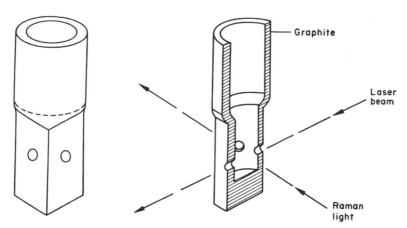

Fig. 19. Raman cell for molten fluorides ($\approx$9 mm o.d. $\times$ 37 mm) (Gilbert *et al.*, Ref. 118).

3.1.1   AlF₃—MF

Gilbert, Mamantov and Begun laid the basis for studies of cryolite-like mixtures by a careful study of the approx. 50–50 mole percent melts of AlF$_3$ with KF—NaF mixtures.[119] The resulting spectrum (Fig. 20, curve (d)) was precisely as expected for a tetrahedral AlF_4^- anion, with one dominant polarized band (ν_1) and three weaker depolarized features, and with the relative positions and intensities of the bands being similar to those of CCl_4. Except for these four

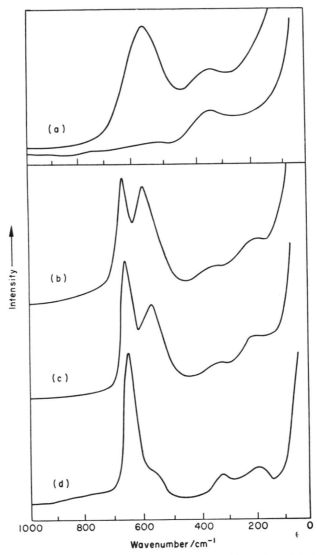

Fig. 20. Raman spectra of AlF_3 containing alkali fluoride melts of different compositions. (a) AlF_3–LiF–NaF (25.0–48.9–26.1 mole per cent) (Li_3AlF_6–Na_3AlF_6 eutectic), 790 °C. The upper and lower curves correspond to the spectra obtained with the polarization plane of the laser beam parallel and perpendicular, respectively, to the plane of observation. (b) AlF_3–NaF (37.5–62.5 mole percent) ($Na_5Al_3F_{14}$, chiolite), 805 °C. (c) AlF_3–NaF (40.6–59.4 mole percent), 760 °C. (d) AlF_3–NaF (46.2–53.8 mole percent), 805 °C. (Gilbert et al., Ref. 120).

bands, assigned as in Table 15, only weak features (535 and 465 cm^{-1}), were observed, these being produced by an impurity the concentration of which could be minimized by subliming the AlF_3.

In a subsequent study of MF-rich mixtures,[120] which yielded data compatible with that from a less extensive investigation by Ratkje and Rytter,[121] Gilbert et al. found evidence for an equilibrium between AlF_4^- and AlF_6^{3-} ions. As can be seen from Fig. 20, the spectrum was slowly transformed from that of AlF_4^- to that of AlF_6^- as the mole percent of AlF_3 was reduced from 46 to 25%. No evidence was found for the AlF_3 species in this concentration range and the dissociation of AlF_6^{3-} into AlF_4^- in the 25% AlF_3 melt was found to be very slight, in agreement with most available data but in contrast to the conclusion reached in an earlier Raman study.[122]

TABLE 15
Vibrational frequencies/cm^{-1} and force constants/10^2 N m^{-1} of AlX_4^- ions in melts[a]

Ion	$v_1(a_1)$	$v_2(e)$	$v_3(t_2)$	$v_4(t_2)$	f_d	f_d/d^2	$f_{d\alpha'}/d^2$	$(f_{d\alpha}-f_{d\alpha'})/d$
AlF_4^-	622	210	760	322	4.33	0.26	−0.10	0.53
$AlCl_4^-$	351	121	490	186	2.58	0.14	−0.04	0.30
$AlBr_4^-$	209	75	409	114	2.06	0.10	−0.02	0.17
AlI_4^-	146	51	336	82	1.59	0.08	−0.02	0.15

[a] Ref. 123.

The vibrational frequencies assigned to the AlF_6^{3-} ion were 555, 390 and 345 cm^{-1} for v_1, v_2 and v_5 respectively. As expected, the v_1 band was strongly polarized as is obvious from curve (a) of Fig. 20. The great breadth of the v_1 band, which seems to decrease as the polarizing power of the alkali metal cation is reduced, was noted by Gilbert et al.[120] as well as by Ratkje and Rytter.[121] The latter authors explain this great breadth using a model analogous to that invoked to explain the differences between the infrared and Raman frequencies for v_1, of molten nitrates (Section 3.4.1 of this review). They suggest that the AlF_6^{3-} species are variously distorted by the range of environments they experience. The v_1 frequency is presumed to be sensitive to the degree of distortion and thus a considerable range of v_1 values is possible, corresponding to the range of perturbations experienced. Since the range of perturbations should be greatest for the cation with greatest polarizing power, the observation of Gilbert et al. that the bandwidth is greatest for the lithium salt is understandable.

The AlX_4^- tetrahedral anion has two triply degenerate modes, v_3 and v_4, as well as a doubly degenerate bending vibration, v_2. The frequencies for the matrix-isolated ion-pairs, $Li^+AlF_4^-$ and $Na^+AlF_4^-$, presented in Table 8 (p. 167) show that the anion is distorted and that the degeneracies are lifted. However, as mentioned in that Section, the splitting of $v_3(t_2)$ is relatively small. These degeneracies are undoubtedly lifted in the ionic melts as well, but the broadness of the melt bands conceals the small splittings that would be observable other-wise. The matrix data indicated that the AlF_4^- ion is, relative to the NO_3^- ion, an insensitive probe of structural features and the melt data confirm this view.

3.1.2 Other AlX$_3$–MX

The ionic melts which form when equimolar quantities of AlX_3 and MX are mixed, where X is Cl, Br or I, are characterized by the presence of a stable tetrahedral MX_4^- anion, as described above for the fluoride case. Complete vibrational frequency assignments have been made for these anions by Begun et al.[123] (Table 15) and these frequencies have been used to derive the valence force field force constants included in Table 15. The data of Rytter et al.[124] support these earlier conclusions reached for the $AlCl_4^-$ system and, further, show cation field effects through values for a range of alkali metal cations. The observed frequencies listed in Table 16 show that $\nu_1(a_1)$ tends to increase with

TABLE 16
Vibrational frequencies/cm^{-1} of the AlCl$_4^-$
ion in melts with alkali metal cations^a

Cation	$\nu_1(a_1)$	$\nu_2(e)$	$\nu_3(t_2)$	$\nu_4(t_2)$
Li$^+$	348	119	512, 498, 473	182
Na^{+b}	351	121	490	184
K$^+$	350	122	487	182
Cs$^+$	344	120	483	178

^{a} Ref. 124.
^{b} From G. Torsi, G. Mamantov and G. M. Begun, *Inorg. Nucl. Chem. Lett.* 6, 553 (1970).

decreasing cation size while the large polarizing power of the Li$^+$ cation is reflected in the splitting of the degenerate $\nu_3(t_2)$ mode into three components. The variation of ν_1 is rationalized in terms of vibrational coupling of the anion with its surroundings; but, since the trend is the same as that observed for nitrate melts (see Section 1.4.1), the cation polarizability model of Brooker and Bredig,[24] which has been applied to the nitrates, might be applicable. The frequencies given in Table 8 (p. 167) show that the trend in the ν_1 frequency for the monomeric $M^+AlX_4^-$ is probably the reverse of that for the melts. It was this situation for the nitrates that prompted the Brooker–Bredig treatment.

Because of the increased ability of the heavier halides (Cl, Br, or I) to bridge between aluminium centres, the structure of the AlX_3–MX melts rich in AlX_3 differs radically from that for the fluoride case. In particular, the spectra at 67% AlX_3 are dominated by a single species that has been identified to be the bridged $Al_2X_7^-$ anion.[123] The data for these species are incomplete because of crowding of the fundamentals in the low frequency region as well as the relatively weak scattering by these systems. Nevertheless, based on the small number of Raman features (Table 17) a symmetric structure is favoured, such as an ethane-like configuration with a co-linear bridging halide.[125] There is some evidence for thermal dissociation of these species, $Al_2X_7^-$, to give increasing amounts of AlX_4^- at higher temperatures.

Rytter *et al.* offer strong evidence for increasing bridging (polymerization) at higher $AlCl_3$ concentrations and propose that $Al_3Cl_{10}^-$ is an important complex ion at 74 mole percent of $AlCl_3$.[124] Of course, as the system composition approaches 100% $AlCl_3$, the dimer Al_2Cl_6 dominates the liquid spectrum.

TABLE 17
Vibrational frequencies of
$Al_2X_7^-$ ions/cm^{-1} [a,b]

$Al_2Cl_7^-$	$Al_2Br_7^-$	$Al_2I_7^-$
435 w		360 w
		288 w, p
		220 w
313 s, p	198 s, p	137 s, p
165 m	104 m	69 m
100 m	60 m	35 m

[a] Ref. 123.
[b] w = weak; p = polarized;
s = strong; m = medium.

3.2 MBF_4, M_2BeF_4, and MgX_2—KX

All four fundamentals of the tetrahedral or distorted-tetrahedral AlX_4^- ions considered in the preceding section are Raman-active, making Raman studies of such systems particularly attractive. In the same sense, the tetrafluoroborate and tetrafluoroberyllate anions are amenable to investigation by Raman scattering. Quist, Bates and Boyd have capitalized on the development of the windowless Raman cell,[117] referred to in the preceding section, to study the BF_4^- and BeF_4^{2-} vibrational spectra in the molten alkali metal salts.[125-128] Using a nickel cell encased in a quartz tube they obtained excellent spectra, such as appear in Fig. 21 for molten $NaBF_4$, with minor problems from contamination with SiF_6^{2-} formed through BF_3 attack of the quartz envelope. It is obvious that the BF_4^- spectrum has the typical tetrahedral pattern so that the assignments presented in Table 18 are straightforward.

No splitting of degenerate BF_4^- modes has been observed for the melts, although the $\nu_2(e)$ and $\nu_4(t_2)$ bands are asymmetric while the $\nu_3(t_2)$ band is extremely broad (ca. 200 cm^{-1}). Thus the individual spectra were interpreted in terms of the anions occupying a distribution of cavities of varying symmetries, with the tetrahedral symmetry being largely preserved. Most attention was

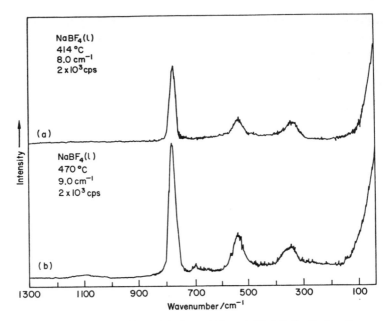

Fig. 21. Raman spectra of molten NaBF₄ at 414 and 470 °C. Radiation from an argon
ion laser (488 nm) was used to excite the spectra (Quist *et al.*, Ref. 126).

directed to the position of the ν_1 band, which was observed to decrease on
melting and also through the series Na to Cs (Table 18), analogous to the
behaviour of ν_1 for nitrates and haloaluminates. The behaviour pattern was
explained in terms of varying F—F non-bonded inter-ionic forces, but it seems
probable that there is a common reason for the similar behaviour observed for
ν_1 for the various classes of melts.

The BeF_4^{2-} spectrum is similar to that of BF_4^- as can be seen by comparison
of Fig. 22 with Figure 21. The vibrational frequencies of the BeF_4^{2-} ion were

TABLE 18
Fundamental frequencies/cm⁻¹ of the
BF₄⁻ ion obtained from the Raman
spectra of molten alkali–metal
tetrafluoroborates[a]

Cation	$\nu_1(a_1)$	$\nu_2(e)$	$\nu_3(t_2)$	$\nu_4(t_2)$
Na⁺	777	360	1070	533
K⁺	766	358	1055	525
Rb⁺	765	357	1050	523
Cs⁺	762	354	1055	520

[a] Ref. 128.

found to be relatively insensitive to the composition (% BeF_2), temperature, and cation, with typical values (those for molten Na_2BeF_4) being 550, 265, 800 and 385 cm^{-1} for ν_1 to ν_4, respectively. The most unusual feature of the spectra was the great bandwidth of the ν_1 band ($Li_2BeF_4 \approx 100$ cm^{-1}, $Na_2BeF_4 \approx 50$ cm^{-1}). This breadth has been related to an unusually large barrier to rotation,

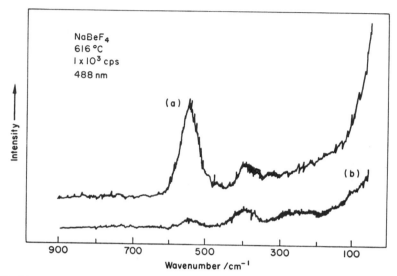

Fig. 22. Raman spectrum of molten Na₂BeF₄ at 616 °C. (a) incident light polarized perpendicular to plane containing slit and laser beam and (b) parallel polarization (Quist *et al.*, Ref. 127).

particularly for the lithium case, but this explanation seems to ignore the fact that an increased barrier would be expected in the solid state for which ν_1 is sharp. An explanation more like that offered for the breadth of ν_1 of $Al_2F_7^-$,[121] and for the difference between the infrared and Raman values for ν_1 of nitrates[52] (see Section 2.1.1), is favoured by this reviewer.

The early Raman studies of molten $MgCl_2$ produced evidence for the existence of polymeric species $[MgCl_2]_n$ with a structure resembling that of the solid.[129] Addition of KCl seems to break up the polymeric units and, at increasing KCl concentrations, $MgCl_3^-$ and possibly $MgCl_4^{2-}$ were found to replace octahedral $MgCl_6^{4-}$ as the dominant species.[129] The conclusion from a more extensive study by Maroni *et al.* which included the bromide and iodide systems as well, was that the principal equilibrium is between the MgX_4^{2-} units and the residual MgX_2 lattice.[130] In a more recent Raman investigation Maroni found all four fundamental bands as expected for the tetrahedral MgX_4^{2-} ion, for X^-/Mg^{2+} mole ratios near 4.0.[131]

The spectra included a strong polarized band (ν_1) along with three weaker depolarized features ($\nu_2-\nu_4$) for each halide system. The frequencies and corresponding Urey–Bradley force constants are presented in Table 19. No evidence was reported for the $MgCl_3^-$ species, the existence of which, like $CdCl_3^-$, has been the subject of some controversy.[132] However, a recent dynamics calculation identifies this unit as a very stable entity that is predominant in a $MgCl_2 \cdot 2KCl$ molten mixture.[133] This result has prompted Sundheim

TABLE 19
Observed Raman frequencies/cm^{-1} and corresponding Urey–Bradley force constants^a/10^2 N m^{-1} for MgX_4^{2-} ions in MgX_2–KX melts^b

Species	$\nu_1(a_1)$	$\nu_2(e)$	$\nu_3(t_2)$	$\nu_4(t_2)$	K	H	F
$MgCl_4^{2-}$	252	100	330	142	0.67	0.01	0.16
$MgBr_4^{2-}$	150	61	290	90	0.61	0.02	0.11
MgI_4^{2-}	107	42	259	60	0.54	0.01	0.08

^{a} K, H and F are the stretching, bending and interaction constants, respectively.
^{b} Ref. 142.

and Woodcock to suggest that three of the Raman bands are produced by this configuration with the fourth band being the result of K^+X^- ion pairs. This analysis also discounts the significance of any force constants for such an ionic system lacking directed chemical bonds.

3.3 ZrF_4– MF and ThF_4–MF

The Raman spectra of ZrF_4 having a range of concentrations in a low-melting molten mixture of LiF–NaF (mole ratio 0.465 : 0.535) have been reported for the lowest temperatures consistent with the various compositions.[134] The Raman spectra are complicated, being composed of broad overlapping bands, but, in general, the evidence is consistent with the existence of equilibria (involving species of differing coordination numbers) that shift as the ZrF_4 concentration is varied. At 33 mole percent ZrF_4 the spectrum resembles that of crystalline Li_2ZrF_6 for which the Zr is known to be six-coordinated. The shift of the symmetric stretching band (≈ 550 cm^{-1}) has been interpreted in terms of higher coordination numbers at lower ZrF_4 concentrations and lower coordination numbers at ZrF_4 concentrations greater than 33%, with no particular evidence for fluoride ion bridging. Coordination numbers ranging from 5 to 8 have been proposed.

Similarly, coordination numbers have been assigned to Th(IV) fluoride species from Raman spectra of ThF_4 mixtures in LiF/NaF melts having a mole ratio of 0.87.[135] Comparison with crystal spectra for Th(IV) having a known coordination number, as in Fig. 23 for a 14 mole percent ThF_4 melt, proved useful. At low ThF_4 concentrations, the ThF_4 and ZrF_4 results were similar, and comparison with data for ZrF_4 and crystalline K_5ThF_9 indicated the presence of an eight-coordinated structure for the 14% ThF_4 melt. At concentrations greater than 25 mole percent the Th(IV) system behaves differently from Zr(IV), and fluoride bridging is presumed to occur such that the coordination number does not decrease below seven.

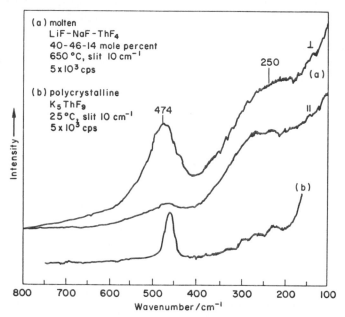

Fig. 23. Raman spectra of (a) molten LiF–NaF–ThF₄ (40–46–14 mole per cent) at 650 °C obtained with perpendicular and parallel polarizations of the incident beam and (b) polycrystalline K₅ThF₉ at 25 °C (Toth and Boyd, Ref. 135).

3.4   (Zn, Cd, Hg)X₂–MX

3.4.1   ZnX₂–MX

Pure liquid $ZnCl_2$ has an extensively bridged three-dimensional network structure with Cl^- tetrahedrally coordinated to the Zn^{2+} ion.[136,137] Angell, Wegdam and van der Elsken have concluded that the short time dynamics of $ZnCl_2$(I) near the melting point are very like those of a solid, since the infrared spectra of the glass or liquid show a remarkable resemblance to the crystal spectra at comparable temperatures.[138] An earlier study by Angell and Wong had indicated that the spectrum of glassy $ZnCl_2$ is most similar to that of the α-crystalline form.[139]

Moyer, Evans and Lo found that addition of KCl to $ZnCl_2$ in a 2:1 ratio leads to the $ZnCl_4^{2-}$ ion, judging from spectra for crystals containing this ion.[137] Their Raman data also supported the contention of Irish and Young[136] that the network structure is dominant in pure $ZnCl_2$ to temperatures well above its melting point. These authors and others have remarked on the analogy between the behaviour of this system and that of the SiO_2 liquid network that breaks up on addition of metal oxide. The initial KCl added apparently acts to limit the polymer unit size, followed by a progressive break-up of the network until the $ZnCl_4^{2-}$ ion results at a 2:1 ratio. Moyer *et al.* found no cause to invoke the presence of $ZnCl_3^-$ as Bues had done for $KCl/CdCl_2$ and $KCl/ZnCl_2$ melts.[140] By contrast, Ellis confirmed the experimental Raman results of Bues and agreed with the contention that both $ZnCl_3^-$ and $ZnCl_4^{2-}$ exist in the molten mixtures.[141] The approximate fundamental frequencies for $ZnCl_4^{2-}$ are 283 (v_1), 124 (v_4) and 75 cm^{-1}(v_2). Ellis also studied $ZnBr_2$ and $ZnBr_2$-KBr systems[136] and obtained Raman data suggesting the presence of structures like those proposed for $ZnCl_2$.

3.4.2 HgX₂–MX

Janz and James, in an early Raman study, found evidence only for molecular HgX_2 species in liquid HgX_2, though the conductivity of this liquid indicates a

TABLE 20
Band assignments and Urey–Bradley force constants^a for species in $HgCl_2$–KCl melts^b

Species	v_1	v_2	v_3	v_4	k_1	k_2	k_3
$HgCl_2$	314		376		2.11	−0.07	0.08
$HgCl_3^-$	282		287	210	1.27	0.21	0.13
$HgCl_4^{2-}$	267	180	276	192	0.82	0.49	0.08

^{a} k_1, bond stretch; k_2, bond bend; k_3, non-bonded interaction. Units are 10^2 N m^{-1}.
^{b} Ref. 138.

small amount of ionization.[142] They reflected on the source of the considerable breadth of the v_1 Raman band and concluded that its origin is not in the presence of species such as $HgCl_3^-$ but in a resonant coupling between neighbouring molecular HgX_2 oscillators. The addition of KCl was accompanied by further band broadening and shifting, and this was interpreted in terms of progressive formation of $HgCl_3^-$ and $HgCl_4^{2-}$ ions.[143] Table 20 lists the frequencies assigned to the fundamental modes of $HgCl_2$, $HgCl_3^-$ and $HgCl_4^{2-}$, along with the Urey–Bradley force constants calculated using these values.

3.4.3 CdX₂–MNO₃

Bues, from a very early Raman study, suggested that both the $CdCl_3^-$ and $CdCl_4^{2-}$ ions are present in $CdCl_2$ mixtures with alkali–metal chlorides.[140] More recently, Clarke, Hartley and Kuroda found that $CdCl_2$ and $CdBr_2$, each in an equimolar molten mixture of KNO_3–$NaNO_3$, produce a single band, regardless of the halide to Cd^{2+} ratio (264 and 164 cm^{-1} for the chloride and bromide systems, respectively).[144] From Job plots, as well as Yoe and Jones plots of their Raman data, they concluded that the dominant equilibria at all compositions are $Cd^{2+} + 3Cl^- \rightleftharpoons CdCl_3^-$ and $Cd^{2+} + 4Br^- \rightleftharpoons CdBr_4^{2-}$.

Small concentrations of $CdBr^+$ and $CdBr_2$ were also indicated at the lower Br^- concentrations with the charged species $CdBr^+$ more favoured, relative to $CdBr_2$, than for aqueous solutions.

3.5 $SnCl_2$–KCl

Like the spectra for $MgCl_2$ and $ZnCl_2$, the Raman bands of molten $SnCl_2$ have been attributed to a lattice network of $SnCl_2$ molecules, with bent $SnCl_2$ units having vibrational frequencies ≈ 225 and $110\ cm^{-1}$.[145,146] Also, addition of KCl breaks up the network and a strong new polarized feature appears near $275\ cm^{-1}$. This has been assigned to ν_1 of a monomeric $SnCl_3^-$ ion by Hathaway and Maroni as well as Clarke and Solomons.

3.6 $LaCl_3$–MCl Melts

Maroni, Hathaway and Papatheodorou have assigned a strong, highly polarized band which appears at $250\ cm^{-1}$ in the anti-Stokes Raman spectrum of $LaCl_3$–MCl melts to the symmetric stretch of the octahedral $LaCl_6^{3-}$ ion.[147] Papatheodorou has recently confirmed the earlier assignment by comparing the melt spectra with that for crystals containing octahedral $LaCl_6^{3-}$ anions.[148] Frequencies of 242 and $106\ cm^{-1}$ were assigned to the $\nu_1(a_g)$ and $\nu_5(t_{2g})$ modes of $LaCl_6^{3-}$ in molten $Cs_2Na[AlCl_6]$.

3.7   (Cu, Ag, Au) X_n—MX

Raman bands for a CuCl–CsCl melt have been found to be temperature- and composition-sensitive by Gilbert et al. who suggest that both two- and four-coordinated Cu^+ is present therein.[149] KCl behaved similarly as a diluent, with bands at $273\ cm^{-1}$ and $250\ cm^{-1}$ being assigned to fundamentals of the $CuCl_2^-$ and $CuCl_4^{3-}$ ions. However, LiCl, probably because Li^+ is comparable with Cu^+ in coordinating ability, does not promote the formation of Cu^+ species with different coordination numbers from that (four) of pure CuCl. At least, added LiCl does not affect band positions.

By contrast, the AgX spectra, with frequency values of 210, 126 and $100\ cm^{-1}$ for Cl, Br and I, respectively, were insensitive to added MX, regardless of the alkali metal, so that the same coordination number is favoured for all compositions. From comparisons with spectra of crystals and solutions a coordination number of four seems likely, this being achieved by edge-sharing of tetrahedra forming polymeric chains.

The Raman spectrum of an $AuCl_3$–KCl melt matches the spectrum for the $AuCl_4^-$ square-planar anion in the solid state.[150] Three bands (339, 318 and $171\ cm^{-1}$) have been observed, as expected, with one strong and polarized (339 cm^{-1}).

3.8   InCl$_2$, In$_2$Cl$_3$ and InCl–4MCl

The chemistry and structure of the indium chloride melts is apparently unusually complex. Unlike most other polyhalide melts discussed in this section, pure InCl$_2$ is apparently an ionic liquid consisting of ions involving the metal atom in different oxidation states, viz. In$^+$InCl$_4$$^-$. The Raman spectrum of the pure melt is that of the tetrahedral InCl$_4$$^-$ species.[151] A strong polarized Raman band at ca. 170 cm^{-1} has been assigned to an In—In stretching mode in both molten In$_2$Cl$_3$ and InCl–4MCl. This may result from In(I) disproportionating to In(III) and In(0), with the latter coordinating to the InCl$_4$$^-$.

REFERENCES

(1)   G. J. Janz and T. R. Kozlowski, *J. Chem. Phys.* **40**, 1699 (1964).
(2)   R. F. Porter and R. C. Schoonmaker, *J. Chem. Phys.* **34**, 29 (1961).
(3)   M. Eisenstadt, G. M. Rothberg and P. Kusch, *J. Chem. Phys.* **29**, 797 (1958).
(4)   A. Snelson and K. S. Pitzer, *J. Phys. Chem.* **67**, 882 (1963).
(5)   M. J. Linevsky, *J. Chem. Phys.* **38**, 658 (1963).
(6)   S. Schlick and O. Schnepp, *J. Chem. Phys.* **41**, 463 (1964).
(7)   R. L. Redington, *J. Chem. Phys.* **44**, 1238 (1966).
(8)   A. Snelson, *J. Chem. Phys.* **46**, 3652 (1966).
(9)   M. Freiberg, A. Ron and O. Schnepp, *J. Phys. Chem.* **72**, 3526 (1968).
(10) A. Snelson, *J. Phys. Chem.* **73**, 1919 (1969).
(11) Z. K. Ismail, R. H. Hauge and J. L. Margrave, *J. Mol. Spectrosc.* **54**, 402 (1975).
(12) Z. K. Ismail, R. H. Hauge and J. L. Margrave, *J. Chem. Phys.* **57**, 5137 (1972).
(13) G. Ritzhaupt and J. P. Devlin, *J. Phys. Chem.* in press (1976).
(14) B. S. Ault and G. C. Pimental, *J. Phys. Chem.* **77**, 1649 (1973).
(15) (a) A. Büchler and J. L. Stauffer, *J. Phys. Chem.* **70**, 4092 (1966); (b) personal communication from A. Büchler.
(16) D. Smith, D. W. James and J. P. Devlin, *J. Chem. Phys.* **54**, 4437 (1971).
(17) N. Smyrl and J. P. Devlin, *J. Chem. Phys.* **60**, 2540 (1974).
(18) G. Ritzhaupt and J. P. Devlin, *J. Chem. Phys.* **62**, 1982 (1975).
(19) H. E. Hallam (Ed.), *Vibrational Spectroscopy of Trapped Species*, Wiley, London, 1973.
(20) K. Butkor and V. Tschassowenny, *Acta Physicochim. URSS*, **5**, 137 (1936).
(21) A. N. Khodchenkov, V. P. Spiridonov and P. A. Akiskin, *Zh. Strukt. Khim.* **6**, 765 (1965).
(22) D. W. James and W. H. Leong, *J. Chem. Phys.* **49**, 5089 (1968).
(23) H. Brintzinger and R. E. Hester, *Inorg. Chem.* **5**, 980 (1966).
(24) M. H. Brooker and M. A. Bredig, *J. Chem. Phys.* **58**, 5319 (1973).
(25) M. E. Jacox and D. E. Milligan, *J. Mol. Spectrosc.* **52**, 363 (1974).
(26) D. W. Berreman, *Phys. Rev.* **130**, 2193 (1963). The value quoted is the average of the transverse and longitudinal mode frequencies.
(27) J. R. Ferraro and A. Walker, *J. Chem. Phys.* **42**, 1273 (1965).
(28) J. K. Wilmshurst and S. Senderoff, *J. Chem. Phys.* **35**, 1078 (1961).
(29) N. Smyrl and J. P. Devlin, *J. Chem. Phys.* **60**, 2540 (1974).
(30) D. J. Gardiner, R. B. Girling and R. E. Hester, *J. Phys. Chem.* **77**, 640 (1973).
(31) D. J. Gardiner, R. B. Girling and R. E. Hester, *J. Mol. Struct.* **13**, 105 (1972).
(32) G. Ritzhaupt and J. P. Devlin, *J. Chem. Phys.* **62**, 1982 (1975).

(33) W. H. Leong and D. W. James, *Aust. J. Chem.* **22**, 499 (1969).
(34) R. F. Porter and E. E. Zeller, *J. Chem. Phys.* **33**, 858 (1960).
(35) S. J. Cyvin, B. N. Cyvin and A. Snelson, *J. Phys. Chem.* **75**, 2609 (1971).
(36) V. P. Spiridonov and E. V. Erokhin, *Zh. Neorg. Khim.* **14**, 636 (1969).
(37) A. Snelson, B. N. Cyvin and S. J. Cyvin, *J. Mol. Struct.* **24**, 165 (1975).
(38) (a) G. L. Vidale, *J. Phys. Chem.* **64**, 314 (1963); (b) W. Klemperer and W. G. Norris, *J. Chem. Phys.* **34**, 1071 (1961).
(39) G. Ritzhaupt and J. P. Devlin, *J. Phys. Chem.* **79**, 2265 (1975).
(40) N. Smyrl and J. P. Devlin, *J. Phys. Chem.* **77**, 3067 (1973).
(41) C. G. Venkatesh, S. A. Rice and A. N. Narten, *Science*, **186**, 927 (1974).
(42) C. G. Venkatesh, S. A. Rice and J. B. Bates, *J. Chem. Phys.* **63**, 1065 (1975).
(43) D. J. Gardiner, R. E. Hester and W. E. L. Grossman, *J. Chem. Phys.* **59**, 175 (1973).
(44) A. T. Lemley and J. J. Lagowski, *J. Phys. Chem.* **78**, 708 (1974).
(45) J. W. Lundeen and R. S. Tobias, *J. Chem. Phys.* **63**, 924 (1975).
(46) D. E. Irish and A. R. Davis, *Can. J. Chem.* **46**, 943 (1968).
(47) D. E. Irish, D. L. Nelson and M. H. Brooker, *J. Chem. Phys.* **54**, 654 (1971).
(48) N. Smyrl and J. P. Devlin, *J. Chem. Phys.* **61**, 1596 (1974).
(49) M. Van Thiel, E. D. Becker and G. C. Pimentel, *J. Chem. Phys.* **27**, 486 (1957).
(50) M. Van Thiel, E. D. Becker and G. C. Pimentel, *J. Chem. Phys.* **27**, 95 (1957).
(51) A. J. Barnes and H. E. Hallam, *Trans. Faraday Soc.* **66**, 1920 (1970).
(52) G. Pollard, N. Smyrl and J. P. Devlin, *J. Phys. Chem.* **76**, 1826 (1972).
(53) D. W. James, W. H. Leong and J. Buur, *Perkin-Elmer News*, No. 19 (1968).
(54) R. E. Hester and K. Krishnan, *J. Chem. Phys.* **49**, 4356 (1968).
(55) J. P. Devlin, P. C. Li and G. Pollard, *J. Chem. Phys.* **52**, 2267 (1970).
(56) K. Williamson, P. Li and J. P. Devlin, *J. Chem. Phys.* **48**, 3891 (1968).
(57) (a) G. H. Wegdam, R. Bonn and J. van der Elsken, *Chem. Phys. Lett.* **2**, 182 (1968); (b) G. H. Wegdam, J. B. te Beek, H. van der Linden and J. van der Elsken, *J. Chem. Phys.* **55**, 5207 (1971).
(58) G. J. Janz and D. W. James, *J. Chem. Phys.* **35**, 739 (1961).
(59) J. B. Bates and G. E. Boyd, *Appl. Spectrosc.* **27**, 204 (1973).
(60) M. H. Brooker, A. S. Quist and G. E. Boyd, *Chem. Phys. Lett.* **9**, 242 (1971).
(61) J. Greenberg and L. J. Hallgren, *J. Chem. Phys.* **33**, 900 (1960).
(62) M. H. Brooker, A. S. Quist and G. E. Boyd, *Chem. Phys. Lett.* **5**, 357 (1970).
(63) J. H. R. Clarke, *Chem. Phys. Lett.* **4**, 39 (1969).
(64) J. P. Devlin and D. W. James, *Chem. Phys. Lett.* **7**, 237 (1970).
(65) D. W. James and J. P. Devlin, *J. Chem. Phys.* **56**, 4688 (1972).
(66) K. Balasubrahmanyam and G. J. Janz, *J. Chem. Phys.* **10**, 4089 (1972).
(67) J. P. Devlin, K. Williamson and G. Austin, *J. Chem. Phys.* **44**, 2203 (1966).
(68) D. W. James and J. P. Devlin, *Aust. J. Chem.* **24**, 743 (1971).
(69) D. W. James and W. H. Leong, *Aust. J. Chem.* **23**, 1087 (1970).
(70) D. W. James and W. H. Leong, *J. Chem. Phys.* **51**, 640 (1969).
(71) G. E. Walrafen and D. E. Irish, *J. Chem. Phys.* **40**, 911 (1964).
(72) C. A. Angell, J. Wong and W. F. Edgell, *J. Chem. Phys.* **51**, 4519 (1969).
(73) R. E. Hester and K. Krishnan, *J. Chem. Soc.* (A) 1955 (1968).
(74) M. Peleg, *J. Phys. Chem.* **77**, 2252 (1973).
(75) P. Li and J. P. Devlin, *J. Chem. Phys.* **49**, 1441 (1968).
(76) A. Eluard, K. Balasubrahmanyam and G. J. Janz, *J. Chem. Phys.* **59**, 2756 (1973).
(77) R. Frech, *J. Chem. Phys.* **61**, 5344 (1974).
(78) J. P. Devlin, D. W. James and R. Frech, *J. Chem. Phys.* **53**, 4394 (1970).
(79) E. Whalley and J. E. Bertie, *J. Chem. Phys.* **46**, 1264 (1967).
(80) E. V. Chisler, *Sov. Phys. Solid State*, **11**, 1032 (1969).

(81) J. P. Devlin, G. Ritzhaupt and T. Hudson, *J. Chem. Phys.* **58**, 817 (1973).

(82) G. Ritzhaupt, personal communication.

(83) J. B. Bates, M. H. Brooker, A. S. Quist and G. E. Boyd, *J. Phys. Chem.* **76**, 1565 (1972).

(84) D. E. Irish, D. L. Nelson and M. H. Brooker, *J. Chem. Phys.* **54**, 654 (1971).

(85) P. C. Van Woerkom, J. DeBleyser and J. C. Leyte, *Chem. Phys. Lett.* **20**, 592 (1973).

(86) M. H. Brooker, *J. Chem. Phys.* **53**, 2670 (1970).

(87) A. C. Gilby, J. Burr, W. Krueger and B. L. Crawford, *J. Phys. Chem.* **70**, 1525 (1966).

(88) D. E. Berreman, *Phys. Rev.* **130**, 2193 (1963).

(89) N. Smyrl, personal communication.

(90) J. W. Lundeen and R. S. Tobias, *J. Chem. Phys.* **63**, 924 (1975).

(91) J. Wong and C. A. Angell, *J. Non-Crystalline Solids*, **11**, 402 (1973).

(92) J. H. R. Clarke and P. J. Hartley, *J. Chem. Soc. Faraday Trans. II*, **68**, 1634 (1972).

(93) D. A. Nissen and B. H. Van Domelen, *J. Phys. Chem.* **79**, 2003 (1975).

(94) J. H. R. Clarke and S. Miller, *Chem. Phys. Lett.* **13**, 97 (1972).

(95) R. G. Gordon, *J. Chem. Phys.* **43**, 1307 (1965); *Adv. Mag. Res.* **3**, 1 (1968).

(96) J. K. Wilmshurst, *J. Chem. Phys.* **36**, 2415 (1962).

(97) D. W. James and W. H. Leong, *Aust. J. Chem.* **23**, 1087 (1970).

(98) B. G. Oliver and G. J. Janz, *J. Phys. Chem.* **75**, 2948 (1971).

(99) J. B. Bates, A. S. Quist and G. E. Boyd, *Chem. Phys. Lett.* **16**, 473 (1972).

(100) V. A. Maroni and E. J. Cairns, *J. Chem. Phys.* **52**, 4915 (1970).

(101) F. L. Whiting, G. Mamantov, G. M. Begun and J. P. Young, *Inorg. Chim. Acta*, **5**, 260 (1971).

(102) A. S. Quist, *Appl. Spectrosc.* **25**, 82 (1971).

(103) R. E. Hester and R. Krishnan, *J. Chem. Phys.* **49**, 4356 (1968).

(104) G. E. Walrafen, *J. Chem. Phys.* **43**, 479 (1965).

(105) J. H. R. Clarke, P. J. Hartley and Y. Kuroda, *Inorg. Chem.* **11**, 29 (1972).

(106) (a) D. L. Rousseau, R. E. Miller and G. E. Leroi, *J. Chem. Phys.* **48**, 3409 (1968); (b) R. E. Miller, R. R. Getty, L. K. Treuil and G. E. Leroi, *J. Chem. Phys.* **81**, 1385 (1969).

(107) J. H. R. Clarke and L. V. Woodcock, *J. Chem. Phys.* **57**, 1006 (1972).

(108) (a) R. Shuker and R. W. Gammon, *Phys. Rev. Lett.* **25**, 222 (1970); (b) R. Shuker and R. W. Gammon, *J. Chem. Phys.* **55**, 4784 (1971).

(109) G. Ritzhaupt and J. P. Devlin, *Chem. Phys. Lett.* **21**, 338 (1973).

(110) T. G. Chang and D. E. Irish, *J. Solution Chem.* **3**, 161 (1974).

(111) G. J. Exarhos, P. J. Miller and W. M. Risen, *J. Chem. Phys.* **60**, 4145 (1974).

(112) J. Wong and C. A. Angell, *Chem. Phys. Lett.* **18**, 221 (1973).

(113) See, for example, C. Haas and D. F. Hornig, *J. Chem. Phys.* **26**, 707 (1957).

(114) (a) F. J. Dyson, *Phys. Rev.* **92**, 1331 (1953); (b) V. M. Bermudez, *J. Chem. Phys.* **54**, 4150 (1971).

(115) R. Shuker and R. W. Gammon, in *Light Scattering in Solids* (M. Balkanski, Ed.), Flammarion Sciences, Paris, 1971, p. 334.

(116) J. P. Devlin and R. Frech, *J. Chem. Phys.* **63**, 1663 (1975).

(117) A. S. Quist, *Appl. Spectrosc.* **25**, 80 (1971).

(118) B. Gilbert, G. Mamantov and G. M. Begun, *Appl. Spectrosc.* **29**, 276 (1975).

(119) B. Gilbert, G. Mamantov and G. M. Begun, *Inorg. Nucl. Chem. Lett.* **10**, 1123 (1974).

(120) B. Gilbert, G. Mamantov and G. M. Begun, *J. Chem. Phys.* **62**, 950 (1975).

(121) S. K. Ratkje and E. Rytter, *J. Phys. Chem.* **78**, 1499 (1974).

(122) C. Solomons, J. H. R. Clarke and J. O. M. Bockris, *J. Chem. Phys.* **49**, 445 (1968).
(123) G. M. Begun, C. R. Boston, G. Torsi and G. Mamantov, *Inorg. Chem.* **10**, 886 (1971).
(124) E. Rytter, H. A. Øye, S. J. Cyvin, B. N. Cyvin and P. Klaboe, *J. Inorg. Nucl. Chem.* **35**, 1185 (1973).
(125) S. J. Cyvin, P. Klaboe, E. Rytter and H. Øye, *J. Chem. Phys.* **52**, 2776 (1970).
(126) A. S. Quist, J. B. Bates and G. E. Boyd, *J. Chem. Phys.* **54**, 4896 (1971).
(127) A. S. Quist, J. B. Bates and G. E. Boyd, *J. Phys. Chem.* **76**, 78 (1972).
(128) J. B. Bates and A. S. Quist, *Spectrochim. Acta*, **31A**, 1317 (1975).
(129) K. Balasubrahmanyam, *J. Chem. Phys.* **44**, 3270 (1966).
(130) V. A. Maroni, E. J. Hathaway and E. J. Cairns, *J. Phys. Chem.* **75**, 155 (1971).
(131) V. A. Maroni, *J. Chem. Phys.* **55**, 4789 (1971).
(132) M. A. Bredig, *Electrochim. Acta*, **5**, 299 (1961).
(133) B. R. Sundheim and L. V. Woodcock, *Chem. Phys. Lett.* **15**, 191 (1972).
(134) L. M. Toth, A. S. Quist and G. E. Boyd, *J. Phys. Chem.* **77**, 1384 (1973).
(135) L. M. Toth and G. E. Boyd, *J. Phys. Chem.* **77**, 2654 (1973).
(136) D. E. Irish and T. F. Young, *J. Chem. Phys.* **43**, 1765 (1965).
(137) J. R. Moyer, J. C. Evans and G. Y.-S. Lo, *J. Electrochem. Soc.* **113**, 158 (1966).
(138) C. A. Angell, G. H. Wedgam and J. van der Elsken, *Spectrochim. Acta*, **30A**, 665 (1974).
(139) C. A. Angell and J. Wong, *J. Chem. Phys.* **53**, 2053 (1970).
(140) W. Bues, *Z. anorg. allgem. Chem.* **279**, 104 (1955).
(141) R. B. Ellis, *J. Electrochem. Soc.* **113**, 485 (1966).
(142) G. J. Janz and D. W. James, *J. Chem. Phys.* **38**, 902 (1963).
(143) G. J. Janz and D. W. James, *J. Chem. Phys.* **38**, 905 (1963).
(144) J. H. R. Clarke, P. J. Hartley and Y. Kuroda, *Inorg. Chem.* **11**, 29 (1972).
(145) J. H. R. Clarke and C. Solomons, *J. Chem. Phys.* **47**, 1823 (1967).
(146) E. J. Hathaway and V. A. Maroni, *J. Phys. Chem.* **76**, 2796 (1972).
(147) V. A. Maroni, E. J. Hathaway and G. N. Papatheodorou, *J. Phys. Chem.* **78**, 1134 (1974).
(148) G. N. Papatheodorou, *Inorg. Nucl. Chem. Lett.* **11**, 483 (1975).
(149) B. Gilbert, K. W. Fung and G. Mamantov, *J. Inorg. Nucl. Chem.* **37**, 921 (1975).
(150) Y. M. Bosworth and R. J. H. Clark, *Inorg. Chem.* **14**, 170 (1975).
(151) J. H. R. Clarke and R. E. Hester, *Inorg. Chem.* **8**, 1113 (1969).
(152) Note added in proof: A revised assignment has recently been suggested, relating the AlF_4^- data much more closely to that of ClO_4^-, e.g. for $^7LiAlF_4$ the ν_3 band is split into components at 649, 817 and 900 cm^{-1} (R. Huglen, personal communication).

Chapter 6

RAMAN AND INFRARED SPECTRAL STUDIES OF ELECTROLYTES

D. E. Irish

Guelph-Waterloo Centre for Graduate Work in Chemistry, Waterloo Campus, Department of Chemistry, University of Waterloo, Waterloo, Ontario, Canada, N2L 3G1

M. H. Brooker

Department of Chemistry, Memorial University, Saint John's, Newfoundland, Canada, A1C 5S7

1 SCOPE

Vibrational spectral studies of electrolyte systems, with a focus on spanning the concentration range from dilute solutions to molten salts, were reviewed in 1971.[1] A comprehensive review by Tobias[2] of studies relevant to inorganic chemistry contains many references which bear on the present theme. Other reviews with a focus on water,[3,4] nonaqueous solvents[5] and electrolytes[6] have appeared and analytical reviews[7,8] draw attention to the recent literature. With this background readily available the present review will concentrate on research published since 1971. More importantly, new methods both of an experimental nature and of treating Raman and infrared data to clarify further the constitution of, and processes occurring in the system will be described in some detail. The review is limited to solutions in aqueous, nonaqueous and mixed solvents; molten salts have been excluded except where the results directly impinge on conclusions for the former systems.

2 THE THERMODYNAMIC PROBLEM

Consider an electrolyte MA, composed of cations M^+ and anions A^-, dissolved in solvent S. Depending on the nature of S and the temperature, the electrolyte may be completely dissociated and dispersed giving a system of MS_m^+ and AS_a^- in medium S; the electrolyte is then described as being 'strong' in that solvent at that temperature. A more common occurrence is the formation of ion pairs or complex ions,† MAS$_x$; the electrolyte from which these arise is said to be 'weak' in that solvent under the specified conditions. The process in the solution is then described as

$$MS_m{}^+ + AS_a{}^- \rightleftharpoons MAS_x + yS \tag{1}$$

From the balance of chemical potentials, the change in standard Gibbs free energy for the process is given by

$$\Delta G_T{}^\circ = -RT \ln K_0, \tag{2}$$

where K_0 is the quotient of activities, $a_{MA}/a_M a_A$, and solvent effects most frequently are not revealed because they are incorporated into the activity coefficients. Knowledge of K_0 permits evaluation of $\Delta G_T{}^\circ$ for the process at temperature T; this ΔG° pertains to a hypothetical process for which all reagents and products are in a defined standard state, e.g. one atmosphere pressure and hypothetical unit concentration.

Recognizing that a is a product of a concentration and an activity coefficient, a_i equals $C_i y_i$, $m_i \gamma_i$, or $X_i f_i$ for species i when concentrations are expressed in mol dm^{-3} (C), mol kg^{-1}(m) or mole fraction (X) respectively. K_0 is then expressed as

$$K_0 = \frac{[MA]}{[M][A]} \frac{y_0}{y_\pm{}^2} = Q_c Q_y \tag{3}$$

or analogous expressions for other concentration scales.‡

Q_c can frequently be measured using vibrational spectroscopy, although measurements have been restricted to relatively concentrated solutions because of low sensitivity. Only in a few cases is knowledge of $y_\pm$ available. Thus evaluation of K_0 or y_0 may not always be possible. Reported equilibrium constants often therefore refer to Q_c (also called β_i for cumulative formation constants, or K_i for step-wise formation constants of species MA$_i$ where i can range from 1 to n).

The classical problem has been concerned with the measurement of K_0 and hence $\Delta G_T{}^0$ for salts, acids, and bases in a variety of solvents, the measurement of α_i, the degree of formation of each species ($\alpha_{MA} = [MA]/[MA]_t$), the temperature-dependence of K_0 which leads to ΔH° for the process, and the pressure-dependence of K_0 which leads to ΔV° for the process. The restriction,

---

† Although the terms ion pair and complex ion are often used interchangeably the Raman spectroscopist can draw an empirical distinction between them. If the inter-ionic bond generates Raman intensity during vibration some covalence exists and the species is considered a complex. If no Raman intensity is detected the interaction is predominantly coulombic and the species can be said to be an ion pair or ion aggregate. In the latter case the association is detected by a perturbation of the spectrum of one of the ions and thus is only detectable if one of the ions is polyatomic. In the former case both ions may be monatomic.

‡ For convenience the common convention of designating the concentration of the species, i, in mol dm^{-3} as [i] is used and is equivalent to the symbol C_i. [i]$_t$ denotes the total, analytical concentration of species i.

imposed by insufficient sensitivity and by the capability of measuring only Q_c (β_i or K_i) by vibrational spectral analysis, severely limits the rigour of interpretations of data so obtained. On the positive side, vibrational spectra provide information about the system at the molecular level: structures of MS_m^+, AS_a^- and MAS_x can often be inferred and the possible alteration of the structure of S itself by the perturbing electrolyte may be sensed. The macroscopic view provided by thermodynamics is filled out by viewing the microscopic. Progress also is being made in the area of solution kinetics by utilizing Raman spectroscopy, which provides unique information about the elementary processes.

2.1   Analysis of a 1:1 Salt

A 1:1 salt can be treated rigorously if the stoichiometric activity coefficients are known.[9] Consider that the salt, of concentration m, is completely dissociated in 1 kg of solvent. The total Gibbs free energy of the system is then

$$G = \frac{1000}{F_s} \mu_s + m\mu_+ + m\mu_- \tag{4}$$

where μ_i are the chemical potentials, F_s is the formula mass of the solvent, S, and $+$ or $-$ imply cations or anions respectively. If an ion pair or complex is formed, MA, and the degree of formation of the free ions is α, the concentrations of constituents are

$$m'_+ = m'_- = \alpha m \tag{5}$$
$$m'_0 = (1-\alpha)m \tag{6}$$

where primes denote quantities which pertain to the case of partial dissociation. The total free energy of the system is now given by

$$G = \frac{1000}{F_s} \mu_s + \alpha m\mu'_+ + \alpha m\mu'_- + (1-\alpha)m\mu'_0 \tag{7}$$

where the zero subscript denotes a quantity relating to the ion pair. Noting the equality of Eqns (4) and (7) and the fact that μ_s is independent of any microscopic description of the dissociation,

$$\mu_+ + \mu_- = \alpha\mu'_+ + \alpha\mu'_- + (1-\alpha)\mu'_0 \tag{8}$$

But since ions and ion pairs are in equilibrium

$$\mu'_+ + \mu'_- = \mu'_0 \tag{9}$$

Thus

$$\mu_+ + \mu_- = \mu'_+ + \mu'_- \tag{10}$$

Equation (10) can be expressed in terms of concentrations and activity coefficients.

$$\mu_+^0 + RT \ln m_+\gamma_+ + \mu_-^0 + RT \ln m_-\gamma_- = \mu_+^{0'} + RT \ln m'_+\gamma'_+ + \mu_-^{0'} + RT \ln m'_-\gamma'_- \tag{11}$$

But the standard states are identical for the two cases being considered, so that:

$$(m_+\gamma_+)(m_-\gamma_-) = (m'_+\gamma'_+)(m'_-\gamma'_-) \qquad (12)$$

or

$$\gamma_+\gamma_- = \alpha\gamma'_+\alpha\gamma'_-$$

or

$$(\gamma_\pm)^2 = \alpha^2(\gamma'_\pm)^2 \qquad (13)$$

Values of the stoichiometric activity coefficients, $(\gamma_\pm)^2$, are frequently available. Thus Eqn (3) can be written in the form

$$K_0 = \frac{m'_0}{m'_+ m'_-} \frac{\gamma'_0}{(\gamma'_\pm)^2}$$

$$= \frac{(1-\alpha)}{m} \frac{\gamma'_0}{(\gamma_\pm)^2} \qquad (14)$$

As we have noted, in favourable cases α can be evaluated from Raman band intensities. Thus the quantity $(1-\alpha)/m(\gamma_\pm)^2$ can be evaluated as a function of concentration. Extrapolation to infinite dilution yields K_0:

$$\lim_{m\to 0} \frac{(1-\alpha)}{m(\gamma_\pm)^2} = \lim_{m\to 0} K_0(\gamma'_0)^{-1} = K_0$$

The extrapolation may not always be possible from the relatively high concentrations studied with Raman spectroscopy. However, knowledge of K_0 from a non-spectroscopic measurement will also provide the means for evaluating the activity coefficient of the ion pair, γ'_0. Thus, in principle, Raman spectroscopy provides a method for evaluation of some interesting thermodynamic quantities. The data can be used to test the validity of γ'_0's obtained from theories such as those of Kirkwood[10] and Bateman et al.[11]

The Raman study of $NaNO_3/D_2O$ provides one example of the application of the above treatment.[12] A Raman line assigned to the ion pair $Na^+NO_3^-$ occurs at 728 cm^{-1} as a shoulder on the side of a line from solvated nitrate ion which occurs at 718 cm^{-1}. Computer techniques[13] were used to partition this contour into the component lines and the ratio of intensities was used to evaluate α. If the partition is correct and the extrapolation to infinite dilution reasonable, K_0 for the ion pair association is 0.060 kg mol^{-1}; γ'_0 falls rapidly from unity and becomes virtually concentration-independent for $m \geqslant 3.5$ with a value of about 0.22. The data do not conform to expressions of the form suggested by Kirkwood[10] and Bateman et al.,[11] but those theories were developed for polar molecules in dilute solution where the solvent could be approximated by a continuum model. It is necessary to obtain γ'_0 values for more salts, and especially for cases where the results are less dependent on the band fitting of a contour of two closely spaced lines, if a significant contribution is to be made to understanding this aspect of the thermodynamics of concentrated electrolyte solutions.

However, there have been few attempts to measure γ_0' directly for such systems and the Raman method appears to be particularly suitable.

2.2   Multi-step Equilibria

In many cases where cations and anions combine, a series of complexes or ion aggregates will form. We will consider mononuclear complexes of the form MA, MA_2, $MA_3 \ldots MA_i \ldots MA_n$ where charges will depend on the particular cation and anion and have been omitted for simplicity. Equilibria are established at each temperature and composition.

$$M \quad +A \rightleftharpoons MA$$
$$MA \quad +A \rightleftharpoons MA_2$$
$$\begin{array}{ccc} \cdot & \cdot & \cdot \\ \cdot & \cdot & \cdot \end{array}$$
$$MA_{i-1}+A \rightleftharpoons MA_i$$
$$\begin{array}{ccc} \cdot & \cdot & \cdot \end{array}$$
$$MA_{n-1}+A \rightleftharpoons MA_n$$

The populations of each constituent can be described by defining the degree of formation of each species, α_i, the cumulative formation constants, β_i, and the stepwise formation constants, K_i:

$$\alpha_i = \frac{[MA_i]}{[M]_t}; \quad \beta_i = \frac{[MA_i]}{[M][A]^i}; \quad K_i = \frac{[MA_i]}{[MA_{i-1}][A]}$$

β_n is related to K_i by

$$\beta_n = \prod_1^n K_i$$

Graphical and statistical methods for evaluating equilibrium constants from a variety of different experimental methods have been extensively described.[14-19] One of these procedures which has been applied to Raman intensity data will be described here.

Consider the case where A is a polyatomic ligand with a vibrational spectrum of its own. Frequently this spectrum is altered significantly by contact with the cation. In such cases the concentrations of the free (f) anion, [A], can often be measured by acquisition of intensity data, I_f, for many solutions with compositions spanning a wide range of $[M]_t$ and $[A]_t$. [A] is given by the expression $[A] = I_f/J_f$. The molar intensity, J_f, is obtained from a separate experiment; solutions of a salt M'A, which is believed to be completely dissociated in the solvent, are prepared and the slope of the plot of I_f against [M'A] is assumed to equal J_f. Frequently the sodium salt is a good choice. In all cases the intensities are divided by that of a suitable reference standard. Choice of an internal standard minimizes errors which may occur from the variation of refractive index and absorption due to colour, in addition to long-term variation in the exciting intensity and problems of reproducing the sample geometry accurately between runs.[20] Perchlorate anion has been most extensively used for this purpose because it does not compete significantly for the cation. When solutions are prepared according to the mole ratio method[15,16] ternary samples of $M(ClO_4)$, NaA and solvent will already contain ClO_4^-. The 935 cm^{-1} band of this anion is an intense and suitable standard. It can be recorded before and after each recording of the sample and its intensity averaged. [A] is then given by

$$[A] = \frac{I_f}{I_{935}} \frac{[ClO_4^-]}{J_f}$$

where J_f has also been measured relative to the perchlorate standard. The expression assumes linearity between I_{935} and perchlorate concentration, an assumption which has been independently verified many times.

From [A] one can compute the concentration of bound A thus: $[A]_b = [A]_t - [A]$. The average ligand number $\bar{n} = [A]_b/[M]_t$ is then obtained. A plot of $\bar{n}$ against [A] should be a smooth, monotonically increasing curve, independent of the concentration of M, if polynuclear species are not present, because $\bar{n}$ is then given by

$$\bar{n} = \frac{\beta_1[A] + 2\beta_2[A]^2 + \ldots}{1 + \beta_1[A] + \beta_2[A]^2 + \ldots}$$

By either graphical or statistical procedures the problem is now to obtain a unique set of β_n which best fits the $\bar{n}$, [A] data. One computer program which has been employed with Raman intensity data is the GAUSS-Z least squares program.[18,21] An average ligand number, $\bar{n}_{calc}$, is calculated from estimated β's, total metal concentrations and [A] data. The program then performs a non-linear least squares refinement of the β's to minimize the sum of the squares of the difference between $\bar{n}_{calc}$ and $\bar{n}_{obs}$.

An example is provided by the treatment of data for the system Cd^{2+}/NO_2^-.[22] The $\bar{n}$ against [A] plot is shown in Fig. 1. The curve is represented by four β's: $\beta_1 = 61.6$, $\beta_2 = 993$, $\beta_3 = 2390$ and $\beta_4 = 1899$. The equilibrium constants are in reasonable agreement with values obtained from dilute solutions by electromotive force measurements[23] and polarography.[24] If the results are to be meaningful it is necessary to obtain many pairs of $\bar{n} - [A]$ data of high reliability. This can strain the present capability of the Raman method, especially when the band of the free anion is overlapped by bands of the complex. For another Raman study, Sr^{2+}/NO_3^-, the data are much more scattered than desirable and the values of β_1 and β_2 are sensitive to the number of data chosen for the analysis.[25] The limitations and pitfalls of these procedures have been dealt with by other authors.[17-19]

Raman spectrometers are now routinely being interfaced to computers. If band halfwidths (FWHH) are independent of composition such that band peak heights are linear functions of species concentrations it should be possible to apply programs such as SQUAD,[26] KEQUIL,[27] SCOGS,[28] or KSEEK,[29]

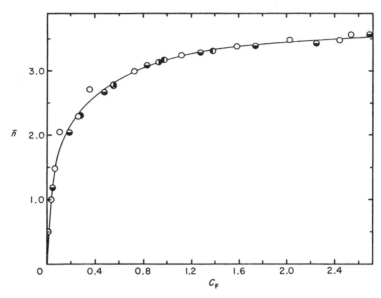

Fig. 1. The average ligand number, $\bar{n}$, plotted against free nitrite concentration for mole ratio experiments: ◑, 1.00 mol dm⁻³ Cd²⁺; ○, 0.90 mol dm⁻³ Cd²⁺; ◔, 0.40 mol dm⁻³ Cd²⁺; ◐, 0.30 mol dm⁻³ Cd²⁺ (Irish and Thorpe, Ref. 22).

developed for treatment of absorbance data, to the digitized Raman intensities. These programs are capable of evaluating stability constants, molar intensities, and concentrations of all species from estimates of the constants, observed intensities, and composition data. To date no successful application to Raman intensity data has come to our attention; convergence was not obtained when the programs were applied to the spectra of a series of solutions containing In^{3+} and Cl^{-}.[30] Again the compatibility of data obtained in successive runs and the choice of a correct baseline are prerequisites to a successful experiment.

The above treatment neglects activity coefficients and dependence on ionic strength. Nixon and Plane[31] drew attention to the constancy of concentration quotients obtained from Raman intensities from concentrated solutions and this constancy has been demonstrated many times since for metal complexing. It is also noteworthy that these constants, obtained for ionic strengths ranging from 3 to 15, appear to equal the thermodynamic constants obtained from data from dilute solutions. There is no question that ionic strength needs to be controlled when concentrations are low (e.g. $C < 0.5$ mol dm⁻³) if a meaningful interpretation is to be obtained, but the ionic medium becomes 'saturated' and ionic strength no longer appears to be an important variable of the system when the composition is best suited to Raman spectroscopy. A fundamental property of concentrated electrolytes may be implied by the Raman results and this deserves exploration.

The development of the constant ionic-medium principle has recently been summarized by Bjerrum[32] and limitations associated with its application to systems for which stability constants are less than ca. $10 \, dm^3 \, mol^{-1}$ are emphasized. Raman spectra which illustrate the degree to which the medium influences equilibria are illustrated in Fig. 2. In Fig. 2(a) the more intense, low-frequency band is the deformation mode of the solvated nitrate ion. The high-frequency shoulder is generated by the ion pairs $Sr^{2+}NO_3^-$ and $Sr^{2+}(NO_3^-)_2$.[25] The ratio of the two signals is not markedly altered when the apparent ionic strength is increased from 3 to 5.2 by the addition of a salt $NaClO_4$, or an acid $HClO_4$. This lack of sensitivity to the medium is the common experience in Raman spectroscopy. On the other hand, in a few cases a large effect has been observed. An example is presented in Fig. 2(b). The low frequency line is the

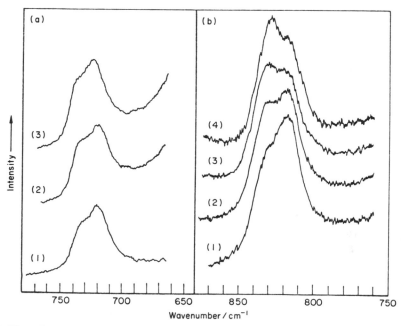

Fig. 2. The effect of ionic strength on equilibria. Panel (a): (1) 1.0 mol dm⁻³ Sr(NO₃)₂; (2) 1.0 mol dm⁻³ Sr(NO₃)₂; 2.2 mol dm⁻³ HClO₄; (3) 1.0 mol dm⁻³ Sr(NO₃)₂; 2.1 mol dm⁻³ NaClO₄. Panel (b): (1) 1.5 mol dm⁻³ Ca(ClO₄)₂; 1.5 mol dm⁻³ NaNO₂; (2) 1.0 mol dm⁻³ NaClO₄ in (1); (3) 2.5 mol dm⁻³ NaClO₄ in (1); (4) 4.0 mol dm⁻³ NaClO₄ in (1).

deformation mode of the solvated nitrite ion. The high frequency shoulder is generated by calcium–nitrite complexes.[33] Addition of $NaClO_4$, which increases the apparent ionic strength from 6 to 10, causes the latter band to increase in intensity to the point where it predominates. The reason for this is not yet entirely clear. The probability that perchlorate ion is successfully and significantly competing for the cation is low; n.m.r. data suggest negligible contact ion-association in the system $Mg(ClO_4)_2$/water.[34] A salt effect of magnitude necessary to account for the observation is also improbable. The consequences of perchlorate association have recently been reviewed by Johansson.[35] He concludes that 'for relatively few central ions has perchlorate association been proven beyond doubt to be of a magnitude that necessitates significant corrections under normal circumstances'. An insensitivity to ionic strength ($0.02 < I < 1.0$ mol dm^{-3}) of the stability of the calcium oxalate complex has also been reported.[36] Fedorov et al.[37] report that an ionic strength increase causes an increase in the complexity of the composition and in the stability of mixed chloronitrato-complexes of cadmium. These few examples indicate that much remains to be learned about ionic interactions in concentrated solution.

2.3 The Problem of Band Overlap

Because of the medium and the motions executed by the species in the liquid phase, vibrational bands tend to be broad. When a new species is formed its characteristic bands are often displaced from those of a reactant by a relatively small amount (e.g. <20 cm^{-1}) and these bands then appear as shoulders, inflexions, or at worst simply intensity contributions to a band of the reactant. Their existence and assignment may sometimes be verified by observing the change in the shape of the contour relative to that of the reactant for a wide range of composition. But if the changes in the band profile reflect changes in the populations of species which are in chemical equilibrium, and if the equilibrium process is to be quantified, individual species intensities must be obtained. One frequently hears statements to the effect that some individuals place no confidence in band fitting. Certainly results from band fitting must be critically examined. But to repudiate the procedure is to surrender the possibility of making progress, because the band overlap problem persists, and the assumptions inherent in band fitting are frequently less severe and physically more reasonable than those introduced into the analysis of other kinds of experimental data. The solution spectroscopist has one important advantage: systematic band fitting can be performed on a series of spectra of solutions with compositions which vary in a regular, defined way. A consistent set of band statistics (positions, FWHH, intensities, Cauchy–Gauss shape ratios) gives the confidence in the result which can never be gained from the band fitting of a single, isolated spectrum.

For band overlap which is not unduly severe, a procedure which combines the knowledge of the investigator and the power of numerical analysis built into a computer—a visual-aided computer procedure called CURVER[13]—is considered by its users to be more powerful than exclusively visual procedures.[38] The alternative is to use completely digital procedures.[39,40] The choice of a suitable model curve is important.[41] Generally a symmetrical shape is adopted. Functions which have been used include Gauss, Cauchy, products or sums of these,[42] or replicas of actual recorded bands.[12] 'Log normal' procedures can allow for possible non-symmetrical band shapes.[43]

One limitation of all band-fitting programs is the possible arbitrariness in the choice of the number of component lines (NC) used to fit the envelope of interest. Frequently the smallest possible number has been used on the grounds that one can always achieve a fit with a larger number, but judgement is required if a physically meaningful result is to be obtained.[44] A new approach is now possible. Bulmer and Shurvell have developed an independent method called factor analysis or principal component analysis (PCA) to evaluate NC[45] and have applied it to infrared spectral data. PCA involves no assumption concerning the band shape. A set of absorbance values A_{ij} is measured for each sample, j, of a series of NS mixtures at wavenumbers designated i. These values, normalized to unit path length, are the sums of the product of molar absorptivities ε_{ik} and species concentrations C_{kj}, where the sum runs from species $k = 1$ to $k = \text{NC}$. Thus

$$A_{ij} = \sum_k^{NC} \varepsilon_{ik} C_{kj}$$

The set of absorbance values is expressed in matrix notation, $\mathbf{A} = \mathbf{EC}$. The dimensions of the matrices are: $\text{NW} \times \text{NS}$ for the absorbance, $\text{NW} \times \text{NC}$ for the molar absorptivity and $\text{NC} \times \text{NS}$ for the concentration, where NW is the number of wavenumbers at which the absorbance was measured and the other quantities are as defined above. Experimental conditions are arranged so that $\text{NW} > \text{NS} > \text{NC}$ for which it has been shown[46] that the rank of $\mathbf{A}$ is equal to NC, provided the spectrum of one of the components is not a linear combination of the spectra of the other components and that the concentration of one or more species cannot be expressed as a linear combination of the concentrations of the other species for all experiments performed.

To obtain the rank and hence solve for NC, the matrix $\mathbf{Q} = \tilde{\mathbf{A}}\mathbf{A}$, with dimensions ($\text{NS} \times \text{NS}$), is obtained and diagonalized; $\tilde{\mathbf{A}}$ is the transpose of $\mathbf{A}$. The number of statistically non-zero eigenvalues equals NC. Four statistical criteria are described in the paper[45] for selecting the eigenvalues which do not arise from experimental error and computational procedures.

The procedure was applied to the study of self-association of acetic acid[45] and trichloroacetic acid[47] in CCl_4 and the formation of a complex between CCl_3D and di-n-butyl ether.[48] The number of component bands given by PCA was compared to that obtained by band fitting and the latter number was adjusted as necessary to obtain physically reasonable results. In one case[47] disagreement between PCA and band fitting caused the authors to examine the Cauchy–Gauss shape ratio of one of the components; the considerable change in this parameter with change in composition suggested the presence of an unresolved component. This example points up how PCA complements and improves band fitting procedures. Data for the CCl_3D di-n-butyl ether complex, normalized to unit concentration and path length, do not exhibit a traditional isosbestic point despite the fact that the PCA method clearly indicated the presence of two absorbing components.[48] This is a consequence of the large difference between the molar absorptivities of the absorbing components. It is shown that normalization of the spectra to unit area generates a 'pseudo-isosbestic' point for such cases. A band-fitting method,[46,49] based on assuming a stoichiometry rather than a band shape, was modified[48] in order to fit decidedly asymmetric component lines to the spectral envelope. From estimates of equilibrium constants and the experimental compositions, species concentrations and molar absorptivities of each absorbing species at each wavenumber were obtained. Absorbances were computed and compared with experimental absorbances. The K's were refined until the sum of squared residuals was below an acceptable level.

The methods described in these papers have direct applicability to many studies of the processes which occur in electrolyte solutions. Band fitting has been extensively applied in the twelve years since the development of the Pitha and Jones programs but the persistent weakness has been the choice of NC. PCA is the most significant advance to date in removing this weakness of the procedure.[50] It has been adapted for use with Raman spectra and applied in the analysis of spectra of aqueous solutions containing a series of chloro-indium(III) complexes.[30,51] PCA provides a virtually unique approach to the difficult task of interpreting such overlapping Raman spectra, providing the heights of Raman bands are proportional to the concentrations of species (i.e. that the FWHH is independent of composition) and that no undesired linear combinations as described earlier exist.

Other ways of detecting band overlap and confirming the conclusions of PCA exist when spectra are obtained in digital form. Butler and Hopkins[44] have considered the consequences of obtaining higher derivatives of the band envelopes. For a series of spectra comparisons of the position of the centroid with respect to the peak maximum, the parts of the FWHH which fall to left and right of the peak maximum, the third moment which provides a measure of band asymmetry, and the second and fourth moments which provide information about the Cauchy–Gauss ratio provide insight into the possible contributions to the observed spectral profiles.[52] These quantities were obtained for the Raman bands arising from chloroindium(III) complexes[30] in order to complement the PCA analysis and attempt to resolve the controversy concerning the number of scattering species.[53] The value of treating band profiles in this way can only be established from the experience gained from investigations of several systems.

2.4   The Effect of Temperature on Chemical Equilibria

Ideally one should be able to obtain useful thermodynamic data from the effect of temperature on the stability constants determined by vibrational spectroscopy. The standard free-energy change, $\Delta G°$, for the formation of a $1:1$ complex is given by

$$\Delta G_T^0 = -RT \ln K_0$$

The standard free-energy change varies with temperature according to the well-known equation of van't Hoff,

$$\frac{d(\ln K_0)}{dT} = \frac{\Delta H°}{RT^2}$$

or

$$\frac{-d(R \ln K_0)}{d\left(\dfrac{1}{T}\right)} = \Delta H°$$

A plot of $(-R \ln K_0)$ versus the reciprocal of the absolute temperature will give the standard enthalpy of formation of the complex, $\Delta H°$, and the standard entropy of complex formation, $\Delta S°$, may be obtained from the definition of G,

$$\Delta S° = \frac{\Delta H° - \Delta G°}{T}$$

In practice, a number of factors militate against the use of vibrational spectroscopy for thermodynamic measurements and very little effort has been devoted to this end.[54–56] (a) Perhaps the most serious problem is again the fact that at the concentrations normally required to obtain infrared and Raman spectra, one does not measure the true equilibrium constant, K_0. Values for $\Delta G°$, $\Delta H°$, $\Delta S°$ thus obtained[54–56] do not refer to any normal standard state and are of qualitative significance only. (b) The effect of temperature is often small, and even temperature changes of as much as 65 °C may result in relative intensity changes of bands due to free and bound species of only 5–10%[57] which is not significantly greater than the experimental error in the intensities, especially since the higher temperature species give rise to broader bands. In this regard there have been several reports[58, 59] concerning the effect of temperature on Raman intensities. (c) Evaluation of $\Delta H°$ and $\Delta S°$ by the van't Hoff equation requires the assumption that the difference between the heat capacities of products and reactants, ΔC_p, is negligible over the temperature range in question since

$$\Delta H_T° = \Delta H_{298}° + \int_{298}^{T} \Delta C_p \, dT$$

$$\Delta S_T° = \Delta S_{298}° + \int_{298}^{T} \frac{\Delta C_p}{T} \, dT$$

Over the temperature range of liquid water, the assumption that $\Delta C_p \approx 0$ is probably not as serious as (a) and (b) above. (d) If two or more complexes exist in solution simultaneously, which is often the case, the problem of evaluating the thermodynamic functions for each process would be greatly complicated. These inadequacies should be kept in mind throughout the discussion which follows.

Al-Baldawi et al.[54] have studied the effect of temperature on the formation of inner sphere $ZnNO_3^+$ in anhydrous methanol. Complex formation was strongly favoured by increased temperature (Fig. 3). Lemley and Plane[55]

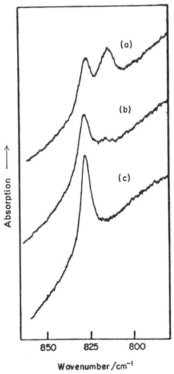

Fig. 3. Infrared spectra, in the 800 cm^{-1} region, of a 1.2 mol dm^{-3} solution of zinc nitrate in anhydrous methanol. Sample temperature: (a) 38, (b) −10, (c) −30 °C (Al-Baldawi et al., Ref. 54).

obtained similar results for inner-sphere $ZnNO_3^+$ in extremely concentrated aqueous $Zn(NO_3)_2$ solutions. Lemley and Plane also report evidence for the presence of an outer-sphere complex, $Zn(H_2O)_6NO_3^+$. Chatterjee et al.[56] have obtained similar results for inner-sphere association of $MgSO_4$ ion pairs. A value of $\Delta H = 2.9 \pm 1$ kcal mol^{-1} (12.1 $\pm$ 4 kJ mol^{-1}) was obtained and this compares favourably with the value of 1.15–1.36 kcal mol^{-1} (4.81–5.69 kJ mol^{-1}) obtained by calorimetry.[60] Thermodynamic parameters obtained by both spectroscopic[54, 56, 61] and classical methods[62−64] are presented in Table 1

TABLE 1
Thermodynamic data[c] for complex formation

System	K / mol^{-1} dm^3	$\Delta G°$/kcal mol^{-1}	$\Delta H°$/kcal mol^{-1}	$\Delta S°$/cal mol^{-1} K^{-1}	Method	Reference
(a) Inner-sphere complexes						
$ZnNO_3^+$ in CH_3OH, 25 °C	3.0	−0.65[a]	+3.0	+12[a]	Infrared	54
$ZnNO_3^+$ in H_2O, 50 °C	4.2	−0.91	+12	+40	Raman	55
$ZnCl^+$ in H_2O, 25 °C, $I = 0$	2.7	0.48	2.83	7.9	Potentiometric	62
$ZnCl^+$ in H_2O, 25 °C, $I = 1.0$	0.73	+0.19	3.1	9.8	Potentiometric	62
$ZnCl^+$ in H_2O, 25 °C, $I = 2.0$	0.67	+0.24	1.6	4.3	Potentiometric	62
$ZnCl^+$ in H_2O, 25 °C, $I = 3.0$	1.0	0	3.6	11.9	Potentiometric	62
$ZnCl^+$ in H_2O, 25 °C, $I = 4.0$	1.4	−0.20	4.1	14.2	Potentiometric	62
$MgSO_4$ in H_2O, 25 °C	0.094[a]	+1.4[a]	2.9	14[a]	Raman	56
$CeSO_4^+$ in H_2O, 25 °C	17.5	−1.69	4.27	20	Calorimetric titration	63
$CeSO_4^+$ in H_2O, 25 °C	20	−1.8	4.2	20	Solvent extraction	63
$EuSO_4^+$ in H_2O, 25 °C	23.8[a]	−1.87	3.88	19.3	Calorimetric titration	63
$EuSO_4^+$ in H_2O, 25 °C	24	−1.9	4.3	21	Solvent extraction	63
(b) Outer-sphere complexes[b]						
$Co(NH_3)_5H_2O.SO_4^+$ in H_2O, 25 °C	1.44	−0.22	−4.0	−13	Spectroscopy (visible)	61
$Zn(H_2O)_6NO_3^+$ in H_2O, 50 °C	0.25	0.89	−3.8	−14.5	Raman	55
$EuNO_3^{2+}$ in H_2O, 25 °C	2.10	−0.41	−0.57	−0.54	Solvent extraction	64

[a] Calculated from available data.
[b] Some doubt exists as to the outer-sphere nature of these complexes. See text.
[c] 1 cal = 4.184 J, I = ionic strength.

for several similar systems. Except for the rather high values of Lemley and Plane for the inner-sphere $ZnNO_3^+$ complex, the $\Delta H°$ and $\Delta S°$ values for the inner-sphere complexes are quite similar. The effect of ionic strength, I, on the $ZnCl^+$ values is not too pronounced, which suggests that even though actual K_0's may not be measurable by vibrational spectroscopy the $\Delta H°$ and $\Delta S°$ values obtained by temperature studies may prove useful. Positive values of $\Delta H°$ and $\Delta S°$ have been interpreted to indicate predominantly inner-sphere complexes.[63,65] Available vibrational data for the $ZnNO_3^{+}$[54,55] and $ZnCl^+$[66] species also support inner-sphere complexes. Most workers have concluded that the lanthanide sulfates form inner-sphere complexes[63,65]; however, from infrared studies of the ν_3 region of sulfate Larsson[67] has calculated that there is only about 12% inner-sphere complexation in 0.1 mol dm^{-3} $Ce_2(SO_4)_3$. Raman studies of these systems would be worthwhile to clarify this point.

Values of $\Delta H°$ and $\Delta S°$ obtained by Lemley and Plane[55] for the outer-sphere $Zn(H_2O)_6NO_3^+$ complex are remarkably similar to the values for the well-documented outer-sphere complex, $Co(NH_3)_5(H_2O)(SO_4)^+$, reported by Taube and Posey.[61] Ahrland[65] has suggested that outer-sphere complexes should be expected to have less positive values for $\Delta H°$ and $\Delta S°$ than inner-sphere complexes. Although it would appear that Ahrland's suggestion is borne out by the present data, there are doubts. One should be aware that the Raman results of Lemley and Plane rely heavily on data obtained by curve resolution of the envelope in the ν_3 NO_3^- region into six components. Sze[68] has shown that consistent fits of this region can be obtained with only four bands and thus questions the significance of the Lemley and Plane analysis. Further discussion of this system is deferred to Section 7.6. Similarly, the outer-sphere $EuNO_3^{2+}$ complex is open to question since Raman results for the similar $CeNO_3^{2+}$ strongly suggest inner-sphere complexes with $K_1 = 1.68$,[69] which is reasonably close to the outer-sphere value of $K_1 = 1.63$ reported by Choppin and Strazik.[64] Hester and Plane[70] have measured the temperature-dependence of the formation of $CaNO_3^+$ by Raman spectroscopy and arrived at a value of $\Delta H° = -0.26$ kcal mol^{-1} (-1.1 kJ mol^{-1}). On the basis of Ahrland's proposal one could be tempted to suggest an outer-sphere complex but all available spectroscopic data indicate that the complex is inner-sphere. Mathieu and Lounsbury[71] also studied spectra of solutions of $Ca(NO_3)_2$ and $Th(NO_3)_4$ over a range of temperatures and in both cases observed that complex formation was favoured at higher temperatures; therefore, positive values of $\Delta H°$ are inferred. It is possible that systematic errors associated with Raman intensity measurements are responsible for the discrepancies between the data of the two groups. At the present time, there appears to be no simple method for differentiating between inner and outer-sphere complexes.

On the basis of the electrostatic model[72-74] one expects an increase in complex formation with increased temperature. A number of non-spectroscopic studies reaffirm this view.[62,75,76] The usual explanation is that because the dielectric constant, ϵ, decreases with increased temperature[77] complex formation is favoured. Linear relationships between $\log K$ and ϵ^{-1} are often observed over small temperature ranges.[72,78,79] The available data (Table 1) for the proposed outer-sphere complexes suggest that, quite unexpectedly, these complexes are less favoured at higher temperatures. Equilibrium constants for $EuNO_3^{2+}$ decrease with increased temperature *and* ionic strength;[64] and both $Zn(H_2O)_6NO_3^+$ and $Co(NH_3)_5(H_2O)(SO_4)^+$ were more dissociated at higher temperatures.[55,61] There are too few data available to draw definite conclusions concerning these unusual results.

Marshall and Quist[78,80] have proposed that the dielectric constant of the solvent may not be the only significant factor in ion–association, and ion–solvent interactions must be considered, while Cobble[81] has stressed that it is the product, ϵT, of the dielectric constant and the absolute temperature, T, raised to an appropriate power that is important in calculations of ion pairing. Marshall and Quist[78,80] have proposed inclusion of the activity coefficient of the solvent in a complete expression for the equilibrium constant, K°,

$$K^\circ = \frac{a_{M^+}a_{A^-}}{a_{MA}a_{H_2O}^k}$$

which is related to the conventional equilibrium constant, K_0, by

$$K^\circ = \frac{K_0}{a_{H_2O}^k}$$

Matheson[82] and Gilkerson[83] have both objected to the Quist and Marshall complete equilibrium constant; however, the simplicity of this approach makes it attractive. The similarity between the complete equilibrium constant of Quist and Marshall and the place exchange equilibrium constant described by Braunstein[84] and employed by Irish and co-workers[12,85] to interpret Raman data is noteworthy. The participation of the solvent in molecular-complex equilibria has also been quantitatively demonstrated by Mehdi *et al.*[86]

At very high and critical temperatures further complications occur since it is necessary to pressurize the system. The dielectric constant of water also increases with increased pressure;[77] consequently, under hydrothermal conditions, temperature and pressure effects will tend to work in opposition. Although very little has been attempted in this difficult area, Franck[87] has reported preliminary Raman studies of HDO and $ZnCl_2$ solutions at very high temperature and pressure, while Buback[88] has investigated liquid ammonia at high temperatures and pressures. Cobble[81] has also discussed the applications of solution chemistry under hydrothermal conditions, and Valyashko[89] has proposed a model for solution structure which accounts for H_2O–H_2O, ion–H_2O and ion–ion interactions and variations of these interactions with temperature.

2.5   The Effect of Pressure on Chemical Equilibria

The application of pressure to a system in which hydrated ions are in equilibrium with complex ions or molecules generally causes a shift to favour the side with greater total charge. This shift is consistent with the fact that the sum of the partial molar volumes of the ions is less than the partial molar volume of the complex or molecules.[90-95] Water molecules in the primary hydration spheres of ions have greater density than those in the bulk solvent or those in the intermediate or 'cluster' zone.[93] This electrostriction results in a volume decrease and more ions will therefore be created in response to the applied pressure stress. Pressure also reduces the molar volume in the intermediate solvation zone and ultimately the molar volume in this region will become less than that in the less compressible electrostricted region. The structure of the primary hydration sphere will then be destroyed.[93]

The technique and scope of high pressure Raman experiments have recently been reviewed by Whalley.[94] Of interest here is the potential of Raman spectroscopy to sense the effect of pressure on ionic equilibria and on solvents. Two-window cells, for collection of the Raman light scattered at 180° to the excitation (back scattering) from liquids under pressure, have been described by Walrafen[96] and Davis and Adams.[97] In later work, Davis and Adams indicated preference for a three-window cell and 90° collection optics.[98] A three-window cell was described by Nicol et al.[99] Four-window cells for study of nonaqueous solutions[100] and condensed gases[101] have also been described.

The use of Raman spectroscopy to sense the effect of pressure on chemical equilibria will be illustrated with several examples. The degree of dissociation of the bisulfate ion is increased by application of pressure.[98]

The direct observation of this equilibrium shift consists of the increase in the intensity of the 982 cm^{-1} line of SO_4^{2-} and the decrease of the intensity of the 1052 cm^{-1} line of HSO_4^- (Fig. 4). The change in this intensity ratio was translated into a change in the concentration quotient for dissociation $Q_v = [SO_4^{2-}][H_3O^+]/[HSO_4^-]$; this quantity almost doubled for a 1000-fold increase in pressure, a change comparable to that inferred from the pressure dependence of the conductivity of sulfuric acid.[102]

The effect of pressure on the equilibrium

$$Mg^{2+} + SO_4^{2-} \rightleftharpoons MgSO_4$$

has been studied.[56] A high-frequency shoulder at 995 cm^{-1} on the more intense 982 cm^{-1} line of SO_4^{2-} was attributed to the formation of the contact ion-pair.[103] One disconcerting aspect of the interpretation is the apparent constancy of the degree of formation of the ion pair (0.11 for $0.1 < C < 2.50$) for a wide composition range.[103] This is possibly related to the difficult task of correctly measuring the intensity of the shoulder. This intensity decreased as anticipated on increase of pressure;[56] pressures of 0.078–1.030 kbar (0.078–

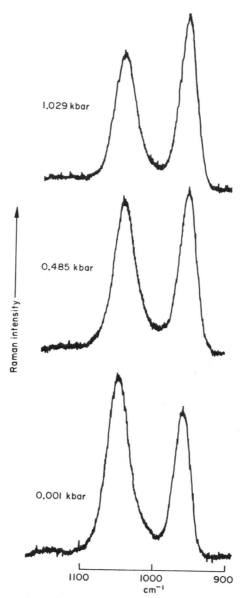

Fig. 4. Raman spectra of a 1.93 mol dm⁻³ KHSO₄ solution, between 900 and 1100 cm⁻¹, recorded at the pressures indicated and 26 °C (Davis *et al.*, Ref. 98).

1.030×10^8 Pa) were applied at four temperatures: 7.0, 10.5, 18.5 and 25.0°C.
Introduction of the concentration quotient $Q_v = [Mg^{2+}][SO_4^{2-}]/[MgSO_4]$ into
the approximate expression

$$RT \left(\frac{\partial \ln Q_v}{\partial P} \right)_{T,P} = -\Delta \bar{V} - RT\beta,$$

where β is the isothermal compressibility of water, gave an approximate value
for $\Delta \bar{V}$, the volume change associated with the ionic equilibrium, of $-20.3 \pm$
1.4 cm^3 mol^{-1}.

This value is much larger than the -7.3 cm^3 mol^{-1} inferred by Fisher[104]
from conductivity data. Millero and Masterton[105] have arrived at a value of
-7.2 to -8.3 cm^3 mol^{-1} at 25°C from consideration of single-ion partial molar
volumes, and have found that the value increases with increasing concentration.
To account for the difference Chatterjee et al.[56] concluded that one cannot
distinguish between solvated sulfate ions and solvent-separated ion-pairs with
Raman spectroscopy, and thus the $\Delta \bar{V}$ measured by this method is a composite
of values for three equilibria

$$Mg^{2+}(aq) + SO_4^{2-}(aq) \rightleftharpoons Mg(H_2OH_2O)SO_4 \rightleftharpoons Mg(H_2O)SO_4 \rightleftharpoons MgSO_4$$

The neglect of activity coefficients and the error in the intensities derived from
band-fitting procedures can also significantly affect the value of $\Delta \bar{V}$. Thermodynamics only provides a relationship between $\Delta \bar{V}°$ and the thermodynamic K; the
volume change refers to a hypothetical process in which all species are in a defined
standard state. Thus one can reasonably ask what physical significance is to be
attached to values obtained by the non-rigorous approach of replacing K by Q
and neglecting the effect of pressure on the activity coefficients? To answer this
question a very large number of good quality Raman intensity data for a wide
range of both composition and pressure must be collected for a system where
there is no ambiguity about the process.

3 THE KINETIC PROBLEM

Ionic equilibria between free ions and ion-pairs or complexes are generally
established in time intervals so short that special techniques must be employed
to gather kinetic data. Raman band profiles are providing a new method for the
study of very fast reaction processes and correlation times of reorientational
motions. Some reactions, such as hydrolysis or atom transfer between ions,
occur slowly; for these, changes in Raman band intensities with time provide a
means of obtaining specific rate constants and rate laws, but this approach has
not been widely used. It is only recently that infrared and Raman studies have
become sufficiently quantitative to compete with electronic spectroscopy but still
the weak signals, poor spectrophotometric accuracy, sample handling problems,
and high costs limit vibrational studies of rate processes to very few systems.
Further developments in technique seem certain to alter this situation, although
the cost factor will remain.

Lephardt and Vilcins[106] have applied Fourier Transform Spectroscopy to infrared studies of the gas phase reaction of N_2O_4–NO_2 mixtures with butadiene and demonstrated the potential of this technique for further studies. Delhaye[107] has developed techniques for obtaining Raman spectra at very high speeds through the use of image intensifiers and Vidicon tubes (see Chapter 4 of this volume). Bridoux et al.[108] have obtained well-resolved spectra with good signal-to-noise ratio in the ms–ns range employing these techniques and Manfait et al.[109] have described a fully digital Raman spectrometer used in synchronism with a multichannel analyser operating in the multiscaler mode. Delhaye, Bridoux and co-workers[107,108,110] have demonstrated the usefulness of the system for applications to Raman spectroscopy of time-evolving samples. The reactions $2\,NOBr \rightleftharpoons 2\,NO + Br_2$ and $2\,NOCl \rightleftharpoons 2\,NO + Cl_2$, for which the half-lives of the reactants are from 1 to 10^3s, were examined in the gas phase.[107] Results have also been presented for Cl_2, Br_2, CO_2, N_2, air, O_2, Me_2CO, $GeCl_4$, and C_2H_2.[110] Sombret and Wallart[111] have employed rapid Raman methods to follow the disproportionation of NaBrO. Raman peaks at 620, 710, and 805 cm^{-1} due to the BrO^-, BrO_2^-, and BrO_3^- species respectively were used to determine the various concentrations of the species present. It was observed that BrO_2^- was produced in the initial step but was subsequently consumed to produce the final product, BrO_3^- (Fig. 5). The reaction was followed over a 10 min period.

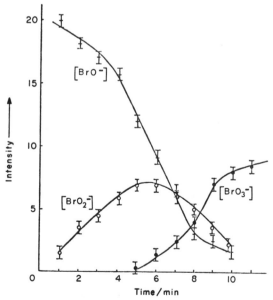

Fig. 5. Evolution of the intensities of the Raman bands for the species BrO^-, BrO_2^- and BrO_3^- as a function of time (min) during decomposition of BrO^- (Sombret and Wallart, Ref. 111).

Sze and Irish[112] have employed conventional Raman spectroscopy to follow the relatively slow rate of hydrolysis of acetonitrile, catalyzed by Hg(II). Raman bands at 2275 and 2305 cm^{-1}, characteristic of CH_3CN bound to Hg^{2+}, were found to decrease in intensity with time and the data were fitted to a second-order rate law: rate = $k[CH_3CN]_b[H_2O]$ with $k = (1.75 \pm 0.10) \times 10^{-6}$ mol^{-1} dm^3 s^{-1} at 25 °C. In the proposed mechanism, a water molecule reacts with the mercury(II)-bound acetonitrile molecule to form a mercury(II)–acetamide complex. Raman lines characteristic of the acetamide intermediate were also detected. Glasoe and Bush[113] have utilized the OH and OD infrared active stretching modes to measure the rate of formation of HOD in the exchange between D_2O and hydrogen in glass and between H_2O and deuterium in glass. Similar quantitative studies of the OH peak of $NaBF_3(OH)$ in molten $NaBF_4$ were employed to determine the stability of BF_3OH^- ion.[114] Walrafen[115] has detected the OH stretching peak in Raman spectra of silica glass.

A number of studies have been undertaken with the aim of elucidating reaction mechanisms. Woodruff and Spiro[116] have employed resonance Raman spectroscopy to detect reaction intermediates in a rapid mixing, continuous flow technique. Clase et al.[117] have studied the products of hydrogenation of aqueous pentacyanocobaltate(II) and the reactions of hydridopentacyanocobaltate(III) with 1,3-butadiene in work directed toward identifying intermediates in $Co(CN)_5^{3-}$ homogeneous catalyzed hydrogenation reactions. Infrared studies have also been used to study reactions in the acetic anhydride-sulfuric acid system[118] and Bukowska and Kecki[119] have correlated the shift in C=O and C—C—C bands with reactivity of acetone molecules in aldolic condensation reactions. Kinugasa et al.[120] have followed the proton transfer from $HClO_4$ to CH_3CN using infrared methods.

It is interesting to note that the Raman effect has been used in a laser temperature-jump apparatus.[121] The stimulated Raman effect in liquid nitrogen was used to shift the radiation of a neodymium-glass laser from 1.06 μm, where absorbance of water is small, to 1.41 μm where water absorbs strongly and could be heated by the laser pulse. The rate constants for the reaction $I_2 + I^- \rightleftharpoons I_3^-$ were measured. Genser and Connick[122] have also studied the rate of exchange for this system by n.m.r. line-broadening techniques.

Dynamic properties of liquids and solutions are determined by intermolecular forces which in turn are responsible for variations in infrared, Raman, and Rayleigh band-shapes. A large number of papers have been devoted to studies of the vibrational and rotational correlation functions which may be obtained from the Fourier transform of infrared and Raman vibrational band contours.[122–128] These studies are outside the scope of this review but a reasonable cross-section of the recent relevant literature has been included. It is interesting to note that in some solutions rotational fine structure of essentially freely rotating molecules has been reported.[129,130] Depolarized Rayleigh light scattering has also been employed to study dynamic processes in liquid systems[131–133] provided that the molecules are not large enough to act as strong scattering centres. Generally, it is assumed that Rayleigh light scattering arises from non-propagating entropy fluctuations due primarily to collision processes, but it has been proposed[134] that the spectral distribution of Rayleigh light scattering (0–3 cm^{-1} region) could permit studies of fast chemical reactions, such as ligand exchange reactions in aqueous solution, e.g.

$$Zn^{2+}(aq) + SO_4^{2-}(aq) \rightleftharpoons ZnSO_4(aq) + H_2O$$

Detailed studies of the Rayleigh scattering from aqueous solutions of $ZnSO_4$, $MnSO_4$ and CsF were undertaken to test this hypothesis but no evidence was found for any additional light scattering due to the fast chemical exchange processes.[135] In all cases the spectra were accounted for by assuming that diffusional concentration fluctuations dominated the light scattering.

In favourable cases infrared and Raman band-shapes can be employed to measure rapid chemical processes. Kreevoy and Mead[136] were able to relate the increase in half-width, w, from that of the dilute solution, w_0, with the mean lifetime of the vibrating species, τ, by the equation

$$w - w_0 = 1.06 \times 10^{-11} (\tau)^{-1}$$

which is identical to that for slow exchange broadening of an n.m.r. line. Chen and Irish[137] have measured the dependence of the halfwidth of the 981 cm^{-1} peak of SO_4^{2-} on H_3O^+ concentration. Halfwidth changes of about 20 cm^{-1} were measured and correlated with proton transfer processes occurring in solution. An apparent rate law

$$\text{rate} = k[H_3O^+](a_w)^x[SO_4^{2-}]$$

was inferred with $k^H = 6.4 \times 10^{11}$ mol^{-1} dm^3 s^{-1} and $k^D = 10.4 \times 10^{11}$ mol^{-1} dm^3 s^{-1}. The viscosity independence of the halfwidth of the 981 cm^{-1} line of SO_4^{2-} further supported the ultra-fast proton exchange mechanism.[138]

Halfwidth changes which accompanied the increase in concentration for aqueous solutions of $LiNO_2$, $NaNO_2$, KNO_2, and $CsNO_2$ were unusual insofar as the values for KNO_2 and $CsNO_2$ decreased with concentration whereas the $LiNO_2$ value increased.[139] The results were interpreted in terms of collision theory; rate constants for encounters between NO_2^- and H_2O decrease in the same order as the solubility: $k_K > k_{Cs} > k_{Na}$. A higher rate of encounters, observed for collisions between $Li^+(aq)$ and NO_2^-, was attributed to solvent-shared ion-pairs.

Since the rates of ligand exchange processes are important to the understanding of vibrational spectroscopic studies of complex formation[54, 140] two of the more suitable reviews on this subject are referenced.[141, 142]

Finally, the hydrogen-bonding studies of Zundel and co-workers[143] will be mentioned, not because they explicitly belong in a section on rate processes, but hydrogen bonding does cause line broadening. Zundel has demonstrated that a continuous absorption is present in the infrared spectra of a number of aqueous and non-aqueous acid and base solutions which is caused by protons or defect protons tunnelling in a double minimum potential well in hydrogen bonds. An extremely high polarizability is associated with the interaction. Experimental findings have demonstrated that as the tunnelling frequency decreases (weaker hydrogen bonds) the infrared continuum disappears.[143] Montrose et al.[144] have employed depolarized Rayleigh scattering to obtain a value of 5×10^{-13} s for the mean lifetime of a hydrogen bond in water.

4   RECENT DEVELOPMENTS IN EXPERIMENTATION

For electrolyte studies, the background spectrum of the solvent or bands of some components may interfere with the measurement of parameters of bands of interest. Difference spectroscopy has been developed to facilitate comparisons of spectra of samples and blanks and to quantify band shifts.

A split-beam, two-cell arrangement has been described by Bodenheimer et al.[145] A rotating, partitioned, cylindrical cell has been described by Kiefer.[146] Sample and reference signal are sent to separate channels of a differential amplifier and the two signals can be balanced electronically. This arrangement is both simpler and provides greater signal-to-noise than the split-beam arrangement. A modification of this system has been used by Gardiner et al. for the study of solutions of electrolytes in formamide.[147] A programmed sample carrier for automated alternate positioning of reference and sample cells in the laser beam has been described by Amy et al.[148] It is particularly well suited for signal accumulation by photon counting and stepwise scanning. The system has been applied in the study of weak signals from samples of nucleosides and nucleotides coordinated to heavy metals.[148-151] Another variation has been described by Covington and Thain.[152] They rotate a cylindrical, partitioned cell and add the signals arising from the two separate compartments. In one compartment the sample of interest is placed. The other contains a sample containing a species to be used as reference. The relative integrated intensity of a line of the sample is thus obtained without using an internal standard and thus without introducing the uncertainty arising from the possible perturbation of an equilibrium of interest by addition of a reference solute. The procedure circumvents problems associated with positioning of two cells and a signal-to-noise improvement was noted; this was attributed to the possible centrifugal removal of dust particles or to a reduction of thermal noise effects.

A novel method for enhancing the intensity of liquids has been described by Walrafen and Stone.[153] Extremely small volumes of liquid are placed in an optical fibre of lengths up to 85 m; a laser beam is transmitted down the fibre by total internal reflection and the light scattered at the fibre end is collected and examined. The Raman intensities of lines of benzene become so great that weak overtones, combinations, and forbidden lines can be detected.[154] The fibre can replace the slit of a conventional spectrometer.[155] The ability to employ this technique for the study of water and aqueous solutions is dependent on developing a fibre with a suitable refractive index or on employing a hollow, straight dielectric waveguide which will transmit radiation with low losses.

Raman spectroscopy has also recently been employed in the study of electrodics and related interfacial phenomena. Fleischmann, Hendra and McQuillan have identified HgO, Hg_2Cl_2, and Hg_2Br_2 on a mercury electrode by their Raman spectra.[156] Subsequent studies were made on a silver–electrolyte interface.[157] Two types of pyridine adsorption, which depend on the potential relative to a standard calomel electrode, were detected; at positive potentials pyridine is believed to be sorbed via the nitrogen atom to the silver because a Raman band at 1025 cm^{-1} is evident, but at more negative potentials a pair of Raman bands at 1008 and 1036 cm^{-1} suggest that pyridine is separated from the electrode by a monolayer of oriented water molecules. Greenler and Slager[158] have outlined methods for obtaining a Raman spectrum of a thin film on a metal surface. Clarke et al.[159] have described the use of laser Raman spectroscopy as a tool for the study of diffusion-controlled electrochemical processes. The reversible reactions of two redox couples, $K_4Fe(CN)_6/K_3Fe(CN)_6$ and quinol/quinone were studied by measuring the Raman intensities of peaks at 856 cm^{-1} quinol, 1666 cm^{-1} quinone, 2096 cm^{-1} ferrocyanide, and 2135 cm^{-1} ferricyanide.

Although Raman spectroscopy has an advantage over conventional infrared methods due to the low Raman scattering of water, infrared attenuated total reflectance (a.t.r.) spectra have been used to study absorbed layers at the interface between a germanium electrode and an aqueous solution of sodium laurate.[160] The properties of a nickel oxide electrode, following charging and discharging, were investigated by infrared spectroscopy.[161] Fourier transform spectroscopy[162, 163] is increasingly being recognized as a powerful technique for obtaining improved infrared spectra of aqueous systems.[164] It has been used in the study of methanol–water mixtures,[165] and for analysis of binary mixtures of nitrate and nitrite with concentrations as low as 0.03 and 0.05 mol dm^{-3} respectively.[166] (The procedure can be compared with the traditional transmission technique.[167, 168]) The use of the CO_2 laser for infrared-absorption spectroscopy is claimed to give an improvement by a factor of 100 over conventional infrared instrumentation, because of the laser power of about 1 watt.[169] Its use has been demonstrated for detection of inorganic anions (8 and 35 g m^{-3}) and sulfate quantitative analysis. In the Raman effect, dilute solutions may sometimes be examined by exploiting the resonance Raman effect.[170, 171] The permanganate and chromate ions have thus been studied at concentrations of 10^{-4}–10^{-3} mol dm^{-3} in a rotating cell.[172] Structural changes, which accompany the colour change of acid-base indicators, have also been elucidated in dilute solution.[173] The detection of pollutants in water by Raman spectroscopy has been discussed.[171, 174] Enhanced Raman intensity may also be obtained from glassy films by the technique of laser trapping.[175]

5 SOLVENTS

5.1 Water

Investigations into the structure of water and aqueous solutions continue to flourish but real progress is tortuously slow. Since a number of excellent reviews have appeared recently[176-182] the present discussion will be somewhat limited.

All water properties seem anomalous but 'anomalous water' or 'Polywater' was most anomalous of all.[183-185] Although Allen[185] has written the 'Requiem for Polywater', unfortunate scars remain. To many, the knowledge that quantum mechanics can be used to prove anything is not a comforting thought. A number of anomalous properties, 'kinks', have also been reported[186-189] for normal water despite the beating this interpretation has received at the hands of Young.[190]

Vaslow[186] has detected critical singularities in measurements of the concentration dependence of apparent molal volumes of alkali metal halides, while Andaloro et al.[187] have measured the temperature dependence of the 1.2 μm combination band of water and observed a 'neatly defined break' occurring at 30–40°C in the Arrhenius plot of integrated intensity; Oder and Goring [188] have reported a similar inflexion point for the 1555 cm^{-1} infrared band. Drost-Hansen[189] has interpreted the thermal anomalies of water as manifestations of an order–disorder phenomenon and discussed the possible role these changes may play in biological systems. Angell et al.[191] have also reported on the anomalous properties of supercooled water from 0 to -38°C and predicted a liquid-state damped λ transition. Unusual effects have been reported for water and aqueous solutions subjected to high-frequency electric and magnetic fields.[192-195] A greater infrared absorbance was claimed for magnetically treated water and this was attributed to an increase in structure due to magnetic ordering. However, subsequent Raman[196] and infrared[197] experiments on water subjected to intense magnetic or electric fields were unable to reproduce the earlier results. Low-intensity, high-frequency (500 MHz) electric fields and magnetic fields of 12 100 G (1.21 T) had no effect on the Raman spectra of water or an aqueous nitrate solution.[196] Electric fields have been observed to increase both the depolarization ratio and scattering intensity for certain Raman modes of organic molecules in the liquid state[196, 198] and an ordering effect of the crystal lattice of $NaNO_2$ subject to an external electric field has been reported.[199] Although the fear of obtaining negative results will undoubtedly delay further studies of these systems, some effort must be devoted to resolving these anomalies.

The vibrational spectrum of pure liquid water is complex and controversy exists over both the number and assignment of peaks and the interpretation in terms of water structure. In the past sceptics have been inclined to say that the number of bands observed depended on the number required by the model. The models can be grouped into two categories: a *mixture model* which describes the liquid as a mixture of at least two distinct species which differ by the number of hydrogen bonds which hold each water to neighbouring molecules,[200–203] and a *continuum model* which assumes the liquid to be completely hydrogen bonded, with a distribution of hydrogen bond angles and bond strengths.[204–208] A review of the situation up to 1971 has been presented.[209] Today most workers seem to agree that there are 'two' classes of OH groups, one of which is considered hydrogen bonded, and one other. There remains the semantic problem of whether to describe the other OH group as non-hydrogen bonded (free) or weakly hydrogen bonded. Most of the theoretical studies support the two-state model[210–217], although Kochnev et al.[218] have criticized the simple structural model and proposed a model involving several types of intermolecular interactions depending on the temperature. Rahman and Stillinger[210] have commented on the presence of a 'dangling' OH group as viewed in a stereoscopically animated representation of the results of their molecular dynamics calculations, while Curnutte and Bandekar[213] were able to reproduce the Raman spectrum of liquid water with greater accuracy when 'broken' hydrogen bonds were introduced into their continuum calculations. At least part of the problem associated with interpreting vibrational spectra of water and aqueous solutions results from the time-scale of the measurement (10^{-13} s) which is of the order of the mean lifetime of a hydrogen bond in liquid water (5×10^{-13} s) recently reported by Montrose et al.[144] from Rayleigh scattering experiments. Unfortunately, attempts to obtain reorientational and vibrational relaxation information from infrared and Raman band-shapes will be complicated by severe band overlap, although David[219] has obtained dipole correlation functions through a Fourier transform of the high frequency side of the ν_3 infrared band of water in organic solvents and confirmed essentially free rotation in chloroform and carbon tetrachloride on a time scale of 0.1 ps. In dioxan a shoulder on the high-frequency side of ν_3 was assigned to a non-hydrogen bonded molecule. In contrast, Wall[208] had previously discussed the transforms of the Raman stretching region of HOD in liquid H_2O in terms of a continuum model.

Both the Raman and infrared spectra of water are extremely broad and contain several inflection points; consequently it is necessary to analyse the data by computerized curve resolution techniques. It has been shown recently that corrections for spectral sensitivity must precede any quantitative analysis of the Raman bandshape[40,220,221] (Fig. 6). Even then, two most recent articles[40,221] on the Raman spectrum of liquid water do not agree as to the number of bands that can be resolved (Table 2). Most of the controversy centres around the band at ca. 3200 cm^{-1} which has often been assigned as a Fermi resonance component of the $\nu_1, 2\nu_2$ pair with the second component at ca. 3400 cm^{-1}.[40,207] Other authors[201,209] have questioned the importance of Fermi resonance and most recently Scherer et al.[220,221] have suggested that the resonance between a broad OH stretching fundamental and a broad distribution of overtone levels gives rise to an 'Evans hole' which appears as a minimum in the envelope at ca. 3340 cm^{-1}. Calculations of the resonance constant for liquid H_2O and D_2O agreed with vapour-phase results.[222]

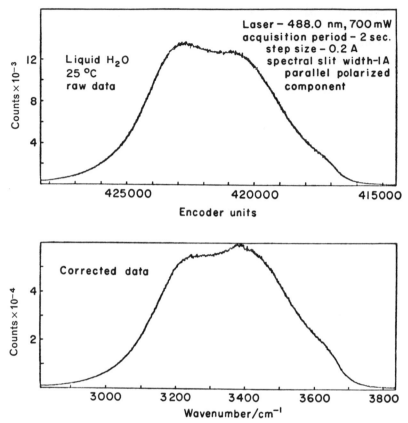

Fig. 6. Parallel polarized component of the Raman spectrum of liquid H_2O in the OH stretching region; observed and corrected spectra (Murphy and Bernstein, Ref. 40).

TABLE 2
Vibrational band positions/cm^{-1} for pure $H_2O_{(l)}$ at 25° C

			Raman		Infrared	
Ref. 40			Ref. 221		Ref. 225	
3215	tetramer ν_1 (a)	3225	$\nu_{dibonded}^{symmetric}$	3230	ν_1	
		3340	$2\nu_2$ (Evans hole)			
3400	tetramer ν_1 (b)	3422	$\nu_{strong\ bonded}^{symmetric}$			
3455	tetramer ν_3	3440	$\nu_{dibonded}^{antisymmetric}$	3450	ν_3	
3545	trimer bonded					
3635	trimer free	3615	$\nu_{weak\ bonded}^{symmetric}$	3630	νweakly bonded or free	

There is some common ground. Murphy and Bernstein[40] interpreted their Raman data on the basis of a mixture of tetrahedrally coordinated water and tricoordinated water.

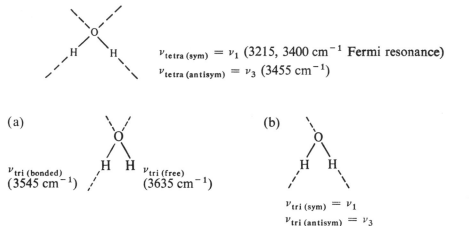

$\nu_{tetra (sym)} = \nu_1$ (3215, 3400 cm^{-1} Fermi resonance)

$\nu_{tetra (antisym)} = \nu_3$ (3455 cm^{-1})

(a)   (b)

$\nu_{tri (bonded)}$
(3545 cm^{-1}) $\nu_{tri (free)}$
                        (3635 cm^{-1})

$\nu_{tri (sym)} = \nu_1$

$\nu_{tri (antisym)} = \nu_3$

(peak positions similar to those of ν_1 and ν_3 tetra)

A simpler model proposed by Scherer et al.[221] has a number of similar features. They also proposed two classes of water, a symmetrical, strong, hydrogen-bonded complex (dibonded),

$\nu_{di (sym)} = \nu_1 = 3225$ cm^{-1}

$\nu_{di (antisym)} = \nu_3 = 3440$ cm^{-1}

and an asymmetrically hydrogen-bonded complex with one strong and one *weak* bond.

$\nu_{bonded} = 3422$ cm^{-1} $\nu_{weak} = 3615$ cm^{-1}

Although Murphy and Bernstein reported a band at 3545 cm^{-1} which Scherer et al. did not resolve, and Scherer et al. favoured assignment of the band at ca.

3200 cm^{-1} to $\nu_{\text{dibonded}}^{\text{sym}}$ rather than a Fermi resonance component, both authors assigned a depolarized band at ca. 3450 cm^{-1} to an antisymmetric ν_3 mode and a component at ca. 3620 cm^{-1} to a weakly bonded (or free) OH group. The position of the ν_3 mode is close to the intensity maximum observed in the infrared spectrum which has been reported at ca. 3410 cm^{-1}.[223-225] This mode gives rise to the most intense band in the infrared spectrum since it has a large dipole–moment derivative, whereas it gives a weak Raman band since it has a small polarizability change. The ν_1 band is difficult to resolve in the infrared spectrum but it has been observed at ca. 3230 cm^{-1}.[225] It may be noted that for pure water the antisymmetric stretching mode occurs at a higher frequency than the symmetric stretching mode, i.e. $\nu_3 > \nu_1$. This is similar to the situation in the gas phase[223] and for water monomers in inert matrices[226-229] and non-polar solvents.[230] (Table 3). Mann et al.[228] have noted that, as

TABLE 3
Band positions/cm^{-1} for water monomers in argon
matrix at 7 K^a

	H$_2$O	D$_2$O	HDO
ν_1	3638.0 ± 1.5	2658.0 ± 1.5	2709.5 ± 1.0
ν_2	1588.5 ± 1.0	1173.5 ± 1.0	1397.0 ± 1.0
ν_3	3734.0 ± 1.0	2771.5 ± 1.0	3687.3 ± 1.0

^{a} Taken from Ref. 226.

monomer water molecules are replaced by dimer and polymer groups in the matrix, ν_1 shifts from 3641 cm^{-1} for the monomer to 3217 cm^{-1} for the polymer, whereas the ν_3 mode shifts from 3729 cm^{-1} for the monomer to 3327 cm^{-1} in the polymer; as a result, ν_3 remains at a higher frequency than ν_1. The assignment of the band at 3217 cm^{-1} to the symmetric stretching mode of the hydrogen-bonded polymer water, ν_{1B}, gives support to the assignment of Scherer et al.[221]

Olander and Rice[231] have suggested that, in amorphous solid water [H$_2$O(as), also known as vitreous ice Iv], 'static and thermal disorder are separate'; hence studies of this phase should provide valuable insight into water structure. Several infrared[232,233] and Raman[175,234] studies have confirmed this view. Venkatish, Rice and Bates[234] have suggested that in ice Iv the water molecules are located in two or three types of distinguishable environments, depending on the details of the assignment. The strong Raman band at ca. 3112 cm^{-1} was assigned to the ν_1 mode of a strongly hydrogen-bonded species on the basis of a depolarization study of Li and Devlin.[175] A component at 3220 cm^{-1} was assigned to the ν_3 mode of a strongly bonded species, whereas weak components at 3370 and 3477 cm^{-1} were assigned to species with bent and weak hydrogen bonds respectively. Fermi resonance involving $2\nu_2$ was considered to have minor significance. Raman spectra obtained from partially deuterated water and ice VI to 10.1 kbar were also consistent with these results.[235] Wong and Whalley[236] have reported the Raman spectra of ice VIII and assigned the bands on the basis of the D_{4h}^{19} space group. The same authors[237] have performed a detailed study of the translational lattice vibrations of the orientationally disordered ice Ih.

Considerable use has been made of dilute (ca. 5%) solutions of H_2O in D_2O and D_2O in H_2O on the assumption that the dilute DOH species will give spectra that are unperturbed by intramolecular coupling. Walrafen and Blatz[238] have also obtained a Raman spectrum for tritiated water, TOH in H_2O. Mundy *et al.*[239] have recently reported that the presence of D_2O and the effect of coupled OD oscillators causes measurable perturbations of the OD vibrations even for solutions containing as little as 1 mole per cent D_2O, which suggests that the results of most HOD studies should be viewed with caution. Most important as far as water models are concerned is the fact that the OH and OD symmetric stretching regions for the dilute HOD species show a marked high frequency shoulder in the Raman spectrum[240] which has been assigned to that fraction of the water molecules which do not have hydrogen-bonded OH groups. Similar infrared studies of Wyss and Falk[241] failed to reveal an analogous high-frequency band and they suggested that the Raman shoulders were due to an asymptotic behaviour of frequency as a function of bonding geometry. Clarke and Glew[242] reanalysed the Wyss and Falk data and concluded that a statistically significant band *was* present near 3600 cm^{-1}. They also calculated that at 10°C, 4.6% of the HOD species had unbonded OH groups. Walrafen[243] has studied the effect of pressure on HDO in H_2O to 7.2 kbar and suggested that increased pressure caused very little change in the fraction of non-hydrogen bonded OH groups. Bondarenko and Gorbatyi[244] studied the infrared spectrum of HOD in D_2O to 550 °C and 500 atm and observed doublet structure in the OH region. Gorbunov and Naberukhim[245] measured the integrated intensity and contour of the OD band for HDO in D_2O and concluded that a mixture model could not explain their spectral data.

Water also gives rise to a number of low frequency modes as well as a variety of combinations and overtones. Walrafen[181] has summarized the evidence for hindered translational modes at ca. 60 cm^{-1} and at ca. 175 cm^{-1}, and a librational mode(s) extending from 300 to 900 cm^{-1}. Walrafen and Blatz[246] have assigned a large number of weak bands observed in H_2O and D_2O between 400 and 4100 cm^{-1}. Oder and Goring[247] have reported an infrared band at 1350 in H_2O and 1000 cm^{-1} in D_2O which they assigned to an overtone of the librational band. The same authors had previously detected an infrared band at 1550 cm^{-1}.[188] Gray *et al.*[248] and James and Irmer[249] have reported techniques for separating Raman scattering from the Rayleigh scattering to obtain information from the 20–200 cm^{-1} region, and Whalley[250] has discussed the origin of the far-infrared spectrum of liquid water. Measurements of the overtone regions in the near-infrared have also been used to investigate the water structure. Péron et al.[251] have studied the overtone region of H_2O and HOD at different temperatures and interpret their data in terms of free OH groups in liquid water, whereas Kleiss et al.[252] have concluded from data obtained for the second overtone region of HOD that the concentration of monomer water is negligible in the liquid. Judging by recent literature[253-256] it appears that the assignment of bands in the overtone region is as difficult as for the fundamental region. The resolution of the near infrared band of HOD into hydrogen-bonded and non-bonded components by Bonner[257] was severely criticized by Giguère.[258] Walrafen and co-workers have reported stimulated Raman spectra for H_2O, D_2O and HDO and solutions of $NaClO_4$ and interpreted the data in terms of a mixture model.[259,260]

Addition of solute molecules to water usually alters the observed vibrational spectrum, and solutes have often been classified as *structure makers* if peaks characteristic of strong hydrogen bonded OH groups increase in relative intensity and as *structure breakers* if peaks due to free OH groups increase.[259-278] These studies have involved the low-frequency regions[268-271] as well as combination bands[264-272] and overtone bands[263,265,266,276,277]. Molecules such as urea[268,269] and ions such as BF_4^-, PF_6^-, ClO_4^-, I^-[4,261,264] are considered as structure breakers, whereas molecules such as sucrose[268] and large organic ions such as tetra-alkylammonium halides[266,267,277,278] are considered as structure makers. It is often found that metal cations have little effect on the water structure.[4]

This interpretation has been criticized by a number of authors who prefer to interpret spectral changes in terms of specific ion–water or molecule–water interaction.[279-286] De Lozé and Baron[283] have stressed the fact that for solutions of salts in water a new structure is built on the basis of specific interactions between ions and molecules. The concepts of structure makers and structure breakers they consider to have meaning only when applied to macroscopic properties like fluidity and dielectric properties. Kęcki and co-workers[287-290] have stressed similar aspects of specific ion–water interactions.

Perhaps the most significant case in point concerns the interpretation of the effect of ClO_4^- ion on the water spectrum. Addition of $LiClO_4$ or $NaClO_4$ to water causes a marked increase in the high frequency region which has been assigned to the 'free' OH group.[4,261,290] The fact that this second component also occurs in the OD region of dilute solutions of HOD in H_2O is strong evidence to suggest a second type of water. Walrafen[262] has assigned this band to the free 'OH' (or OD) and attributed the intensity increase to the structure breaking ability of ClO_4^-. Lilley[4] expanded on this view in a recent review of the pertinent information. On the other hand a number of workers, notably Brink and Falk[279] and Symons and Waddington[280,281] prefer to consider the new component as being due to a water molecule hydrogen-bonded to perchlorate. Symons and Waddington[281] have arrived at a 'hydration' number of four for perchlorate and fluoroborate ions in aqueous solutions. Kecki[287-290] prefers to assign the new peak to a water molecule that is trapped between the cation and the anion.

$$M^+ \text{---} O \underset{\diagdown}{\overset{\diagup}{}} \begin{array}{l} H \\ H \text{---} ClO_4^- \end{array}$$

Subramanian and Fisher[265] have pointed out that hydrogen bonding to ClO_4^- is expected to be weak and interpret their near-infrared results in favour of the OH being free. At this point, evidence seems to favour two classes of OH groups in liquid water, each with a wide range of energy distributions, but whether one chooses to call the OH group associated with the high frequency mode a 'free' or a 'weak' hydrogen-bonded group appears to be a matter of personal preference.

5.2 Liquid Ammonia

Solvent properties of liquid ammonia have been the subject of a number of recent investigations. Although most of the studies were undertaken with the aim of providing information on hydrogen bonding and ion-pair formation to complement aqueous solution studies[291-305] the unusual ability of liquid ammonia to dissolve alkali metals has prompted several spectroscopic studies of these systems.[306,307] The ammonia molecule has C_{3v} symmetry and should exhibit four coincident lines in its infrared and Raman spectra. In the symmetric stretching region the vibrational spectrum is complicated by the effects of hydrogen bonding and Fermi resonance, similar to, but not quite as severe as that found for water. The most widely adopted assingment is presented in Table 4. The most prominent feature of the Raman spectrum is a doublet structure consisting of two strongly polarized bands at ca. 3300 and 3214 cm^{-1} which have

TABLE 4
Band positions/cm^{-1} and depolarization data for liquid ammonia^a

3385 dp	v_3 (e)
3300 p ($\rho \approx 0.05$)	$v_1{}^b(a_1)$
3270 p ($\rho \approx 0.05$)	v'
3214 p ($\rho \approx 0.05$)	$2v_4{}^b$
1640 dp	v_4 (e)
1046 p	$v_2{}^c(a_1)$

^{a} Band positions from Ref. 291; depolarization data from Ref. 292.
^{b} Schwartz and Wang (Ref. 292) argue for the interchange of these assignments.
^{c} A doublet structure has been reported for this band (Ref. 306).

been assigned to the symmetric stretching vibration, ν_1, and the overtone, $2\nu_4$, in Fermi resonance. A broad band at ca. 3270 cm^{-1} has been resolved from the envelope and assigned specifically to the symmetric stretching mode of a hydrogen-bonded ammonia species of C_s symmetry[291-298] which is different from bulk ammonia. However, the effect of temperature on peak positions and halfwidths suggested that 'bulk' ammonia molecules are also influenced by hydrogen bonding.[292] Again, as for water, the assignment of the ammonia spectrum has been the subject of controversy. Birchall and Drummond[299] have suggested that the usual assignment of ν_1 and $2\nu_4$ should be reversed, i.e. $\nu_1 \approx 3215$ cm^{-1} and $2\nu_4 \approx 3300$ cm^{-1}. This is more consistent with the fact that ν_4 is ≈ 1640 cm^{-1} which would put $2\nu_4 \approx 3280$ cm^{-1}, but it is the opposite of the gas phase assignment.[308] Depolarization data offer no help since both bands have very small depolarization ratios. In an effort to resolve this problem, Schwartz and Wang[292] studied the N—H stretching region as a function of temperature and the resonance interaction was quantitatively analysed at all temperatures by means of the utilization of a coupled damped-oscillator model. As the temperature was lowered, the intensity of the band at ca. 3220 cm^{-1} increased at the expense of the intensity of the band at ca. 3300 cm^{-1}. In the absence of Fermi resonance ν_1 would be expected to be more intense than $2\nu_4$.

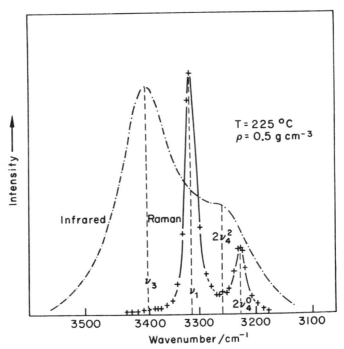

Fig. 7. Infrared and Raman spectra of NH₃ at 225 °C and a density of 0.5 g cm⁻³ (Bubach, Ref. 88).

If thermal broadening was the important factor then at lower temperatures the effects of Fermi resonance should decrease, which appeared to be the case. However, Buback[88] and Buback and Franck[301] have performed detailed infrared and Raman studies of ammonia over a wide range of temperatures and pressures. They observed that the frequency of the 3310 cm^{-1} band increased with decreased density; the 3220 cm^{-1} band position remained essentially constant. Buback and Franck assigned the bands in the usual way. The effects of Fermi resonance appear to have been decreased by the upward frequency shift of the ν_1 component; consequently the conclusions of Schwartz and Wang are open to question. Gardiner et al.[294] have also suggested that the effects of Fermi resonance are relatively unimportant. Recently, Lundeen and Koehler[300] evaluated both models and favoured the Schwartz and Wang assignment.

Roberts and Bettignies[297] studied the Raman spectrum of ammonia in hexadeuteriobenzene; they did not find any evidence for specific hydrogen-bonded interactions between NH_3 and C_6D_6 but did observe a decrease in the relative intensity of the ν_1 and ν_3 modes of ammonia which they attributed to the breaking up of the hydrogen-bonded structure of the C_6D_6 molecules. Cugley and Pullin[302] have observed that NH_3 rotates freely in an argon matrix but not in an N_2 matrix. Gardiner et al.[294] reported essentially free rotation for dilute solutions of NH_3 in CCl_4, but at higher concentrations and in liquid CH_3CN self-association and intermolecular association both occur. Ault and Pimentel[303] have reported the formation of the NH_3HCl hydrogen-bonded complex in matrix isolation studies.

Vibrational spectroscopic studies of the effect of various salts on the hydrogen-bonded structure of liquid ammonia have also been reported.[291, 293, 295, 296, 298] The two-species model similar to that proposed for water appears to offer the most reasonable interpretation of the results. Lagowski and co-workers[295, 296] have studied NaI and $NaClO_4$ solutions in NH_3, ND_3 and ND_2H and found that ClO_4^- ions decrease the H-bonding interactions, whereas I^- exhibits the opposite effect. In general the fundamental vibrational frequencies of liquid ammonia are perturbed primarily by anion interaction, although the symmetric bending mode (ν_2) does exhibit strong cation dependence.[291] Vibrational spectra of the nitrate and thiocyanate ions imply that the NO_3^- ... NH_3 interaction is weaker than NH_3 ... SCN^- interaction.[293] Low-frequency bands due to the symmetric M—N stretching vibration of the solvated cation have been observed for a number of salts.[291, 298, 304]

The dielectric constant (relative permittivity) of liquid ammonia is ≈ 23 at $-33\,°C$ which is considerably lower than the value for water; consequently, ion-pair formation should be more favourable than for aqueous solutions. Raman studies of a number of nitrate and thiocyanate salts confirm this view.[291, 293, 298, 304] The nitrate results are very similar to those obtained for aqueous solutions (Section 7.6) (Table 5). For ammonia solutions of KNO_3 and NH_4NO_3 only one band is observed in the ν_4 region (at ca. 709 cm^{-1}) and the ν_3 region consists of a broad doublet with splitting of ca. 35 cm^{-1}.[291, 293, 304, 305, 396] This is consistent with the view that long-lived ion-pairs are not present in these solutions. The splitting of the degenerate ν_3 mode is ca. 21 cm^{-1} less than the value (ca. 56 cm^{-1}) for analogous aqueous solutions. This reflects weaker hydrogen-bonding and a somewhat more

TABLE 5
Band positions/cm^{-1} and assignments for the nitrate fundamentals of ammonia solutions of nitrate salts

Cation	ν_4	ν_1	ν_3	Ref.
Li$^+$	714, 732	1047	1349, 1404	298
	711, 719	1045	1340, 1385	293
Na$^+$	707, 717	1044	1350, 1383	304
	709, 719	1044	1347, 1390	293
K$^+$	710	1044	1346, 1382	304
NH$_4^+$	712	1044	1340, 1380	293
	709	1037	1335	298
Ag$^+$	707	1043	1344, 1370	304
Ca^{2+}	708, 730	1044	1350, 1380	291
	707, 728	1045	1334, 1371, 1428	304
Sr^{2+}	708, 723	1044		291
Ba^{2+}	709, 719	1044	1345, 1390	291

symmetric field about the nitrate ion. Inner-sphere ion-pairing occurs for a number of salts, as evidenced by the occurrence of a new depolarized band at ca. 720 cm^{-1} and an increase in the complexity of the ν_3 region (Table 5). A weak peak at ca. 260 cm^{-1} has been assigned to the Ca—ONO$_2$ stretching mode but has not been observed for the other salts.[304]

Vibrational spectroscopy has been used to investigate the nature of alkali metal–ammonia solutions. Although Smith and Koehler[306] were unable to detect any changes in the liquid ammonia spectrum for alkali metal concentrations of 0–50×10^{-4} mol dm^{-3}, Rusch and Lagowski[307] have reported that the N—H stretching frequency of the solvent shifts to lower energy with increasing concentration of lithium and potassium over the concentration range 5×10^{-3} to 5×10^{-2} mol dm^{-3}. The results were interpreted in terms of a solvent-containing species in the presence of solvated electrons.

5.3   Acetonitrile, Dioxan, and Other Solvents

An increasing number of workers are concentrating on non-aqueous solvents and a large number of infrared and Raman studies of these systems have been reported. Cox[309] has reviewed the physical properties of a number of aprotic solvents, while Irish[5] has summarized many of the infrared and Raman studies of organic solvents. In Table 6 we have extended the original Table of vibrational

TABLE 6
References to vibrational assignments for non-aqueous solvents

Solvent	Formula	Reference
Acetic acid	CH_3COOH	1. (a) J. T. Bulmer and H. F. Shurvell, *J. Phys. Chem.* **77**, 256 (1973).
Acetone	CH_3COCH_3	2. (a) P. F. Krause, B. G. Slagola and J. E. Katon, *J. Chem. Phys.* **61**, 5331 (1974).
		(b) J. E. Griffiths, *J. Chem. Phys.* **60**, 2556 (1974).
		(c) M. K. Wong, W. J. McKinney and A. I. Popov, *J. Phys. Chem.* **75**, 56 (1971).
Acetonitrile	CH_3CN	3. (a) A. Loewenschuss and N. Yellin, *Spectrochim. Acta* **31A**, 207 (1975).
		(b) T. B. Freedman and E. R. Nixon, *Spectrochim. Acta* **28A**, 1375 (1972).
		(c) M. Schwartz and C. H. Wang, *Chem. Phys. Lett.* **29**, 383 (1974).
		(d) S. Higuchi, H. Tsuyama, S. Tanaka and H. Kamada, *Spectrochim. Acta* **31A**, 1011 (1975).
		(e) J. E. Griffiths, *J. Chem. Phys.* **59**, 751 (1973); **60**, 2556 (1974).
		(f) W. G. Rothschild, *J. Chem. Phys.* **57**, 991 (1972).
		(g) G. D. Patterson and J. E. Griffiths, *J. Chem. Phys.* **63**, 2406 (1975).
		(h) M. P. Marzocchi and S. Dobos, *Spectrochim. Acta* **30A**, 1437 (1974).
		(i) K. Balasubrahmanyam and G. J. Janz, *J. Amer. Chem. Soc.* **92**, 4189 (1970).
		(j) Y. Sze, Ph.D. Thesis, University of Waterloo, Waterloo, Ontario, Canada, 1973.
		(k) T. G. Chang and D. E. Irish, *J. Solution Chem.* **3**, 161 (1974).
		(l) G. J. Janz and M. A. Muller, *J. Solution Chem.* **4**, 285 (1975).
		(m) M. H. Baron and C. de Lozé, *J. Chim. Phys., Phys.-Chim. Biol.* **68**, 1293 (1971); **69**, 1084 (1972).
Benzene	C_6H_6	4. (a) 3(g).
Benzonitrile	C_6H_5CN	5. (a) 3(f).
Butyl alcohol	$(CH_3)_3COH$	6. (a) E. E. Tucker and E. D. Becker, *J. Phys. Chem.* **77**, 1783 (1973).
		(b) Y. Sassa and T. Katayama, *J. Chem. Eng. (Japan)* **7**, 1 (1974).
Butyl ether	$(C_4H_9)_2O$	7. (a) J. T. Bulmer and H. F. Shurvell, *J. Phys. Chem.* **77**, 2085 (1973).
Carbon disulphide	CS_2	8. (a) H. W. Kroto and J. J. C. Teixeira-Dias, *Spectrochim. Acta* **28A**, 1497 (1972).
		(b) S. V. Ribnikar and O. S. Puzic, *Spectrochim. Acta* **29A**, 307 (1973).
Carbon tetrachloride	CCl_4	9. (a) P. K. Glasoe, S. Hallock, M. Hove and J. M. Duke, *Spectrochim. Acta* **27A**, 2309 (1971).
		(b) J. Guilleme, M. Chabanel and B. Wajtkowiak, *Spectrochim. Acta* **27A**, 2355 (1971).
		(c) S. Sunder and R. E. D. McClung, *Chem. Phys.* **2**, 467 (1973).

TABLE 6—*Cont.*

Solvent	Formula	Reference
Carbon tetrafluoride	CF_4	10. (a) A. C. Jeannotte, D. Legler and J. Overend, *Spectrochim. Acta* **29A**, 1915 (1973).
		(b) F. P. Daly, A. G. Hopkins and C. W. Brown, *Spectrochim. Acta* **30A**, 2159 (1974).
		(c) R. Akhmedzhanov, V. V. Bertsev, M. O. Bulanin and L. A. Zhigula, *Opt. Spectrosc.* **36**, 709 (1974).
Chloroacetic acid	CCl_3COOH	11. (a) M. Obradovic, T. Solmajer and D. Hadzi, *J. Mol. Struct.* **21**, 397 (1974).
Chloroform	CCl_3H	12. (a) W. G. Rothschild, G. J. Rosasco and R. C. Livingston, *J. Chem. Phys.* **62**, 1253 (1975).
		(b) 3(g).
		(c) 7(a).
N,N-dimethyl-acetamide	$(CH_3)_2NCOCH_3$	13. (a) M. H. Baron, J. Corset, C. de Lozé and M. L. Josien, *Compt. Rend. Acad. Sci.* (*Paris*) **274C**, 1321 (1972).
Dimethyl carbonate	$(CH_3)_2CO_3$	14. (a) J. E. Katon and M. D. Cohen, *Can. J. Chem.* **53**, 1378 (1975).
N,N-dimethyl-formamide	$(CH_3)_2NCHO$	15. (a) S. M. Petrov and V. S. Pilyrigen, *Russ. J. Phys. Chem.* **45**, 1231 (1971).
Dimethyl sulfoxide	CH_3SOCH_3	16. (a) 11(a).
		(b) J. R. Scherer, M. K. Go and S. Kint, *J. Phys. Chem.* **77**, 2108 (1973).
		(c) L. Singuret and M. Strat, *Acta Phys. Pol.* **A47**, 391 (1975).
p-Dioxan	$\overline{OCH_2CH_2OCH_2CH_2}$	17. (a) 3(f).
		(b) 3(j).
Ethanol	CH_3CH_2OH	18. (a) A. N. Fletcher, *J. Phys. Chem.* **76**, 2562 (1972).
		(b) 2(b).
Ethylene carbonate	(structure shown)	19. (a) B. Fortunato, P. Mirone and G. Fini, *Spectrochim. Acta* **27A**, 1917 (1971).
		(b) G. Fini and P. Mirone, *J. Chem. Soc. Faraday Trans. II* **70**, 1767 (1974).
		(c) G. Fini, P. Mirone and B. Fortunato, *J. Chem. Soc. Faraday Trans. II* **69**, 1243 (1973).
Ethylenediamine (1,2-ethanediamine)	$NH_2CH_2CH_2$-NH_2	20. (a) A. L. Borring and K. Rasmussen, *Spectrochim. Acta* **31A**, 889, 895 (1975).
		(b) Y. Omura and T. Shimanouchi, *J. Mol. Spectrosc.* **55**, 430 (1975).
Ethyl fluoroformate	C_2H_5FCO	21. (a) S. W. Charles, G. I. L. Jones, N. L. Owen and L. A. West, *J. Mol. Struct.* **26**, 249 (1975).
Ethyl propiolate	$C_2H_5COOC_2H_5$	22. (a) 21(a).
Fluoroform	CF_3H	23. (a) J. DeZwann, D. W. Hess and C. S. Johnson, *J. Chem. Phys.* **63**, 422 (1975).
Formaldehyde	H_2CO	24. (a) H. Khoshko, S. J. Hemple and E. R. Nixon, *Spectrochim. Acta* **30A**, 863 (1974).
Formamide	$HCONH_2$	25. (a) D. J. Gardiner, R. B. Girling and R. E. Hester, *J. Chem. Soc. Faraday Trans. II* **71**, 709 (1975).
		(b) K. Itoh and T. Shimanouchi, *J. Mol. Spectrosc.* **42**, 86 (1972).

For ethylene carbonate the structure is drawn as a carbonyl carbon:

$$
\begin{array}{c}
O \\
\parallel \\
C \\
O \quad O \\
\mid \quad \mid \\
H_2C\text{—}CH_2
\end{array}
$$

TABLE 6—*Cont.*

Solvent	Formula	Reference
Formic acid	HCOOH	26. (a) W. G. Rothschild, *J. Chem. Phys.* **61**, 3422 (1974).
		(b) B. M. Rode, *Chem. Phys. Lett.* **32**, 34 (1975).
Glycerol and other polyols	$C_3H_5(OH)_3$	27. (a) C. H. Wang and R. B. Wright, *J. Chem. Phys.* **55**, 3300 (1971).
		(b) L. D. Vink, L. Cambon and R. Lafont, *Compt. Rend. Acad. Sci.* (*Paris*) **C267**, 1024 (1968).
		(c) J. Knoeck, *J. Inorg. Nucl. Chem.* **35**, 823 (1973).
		(d) R. P. Oertel, *Inorg. Chem.* **11**, 544 (1972).
Hydrogen peroxide	H_2O_2	28. (a) J. L. Arnau, P. A. Giguère, M. Abe and R. C. Taylor, *Spectrochim. Acta* **30A**, 777 (1974).
		(b) H. Chen and P. A. Giguère, *Spectrochim. Acta* **29A**, 1611 (1973).
Methanol	CH_3OH	29. (a) R. T. Yang and M. J. D. Low, *Spectrochim. Acta* **30A**, 1787 (1974).
		(b) J. R. Durig, C. B. Pate, Y. S. Li and D. J. Antion, *J. Chem. Phys.* **54**, 4863 (1971).
Methyl acetate	CH_3COOCH_3	30. (a) W. O. George, T. E. Houston and W. C. Harris, *Spectrochim. Acta* **30A**, 1035 (1974).
Methyl formate	CH_3CHO	31. (a) H. V. Venkatasetty, *J. Electrochem. Soc.* **122**, 245 (1975).
Methyl iodide	CH_3I	32. (a) 3(g).
		(b) H. S. Goldberg and P. S. Pershan, *J. Chem. Phys.* **58**, 3816 (1973).
		(c) J. H. Campbell, J. F. Fisher and J. Jonas, *J. Chem. Phys.* **61** 346 (1974).
Nitrogen dioxide	NO_2 (and N_2O_4)	33. (a) D. E. Tevault and L. Andrews, *Spectrochim. Acta* **30A**, 969 (1974).
		(b) R. Audinos, *Rev. Chim. Minerale* **10**, 701 (1973).
Propanol	C_3H_7OH	34. (a) 2(b).
		(b) 3(f).
Propylene carbonate	$$\begin{array}{c} O \\ \parallel \\ C \\ \diagup\;\;\diagdown \\ O\;\;\;\;O \\ \mid\;\;\;\;\mid \\ H_2C\!-\!CH \\ \mid \\ CH_3 \end{array}$$	35. (a) 18(a), 18(c).
		(b) M. S. Greenberg, D. M. Wied and A. I. Popov, *Spectrochim. Acta* **29A**, 1927 (1973).
Pyridine	C_5H_5N	36. (a) J. Rouvière, B. Dimon, B. Brun and J. Salvinien, *Compt. Rend. Acad. Sci.* (*Paris*) **274C**, 458 (1972).
		(b) P. R. Hardy and A. I. Popov, *Spectrochim. Acta* **28A**, 1545 (1972).
Silicon tetrachloride	$SiCl_4$	37. (a) J. E. Griffiths, *Spectrochim. Acta* **30A**, 169 (1974).
		(b) J. A. Creighton and T. J. Sinclair, *Spectrochim. Acta* **29A**, 817 (1973).
Sulfur dichloride and disulfur dichloride	SCl_2 (S_2Cl_2)	38. (a) S. G. Frankiss and D. J. Harrison, *Spectrochim. Acta* **31A**, 161 (1975).

studies of non-aqueous solvents as compiled by Irish.[5] The Table provides reference to information concerning peak positions, halfwidths, assignments, and in certain cases, the effect of molecular association and molecular reorientation on the band-shapes. A number of the studies were performed primarily to investigate the nature of solute–solute and solute–solvent interactions and although only small sampling of this topic can be presented in this review the reader should be aware that replacing water with a non-aqueous solvent does not always simplify the problem. For instance, Szezepianak and Orville-Thomas[310] have observed pronounced solute–solvent interactions between phenol and a variety of fluorinated and mixed 'inert' solvents. Self-association of the solutes benzoic acid[311] and acetic acid[45] has been observed in CCl_4 solutions, while Sassa and Katayama[312] have studied the effects of solvent–solvent and solute–solvent interactions in a number of alcohol solvents and Fini and Mirone[313] have demonstrated the effects of strong intermolecular coupling between molecules in the dipolar aprotic liquids, ethylene and propylene carbonates. The existence of two major conformers has been reported for dimethyl carbonate solutions[314] and ethylenediamine.[315] Choppin and Downey[316] reported evidence for water–chloroform interaction, while Burneau and Corset[317] have inferred a similar acetone–water interaction. Many organic liquids exhibit low-frequency infrared and Raman peaks which appear to be due to collision interactions, hindered rotatory motions, or intermolecular complex formation.[318–321] Similar bands are observed in nearly all liquids and should not be interpreted as evidence for solid-like quasi-crystalline structure. Acetonitrile and dioxan will be discussed in more detail.

Acetonitrile is finding increasing use as a non-aqueous solvent in investigations of ion–solute and ion-pair interactions. Acetonitrile is a fairly powerful donor ligand for metal ions[68,322,323] and evidence has been obtained for direct interactions with a number of cations, including such large monovalent cations as K^+ and Rb^+.[322] Specific effects of solvent–ion interactions on ion-pair formation have been investigated and for CH_3CN/H_2O mixed solvents the competitive nature of the solvation process was studied. The vibrational spectrum of CH_3CN is tabulated in Table 7 together with values for CH_3CN in an aqueous solution, approximate values for complexed CH_3CN, and tentative assignments. Addition of water to acetonitrile causes small shifts in band maxima (e.g. ν_2 shifts from 2254 to 2258 cm^{-1}), but no new bands were observed.[68] Interaction between water and acetonitrile has been inferred from studies of water and acetonitrile and their solutions in CCl_4.[324,325] Much more pronounced changes occur in the acetonitrile spectrum when the $M(CH_3CN)^{n+}$ solvate is formed. Except for those due to CH_3 bending and stretching modes, all of the CH_3CN bands appear as doublets (Table 7, Fig. 8). The exact frequencies depend upon the nature of the metal cation; for instance, for free acetonitrile the $C\equiv N$ stretch is at 2254 cm^{-1}, for $Ag(CH_3CN)^+$, 2270 cm^{-1}[326,327] (Table 7), and for $Zn(CH_3CN)^{2+}$, 2290 cm^{-1}.[68] In very concentrated solutions of $Zn(NO_3)_2$ in CH_3CN/H_2O, a shoulder, which appears at

TABLE 7
Raman band positions/cm^{-1} for acetonitrile^a

5 H$_2$O:1 CH$_3$CN	CH$_3$CN	CH$_3$CN—M^b	Assignment
383	379	395^c	ν_8 C—C≡N bend
755	751	785^c	$2\nu_8$
923	921	938^c	ν_4 C—C stretch
≈1040	≈1040	1035^d	ν_7 CH$_2$ antisymmetric rock (observed in infrared)
1375	1375	1372	ν_3 CH$_3$ symmetric bend
1410	1412	1412^d	$\nu_7 + \nu_8$
1442	1449	1444^d	ν_6 CH$_3$ antisymmetric bend
2258	2254	2290^c	ν_2 C≡N stretch
2297	2294	2315^c	$(\nu_3 + \nu_4)^e$
2945	2945	2945^d	ν_1 CH$_3$ symmetric stretch
3005	3004	3005^d	ν_5 CH$_3$ antisymmetric stretch

^{a} Values and assignments taken from Ref. 68.
^{b} Approximate values for acetonitrile bound to a bivalent metal cation.
^{c} If both free and bound species are present these bands give well-resolved doublets.
^{d} Free and bound CH$_3$CN bands are essentially coincident.
^{e} Possibly in Fermi resonance with ν_2.

ca. 2263 cm^{-1} on the ν_2 C≡N stretching band, is considered to arise from discrete water–acetonitrile interaction.[68] A word of warning is in order before leaving acetonitrile, since the normally slow hydrolysis of this molecule

$$RCN + 2H_2O \rightarrow RCOOH + NH_3$$

may be catalyzed by certain species, e.g. Hg^{2+}, Ni, ZnCl$_2$.[68,328]

Dioxan is an unusual liquid. In accordance with its symmetric structure (point group C_{2h}), its dipole moment is essentially zero, and it has a very low dielectric constant. These particular properties combined with the fact that dioxan is

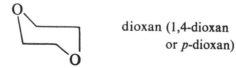

dioxan (1,4-dioxan
or *p*-dioxan)

miscible in all proportions with such a highly polar solvent as water makes dioxan–water mixtures very suitable for studies of the behaviour of electrolytes in media of varying dielectric constant. The need for such studies to test the validity of current solution theories has been discussed earlier. Although dioxan–water mixtures obscure a considerable portion of the vibrational spectral region, a sufficient number of windows exist so that in favourable cases solvent–solvent, ion–solvent, and ion–ion interactions may still be investigated. Peak positions for pure dioxan are listed in Table 8 together with peak positions for

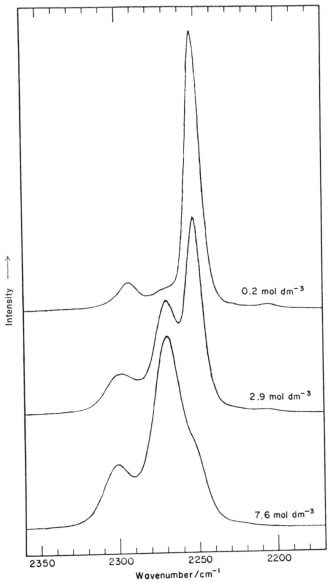

Fig. 8. Raman spectra of the CN region of acetonitrile for AgNO₃/CH₃CN solutions of the designated concentrations (Chang and Irish).

$2H_2O:1C_4H_8O_2$, approximate positions of $M(C_4H_8O_2)^{n+}$ bands where they differ from those of free dioxan, and tentative assignments. Large shifts occur for the ring vibrations at 435, 835 and 1110 cm^{-1}. These modes have been shown to have major contributions from the C—O—C vibrations;[328] thus interaction with water at the oxygen ends of dioxan has been suggested.[68]

TABLE 8
Vibrational band positions/cm^{-1} for dioxan[a]

2 H$_2$O/1 dioxan Raman	infrared	Dioxan (pure) Raman	infrared	M-dioxan[b] Raman	infrared	Assignment
(270)^c		(270)^c				
419		421				ν_{10} a_g ring bend
439		435				ν_9 a_g ring bend
487		488				ν_{27} b_g ring bend
(615)^c	615	(615)^c	614		625	ν_{35} b_u ring bend
833	(835)^d	835	(835)^d	825		ν_8 a_g ring stretch
852		852				ν_{26} b_g CH$_2$ rock
	872		873		863	ν_{18} a_u ring stretch
(890)^c	890	(890)^c	888			ν_{34} b_u CH$_2$ rock
1015	(1015)^d	1015	(1015)^d			ν_7 a_g CH$_2$ rock
	1048		1049			ν_{33} b_u ring stretch
	1081		1082			ν_{17} a_u CH$_2$ rock
1101		1110				ν_{25} b_g ring stretch
	1118		1119			ν_{16} a_u ring stretch
1128		1128				ν_6 a_g ring stretch
1219		1217				ν_{24} b_g CH$_2$ twist
	1256		1252			ν_{15} a_u CH$_2$ twist
	1292		1287			ν_{32} b_u CH$_2$ twist
1307		1304				ν_5 a_g CH$_2$ twist
1335		1336				ν_{23} b_g CH$_2$ wag
1339						ν_4 a_g CH$_2$ wag
	1369		1365			ν_{14} a_u CH$_2$ wag
	1377		1375			ν_{31} b_u CH$_2$ wag
1445		1444				ν_3 a_g CH$_2$ scissors
	1445		1444			ν_{13} a_u CH$_2$ scissors
	1457		1454			ν_{30} b_u CH$_2$ scissors
1460		1462				ν_{22} b_g CH$_2$ scissors
2863		2856				ν_2 a_g CH$_2$ stretch; ν_{21} b_g CH$_2$ stretch
2975		2967				ν_1 a_g CH$_2$ stretch; ν_{20} b_g CH$_2$ stretch

[a] Band positions taken from Ref. 68.
Assignments from O. H. Ellestad, P. Klaboe and G. Hagen, *Spectrochim. Acta* **27A**, 1025 (1971).
[b] Approximate values listed for Hg(dioxan)$^{2+}$ for doublet bands only.
[c] Infrared mode observed due to perturbation of C_{2h} symmetry.
[d] Raman mode observed due to perturbation of C_{2h} symmetry.

The upward displacement of the CH$_2$ stretching modes has been attributed to the change in the CH$_2$ force constants due to the interaction at the C—O—C groups.[68] The existence of 2:1 and 1:1 dioxan–water complexes has been inferred from infrared studies of the O—H stretching region of dilute H$_2$O–dioxan solutions in CCl$_4$.[329] Similar complexes have been proposed for solutions of high water content[325] but the complexity of the OH region makes such claims tenuous. Choppin and Violante[330] have proposed a three-species model after examining the absorption spectra of water–acetone and acetonitrile in which bands were assigned to species in which zero, one, and two hydrogen atoms of water are involved in hydrogen bonding with other water molecules with little dioxan–water interaction. Burneau and Corset[331] have criticized the far-infrared assignments and reassigned at least one peak to a simultaneous transition, $\nu_{OH}(H_2O) + \nu_{CH_3}$ (base). Sze[68] concluded that there was not enough evidence to suggest specific, spectroscopically distinct dioxan–water species since no new bands were detected, but the large shifts of the ring vibrations indicated significant interaction. Although evidence exists for formation of weak Li^+, Na^+, K^+ complexes with dioxan[332] the ability of dioxan to complex is considerably less than that for CH_3CN; consequently, the addition of electrolytes to dioxan–water solutions seldom causes doubling of dioxan bands. Sze[68] observed doublets at 615, 625 cm^{-1}, 825, 832 cm^{-1}, and 863, 872 cm^{-1} for the $Hg(NO_3)_2/C_4H_8O_2/H_2O$ system, which suggested the presence of two dioxan species. Again, since the affected modes were associated with ring vibrations, it was concluded that the interaction probably occurs at oxygen sites.

6   ION SOLVATION

6.1   Cation Solvation

Solvent molecules in the immediate vicinity of an ion will experience a different potential from that of the bulk solvent and it is of considerable interest to determine if the ion–solvent interactions are less than, equal to, or greater than any ion–ion or solvent–solvent interactions. Cations with high polarizing power (Z/r) often order the solvent molecules into well-defined coordination spheres, with relatively high thermodynamic stability and long mean lifetimes. Lincoln[333] and Hinton and Amis[334] have summarized the characteristic first coordination numbers for a number of cations in different solvents, while Hunt[142] has reviewed some of the work related to the kinetic stability of solvated cations. Inelastic neutron scattering has also been employed to obtain information about hydrated cations and the effect of anions on the hydration shell.[335] A monograph on solvent effects on chemical phenomena is also of interest.[336] Vibrational spectroscopy can provide information through interpretation of variations of band positions, intensities, and halfwidths of both the solute and solvent bands over a wide range of composition and temperature. In favourable cases the ion–solvent interaction may generate new bands characteristic of a true complex. These bands may be due primarily to ligand modes shifted to slightly different peak positions by the influence of the force field of the ion, or they may be due to a cation–solvent vibrational mode. The doubling of the acetonitrile modes due to complexation with Zn^{2+} has already been noted (Section 5.3). Sze[68] also assigned a weak Raman band at ca. 180 cm^{-1} to a Zn—N symmetric stretching vibration of the $Zn(CH_3CN)_x^{2+}$ complex ion. Similar observations have been reported for a number of different solvated cations.

6.1.1 Hydrates

Complexation of water by a cation does not substantially alter the internal fundamental frequencies of water from those characteristic of pure water.[4,337] Normal coordinate calculations of Kistenmacher et al.[338] for complexes of the type X---H_2O ($X=F^-$, Cl^-, Li^+, Na^+, K^+) show that, to a good approximation, the ion and the water molecule could be assumed to be essentially uncoupled, and that the frequencies characteristic of the complex were nearly independent of the H_2O force constants. Since little information about aqueous hydrates can be obtained from the fundamental region the search for bands due to ion–water vibrations takes on added importance. To date, the metal–oxygen symmetric stretching vibration has been detected by Raman spectroscopy for a large number of aqueous hydrated cations (Table 9). The antisymmetric stretching mode expected to give a band in the infrared spectrum appears to be obscured

TABLE 9
Observed Raman band positions/cm^{-1} for M—O vibrations of hydrated cations in aqueous solution

Species	Wavenumber /cm^{-1}	Pol.	Mode	Reference
Be(II)	535	p	$\nu_1(a_1)^a$	
	82	dp	$\nu_2(e)$	
	880	dp	$\nu_3(t_2)$	367, 603
	355	dp	$\nu_4(t_2)$	
Mg(II)	362	p	$\nu_1(a_{1g})^b$	361
Co(II)	380	p	$\nu_1(a_{1g})^b$	c
Ni(II)	390	p	$\nu_1(a_{1g})^b$	c
Cu(II)	436	p	$\nu_1(a_{1g})^b$	622
Zn(II)	360	p	$\nu_1(a_{1g})^b$	361
Cd(II)	348	p		621
Hg(II)	362	p		623
ClCH$_2$Hg$^+$	462	p		631
Al(III)	532	p	$\nu_1(a_{1g})^b$	370
	344	dp	ν_2 or $\nu_5(t_{2g})$	
Cr(III)	500	p	$\nu_1(a_{1g})^b$	c
Fe(III)	510	p	$\nu_1(a_{1g})^b$	633
	308	dp	$\nu_2(e_g)$	
In(III)	400	p		566
Tl(III)	≈ 450	p		372
Bi(III)	390	p		634
Ce(IV)	394	?		636
Th(IV)	420	p		637

^{a} Assignments based on tetrahedral $Be(H_2O)_4^{2+}$ cation.
^{b} Assignments based on octahedral $M(H_2O)_6^{n+}$ cation.
^{c} C.-H. Huang and M. H. Brooker, unpublished work.

by low-frequency water modes and background absorption for hydrates in solution, but a number of workers have reported bands due to this mode for solid hydrates.[339–349] A complete single-crystal infrared and Raman study of [Ni(H$_2$O)$_6$][SnCl$_6$] has established the assignments for the hexa-aquo cation.[348] In this study the assignments were aided by the high crystal symmetry, but for most crystals the assignments are complicated by overlap with bands due to lattice modes and perturbations due to low crystal symmetry.[340,341,344,345,349]

Inspection of Table 9 suggests that bands due to metal–oxygen symmetric stretching can only be detected for hydrates with small cations which are capable of a significant distortion of the potential energy surface at the oxygen end of a water molecule, so that the metal–oxygen vibration has an associated polarizability change. The 'softer' cations such as Zn^{2+} and Hg^{2+} would be expected to give interactions having relatively high polarizability, but the fact that 'harder' cations such as Mg^{2+} and Al^{3+} exhibit bands suggest that cation polarizability is not a dominant factor. It is noteworthy that no comparable Raman bands have been reported for cations with Pauling radii greater than 1.0 Å (0.1 nm), including a large number of ions considered to be strongly hydrated (i.e. lanthanide(III) ions).

Of the alkali metal cations, only the small Li^+ is normally considered to be strongly hydrated, although Na^+ and K^+ may also be weakly hydrated. Cogley et al.[350] have reported association constants for water with Li^+, Na^+, K^+ and Cl^- from n.m.r. data in propylene carbonate; normal coordinate calculations for the Li^+—, Na^+—, and K^+–H$_2$O complexes place the symmetric stretching frequencies at 444.3, 228.8, and 176.1 cm^{-1}, respectively.[338] A coordination number of 4 has been suggested for Na^+ from ^{23}Na n.m.r. data.[351] Matrix isolation studies of Devlin and co-workers[352–355] also suggest hydration of the alkali metal ions. Neutron and X-ray diffraction patterns[356,357] of aqueous LiCl solutions were consistent with the Li(H$_2$O)$_4{}^+$ tetrahedral species, and ab initio calculations[358] predicted the same species. Molecular dynamics studies[359] of LiCl solutions predicted a hydration sphere containing 5.5 H$_2$O molecules. Leifer and Hogfeldt[360] have also suggested from ion activity functions that the Li(H$_2$O)$_4{}^+$ species is very stable in aqueous solution. Raman studies of aqueous nitrates have shown that H$_2$O is only displaced from the coordination sphere of Li^+ and Na^+ at high concentrations and coordination numbers of about 3–4 have been inferred.[12,33,85] Failure to detect the cation–water vibration does not mean that hydrated cations are not formed. With the overwhelming evidence for the Li(H$_2$O)$_4{}^+$ species, it seems possible that with improved detection devices and signal-averaging techniques one might expect to detect a Li^+–water band.

Raman bands have been detected for the aqueous hydrates of Mg^{2+} and Be^{2+} but have not been reported for the other alkaline earth cations. A weak band ≈ 390 cm^{-1} observed for concentrated Ca(NO$_2$)$_2$ solutions was tentatively assigned to the Ca^{2+}–H$_2$O mode,[33] while Schropfer[342] assigned an infrared band at 440 cm^{-1} (330 cm^{-1} in D$_2$O) in solid CaSO$_3$·$\frac{1}{2}$H$_2$O to a similar mode. The Sr^{2+}–H$_2$O stretching mode of solid Sr(H$_2$O)$_6$Cl$_2$ has also been assigned.[349]

The peak at 362 cm^{-1} observed for Mg^{2+}-containing solutions has been assigned to the Mg(H$_2$O)$_6$$^{2+}$ octahedral species. A marked temperature-dependence of the peak position was reported and attributed to weakening of the Mg^{2+}–water bond with increased temperature.[51,361] Sensitivity was enhanced by multiple-scan averaging and spectral analyses were performed by digital computer methods.[362] Detailed studies of the magnesium nitrate–water system indicate that the Mg(H$_2$O)$_6$$^{2+}$ ion is very stable and NO$_3$$^-$ does not enter the coordination sphere until it is required to do so for stoichiometric reasons.[363,364] Green and Sheppard[365] have studied the preferential solvation of Mg^{2+} ion in acetone–water mixtures by n.m.r. The octahedral complex Mg(H$_2$O)$_6$$^{2+}$ was the most stable, although both acetone and ClO$_4$$^-$ were able to enter the coordination sphere. Covington and Covington[366] in a similar study reported an overall coordination number of 6.0±0.4. Both groups of workers were able to obtain equilibrium constants for the solvation change from water to acetone.

Most authors have assigned the vibrational spectrum of hydrated Be^{2+} to the tetrahedral ion Be(H$_2$O)$_4$$^{2+}$ although the detailed data and the assignments differ. More bands are observed than are required for the tetrahedral model. Irish and Chang[367] have assigned peaks at 535, 82, 880, and 355 cm^{-1} to the $\nu_1(a_1)$, $\nu_2(e)$, $\nu_3(t_2)$, and $\nu_4(t_2)$ modes of the tetrahedral species. An additional pH-dependent Raman band at 490 cm^{-1} was attributed to a hydrolysis product, while Raman bands at 420 cm^{-1} (depolarized) and 466 cm^{-1} (polarized) were tentatively assigned to the structure beyond the first coordination sphere of Be^{2+}. Bertin and Derouault[368] did not detect the infrared band at about 880 cm^{-1} reported by Irish[367] and by Grigor'ev et al.,[369] but in acidic solution they observed an infrared band at 990 cm^{-1} (880 cm^{-1} in D$_2$O). Raman bands at 534 and 357 cm^{-1} (512 and 330 cm^{-1} in D$_2$O) were assigned to the ν_1 and ν_4 modes. Bands observed at 515, 415, and 1170 cm^{-1} in neutral solutions were assigned to a cyclic hydroxy complex Be$_3$(OH)$_3$(H$_2$O)$_6$$^{3+}$. Marques et al.[370] reported bands at 528 and 348 cm^{-1} for 2.6 mol dm^{-3} Be(NO$_3$)$_2$ and 533 and 351 cm^{-1} in 2.2 mol dm^{-3} BeSO$_4$, which they assigned to the ν_1 and ν_3' modes of an *octahedral* complex. A weak band at 765 cm^{-1} was assigned to the ν_1 mode of Be(H$_2$O)$_4$$^{2+}$. Gardiner et al.[371] assigned bands at 526 and 335 cm^{-1} to the ν_1 and ν_4 modes of the tetrahedral species and a band at 467 cm^{-1} (and perhaps 355 cm^{-1}) to a hydrolysis product. Although there is fair agreement for the major features, the disagreement for the minor features suggests that the problem may be due to the presence of impurities or to anion- and H$_3$O$^+$-dependence of the frequencies.

The Al^{3+} and Fe^{3+} ions exhibit a two-band spectrum, with the polarized high-frequency band assigned to the a_{1g} mode of an octahedral species and the low-frequency band assigned to either a t_{2g} or e_g mode. The t_{2g} assignment seems preferable since for other octahedral complexes the t_{2g} mode is more intense than the e_g mode. It is interesting to note that for the small highly-charged ions Al^{3+}, Fe^{3+}, and Cr^{3+}, the frequency of the symmetric stretch is at about 500 cm^{-1}. In a study of the aqueous thallium(III) chloride system, Spiro[372] observed a band at 450 cm^{-1} which he assigned to a Tl^{3+}–H$_2$O mode. The fact that addition of *two* moles of Cl$^-$ reduced the intensity of this band to zero was interpreted as evidence for a distorted octahedral (D_{4h}) arrangement of water molecules about Tl^{3+}, with the two axial water molecules contributing all of the intensity to the Tl^{3+} water band, and with the four equatorial water molecules being less tightly coordinated. No Raman bands have been observed for the Ln^{3+}–H$_2$O vibrations, and although these ions are usually considered to be eight- or nine-coordinated,[373] the interaction must be essentially electrostatic.

The lifetime of aqueous hydrates is also of interest to the spectroscopist, since a sufficiently labile molecule may undergo complete environmental averaging with the bulk solvent and hence make no contribution to the coordination number determined by a particular method. A number of recent solvent-exchange studies have been performed. The half-life of exchange varies from very long-lived Cr(H$_2$O)$_6$$^{3+}$ ($t_{\frac{1}{2}} \approx 40$ hours) to the very short-lived Ni(H$_2$O)$_6$$^{2+}$ ($t_{\frac{1}{2}} \approx 10^{-5}$ s) and Co(H$_2$O)$_6$$^{2+}$ ($t_{\frac{1}{2}} \approx 10^{-7}$ s).[142,333] Of interest to the chemist is the catalytic action of ions such as IO$_3$$^-$, NO$_3$$^-$, NO$_2$$^-$, and Cl$^-$.[374,375] For instance, Green and Sheppard[365] reported that in acetone–water mixtures, the hydrated magnesium ion underwent a more rapid exchange of water molecules in the presence of NO$_3$$^-$ than in the presence of ClO$_4$$^-$. Previous Raman studies by Al-Baldawi *et al.*[54] suggested that NO$_3$$^-$ enhances the exchange rate of the Zn^{2+}–CH$_3$OH complex in anhydrous methanol.

6.1.2 Ammoniates

Although less work on the ammoniates has been reported, ammonia appears to form stronger complexes than water. The internal modes of NH$_3$ are not significantly affected by complexation with cations (Section 5.2), so it is difficult to separate bands of complexed ammonia from those of bulk ammonia. Infrared and Raman spectra of solid ammoniated salts have been reported and peaks assigned to the M—N vibrations of ammoniate complexes.[376–378] Again, sampling problems appear to have prevented detection of the infrared-active antisymmetric M—N vibration and only a few polarized Raman bands of the symmetric-stretching mode have been reported (Table 10). Lundeen and Tobias[304] observed two polarized bands for Ag$^+$ solutions in liquid ammonia and assigned these to the two a_g modes of an Ag(NH$_3$)$_6$$^+$ species with D_{4h} symmetry. An interesting finding is the presence of M—NH$_3$ bands for Li$^+$, Na$^+$, Ca^{2+}, Sr^{2+}, and Ba^{2+}, where none had been observed for the hydrates. Vibrational spectra of M$^+$NO$_3$$^-$ ion pairs variously hydrated and ammoniated in an argon matrix also suggested strong ammonia solvates with Li$^+$, Na$^+$, and K$^+$.[352–355]

6.1.3 Other solvates

Evidence for cation solvation has been reported for a number of other solvents. Whereas for aqueous and ammonia solutions Raman bands were more easily detected than infrared bands because of the low Raman background scattering

TABLE 10
Band positions/cm^{-1} for M—N vibrations
of M(NH$_3$)$_x$$^{n+}$

Ion	Ref. 291	Ref. 298^a	Ref. 304
Li$^+$	241	245, 346, 538	
Na$^+$	194		
Ag$^+$			296, 329
Mg^{2+}	328		
Ca^{2+}	266		260
Sr^{2+}	243		
Ba^{2+}	215		

^{a} For a mole ratio LiNO$_3$:NH$_3$ = 1:6.4, the band positions were reported to be concentration-dependent.

compared with the strong infrared absorption, for most organic solvents the infrared background absorption is much less and infrared bands are more easily observed. Only a few M—N or M—O symmetric-stretching Raman modes have been observed for organic solvates. Sze[68] has tentatively assigned a band at 168 cm^{-1} to a Hg^{2+}–dioxan mode and a weak band at 180 cm^{-1} to a Zn^{2+}–acetonitrile mode. In both cases doublet structures of the dioxan and aceto-nitrile bands confirmed the existence of metal ion-solvates (Section 5.3). Although the ionic nature of the cation–solvent interactions seems to preclude the detection of most metal–solvent vibrations by Raman spectroscopy, the far-infrared 'windows' of these solvents have permitted detection of a number of vibrations due to 'cations in solvation cages'. Often in these cases a splitting of certain bands due to the internal modes of the solvent attests to the specificity of the cation–solvent interactions. Work in this field has been reviewed by Irish,[5] Edgell[379] and Popov.[380] Generally, these ion-cage vibrations have the following characteristics: the bands are broad and of medium intensity, the band frequency varies with the solvent and with the cation but is independent of the anion (unless a contact ion-pair is formed), the band frequencies are about 400 cm^{-1} for Li$^+$, 200 cm^{-1} for NH$_4$$^+$, 180 cm^{-1} for Na$^+$ and about 150 cm^{-1} for K$^+$. Much of the recent work in this area[381–393] has been reported by Popov and co-workers.[381–386]

Recently, Baum and Popov[381] have studied the solvation of lithium ion by acetone in acetone–nitromethane solutions by Raman, infrared and n.m.r. spectroscopic techniques. An infrared band at 425 cm^{-1} was assigned to the Li$^+$–acetone vibration. Acetone bands at 390 cm^{-1} (infrared) and 789 cm^{-1} (Raman) were shifted to 369 cm^{-1} and 803 cm^{-1} for the Li$^+$–acetone complex. The 369 cm^{-1} band had previously been mis-assigned to a Li$^+$–nitromethane mode.[391] Quantitative intensity studies were consistent with the formation of a 4:1 acetone, Li$^+$ complex, and estimates of the stepwise stability constants for complexation of Li$^+$ by acetone in nitromethane solutions were $K_1 = 19.1$,

$K_2 = 2.5$, $K_3 = 1.3$, and $K_4 = 0.6$. The Li^+ was preferentially solvated by acetone in the acetone–nitromethane solutions. Similar studies of the Li^+ and NH_4^+ solvation by pyridine have been reported by Rouviere and co-workers.[392] Infrared bands at 420 and 195 cm^{-1} were assigned to the Li^+ and NH_4^+ 'cage' vibrations, the 992 cm^{-1} pyridine mode shifted to 1004 cm^{-1} for the Li^+– pyridine complex, and a coordination number of four was reported for Li^+. Cation-solvent vibrational bands have been reported for ions in propylene carbonate,[385, 387] sulfolane,[388] tetrahydrofuran,[389] acetonitrile,[381, 391] dimethyl sulfoxide (DMSO),[384, 390] and pyridine.[386, 392]

Measurement of bands due to solvent modes of metal–solvent complexes have also been used to characterize the ion solvation. Perilygen and Klimchuk[394] used bands in the 1000–1500 and 1650–3000 cm^{-1} regions of acetone to arrive at the conclusion that the coordination numbers of the Na^+, Li^+, and Mg^{2+} ions are four, four, and six, respectively. A hydration number of four was also derived from concentration studies in tetrahydrofuran for Na^+ by measuring infrared absorption in the 900–1150 cm^{-1} region.[395]

Baron et al.[396] observed three bands in the CO region of N,N-dimethylacetamide when Li^+ or Ba^{2+} salts were added. A solvent dimer absorbed at 1658 cm^{-1}, the monomer at 1643 cm^{-1}, and the cation–solvent species at 1627 cm^{-1} (Li^+) or 1620 cm^{-1} (Ba^{2+}). Coetzee and Sharpe[322] have reported infrared and n.m.r. studies of solute–solvent interactions for a number of aprotic solvents. Ion–solvent interactions have been reported for LiCl in formic acid.[397] Regis and Corset[398] have shown that Li^+ is preferentially solvated by acetonitrile in acetonitrile–nitromethane mixtures, and Covington et al.[399] have demonstrated the preference of Li^+ for water in water–DMSO mixtures; the competitive solvation of cations in water–acetonitrile systems has also been studied.[400] Association of DMSO with water has been studied by Raman spectroscopy.[401]

Far-infrared and Raman spectra have recently been reported for lithium and sodium cryptates in non-aqueous solvents.[402] Cryptates are formed as an inclusion-type complex when alkali–metal cations are trapped inside unusual macro-bicyclic ligands called cryptands. These have the form:

C222, $a = b = c = 1$; C221, $a = 0$, $b = c = 1$; C211, $a = b = 0$, $c = 1$.

Far-infrared bands were assigned to the cation 'cage' vibration. For the Na^+ cryptates C222 and C221 bands were observed at (234 ± 2) and (218 ± 1) cm^{-1}, and for the Li^+ cryptates C221 and C211 bands were observed at (243 ± 3) and (348 ± 1) cm^{-1}. Failure to detect Raman bands due to the cation–ligand vibration attests to the electrostatic nature of the interaction. Related n.m.r. studies have been reported.[403]

6.2 Anion Solvation

Although the preceding discussion strongly supports the concept of specific cation solvation, the evidence in favour of anion solvation is much less compelling. Nevertheless, a growing number of workers are interpreting their data in terms of anion–solvate complexes. Anions are generally larger than cations. Therefore, except for F^-, the polarizing power, and thus the thermodynamic stability of anion solvates, is expected to be much less than for cations. One also expects greater lability of solvent molecules in the hydration sphere of the anion. Although anion–solvent stretching modes have not been observed, it has previously been noted (Sections 5.1 and 5.2) that anions have a considerable effect on the positions and halfwidths of the bands due to the stretching modes of H_2O and NH_3. Symons and Waddington[404] studied the infrared spectra of perchlorates and fluoroborates and assigned new bands at frequencies higher than those of the stretching modes of pure water to $ClO_4^- - H_2O$ and $BF_4^- - H_2O$ complexes. Hydration numbers of four were calculated from intensity measurements. Lemley and Lagowski[293] have studied the Raman spectra of ammonia solutions of $NaNO_3$, NaSCN, NH_4NO_3, NH_4SCN, $LiNO_3$, and LiSCN and observed that anions dominate the interaction with the solvent for the sodium and ammonium salts. A discrete $NH_3 . SCN^-$ complex was proposed. In the ν_2 region of the NH_3 spectrum a band at 1120 cm^{-1} was assigned to H-bonded ammonia shifted from the 1060 cm^{-1} value of uncomplexed ammonia, and the ν_3 S—C mode of SCN^- was shifted to about 740 cm^{-1} from the value the uncomplexed SCN^- of about 750 cm^{-1}. Interaction through sulfur was implied.

Hydrogen-bonding effects have also been reported for the nitrate ion in various solvents.[5,405,406] Davis et al.[5,405] reported a band due to the hydrogen-bonded $CCl_3H---NO_3^-$ species when tetraphenylarsonium nitrate was dissolved in chloroform. Findlay and Symons[406] observed that the addition of methanol to solutions of tetrabutylammonium nitrate in methylene chloride causes the singlet band at 1352 cm^{-1}, characteristic of the ν_3 mode of NO_3^- in aprotic solvents, to be lost and replaced by a doublet with components at 1334 and 1405 cm^{-1}. The effect was explained by postulating the existence of a $1:1$ $CH_3OH---NO_3^-$ complex with symmetry lower than D_{3h}, which lifts the degeneracy of the $\nu_3(e')$ mode (Section 7). In a reverse titration, the O—H stretching band at 3620 cm^{-1}, characteristic of non-hydrogen-bonded methanol, was replaced by a broader band at ca. 3405 cm^{-1} which was assigned to the $1:1$ hydrogen-bonded solvate. A doublet structure in the ν_3 region of the spectrum

of NO_3^- in H_2O has been interpreted in terms of a H_2O---NO_3^- complex.[407]
The possibility that the rotatory motion of the nitrate ion in a solvent cage
contributes significantly to this doublet structure[367] has been tested and
rejected.[408] Rotational motions of the ion may produce a difference in band
centres between infrared and Raman spectra, but a symmetry-lowering resulting
from H_2O—NO_3^- binding is inferred to be the cause of the splitting of the ν_3
band. Similar complexes could explain the doubling of bands due to ν_3 modes for
aqueous carbonates and chlorates. Relatively strong unsymmetrical interactions
have also been suggested from studies of gas-phase hydration of NO_3^-[409] and
Hertz[410] has shown through n.m.r. studies that the hydration sphere of F^- ion
has the unsymmetrical structure HOH---F^- not the symmetrical arrangement

$O\overset{\displaystyle /H}{\underset{\displaystyle \backslash H}{<}}F^-$. Harmon and Gennick[411] studied the monohydrates of tetra-

methylammonium fluoride and hydroxide by infrared spectroscopy. Intense low-
frequency bands have been assigned to tightly coordinated water attributed to
the species $(F^-H_2O)_2^{2-}$ and $(OH^-H_2O)_2^{2-}$. Kistenmacher et al.[338] have
calculated the heat of formation and the normal modes for Li^+, Na^+, K^+, F^-,
and Cl^- ion complexes with a single water molecule. The values of the
Hartree-Fock binding energies were -35.2, -24.0, -16.6, -23.7, and -11.9
kcal mol^{-1}, respectively (i.e. -147, -100, -69.4, -99.2, and -49.8 kJ mol^{-1},
respectively). These results, together with the normal coordinate calculations,
could be interpreted to suggest that F^- should form hydrates with a strength
comparable to that of Na^+, while Cl^- should bind somewhat more weakly to
water than K^+ does.

Other physicochemical studies suggest anion hydration. Neutron and X-ray
diffraction data for aqueous LiCl suggest octahedral coordination of oxygen
atoms about Cl^-.[356] Molecular dynamics calculations based on LiCl solutions
also support octahedral coordination of Cl^- ion.[359] Hydrogen bonding
between water and anions such as SO_4^{2-} and NO_3^- is often reported to exist
in crystal hydrates,[345,412] and anomalous isotope shifts observed for PO_4^{3-}
and $B(OH)_4^-$ ions in aqueous solution have been attributed to hydrogen bonding.[413,414] Cogley et al.[350] have calculated an equilibrium constant for the
formation of a Cl^----H_2O complex in propylene carbonate solutions which
is of the same order of magnitude as the Li^+---H_2O equilibrium constant.
Finally, studies of the overtone region of the infrared spectrum of H_2O for
aqueous CO_3^{2-} and SO_4^{2-} solutions were interpreted to indicate that CO_3^{2-}
and SO_4^{2-} ions distort the configuration of H_2O molecules surrounding cations
in hydration shells.[415] The results are consistent with the small molar volumes,
$\bar{V}°$, for CO_3^{2-} and SO_4^{2-} and suggest that F^- and OH^- should show a similar
effect.[416] The molar volume of NO_3^- in aqueous solution is about the same as
its value in the solid, which suggests that NO_3^- forms hydrogen-bonds with
water about as well as water forms hydrogen-bonds with water. The small
frequency shift in the bands due to O—H stretching which accompanies addition
of NO_3^- to water is consistent with this idea (Section 5.1).

7 VIBRATIONAL SPECTRAL STUDIES OF SELECTED SYSTEMS

7.1 Acids

Three objectives of the study of the vibrational spectra of acids are: the measurement of the degree of formation (α) of the free ions from the acid and hence the estimation of acidity constants (K_a) of moderately strong acids; the determination of structures; and the elucidation of proton-transfer processes by measurement of band shapes. The latter topic has been briefly discussed in Section 3; here we stress the progress in the first two areas.

To measure α the usual practice is to compare the intensity of an isolated band of a supposedly free ion in the acid system with the intensity of a band from a salt containing the free ion and believed to be totally ionized in the chosen solvent.[20] In some cases a band common to the acid and the free ion is employed as an internal intensity standard.[417–420] In other cases, a cell replacement technique has been used to obtain intensity ratios relative to an external standard.[137] A rotating, partitioned cell[152] has also been used as described in Section 4. Following measurement of α, extrapolation procedures, sometimes using stoichiometric activity coefficients as discussed in Section 2.1, are used to estimate K_a. Limitations imposed by instrumentation, band overlap, and uncertainty in the extrapolation, limit the accuracy of K_a to probably $\pm 5\%$. It

TABLE 11
Vibrational spectral studies of the dissociation of acids

System	Species observed	Raman band/cm^{-1}	K_a at 298 K /mol dm^{-3}	References
CH_2FCOOH	$CH_2FCO_2^-$	1340	$(3.0 \pm 0.5) \times 10^{-3}$	417
CF_3COOH	$CF_3CO_2^-$	1438	4—8	418
CCl_3COOH	$CCl_3CO_2^-$	1348	2—5	418
		1344	3.2	419
$MeSO_3H$	$MeSO_3^-$	1046	83 ± 2	420
$EtSO_3H$	$EtSO_3^-$	≈ 1046	48 ± 2	420
$PrSO_3H$	$PrSO_3^-$	≈ 1046	34 ± 6	420
HSO_4^-	SO_4^{2-}	980	0.010	137
			0.0112 mol kg^{-1}	424, 425
HNO_3	NO_3^-	1049	α/c data	152
			24	423

is useful, however, to be able to map α over a wide range of acid concentrations and composition by Raman spectroscopy and thus to elucidate the constitution of a concentrated solution. A list of recent studies is presented in Table 11. (This extends Table 1 of Ref. 20.)

Many acids are ionogens[421] and only become ionic when they react with a solvent. Ionization must precede dissociation, and the following scheme can be postulated:[418,422]

$$S + HA \xrightleftharpoons{K_i} SH^+ . A^- \xrightleftharpoons{K_d} SH^+ + A^-$$

The equilibrium constant for the overall process, which is the process normally considered in discussions of acidity, is the product $K_i K_d = K_a$ of the ionization constant and the dissociation constant. This scheme implies the possible existence of ion pairs $SH^+ A^-$ in addition to the 'free' ions, their concentration depending on the relative magnitudes of K_i and K_d. Covington et al.[418] have pointed out that if the Raman spectra of A^- and $SH_2^+ A^-$ are indistinguishable one can expect Raman (and n.m.r.) spectra to yield K_a in the limit of zero concentration, but conductivity and indicator methods may yield a different 'K' defined by $K_i K_d/(1 + K_i)$, because the ion-pair is electrically neutral.

Some experimental evidence for this ion-pair has come from studies of HSO_4^- and HNO_3. In the Raman spectra of HSO_4^-/H_2O solutions there is a confusing array of overlapping bands in the region 800–1300 cm^{-1}. By computer procedures bands characteristic of the HSO_4^- and SO_4^{2-} ions were separated and identified.[137] However, if one makes the reasonable assumption, borne out by many other studies of other species, that Raman bands have a symmetrical profile about the band maximum, then two additional bands must be invoked to achieve an acceptable fit. One of these occurs at 948 cm^{-1}, just below the 980 cm^{-1} frequency of the symmetrical stretch of SO_4^{2-}. It has been assigned to the species $H_3O^+ SO_4^{2-}$. This assignment is reasonable. Compare, for example, nitrate spectra which have been more exhaustively studied. When a cation binds to NO_3^- there are many examples where a new band of the ion-pair occurs just below or just above the 1048 cm^{-1} frequency of the free NO_3^- ion: $Hg^{2+} NO_3^-$, 1048 and 1033 cm^{-1};[68] $Zn^{2+} NO_3^-$, 1048 and 1036 cm^{-1};[68] $Sr^{2+} NO_3^-$, 1048 and 1051 cm^{-1}.[25] When SO_4^{2-} binds to Mg^{2+}, bands are observed at 982 and 995 cm^{-1}.[103] Thus the perturbation of SO_4^{2-} by H_3O^+, which occurs when an ion-pair forms, can be expected to generate a new line near 980 cm^{-1}. The 948 cm^{-1} band was also reported in the infrared spectrum where the overlap is minimized because the 980 cm^{-1} band is forbidden.[137] Additional evidence comes from studies of nitric acid, where there are fewer overlapping bands.[423] Prior to reaching concentrations where bands of molecular HNO_3 are evident, a band at 1036 cm^{-1} appears as an unsymmetrical shoulder on the 1048 cm^{-1} line of NO_3^-; this band also changes in intensity with composition in a manner consistent with the assignment to the ion-pair $H_3O^+ NO_3^-$.

Although the amassed evidence strongly suggests the correctness of the assignment, an alternative interpretation has been suggested. Turner[424] apparently detected a band at about 950 cm^{-1} in the spectrum of $HSO_4^-/water$ systems, in reasonable agreement with the observations reported above. However, by broadening the wings of the 980 cm^{-1} band of SO_4^{2-} he was able to include the 950 cm^{-1} band therein and thus he chose to ignore it. Such a procedure is relatively simple to apply because an equivalent contribution can be taken from the second, somewhat more intense, additional band at about 1030 cm^{-1} on the side of the 980 cm^{-1} band (a band assigned by Chen and Irish[137] to HSO_4^- and by Turner[424] to a form of HSO_4^- differing in the manner of hydration from the majority of bisulphate ions present). The procedure is not necessarily correct, however, and it is doubtful if sufficient precision is obtainable from a Du Pont curve analyser to warrant the conclusion that the 950 cm^{-1} line is an artifact of the procedure. The statement[425] 'The 948 cm^{-1} line vanishes if it is only assumed that all lines are symmetrical' is clearly not correct because the 948 cm^{-1} band was originally discovered by assuming symmetrical band shapes. Obviously the resolution of the difference of opinion concerning the existence of a band due to $H_3O^+SO_4^{2-}$ is not likely to come from Raman spectroscopy because the natural breadth of the bands and the severity of the overlap precludes the gathering of 'conclusive' data by improved instrumentation.

In a second study, Turner[425] implied the existence of the ion pair from consideration of the behaviour of intensity data when subjected to extrapolation procedures. Hopefully, other methods will yield results which eventually will lead to a better understanding. But, contrary to one stated opinion,[424] the validity of the interpretation of Raman band broadening in terms of proton transfer processes does not rest on direct observation of bands from the ion-pair.

In aqueous acid solutions the vibrational spectrum of H_3O^+ is obscured by the high rate of proton transfer between solvent molecules,[202] but vibrational spectroscopic studies have been reported for $H(H_2O)_n^+$ in hydrates of the type $HX.nH_2O$ (X = Cl or Br; n = 1–4)[426] and H_3O^+ and D_3O^+ in $H_3O^+CH_3C_6$-$H_4SO_3^-$ and $D_3O^+CH_3C_6H_4SO_3^-$.[427] In the latter case the assignments are supported by normal-coordinate calculations. Huong and Desbat[428] have contrasted the vibrational spectrum of H_3O^+ in $H_3O^+SbCl_6^-$, in which hydrogen bonding is weak,[429] with spectra of $H_3O^+Cl^-$ and $H_3O^+Br^-$, in which hydrogen bonding is strong. The results of these studies are summarized in Table 12. The results indicate that $\nu_1 > \nu_3$; this order is the inverse of that known for molecules such as NH_3 with C_{3v} symmetry (see Table 4). It is also clear that ν_1 and ν_3 are sensitive to the hydrogen-bonding donor–acceptor distances and thus one cannot ascribe fixed stretching frequencies for ν_1 and ν_3. Calculation shows that the ν_1/ν_3 trend could be reversed if the hydrogen bonding interaction were sufficiently weak[427] but the experimental results[429] do not support this. It is also clear that the results are sensitive to the manner of preparation and the composition of the samples.[426,428] Assignments for the species $H_5O_2^+$ have been inferred from studies of the di- and tri-hydrates of HCl and HBr[426,430] and for the species $H_7O_3^+$ from the tri-hydrates of $HClO_4$ and HNO_3.[431] Giguère and Madec[432] have reported Raman data for the H_3O^+ ---Cl^- ion-pair in an equimolar mixture of H_2O, HCl and SO_2.

Zundel and co-workers[143,433–435] have continued their studies of the

TABLE 12
Fundamental frequencies/cm^{-1} of the H_3O^+ ion

Assignment C_{3v}	$H_3O^+SbCl_6^-$ (CH$_2$Cl$_2$ solution, 298 K) (Ref. 429)	$H_3O^+SbCl_6^-$ (s, 77 K) (Ref. 429)	$H_3O^+Br^-$ (s, 77 K) (Ref. 428)	$H_3O^+Cl^-$ (s, 77 K) (Ref. 428)	$H_3O^+CH_3C_6H_4SO_3^-$ (s, $\approx$298 K) (Ref. 427)
$\nu_1(a_1)$	3560	3509	2900	2895	2700
$\nu_3(e)$	3510	3463	$\begin{cases}2700\\2570\end{cases}$	$\begin{cases}2630\\2525\end{cases}$	2600
$\nu_4(e)$	1600	1604	1605	$\begin{cases}1650\\1615\end{cases}$	1665
$\nu_2(a_1)$	1095	1095	970	970	1130

vibrational spectra of hydrogen-bonded species. They have observed that, in liquid systems in which BN^+---B hydrogen-bonds with a symmetrical double-minimum potential well, a continuous infrared absorption is observed. This has been attributed to a continuous energy distribution of the protons caused by various interactions resulting from the extremely high polarizabilities of these hydrogen-bonds.[143] A similar interpretation has been invoked to explain the continuous scattering observed in the Raman spectra of pure water and aqueous HCl solutions.[143,433]

Several studies of how the solvent modifies the rotation–vibration band profiles of diatomic molecules have been reported. These include studies of the acids HCl,[436] DCl,[436,437] HBr,[436] DBr[436] and HF.[438] In inert solvents, molecular perturbations are equivalent to those for gases at high pressures; for a polar solvent, the rotational correlation function must be calculated in the same manner as for the pure liquid.[436] The frequency shift of ν_{H-F} due to hydrogen-bonding is larger than that of other proton donors and correlates with the base strength of the solvent.[439] Enthalpies of complex formation have been estimated from the data. The acid–base interaction of CH_3CN and $HClO_4$, which commences with hydrogen-bonding, followed by slow proton transfer, has been followed by infrared spectroscopy.[440]

Four isotopic HNO_3 molecules have been studied in a N_2 matrix and vibrational assignments have been made for both the monomer and the dimer.[441] Vibrations of a hydrogen dinitrate ion $H(NO_3)_2^-$ have been reported;[442,443] ab initio calculations of the configurations and of the proton potential curves indicate that the energy differences between a configuration with a short hydrogen-bond and one with tetrahedral coordination of the hydrogen ion are small.[444] The constitution of concentrated N_2O_4—HNO_3—H_2O solutions has been explored by Raman spectroscopic techniques.[445,446]

Raman spectra of bicarbonate and carbonate ions in the presence of alkali metal cations provide no evidence for anion–cation association[447] although e.m.f. data have been interpreted assuming the presence of the species $NaHCO_3$

and $NaCO_3^-$.[448] Hydrogen–deuterium exchange on the bicarbonate ion in H_2O–D_2O mixtures has been followed by Raman spectroscopy and concentration quotients for the pertinent reactions have been calculated.[447] Infrared spectra of H_2O and CO_2 trapped together in a N_2 matrix show a non-hydrogen-bonded water–CO_2 complex[449] consistent with results from other solution studies.[447b]

Raman spectra of acetic acid, acetic acid-d_1, acetic acid-d_3 and perdeuteriated acetic acid in the polycrystalline state have been reported,[450] and also those of the acetic acid–fluorosulfuric acid compound.[451] Infrared spectra of matrix-isolated trifluoroacetic acid and its anhydride have been discussed.[452] In addition to recent work on the self-association of carboxylic acids,[45,47,48] the work of Guilleme et al.[453] and of Glasoe et al.[454] is noteworthy; the latter is concerned with the question of the relative strengths of hydrogen and deuterium intermolecular bonds. Molecular reorientation in carboxylic acids and its dependence on intermolecular interactions and dimerization have been studied by depolarized Rayleigh scattering.[455]

7.2 Hydroxides, Zincates, Aluminates, Vanadates, and Silicates

The frequency of the OH^- stretching vibration occurs at 3663 cm^{-1} in the spectrum of crystalline LiOH.[456,457] A complete analysis of the single-crystal spectrum has been performed;[456] bands at 419 cm^{-1} (e_u(i.r.)) and at 287 cm^{-1} (e_g(R)) were assigned to librational modes with the symmetries indicated. Cation–anion layer vibrations were assigned at 519 and 620 cm^{-1}. Sharma[458,459] has studied the low-frequency Raman spectra of concentrated solutions of alkali metal hydroxides. For 17.16 mol dm^{-3} NaOH broad bands were observed at 292 cm^{-1} (polarized) and 322 cm^{-1}; for 16.34 mol dm^{-3} KOH bands at 282 cm^{-1} (polarized) and 310 cm^{-1} were observed. These were only slightly shifted when CH_3OH was used as solvent. Intensity studies indicated that these Raman bands only appear when the concentrations exceed 3.6 mol dm^{-3} KOH and 4.4 mol dm^{-3} NaOH. The bands were assigned to ion-pairs or clusters. For LiOH solutions no bands were observed and it was concluded that the strongly solvated Li^+ cations retain their hydration spheres intact in alkaline medium.

In earlier studies of ZnO/MOH solutions, bands at the above positions were assigned to t_2 and e modes of the tetrahedral $Zn(OH)_4^{2-}$ ion.[460,461] Sharma[459] has shown that these bands are absent in spectra from ZnO/LiOH solutions and thus only two bands at approximately 470 cm^{-1} (polarized) and 430 cm^{-1} (depolarized) can be attributed to zinc-containing species. An intensity-ratio change with composition points to two different species. The 470 cm^{-1} band was assigned to linear ZnO_2^{2-}, perturbed slightly by Na^+ and K^+ but less so by Li^+(aq). The 430 cm^{-1} band was assigned to polynuclear aggregates which are broken up by addition of OH^- and by dilution. These assignments are analogous to those for polynuclear aggregates and $ZnCl_4^{2-}$ species in concentrated $ZnCl_2$ solutions.[462] Briggs *et al.*[463] also distinguished between bands at 283 and 310 cm^{-1} (assigned to bands in the spectrum of KOH solution) and bands at 430 and 471 cm^{-1}. However, they failed to note that the latter two bands could arise from two different species and they retained the assignment to $Zn(OH)_4^{2-}$, partly basing this conclusion on potentiometric data and partly on the fact that the 435 cm^{-1} infrared band is coincident with one Raman band. But if the latter is attributed to different species (viz. the polynuclear aggregates) their argument is weak. They do provide evidence for aggregates which slowly break down on standing (ageing effect). It appears that the constitution of these concentrated solutions is extremely complex and time-dependent, but had the Sharma model been available to Briggs *et al.* they could possibly have adapted it to account for their observations instead of invoking the species $Zn(OH)_4^{2-}$. In an analogous system, $HCdO_2^-$ has been postulated.[464] Solids containing ZnO_2 units are known.[465]

Evidence is available which supports the view that aluminate solutions contain AlO_2^- species at high pH.[458,466] For $8 < pH < 12.5$, $Al(OH)_4^-$ is not believed to have T_d symmetry and, in fact, a polymeric species may also exist in this system.[466] Both zincate and aluminate break down NaOH and KOH clusters.[458] Kopylova and co-workers[467,468] assign bands at 636 cm^{-1} (R) and 740 cm^{-1} (i.r.) to the $\nu_1(a_1)$ and $\nu_3(t_2)$ modes of $Al(OH)_4^-$ and bands at 900–920, 550, and 740 cm^{-1} to linear polymers. Complexes are not believed to be associated by hydrogen bonds. Their studies also dwell on ageing.[469]

Evidence for $VO(OH)_3^-$ in basic aqueous solution has been advanced by Iannuzzi and Rieger.[470] The ion has a Raman band at 987 cm^{-1} whereas the aquo-ion has one at 1001 cm^{-1}, and hydrated VO_2 has one at 968 cm^{-1}. Raman spectra of aqueous solutions containing sodium silicate indicate that the monomeric anions present in solution result from deprotonation of $Si(OH)_4$; they are $SiO(OH)_3^-$, $SiO_2(OH)_2^{2-}$, and $SiO_3(OH)^{3-}$ with concentrations dependent on the Na_2O–SiO_2 mole ratio. Possible structures of polymers also are discussed.[471] In the spectrum of fused silica a Raman band near 3690 cm^{-1} was assigned to Si—OH groups by Walrafen.[115] In contrast to this, hydrothermal α-quartz was found to contain hydrogen-bonded OH...OH$^-$ units of hydrated OH$^-$ ions with a Raman band at 3590 cm^{-1} and an infrared band at 3585 cm^{-1} and H_2O molecules engaged in various kinds of hydrogen-bonding with bands between 3000 and 3525 cm^{-1}.[472]

7.3 Halides

Many reports of investigations of the interactions of halide ions with metal cations in solution have appeared; the investigations are prompted by the desire to characterize and analyse species in solutions of industrial and biological importance and the hope of further elucidating basic bonding principles. Although ion-pairs have been inferred from thermodynamic and kinetic measurements of aqueous and aqueous–acetone solutions of alkali metal halides,[473–476] no confirmation of this has been achieved by Raman studies, even for molten lithium chloride. It would appear that even the $Li^+ \dots Cl^-$ interaction is too ionic to induce a sufficiently large polarizability change to give rise to a Raman band. On the other hand, Raman spectra of molten Li_2BeF_4, Na_2BeF_4,[477] and K_2MgCl_4 and Cs_2MgCl_4[478] exhibit the four bands expected for the discrete tetrahedral species BeF_4^{2-} (tetrafluoroberyllate ion) and $MgCl_4^{2-}$ (tetrachloromagnesate ion). The BeF_4^{2-} ion is relatively stable in aqueous solution, provided an excess of F^- ion is added to prevent the hydrolysis or solvolysis reaction.[479] Hogben et al.[480] have investigated solutions containing fluoride and beryllium ion in the ratios between 5 and 0.5 by ^{19}F n.m.r. and were able to detect signals due to BeF_4^{2-}, BeF_3^-, BeF_2 and BeF^+. Approximate equilibrium constants for the dissociations were reported. Tetrachloromagnesate does not appear to exist in any appreciable concentration in aqueous solution due to the stability of the $Mg(H_2O)_6^{2+}$ species. Havel and Högfeldt[481] have employed e.m.f. titrations and vapour phase osmometry to measure the equilibrium constants for the formation of $MgCl^+$ and $MgBr^+$ in aqueous solution and obtained the rather small values of $\log K_1 = -0.98$, and -1.45, respectively. A study of the Cs_2MgCl_4 system from dilute solution to molten salt should prove interesting since at some point the octahedral coordination of $Mg(H_2O)_6^{2+}$ gives way to the tetrahedral coordination of $MgCl_4^{2-}$. Matrix isolation studies of some alkaline-earth halides have also been reported.[482–484]

Raman spectra of the tetrafluoroborate ion reveal that the species exists as a discrete tetrahedral ion in solid and molten alkali–metal tetrafluoroborates, and in aqueous solutions of these salts[485–487] (cf. earlier potentiometric studies[488]). The preparation of the alkali–metal tetrachloroborates and a study of their Raman spectra have also been reported.[489]

Alkali chloroaluminate melts exhibit evidence for a large number of species including Al_2Cl_6, $AlCl_4^-$, and $Al_2Cl_7^-$;[490,491] however, the $Al(H_2O)_6^{3+}$ species dominates the aqueous solution chemistry and no evidence has been reported for aqueous aluminium chloride complexes. Molten cryolite, Na_3AlF_6, has been studied by Raman spectroscopy. The spectra have been interpreted in terms of an equilibrium between the tetrahedral AlF_4^- and the octahedral AlF_6^{3-} species.[492] Quantitative studies of band intensities were used to estimate a dissociation constant for $AlF_6^{3-} \rightleftharpoons AlF_4^- + 2F^-$. In this case Raman spectroscopy was able to resolve a problem of considerable controversy. Infrared spectra of matrix-isolated AlF_3[493] and gallium trihalides[494] have also been reported and interpreted in terms of molecules with planar D_{3h} symmetry. Unlike Al^{3+} and Ga^{3+}, In^{3+} and Tl^{3+} ions are not as strongly hydrated in aqueous solution and the coordinated water molecule of the hexaquo-complex is sequentially replaced until the stable tetrahedral MCl_4^- ion is formed.[30,51,495–499] Work and Good[500] have assigned the infrared spectra of $GaCl_4^-$ and $GaBr_4^-$ in benzene solution, while Raman studies have shown the

$GaCl_4^-$ species to be tetrahedral;[496,497,501] bridge complexes have been detected in the melts.[501] Chloride exchange processes on gallium(III) in concentrated aqueous chloride solutions have been investigated by ^{35}Cl and ^{71}Ga n.m.r.[495] Raman spectra of molten $InCl_3$–KCl mixtures were reported to contain $InCl_4^-$, $In_2Cl_7^-$ and $In_2Cl_6^-$.[502] Davies et al.[503] have reported Raman spectra for a number of indium bromide solids. Campbell[504] has reported thermodynamic properties of concentrated aqueous solutions. Conductance data indicated that from 6 to 0.5 mol kg^{-1}, indium chloride behaves as a binary electrolyte

$$InCl_3 \rightleftharpoons InCl_2^+ + Cl^-$$

and an ionization constant of 14.5×10^{-2} was calculated. Quantitative Raman studies of the indium(III)–chloride aqueous system over a wide range of In^{3+}/Cl^- ratios gave clear evidence for four species.[30,51] Early Raman frequency and intensity measurements on aqueous indium(III) halide solutions indicated the presence of $InCl^{2+}$, $InCl_2^+$, and $InCl_4^-$ in the case of chloro-complexation, and $InBr^{2+}$, $InBr_2^+$ and $InBr_3$ for bromo-complexation. It was suggested that the $InCl_4^-$ was not tetrahedral but also contained coordinated water in its first coordination sphere.[498] A study of the thallium(III) chloride system suggested the presence of five species.[499] A major obstacle to the measurement of stepwise stability constants for metal halide complexes from Raman data is the difficulty associated with the measurement of molar intensity values (J)—a consequence of the severe band overlaps.[30,51,498,499] Spiro[499] attempted to estimate J values for $TlCl_4^-$ and $TlCl_{4+n}^{-(n+1)}$, where n is either 1 or 2, while studying the aqueous thallium(III)–chloride system; he found that the extra chloride(s) on $TlCl_4^-$ *reduced* the J value by more than a factor of four $[J_{4(305 \text{ cm}^{-1})} = 11.0, J_{4+n(305 \text{ cm}^{-1})} = 2.25]$. Large changes of J values imply significant changes in the cation–halide interaction and may provide information relating to the symmetry of the species if they can be obtained. Principal component analysis (PCA) should aid in the extraction of this information from Raman intensity measurements (Section 2.3).

In other studies, evidence has been obtained for lead(II) chloride complexes in molten $PbCl_2$,[505] while e.m.f. evidence has been obtained for a halide complex of triphenyllead(IV) and diphenyllead(IV) ions in methanol solutions.[506] Raman spectra of dimethyltin(IV) and dimethylthallium(III) in single crystals and aqueous solutions have been reported and C—Sn, C—Tl bond polarizabilities derived.[507] Raman studies have been used to complement e.m.f. and n.m.r. studies of the hydrolysis of aquodimethyllead(IV) ion.[508] Further Raman studies of CCl_4,[509] CF_4,[510] $SiCl_4$,[510–513] and SnI_4[514] have been reported. The band contour of the symmetric stretching mode of $SiCl_4$ has been attributed to the effect of strong, intermolecular interactions[511,512] although previously the anomalous shape had been attributed to the existence of hot bands.[513] The Fermi doublet between ν_3 and $2\nu_4$ was found to be temperature-dependent for CF_4 in argon solutions.[510] Raman spectra of bismuth(III) chloride complexes have been studied in aqueous solution and as trioctylamine extracts.[515] Raman spectra of gaseous $BiCl_3$ were consistent with C_{3v} symmetry,[516] and the ions BiX_4^-, BiX_5^{2-} and $Bi_2X_9^{3-}$ have been reported to be ion-paired to quaternary ammonium cations in benzene solution.[517] Lanthanum(III) halide complexes have been detected in the Raman spectrum of molten mixtures[518] but studies of aqueous solutions of lanthanide halides failed to reveal any evidence for ion pairs.[286] X-ray diffraction studies of aqueous $LaCl_3$ solutions indicate that each La^{3+} has eight nearest (oxygen) neighbours with an average La—O distance of 0.248 nm. The ion-pair La—Cl distance was about 0.47 nm, which suggests that only outer-sphere ion-pairs are formed.

Transition metal cations are relatively strongly hydrated, but halide complexes do form in appreciable amounts at moderately high concentrations. Stability constants for a number of chloro- and bromo-complexes of the bivalent transition metal ions have recently been determined at ionic strength 1.0 by a kinetic method.[520] Where comparisons are possible, the results are consistent with earlier thermodynamic measurements.[521, 522] At low ionic strength, K_1 values of around 1 are suggested. It has been suggested that these complexes are predominantly of the outer-sphere type.[520] Further support for this suggestion comes from the fact that the values quoted for MNO_3^+ complexes[520] are an order of magnitude greater than similar values measured by Raman spectroscopy (Section 7.6). Makashev et al.[523] have attempted to estimate the contribution of inner- and outer-sphere copper(II) chloro-complexes to the overall absorption coefficients in the visible region. In concentrated solutions, inner-sphere complexation does become important, possibly because of a large increase in the formation constants with increased ionic strength. Formation constants for the chloro-complexes of zinc were found to increase with temperature and ionic strength.[62] Similar observations have been reported for iron(III) chloro-complexes.[524] Ohlson and Vannerberg[525] used electronic spectroscopy to measure stability constants of copper(II) chloro-complexes in 9 mol dm^{-3} H_2SO_4 and reported a value of β_1 about eight times larger than that reported at ionic strength 1.0.[520] In addition, formation constants for $CuCl_2$, $CuCl_3^-$, and $CuCl_4^{2-}$ were obtained. It is well known that $ZnCl_4^{2-}$ is present in aqueous $ZnCl_2$ solutions and, in fact, the anhydrous complex salts, Cs_2ZnCl_4 and Cs_2CuCl_4, can be crystallized from an aqueous mixture containing two moles $CsCl$ to one mole of the hydrated zinc or copper chloride.[526, 527] Studies of the nickel(II) and copper(II) chloride system at elevated temperatures and pressures indicate that tetrahedral complexes are dominant at high temperatures and pressures. For the nickel(II) system the dominant species were found to be $NiCl_2(H_2O)_2$ and $NiCl_3 \cdot H_2O^-$,[528] whereas for the copper(II) system with excess $LiCl$ the $CuCl_4^{2-}$ species prevailed even at room temperature.[529] The transitions from hexaquo- to tetrachloro-complexes were described by the sequence

$$Cu(H_2O)_6^{2+} \rightleftharpoons Cu(H_2O)_5Cl^+ \rightleftharpoons Cu(H_2O)_4Cl_2 \rightleftharpoons Cu(H_2O)_3Cl_3^- \rightleftharpoons$$
$$Cu(H_2O)_2Cl_4^{2-} \rightleftharpoons CuCl_4^{2-}$$

Studies of the electronic spectra of $NiCl_2$ in DMSO indicated the presence of $Ni(DMSO)_6^{2+}$, $NiCl(DMSO)_5^+$, $NiCl_2(DMSO)_4$, and $NiCl_3(DMSO)^-$, but not $NiCl_4^{2-}$.[530]

Infrared[527] and Raman[526] spectra of a number of solid chloro-complexes of the type A_2MCl_4 and A_3MCl_5 (A = Rb or Cs; M = Fe, Co, Ni, Cu, or Zn) known to contain distorted MCl_4^{2-} tetrahedra have been examined, but Raman studies of the aqueous complexes have been restricted to the ions, Fe^{3+}, Zn^{2+}, Cd^{2+} and Hg^{2+}. The conclusion of a number of Raman studies of concentrated ferric chloride solutions is that the tetrahedral $FeCl_4^-$ species dominates the spectrum, but that several different minor species are also present.[531-533] Marston and Bush[531] suggested that a complex of stoichiometry $FeCl_3$ exists in less concentrated solutions and proposed a D_{3h} trigonal–bipyramidal structure with water molecules in the axial positions. Sharma[532] has suggested that appreciable concentrations of $Fe(H_2O)_4Cl_2^+$ and a polymeric species of the type $FeCl_5 \cdot H_2O^{2-}$ or $FeCl_6^{3-}$ may exist along with the $FeCl_4^-$ complex, depending on the concentration. Binuclear complexes, $Fe_2Cl_7^-$ and Fe_2Cl_6, have been proposed from spectrophotometric and potentiometric studies of the KCl–$FeCl_3$ melts.[534]

Recent studies of the Raman spectra of molten Cs_2ZnCl_4[535] and aqueous $ZnCl_2$ solutions[66] have been interpreted in favour of a tetrahedral $ZnCl_4^{2-}$ species. Only two bands were observed at ca. 277 and 100 cm^{-1} and it was suggested that in both the aqueous and the molten state the four tetrahedral modes of $ZnCl_4^{2-}$ merged into two broad bands, with ν_1 coalescing with ν_3, and ν_2 with ν_4. This explanation appears to be reasonable since ν_3 is normally very weak, and in solid Cs_2ZnCl_4 the ν_1 and ν_3 bands overlap considerably.[526,536]

The coalescence of ν_2 and ν_4 is more surprising since in solid Cs_2ZnCl_4 the bands are at 115 and 140 cm^{-1} and studies of Cs_2MgCl_4 suggest that the ν_2 and ν_4 bands are not very temperature-sensitive and, in fact, can be resolved in the spectrum of molten Cs_2MgCl_4.[478] A four-band spectrum has also been observed for $ZnBr_4^{2-}$ in aqueous solution, and ν_2 and ν_4 bands were clearly resolved.[537] Although the Cs_2ZnCl_4 crystal contains the tetrahedral $ZnCl_4^{2-}$ species with only a slight distortion from tetrahedral,[538] there is no compelling reason to believe that this must be the species present in the melt or in aqueous solution. It is possible that contributions due to polymeric species in molten Cs_2ZnCl_4 and to $ZnCl_4(H_2O)_n^{2-}$ in aqueous solution (suggested by Irish et al.[462]) affect the ν_2 and ν_4 band resolution of $ZnCl_4^{2-}$. Angell et al.[539] have measured the far-infrared spectra of liquid, glass, and crystalline $ZnCl_2$ and interpreted their spectra in terms of a basic tetrahedral group linked through chloride bridges. Less information is available on the mono-, di-, and tri-halo-complexes, although Macklin and Plane[537] attempted to identify these complexes for aqueous bromo-complexes of zinc(II), cadmium(II) and mercury-(II) from frequency shifts. Values for the stability constants of the species $ZnCl^+$, $ZnCl_2$ and $ZnBr^+$ and $ZnBr_2$ have been determined by e.m.f. measurements for aqueous ammonium chloride melts.[540]

Coordination of cadmium(II) with chloride and bromide ions has been studied (Raman spectroscopy) in molten $KAlCl_4$[541] and in molten $LiNO_3/KNO_3$ mixtures.[542] In the former study, the $CdCl_4^{2-}$ species was found to predominate, while in the latter study $CdCl_3^-$ and $CdBr_4^{2-}$ predominated, with evidence for $CdBr^+$, $CdBr_2$ and $CdCl_3^-$. Yellin and Marcus[543] have studied the stability of a number of mixed bromo-iodo- and cyano-iodo-complexes of cadmium(II) and mercury(II) in aqueous solution.

Polyatomic halide ions have also been subjected to studies by Raman spectroscopy. The I_3^- ion has been studied in solid phase[544, 545] and in solution in acetonitrile[544] and the results have been interpreted in terms of a linear I_3^- ion. Loos and Jones[546] have studied the effect of KI on the Raman spectrum of I_3^- and noted that with increased concentration of KI, the 114 cm^{-1} band characteristic of I_3^- decreased in intensity while a new band appeared at 155 cm^{-1}. The 155 cm^{-1} band was assigned to higher polyhalides of the type I_4^{2-}, I_5^-, or I_6^{2-}. In this regard it has been shown by X-ray crystallography that linear I_{16}^{4-} ions exist in $(\text{theobromine})_2H_2I_8$.[547] Mixed polyatomic halides have also been investigated.[548, 549] Delhaye et al.[549] have studied the interaction of bromine with halide ions in acetonitrile and water solvents. Interestingly, the HF_2^- ion is stable enough in aqueous solution to permit the measurement of its spectrum.[550]

7.4 Halates, Perhalates

Vibrational spectra of the halates and perhalates have not been as extensively investigated as the nitrates but nevertheless they have been quite well characterized (Table 13).[551, 552] The less stable halites and hypohalites are less well known.[111, 551] Infrared and Raman spectra of solid alkali metal chlorates[551–555] and bromates[556, 557] have been interpreted on the basis of factor group analysis of the unit cell. Similar studies have been performed for the

TABLE 13
Band positions/cm⁻¹ and assignments for aqueous perhalates^a and halates^b

Ion	$v_3(t_2)$	$v_1(a_1)$	$v_2(e)$	$v_4(t_2)$
ClO_4^-	1120	935	460	625
BrO_4^-	883	798	331	410
	$v_3(e)$	$v_1(a)$	$v_2(a)$	$v_4(e)$
ClO_3^-	977^c	933	608	477
BrO_3^-	805	805	418	358
IO_3^-	775	805	358	320

^{a} Ref. 552.
^{b} Ref. 563.
^{c} Average of two components.

alkaline earth hydrated chlorates.[558] Studies of alkali metal iodates,[559] and matrix-isolation studies of $M^+ClO_3^-$ and $M^+ClO_4^-$ ion-pairs have also been reported.[560,561] Site and correlation field splittings are of similar magnitudes to those observed for the nitrate ion and indicate that, like NO_3^-, the ν_3 mode of XO_3^- ions is extremely sensitive to the environment.

Limited Raman studies of aqueous chlorates indicate that the $\nu_3(e)$ mode gives a doublet even in spectra from dilute solution[562–564] and suggest that, as for NO_3^-, the interaction with water is sufficient to lift the degeneracy. In concentrated solutions of $LiClO_3$,[562] $Mg(ClO_3)_2$,[564] $Ca(ClO_3)_2$ and perhaps $Zn(ClO_3)_2$[565] the $\nu_4(e)$ band shows a shoulder at slightly higher frequency. For example, in 10.6 mol dm^{-3} $LiClO_3$ solution two bands are observed at 503 and 483 cm^{-1}, whereas for solutions less than 5 mol dm^{-3} only a single band at 483 cm^{-1} was observed. Although no quantitative intensity studies of this region have been performed, the results are reminiscent of those for nitrate systems and suggest that this region may be useful for measurements of stability constants if it can be shown that the high-frequency component is due to the ion pair. Studies of BrO_3^- and IO_3^- complexes should also be possible.

The perchlorate ion is often used in Raman spectroscopy as an internal standard because of its apparent inability to form inner-sphere ion-pairs with most cations. Even for $In(ClO_4)_3$ solutions there was no evidence for perturbation of the four-band spectrum of tetrahedral ClO_4^-.[566] No evidence has been reported to indicate that the ν_3 band of ClO_4^- is a doublet in dilute solutions and the spectrum of the ν_3 region of 2.0 mol dm^{-3} $NaClO_4$ recorded by one of the authors (MHB) failed to reveal a doublet structure. However, $M^+ClO_4^-$ ion-pairs in matrix isolation do show pronounced splittings of the ν_3 band.[561] A possible explanation for the difference between the ν_3 region of ClO_4^-(aq) and ClO_3^-(aq) is that the ClO_4^-(aq) is less strongly hydrogen-bonded to the water. Inner- and outer-sphere perchlorate complexes have been proposed in non-aqueous systems.[35,567–570] Inner-sphere ion-pairing had been proposed for $Zn^{2+}ClO_4^-$ in methanol from n.m.r. studies,[568] but subsequent analogous studies of $Zn^{2+}NO_3^-$ in methanol, using data from n.m.r., Raman and infrared spectroscopy, suggested the need for a modified interpretation of concentration-dependent solvation numbers; solvent-separated species were invoked because vibrational spectroscopy failed to confirm contact ion-pairs.[54] Ultrasonic studies of Ni(II), Cu(II), and Zn(II) perchlorates in acetonitrile suggested inner-sphere coordination with Cu(II) and Zn(II) but outer-sphere coordination with Ni(II).[569] It is possible that Raman studies can help to resolve the role perchlorate plays as a ligand in solution.

7.5   Carbonates and Bicarbonates

Infrared and Raman spectra have been reported for a number of alkali metal carbonate and bicarbonate solids.[571–573] For carbonates the site and correlation field effects are similar in magnitude to those of nitrate. A study of the alkali metal carbonates as molten salts and as dilute aqueous solutions revealed a doublet structure for the ν_3 region analogous to that observed for molten and aqueous nitrates.[573] The infrared and Raman band maxima did not coincide (for Na_2CO_3(aq), Raman 1381 and 1430 cm^{-1}; infrared 1356 and 1397 cm^{-1}) and the relative intensity of the high-frequency component was greater in the Raman than in the infrared spectrum. Similar findings have been reported by Oliver and Davis.[447] Oliver and Davis have used the intensities of the 1017 cm^{-1} bicarbonate band and the 1062 cm^{-1} carbonate band to study quantitatively the bicarbonate–carbonate equilibrium and qualitatively to study the CO_2–H_2O system.[447]

The CO_2–H_2O system has also been studied by P-jump and T-jump methods.[574] The effect of coordination on the vibrational spectrum of CO_3^{2-} has been calculated by Taravel et al.[575] and although CO_3^{2-} complexes readily form they are insufficiently soluble to be studied in aqueous solution. The dynamics of the magnesium–bicarbonate/carbonate interactions have been studied by Patel et al.[576] Sodium bicarbonate and carbonate ion-pairs have been suggested from thermodynamic measurements[577] but no evidence of ion-pairing was found in the Raman studies of the molten or aqueous carbonates or of the aqueous bicarbonates.

7.6 Nitrates

The nitrate ion has proven extremely useful as a spectroscopic 'probe' for investigation of solution structure at the microscopic level. Interactions of nitrate ion with other species modifies the vibrational spectrum in a manner that depends on the nature of the interaction. Correct interpretation of the spectral changes can provide information about the nitrate environment and ultimately provide a link between the microscopic measurement and the classical macroscopic thermodynamic parameters. Several reviews have appeared on the subject and should be consulted for background information.[1,5,8,578]

The hypothetical 'free' NO_3^- species has D_{3h} symmetry and should exhibit a four-band spectrum $\nu_1(a_1')$, ≈ 1050 cm^{-1}, Raman-active only; $\nu_2(a_2'')$, ≈ 830 cm^{-1}, infrared-active only; $\nu_3(e')$, ≈ 1380 cm^{-1} Raman- and infrared-active; $\nu_4(e')$, ≈ 716 cm^{-1}, Raman- and infrared-active. However, even in dilute aqueous solution, the spectra of alkali metal nitrates indicate the appearance of forbidden modes and a doubling of the $\nu_3(e')$ band, with broad depolarized components at 1348 and 1406 cm^{-1} (Raman), and 1347 and 1395 cm^{-1} (infrared)[1] (Fig. 9). The band centred at 1347 cm^{-1} is more intense than the peak at 1395 cm^{-1} in the infrared spectrum (intensity ratio I(1347)/I(1395) = 1.3), whereas in the Raman spectrum the 1348 cm^{-1} band is less intense than the 1406 cm^{-1} band (intensity ratio I(1348)/I(1406) = 0.63).[406–408] A similar broad doublet structure has been observed for dilute nitrate solutions in liquid ammonia,[291,293,296,304,305] formamide,[147] and methanol,[406] for high-temperature disordered alkali–metal nitrate solids,[579–581] and for molten alkali–metal nitrates.[580–586] For solutions

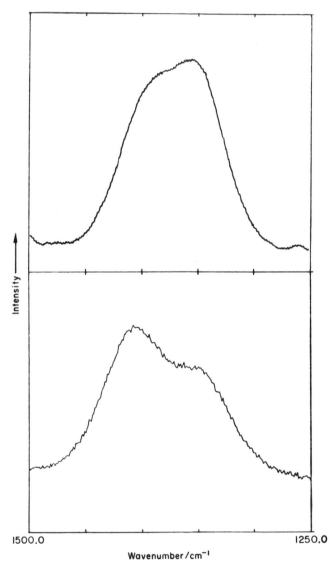

Fig. 9. The ν_3 band of the nitrate ion from 0.50 mol dm⁻³ NaNO₃. Upper: infrared.
Lower: Raman, after averaging 36 scans (Irish and Bulmer, in Lockwood, Ref. 408).

of tetra-*n*-butylammonium nitrate in methylene chloride, dimethyl sulphoxide, and methyl cyanide[406] and for tetraphenylarsonium nitrate in chloroform,[405] only a single band at ca. 1350 cm⁻¹ has been detected.

It seems unlikely that the doublet structure is due to ion-pair formation since the band profile has been found to be insensitive to both the nature of the cation and the concentration for solutions less concentrated than 1 mol dm⁻³. A specific NO_3^- ... H_2O hydrogen-bonded complex has been proposed[405–407] but this is not fully consistent with the observation of Davis et al.[405] who found only a single band at ca. 1360 cm^{-1} for the nitrate ion in chloroform, although strong evidence was presented for the Cl_3C—H ... NO_3^- hydrogen-bonded species. The chloroform C—H stretch shifted from 3034 cm^{-1} to 2984 cm^{-1} when hydrogen-bonded to the nitrate.[5] It is possible that stronger hydrogen-bonding occurs in water and methanol and this results in the splitting of the ν_3 band. For solutions of tetra-n-butylammonium nitrate and methanol (0.1 mol dm^{-3}) in methylene chloride a broad band at ca. 3405 cm^{-1} was assigned to a hydrogen-bond OH stretching mode of a 1:1 solvate while the non-hydrogen-bonded OH stretch occurred at 3620 cm^{-1}. The nitrate ion in water does not significantly alter the position of the OH stretching mode[407] and this could be interpreted in terms of the nitrate ion forming hydrogen bonds with water, of equal strength to the water–water hydrogen bonds. A relatively strong, hydrogen-bonded, nitrate–water interaction would also account for the weak water band at ca. 690 cm^{-1} observed only for aqueous nitrate solutions.[85,407] Jenkins and Waddington[587] have calculated the charge on the oxygen atom of the nitrate group to be -0.72 e, which is sufficient for a reasonably strong nitrate–water interaction. The smaller splitting of about 35 cm^{-1} for the ν_3 band in the spectrum from a solution in dilute ammonia would be consistent with this view since weaker hydrogen-bonding is expected in ammonia. Single crystal X-ray studies[588–593] of hydrated nitrate salts also suggest that relatively short O ... H—O bonds (ca. 0.27 nm) between water oxygen atoms and the nitrate oxygen atoms can be interpreted in terms of hydrogen-bonding.

The question arises as to whether it is the hydrogen-bonding or the field asymmetry associated with the interaction that is most important in lifting the degeneracy of the $\nu_3(e')$ mode. Field asymmetry (site-splitting) could also be the cause of the doublet structure in the high temperature disordered solids and the molten salts. Devlin and co-workers[352–355,584] measured the effects of different cations and matrices on the site perturbations of the ion-pairs formed in matrix-isolation studies and have demonstrated that the ν_3 region of the nitrate ion is extremely sensitive to field asymmetry. Solvation of the cation with water and ammonia was found to reduce the magnitude of the split of the ν_3 components.[354]

Although the hydrogen-bonding or field asymmetry model can explain the doublet structure, a specific model with well-defined symmetry is not suggested since both components of ν_3 remain depolarized. It seems quite possible that the nitrate ion is undergoing rapid oscillatory motions such that on the time scale of the measurement (10^{-13} s), it is not ordered with respect to the field (or hydrogen-bonds). Accurate X-ray diffraction studies of alkali-metal nitrate crystals indicate that even at room temperature, the root-mean-squared oscillation about the C_3 axis is about 8°,[594,595] which creates doubt about the validity of the harmonic approximation for a description of atomic motion. It has also been suggested[596] that the positions of the oxygen atoms for high-temperature

$NaNO_3$ solid are best described as an annulus of negative charge. Hindered rotation cannot be entirely ruled out, but Lockwood[408] has shown that a free rotation, 'gas phase' model with O, P, Q, R and S branches cannot account for the envelope in the ν_3 region in a quantitative way.

Many alternative explanations for the ν_3 doublet structure have been proposed. It has been suggested that the component at 1400 cm^{-1} observed in molten salts and high-temperature solids[352,353,580,584] is due to a longitudinal optical (LO) mode associated with long-range, transition-dipole interactions of neighbouring nitrate groups. An LO mode occurs in a crystal at higher frequencies than the corresponding transverse optic (TO) mode due to an increase in the force constant that occurs when the phonon (a wave-like motion in the solid) has its electric displacement vector in the same direction as the phonon propagation. Not only does this proposal preclude a common explanation from dilute solution to molten salts, but it is not consistent with dilution studies of molten nitrates which indicate that the nitrate spectrum is influenced only by nearest neighbour *cations*.[585] Further, it should be noted that for molten $LiNO_3$ the rather large value of the splitting of ν_3 of about 110 cm^{-1} may well be partly caused by the presence of ion pairs, since the ν_4 region of the spectrum shows a band at ca. 740 cm^{-1} which is diagnostic of such pairs.[85,585,597] This possibility was not considered in the interpretation of dilution studies of $LiNO_3$ with $LiClO_3$,[352-354,584] nor was the possibility that $Li^+ClO_3^-$ pairs could form, as has been proposed by Oliver and Janz.[562] Transient $Li^+NO_3^-$ ion pairs have been invoked by a number of workers to explain molten salt, Raman[582,585,598] and n.m.r.[599] data. The similarity of the ν_3 TO/LO separation for solid $LiNO_3$ with the band separation observed in the molten salt may well be fortuitous. The fact that the shape of the ν_3 doublet envelope does not change appreciably from high-temperature disordered solids, to melts, to dilute aqueous solution, suggests a common origin for the doublet structure. The similar ν_3 modes of CO_3^{2-}[447,573] and ClO_3^-[562,563] also show doublet structure and, although these ions have not been studied in as great detail as has the NO_3^- ion, it has been observed that, as with NO_3^- ion, the doublet structure is retained even for dilute aqueous solutions. The fact that the ν_3 mode of each of these ions is associated with a large transition dipole may be significant, but the exact role this plays is difficult to ascertain. Perchlorate ion also has a large transition dipole associated with the ν_3 mode; although the band due to this mode is extremely broad in the aqueous solution spectrum it does not appear to be split. (The spherical ClO_4^- ion may be less susceptible to asymmetric field distortion.) LO modes are observed clearly in the Raman spectra of non-centrosymmetric ordered crystals[553,554,579] but the attempt to carry this interpretation over to liquids may not be valid. In ordered crystals, sharp lines are usually observed in the ν_3 region for both LO and TO modes because only the zone-centre wave-vector, $\mathbf{k} \approx 0$ modes (in-phase motions of the lattice) are active in the vibrational spectrum. In melts and aqueous solution $\mathbf{k}$ loses its meaning and all modes are active regardless of phase; consequently, a density of states is observed which will show a distribution of modes with all energies (or environments). Because the ν_3 antisymmetric stretching modes are so sensitive to the environment, very broad peaks may be observed but a splitting into transverse optic and longitudinal optic modes due to charge bunching is difficult to support in melts or aqueous solutions.

Fermi resonance of ν_3 with $2\nu_4$ can also be ruled out as an explanation for the doublet structure since $^{15}NO_3^-$ studies in dilute aqueous solution show that *both* components of the ν_3 doublet shift by comparable amounts, about 30 cm^{-1}, whereas ν_4 is unshifted.[600,601] Jahn–Teller distortion[581,602] has also been proposed, but this does not seem likely since there are several cases where the ν_3 band is clearly a singlet.[405,406]

The cation-dependence of the ν_3 region in spectra from concentrated aqueous solutions that do not contain significant specific inner-sphere or contact ion-pairs is also consistent with an asymmetric-field splitting model. It has been observed that in nitrate solutions of $Li(H_2O)_4^+$,[85,407] $Be(H_2O)_4^{2+}$,[367,371,603] $Mg(H_2O)_6^{2+}$,[334,363,364,367,603,604] $Al(H_2O)_6^{3+}$[371,604] and $Zn(H_2O)_6^{2+}$ [55,68] the separation of the components of the ν_3 band increases with increasing concentration of cation. This does not appear to be due to contact ion-pairs since the band at 740 cm^{-1}, characteristic of contact ion-pairs, cannot be detected. Two interpretations seem attractive to us. (a) Discrete solvent-separated ion-pairs may be formed which exist for a time that is long compared with the measurement time. In such a case the doublet structure should be a quartet, with two bands from the solvated nitrate and two from the outer-sphere ion-pair. Lemley and Plane[55] have curve-resolved their Raman spectra of $Zn(NO_3)_2$ solutions in this way and obtained a stability constant for the outer-sphere complex $Zn(H_2O)_6(NO_3)^+$. Chang,[603] Irish,[367] and Gardiner et al.[371] have proposed a similar model for $Be(H_2O)_4(NO_3)^+$. (b) It is also possible that discrete species are not formed and the increase in the separation of the ν_3 components is merely due to the gradual increase in the field strength acting on the solvated nitrate group due to the increased polarization of the water molecule by the cation. Essentially, this second explanation means that the rate of formation and breakage of outer-sphere complexes would be too fast to observe. Sze[68] has also studied the aqueous $Zn(NO_3)_2$ system and concluded that, contrary to the results of Lemley and Plane (above), better fits to the ν_3 envelope were obtained if the peak positions and halfwidths were allowed to vary. Sze's results suggest that outer-sphere ion-pairs cannot be detected by Raman spectroscopy. In this regard, Larsson[67] has proposed that similar studies of the ν_3 mode of sulfate could be used to measure outer-sphere ion-pairs, but subsequent studies[605] were not consistent with conclusions based on infrared bandwidths. One hopes that Raman spectroscopy will provide a method of detecting outer-sphere ion-pairs since all other methods have proved to be inconclusive, but one cannot be over optimistic about this since the curve-resolving methods required to analyse the broad envelopes normally obtained will leave us with, at best, a very slippery handle.

The transition to inner-sphere associations results in more pronounced alterations to the nitrate spectrum. Doubling of all the bands due to the nitrate ion occurs, although for some systems the separation of the components is undetectable. Usually the peaks due to the complex have frequencies close to the values for anhydrous solids.[606,607] Appearance of a second band in the ν_4 region at ca. 740 cm^{-1} seems to be the best diagnostic feature of inner-sphere ion-association.[597,604] It should be pointed out that all evidence to date indicates that aqueous complex formation does not remove the degeneracy of the $\nu_4(e')$ mode as has been suggested.[352,353,584,608] This implies that, for the complex ions of symmetry lower than C_3, both components of the ν_4 band are shifted to higher frequencies ≈ 740 cm^{-1} and away from the band at 717 cm^{-1} due to solvated nitrate. Occasionally, more than one component can be resolved in the 740 cm^{-1} region but this is believed to be due to complexes containing different numbers of nitrate groups[364] rather than the lifting of the degeneracy of an e' fundamental of one group. Strong evidence to support this view comes from careful quantitative Raman studies discussed below. A summary of the major features of the nitrate spectrum for the various environments is given in Table 14. A more detailed account has been given elsewhere.[1,578] Several important aspects warrant further comment. The inner-sphere ion-pair is characterized by

TABLE 14
Summary of Raman band positions/cm^{-1} for NO$_3^-$ in various environments[a]

NO$_3^-$(aq) solvate	M$^+$(H$_2$O)NO$_3^-$ solvent-separated ion-pair	M$^+$NO$_3^-$ ion-pair	M—ONO$_2$ monodentate complex	bidentate complex
			280 p	230 p
717 dp	717 dp			
		740 dp	750 p	750 p
		815[b]	810[b]	810[b]
830[b]	830[b]			
		(1040—1060)p[c]	1040 p	1040 p
1048 p	1048 p			
				1300 dp
		1320 dp	1320 p	
1350 dp	1350 dp			
1400 dp				
	1420 dp			
		1450 dp	1450 dp	
				1500 p

[a] Approximate values only, values are often concentration-dependent.
[b] Infrared values. Weak Raman bands are often observed at similar frequencies.
[c] Cation-dependent.

a nominal doubling of the number of bands. However, the non-specific nature of the interaction is characterized by the absence of a metal–oxygen band and the depolarized nature of the new bands in the v_4 and v_3 regions. The aqueous calcium nitrate system seems to exemplify best the classical ion-pair.[608,609] Apparently, the cation does not fully restrict the rotational freedom of the NO_3^- group.[408] The transition from ion-pair to complex-ion is gradual and is characterized by the appearance of a polarized band due to a metal–oxygen vibration and a decrease in the depolarization ratio for bands in the v_3 and v_4 regions. Normal-coordinate calculations[575,610] have demonstrated that for unidentate binding the lower frequency band in the v_3 region should be Raman polarized, while the higher frequency mode is polarized in the spectrum of the bidentate complex. The bidentate complex appears to become the dominant species in extremely concentrated solutions[344,363,364] and most solid nitrates adopt a bidentate arrangement.[344,578,606,611,617] Proposed rules[578,614] for differentiating monodentate and bidentate coordination have been questioned by James and Kimber[617] and Brooker.[615]

In the gas phase, $Li^+NO_3^-$ and $Na^+NO_3^-$ ion-pairs have been reported to have unidentate nitrate groups,[618] whereas $Tl^+NO_3^-$ and $Cs^+NO_3^-$ may be bidentate.[619,620] Ishchenko et al.[619] have proposed that the gas phase ion-pair may not have a specific geometry and have suggested that both ions are free to move with respect to one another with the geometries of greatest importance being those for which the ion pairs have the C_s, C_{2v} and C_{3v} symmetries. This suggestion is similar to the proposed non-specific model for solutions containing ion pairs. Some success has been achieved in assigning spectra of true complexes to specific models, usually with C_{2v} symmetry[621,622] but occasionally with D_{2h} symmetry[623] or C_s symmetry.[624]

A significant advance in recent years has been the use of vibrational spectroscopy in a quantitative manner to determine stability constants and other thermodynamic parameters. Stability constants for metal–nitrate systems measured to date are listed in Table 15 together with major spectral observations. Quantitative studies have been performed by measurement of the 'free' and 'bound' nitrate concentrations from accurate intensity measurements in each of the nitrate fundamental regions[68,407,603,605,608,609,621-637] but only occasionally has more than one region been used within a single system.[68,622,624] The 700 cm^{-1} Raman region has proven most useful since clear separation of the bands due to free and bound nitrates simplifies the intensity measurements. The plots of the total Raman intensity in the v_4 region versus concentration are either linear or have a slight positive deviation from linearity at higher concentrations which suggests that $J_{b1} = J_f$ and $J_{b2} \geqslant 2J_f$.[25,68,69,364,609] In general, J_f is known and the intensity of the band due to solvated nitrate (717 cm^{-1}) can be employed to calculate $[NO_3^-]_f$; $[NO_3^-]_b$ can be obtained from $[NO_3^-]_t - [NO_3^-]_f = [NO_3^-]_b$. Analogous results are obtained in the v_1 region if the bands due to free and bound nitrate can be resolved. One might tend to have more confidence in the results calculated from the data on the v_1

TABLE 15
Summary of formation constants and spectroscopic data for metal nitrates at 25 °C

Cation	β_1	β_2	M—O	Characteristic Raman bands/cm^{-1} of the *complex*				Reference
				ν_1	ν_2 (infrared)	ν_3	ν_4	
Li$^+$	≈0.09[a] (0.24)[b]			1056 p	832	1389 dp	737 dp	85
Na$^+$	0.060 (2.98)[b]			1051 p	831	1368 p 1415 dp	728 p	12
Ag$^+$	0.10			1041 p	818	1307 p 1427 dp	728 dp	624
Ag$^+$ (acetonitrile)	1.10		110 dp	1037 p	824	1304 p	723 dp	326
Ag$^+$ (acetonitrile)	84 (70)[c]		120 dp	1037 p	obscured	obscured 1304	722 dp	327
Be^{2+}	≈0.4[a]	evidence for β_2		1053 p 1035 p	824 819	1325 p, 1281 p 1435 dp, 1515 dp,	725 dp	603
Mg^{2+}	<0.02[a] ≈0.2[a] (95 °C)			1039 p 1064 p	821	1330 p, 1377 dp 1466 dp, 1515 p	740 dp 759 dp	364
Ca^{2+}	0.13	0.036		1049 p	820	1355 dp 1435 dp	738 dp	609
Ca^{2+} (2H$_2$O:1 dioxan)	3.99	0.31				obscured	735 dp	609
Sr^{2+}	0.76	0.10		1051 p		1367 dp 1435 dp	733 dp	25
Zn^{2+}	4.2 (50 °C) (inner sphere) 0.25 (50 °C) (outer sphere)		260 p	1033 p ≈1048 p		1312 p 1490 dp 1360 p 1455 dp	≈755 p ≈723 dp	55 55
Zn^{2+}	0.02		285 p	1035 p		1310 p, 1335 p 1480 dp, 1428 dp	749 p 758 dp	68
Zn^{2+} (methanol)	2.6	0.13		obscured	817	1310 p obscured	753 dp	54
Zn^{2+} (2H$_2$O:1 dioxan)	0.22			1028 p	816	obscured	750	68

Ion								Ref
Zn²⁺ (4H₂O:1 acetonitrile)	0.090		265 p	1037 p	815	1320 p, 1490 dp	753 p	68
Cd²⁺	0.38 (44 °C)	0.042			818	1324 p, 1452 dp	740 p	621
Hg²⁺	2.2		270 p	1034 p	810	1295 p, 1460 dp	740 p	68
Hg²⁺ (2H₂O:1 dioxan)	5.6	2.8	270 p, 240 p	1033 p	811	obscured	739	68
CH₃Hg⁺	0.040 (0 °C)		292 p	1000 p		1282 p, 1502 dp	745	630
ClCH₂Hg⁺	3.3		300 p			1290, 1485		631
Ni²⁺	≈0.02						740 dp	600
Cu²⁺	0.07		272 p	1040 p	805	1315 p, 1420 dp	757 p	622
Sc³⁺	evidence for β_1 and β_2		278–287 p	1031 p		1297, 1420 dp, 1540 p	757 p	632
Fe³⁺	≈0.1[a]		282 p	1054 p		1337 p, 1427 dp	740 dp	633
Bi³⁺	evidence for β_1 to β_4		239 p	1036 p	810	1294 dp	747 p	634
In³⁺			270 p	1040 p		1500 p, 1450 dp, 1315 p, 1510 dp	750 p	566
Ce³⁺	1.68	1.17		1044 p	820	1299 dp, 1325 p, 1487 p, 1456 dp	742 dp	69
Gd³⁺	<0.8[d]	4.6[d]		1044 p	818	1299 dp, 1318 p, 1506 p, 1475 dp	750 dp	635
Ce⁴⁺		$\beta_4 \approx 0.3$[a]	238 p		807	1294 dp, 1538 p	748 p	636
Th⁴⁺	1.34,[e] 1.0[a,f]	6.3[a,e] 1.6[a,f]	230 p	1038 p	806	1303 p, 1444, 1534 p, 1492 p	753 dp	637

[a] Estimated from limited data in the reference.
[b] Place-exchange equilibrium constants.
[c] Determined by conductance.
[d] There is evidence to suggest that the quoted values may be unreliable.
[e] Calculated from approx. 1050 cm⁻¹ data.
[f] Calculated from approx. 700 cm⁻¹ data.

region than for those on the ν_4 region since the symmetric stretching mode is non-degenerate and the problem of loss of degeneracy is avoided; however, clear resolution of the two components is not always possible. Again the linearity of plots of the total band intensity in the 1050 cm^{-1} region versus concentration[327,364] suggests that $J_f \approx J_b$. In some systems stability constants have been calculated from data in both the ν_1 and ν_4 regions and identical values obtained, which further supports the proposal that in most systems the complex does not contribute intensity at 717 cm^{-1}.[68,622,624] The ν_3 Raman region[621] and the ν_2 infrared region[54] have also been used to calculate stability constants. It would appear that the ν_1, ν_3 and ν_4 infrared regions are unsuitable for quantitative work. The transition dipole of the ν_4 normal mode of the nitrate ion is extremely cation-sensitive, as can be seen from the large intensity increases for increasing values of z/r for the alkali–metal and alkaline–earth solids.[606,607] As a result of the large molar intensity the infrared band at ca. 740 cm^{-1} due to the complex is often observed when the band due to free nitrate at ca. 718 cm^{-1} cannot be detected.

Values of β_1 listed in Table 15 for Li$^+$, Na$^+$ and Ag$^+$ are in good agreement with available conductivity data.[12,327,638] The fact that the place exchange equilibrium constant for NaNO$_3$ is larger than for LiNO$_3$ reflects the fact that Li$^+$ is more strongly hydrated and does not as easily accept a nitrate ion into the coordination sphere. Failure to detect inner-sphere association for KNO$_3$, RbNO$_3$, CsNO$_3$, and TlNO$_3$ does not mean that NO$_3^-$ does not come in contact with the cation. It is more likely that the ion-pairs do not exist long enough to be detected (i.e. they are essentially collision-complexes) and/or that the peak positions for ion-pairs are almost identical to those of the solvated nitrate ion. Association constants for ion-pair formation of Tl$^+$NO$_3^-$ (1.9) and Rb$^+$NO$_3^-$ (0.8) have been estimated by Masterton et al.[639] from density data and for Tl$^+$NO$_3^-$ (0.26) by Fedorenko et al.[640] from solubility studies.

The difference between the values of β_1 for Ag$^+$NO$_3^-$ in acetonitrile as measured by Janz and Muller[327] (84), and by Chang and Irish,[326] (1.1) (Table 15) can be explained. Values of the ratio of I_f/I_{ip}, measured from two different spectral regions, for bands assigned to 'free' and 'ion-paired' nitrate are plotted in Fig. 10, together with the ratio calculated from the value of $\beta_1 = 70$ obtained from conductivity data.[327] For the ν_1 Raman region the results of both groups fall close to the curve calculated from conductance data but the I_f/I_{ip} ratio for the ν_4 Raman region as measured by Chang and Irish is too high. An infrared band intensity ratio is in good agreement with the ν_1 Raman result. Consequently, the value of β_1 obtained by Chang and Irish is probably too low. A number of factors could be responsible for this problem. In dilute solutions the weak ν_4 region is difficult to measure and the results may reflect a large systematic error in curve resolution or baseline subtraction. It is possible that the ion-pair contributes intensity at about 710 cm^{-1}, but if this is the case it would be the first confirmed example of the removal of degeneracy of ν_4 for nitrate complexes in solution. A weak band due to acetonitrile may also contribute intensity in the 710 cm^{-1} region. It would appear that the 1050 cm^{-1} region provides the best measure of ion-pairing in this system despite interference from the 1041 cm^{-1} line of the solvent. The linearity of the plot of total intensity of the 1050 cm^{-1} band versus nitrate ion concentration suggests that $J_{1037(ip)} = J_{1042(f)}$. Both groups of workers reported a depolarized Raman band at ca. 110 cm^{-1}. This has been assigned to a librational mode of the hindered NO_3^- group in the coordination sphere of the Ag^+. Depolarization data support a $C_s(\sigma_v)$ geometry for the ion-pair.[326]

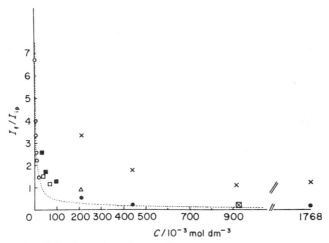

Fig. 10. The ratio of the intensity of a specified band of the free nitrate ion, I_f, to that of the corresponding band of the ion-paired nitrate ion, I_{ip}, plotted against concentration of $AgNO_3$ in acetonitrile in the dilute solution range. I_{1042}/I_{1037}: ○ tabulated in Ref. 327; □ quoted in text of Ref. 327; ■ Ref. 626; ● Ref. 603. I_{706}/I_{723}: × Raman; ⊠ infrared: Ref. 603. I_{833}/I_{824}: △ Ref. 603. Dotted line calculated from conductivity data (Ref. 327).

Values of formation constants have also been obtained for aqueous solutions of the alkaline-earth nitrates. The trend $\beta_1(Mg^{2+}) < \beta_1(Ca^{2+}) < \beta_1(Sr^{2+})$ is as expected on the basis of hydration energies. Since magnesium forms a well-defined $Mg(H_2O)_6^{2+}$ species, water competes more effectively for the positions in the coordination sphere. Raman studies of the dehydration of $Mg(NO_3)_2 \cdot 6H_2O$ corroborate this view.[344,363,364,641] Calcium and strontium, on the other hand, have poorly-defined hydration spheres and ion-pairs are more readily formed. Barium should also form ion-pairs with nitrate ion, but these have not been detected to date, possibly because the salt solubility is too low or because the band due to the ion-pair cannot be resolved. In the spectrum of solid $Ba(NO_3)_2$ the ν_4 band is at about 723 cm^{-1}.[606] Fedorov et al.[642] have measured stability constants for $Ca(NO_3)_2$, $Sr(NO_3)_2$ and $Ba(NO_3)_2$ by solubility methods. At ionic strength 1.0 the values are: $\beta_1 = 0.88$, $\beta_2 = 0.30$ for calcium; $\beta_1 =$

1.12, $\beta_2 = 0.50$ for strontium; and $\beta_1 = 1.44$, $\beta_2 = 0.93$ for barium. Conductance studies of magnesium nitrate solutions have also been reported.[643] The $Be(NO_3)_2$ results warrant some discussion. The value of $\beta_1 \approx 0.4$ (Table 15) has been calculated from the Raman data of Chang[603] for the ν_4 region. In this work bands were resolved at 717 cm^{-1} (free ion) and 725 cm^{-1} (ion pair). It has been suggested that the beryllium nitrate system may represent the most favourable situation for outer-sphere ion-pair formation.[367,371,603] Large splittings in the ν_3 region and the polarized nature of the peak at 1325 cm^{-1}, together with the absence of the 740 cm^{-1} band, suggested a structure of type $Be(H_2O)_4-(NO_3)^+$. At higher concentrations new bands appear which may be due to inner-sphere ion-pairing. An alternative view is that inner-sphere ion-pairing may occur even at moderate concentrations, but the strong interaction between the Be^{2+} and the remaining three water molecules may greatly diminish the polarization of the nitrate group. This could reduce the position of the inner-sphere ν_4 to 725 cm^{-1}. Devlin and co-workers[352-354] have reported similar reductions in polarizing power of alkali metal ions due to solvation with water and ammonia. Formation of complex compounds between beryllium and alkali metal nitrates from aqueous solution has been reported.[644] Chang[603] has reported that the molar intensity of the symmetric stretching vibrations of $Be(H_2O)_4^{2+}$ is almost constant over a wide range of $Be(NO_3)_2$ concentrations, which would imply the formation of an outer-sphere ion-pair, if all four Be—O bonds contributed to the intensity. Outer-sphere ion-pairing has also been suggested for the aqueous aluminium and zinc nitrate systems.[55,371] Completion of the X-ray study for $Be(NO_3)_2.4H_2O$ may help to resolve this problem.[593]

Values of β_1 and β_2 for Gd^{3+} and Th^{4+} are remarkable in that in two cases the authors[635,637] have reported that $K_2 > K_1$, which is contrary to the usual step-wise formation of complexes. However, the values quoted by the authors are probably not correct, since a plot of $\bar{n}$ versus $[NO_3^-]_f$ for each of these systems (from the authors' published data) shows that the data for the various molar ratio, stoichiometric, and continuous variation compositions, do not fall on the same curve (Figs 11 and 12); this indicates either faulty data or that the complex formation is strongly dependent on ionic strength. For $Gd(NO_3)_3$ a value of $\beta_1 = 4 \pm 1$ can be calculated from the data for $\bar{n} < 0.58$. The high value for β_2 of Th^{4+} may be due to curve resolving problems associated with analysis of the 1050 cm^{-1} band data employed by the authors. A lower value of $\beta_2 = 1.6$ can be calculated from the published data for the 700 cm^{-1} region. A Raman study of the cerium(III) nitrate system indicated that its behaviour is normal; no evidence for strong ionic-strength effects was presented.[69]

Stability constants have also been calculated for a number of lanthanides by other techniques and values of β_1 around 1 or 2 are usually observed.[64,645-649] A qualitative Raman study of aqueous $La(NO_3)_3$ and $Lu(NO_3)_3$ has also been made.[650] Accurately quantitative studies of the vibrational spectra of lanthanide and actinide nitrates should provide valuable data to test currently

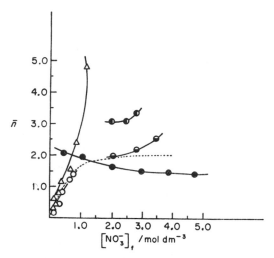

Fig. 11. Formation curve for the aqueous gadolinium(III) nitrate system from the data of Ref. 635. ● stoichiometric solutions; △ Job data; ○ molar ratio data, $[Gd^{3+}]$ = 2.0 mol dm⁻³; ◐ molar ratio data, $[Gd^{3+}]$ = 1.0 mol dm⁻³; ◑ molar ratio data, $[Gd^{3+}]$ = 0.5 mol dm⁻³. Dotted line calculated from β_1 = 4.6.

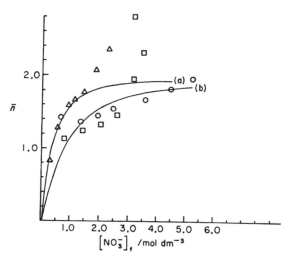

Fig. 12. Formation curve for the aqueous thorium(IV) nitrate system from data of Ref. 637. △ Molar ratio data (1050 cm⁻¹ data); ○ stoichiometric solutions (1050 cm⁻¹ data); □ stoichiometric solutions (700 cm⁻¹ data). (a) Calculated for β_1 = 1.3, β_2 = 6.3. (b) Calculated for β_1 = 1.0, β_2 = 1.6.

accepted theories of aqueous electrolytes and will be aided considerably by the excellent thermodynamic studies that are being performed on these systems.[651-653]

In a number of cases the β values determined by Raman spectroscopy are in excellent agreement with values determined by conventional methods. For instance, the stability constants for mercury(II) nitrate obtained by Sze[68] using Raman spectroscopy ($\beta_1 = 2.21$, $\beta_2 = 0.042$) are in excellent agreement with values ($\beta_1 = 2.24$ and $\beta_2 = 0$) obtained by Hietanen and Sillén[654] using an e.m.f. method. Similarly for $Ce(NO_3)_3$, the β_1 value of 1.68 obtained by Nelson and Irish[69] compares favourably with the value of 1.63 obtained by Choppin and Strazik.[64] Riddell et al.[12] have shown that the degree of ion-pair formation in aqueous $NaNO_3$ as measured by Raman methods is in excellent agreement with that deduced from conductivity studies. Janz and Muller[327] had similar success for $AgNO_3$ in acetonitrile.

Studies of nitrate ion-pair formation have also been performed for non-aqueous solutions, such as liquid ammonia,[291,293,296,304] methanol,[54] acetonitrile[326,327,603,609,625] and dioxan–water mixtures.[68,609] Ion-pair formation is strongly favoured in solvents with low dielectric constants (permittivities) but the change in dielectric constant in itself cannot explain the values of the stability constants measured for the different systems. Association constants ($\beta_1 = 2.6$, $\beta_2 = 0.13$) for $Zn(NO_3)_2$ in anhydrous methanol, $\epsilon = 33.6$, have been obtained from infrared studies,[54] yet Sze[68] has noted that for the same solute in a 4:1 mixture of water:dioxan as solvent (for which the dielectric constant is about the same, $\epsilon = 33.0$), the association constant $\beta_1 = 0.07$, i.e. only about 1/40 of the methanol value. Similarly, a study of $Ca(NO_3)_2$ complexing in dioxan–water mixtures[609] demonstrated that the values of β_1 and β_2 increase with decreased water concentration (lower ϵ values), but a plot of ϵ^{-1} v. log K_1 is certainly not linear. These results suggest that for many strongly hydrated cations the well-defined hydration sphere is not as readily disrupted as predicted by a simple electrostatic model. Studies of a number of aqueous systems in the extremely concentrated solution range suggest that the nitrate ion only enters the coordination sphere when water concentration is insufficient to complete the hydration sphere.[363,364,655]

7.7   Nitrites

In recent years a number of quantitative and qualitative vibrational spectroscopic studies of aqueous metal nitrite systems have been reported. The nitrite ion has C_{2v} symmetry and the 'free' ion should give rise to three infrared- and Raman-active fundamental vibrational modes: $\nu_1(a_1)$, symmetric stretch ≈ 1330 cm^{-1}, $\nu_3(b_1)$, antisymmetric stretch, ≈ 1240 cm^{-1}; and $\nu_2(a_1)$, symmetric bend (deformation), 817 cm^{-1}. Although for many species the antisymmetric stretching frequency is higher than the symmetric stretching frequency, it should be emphasized that for nitrite ion the reverse is true.[168] Interaction between the nitrite ion and a cation may be through the oxygen atom (nitrito) or through the nitrogen atom (nitro). Bridging complexes are also possible but would be unlikely to occur in aqueous solution. The nitrito-linkage may be monodentate

$$M—O\overset{\displaystyle /N\diagdown}{\diagup}O \quad \text{or bidentate (chelate)} \quad M\overset{\displaystyle /O\diagdown}{\underset{\displaystyle \diagdown O\diagup}{\diagup}}N.$$ It would appear that nitrito

linkages are characterized by high values for the bending mode ≈ 860 cm^{-1} and low values for the symmetric stretch ≈ 1050–1250 cm^{-1};[656–658] however, the nitrite spectrum is not as well characterized as the nitrate spectrum and for many systems no clear pattern can be established.[22,33,57]

Although the nitrite is a somewhat stronger ligand than nitrate and may show more versatility due to its ambidentate nature, studies of nitrite solutions are hampered by stability problems[659,660] because in acidic solution decomposition of nitrous acid occurs:

$$3NO_2^- + 2H^+ \rightarrow NO_3^- + 2NO + H_2O$$

Aqueous alkali–metal nitrite solutions have been studied by infrared and Raman spectroscopy;[139] whereas, for aqueous solutions of NaNO$_3$ and LiNO$_3$, there is spectral evidence for contact ion-pairing (Section 7.6), no bands characteristic of contact Li$^+$NO$_2^-$ or Na$^+$NO$_2^-$ ion-pairs were detected. Band positions for the three normal modes were found to be concentration-dependent and shifted toward the solid-state values. Band intensities were found to increase linearly with concentration. The data were interpreted in terms of solvent-shared interactions for LiNO$_2$ and rapid disordered collisions and exchanges for KNO$_2$ and CsNO$_2$.

Evidence for the existence of discrete ion-pairs for a number of aqueous bivalent and tervalent metal nitrites have been obtained by infrared and Raman spectroscopy.[22,33,57,657,661–664] The most obvious diagnostic change in the vibrational spectrum is the doubling of the number of bands in the ν_2 region (Table 16). In addition to the ν_2 band of solvated nitrite a band occurs anywhere from 830 to 870 cm^{-1}; it has been assigned to nitrite ion in the coordination sphere of the cation on the basis of concentration studies (Fig. 13). It has been suggested that the presence of the high-frequency band (≈ 870 cm^{-1}) indicates a nitrito-linkage (perhaps a chelate), whereas the low-frequency band (≈ 840 cm^{-1}) indicates nitro-coordination.[656,657] If this is true then some systems may contain equilibrium concentrations of species with both types of bonding (Table 16).[22,57] Although the presence of a band at ca. 860 cm^{-1} has usually been interpreted as being characteristic of a bidentate nitrito-linkage (chelate), Green and Bell[658] have shown that a band observed at a similar position in the NiL$_2$(NO$_2$)$_2$ spectrum is definitely due to unidentate nitrito complexes. The ν_1 and ν_3 regions are less diagnostic and in several cases the bands from bound and free nitrite appear to be coincident.[22,33,664]

Several studies have been devoted to quantitative measurements of band intensities and subsequent evaluation of stability constants. A summary of the

TABLE 16
Summary of formation constants and spectroscopic data for aqueous nitrites (25 °C)

Cation	β_1	β_2	β_3	β_4	β_5	Characteristic vibrational bands/cm^{-1} of the complex			Method	Ref.
						ν_1	ν_2	ν_3		
Mg^{2+}	0.061						837 p	≈1370 dp	Raman	33
Ca^{2+}	0.535^a	0.167^a				≈1330 p	833 p	≈1370 dp	Raman	33
Ni^{2+}	2.2	0.45	0.65			1258	842	1370	infrared	57
							871 w	1430		
	0	0.15	0				842 p	1370 dp	Raman	57
		0.16^b (Ref. 662)					871 w, p	1430 dp		
Cu^{2+}	9^b	22.5^b	27^b	20^b	9.3^b		840	1380	infrared	662
Zn^{2+}	1.4	1.26				≈1330 p	867 p	1390 dp	Raman	657
Cd^{2+}	61.6	993	2390	1899		≈1330 p	845 w, p	1230	Raman	22
							861 p			
Hg^{2+}	evidence for $\beta_4 = 1.58 \times 10^{11}$ (Ref.660)					1330	861	1220	infrared	663
						1328 m	857 p	1209 w	Raman	664
Cr^{3+}	63^b	569^b	1701^b			1050	850	1450	infrared	662

^{a} Measured at ionic strength 5.8. The values of β's are extremely dependent on the ionic strength.
^{b} Calculated from electronic spectra.

data is presented in Table 16. The aqueous $Zn(NO_2)_2$ system was studied by Raman spectroscopy over a wide range of solution composition.[657] Step-wise formation of $Zn(NO_2)^+$ and $Zn(NO_2)_2$ was reported, with $\beta_1 = 1.4$, and $\beta_2 = 1.2_6$, determined from the intensity data in the 800 cm^{-1} region. The increased complexing ability of the nitrite ligand compared with nitrate ion is shown by these studies because for $Zn(NO_3)^+$, $\beta_1 = 0.02$. Raman studies of the aqueous $Cd(NO_2)_2$ system have also indicated considerable complex formation, with $\beta_1 = 61.6$, $\beta_2 = 993$, $\beta_3 = 2390$, and $\beta_4 = 1899$.[22] The excellent agreement between the β values determined by Raman spectroscopy and those measured by potentiometric and polarographic methods suggests that many of the goals of quantitative Raman spectroscopy (Section 1) may well be realized. Raman spectra of solutions containing mercury(II) and nitrite have been interpreted in terms of two species, viz. $Hg(NO_2)_2$ and $Hg(NO_2)_4^{2-}$.[664] It is known that the latter complex is particularly stable; it has a stability constant of about 10^{11}.[660] The nitrite ions are arranged around Hg^{2+} in bidentate fashion in the solid and probably also in solution.[664] The band due to the deformation mode occurs at 875 cm^{-1} (cf. 861 cm^{-1} for Cd^{2+}/NO_2^-) and Hg—O vibrations were reported at 293 cm^{-1} (1:2 stoichiometry) and 261 cm^{-1} (1:4 stoichiometry) (cf. 240 cm^{-1} for Cd^{2+}/NO_2^-). The shift may relate to the replacement of water in the first coordination sphere of the lower complexes of Hg^{2+}. For Zn^{2+} the band is at 360 cm^{-1} and only two nitrites at most

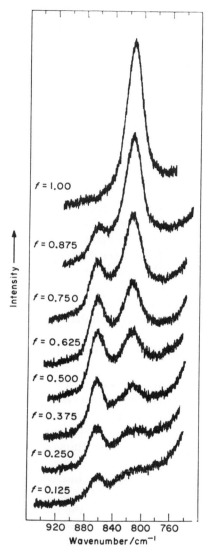

Fig. 13. Raman bands of the free NO_2^- ion (815 cm^{-1}) and complexed NO_2^- ion (867 cm^{-1}) for solution compositions designated by the Job variable, $f = [NO_2^-]/\{[NO_2^-]+[Zn^{2+}]\}$, where the denominator is constant at 2.0 mol dm^{-3} (Brooker and Irish, Ref. 657).

are binding to the cation;[657] the other sites probably are occupied by water molecules. Mercury(II) apparently binds to NO_2^- more strongly than does cadmium(II), and the stability constants also are larger.[660]

Stability constants also have been evaluated for aqueous $Ca(NO_2)_2$ and $Mg(NO_2)_2$ systems and it was noted that ion-pair formation in $Ca(NO_2)_2$ is extremely dependent on ionic strength (Fig. 2).[33] The β values for $Ni(NO_2)_2$ are unusual. The infrared and Raman studies do not lead to the same conclusions.[57] Raman intensity data suggested the presence of only $Ni(NO_2)_2 \cdot 4H_2O$ with $\beta_2 = 0.15 \pm 0.02$, which was in excellent agreement with the value of $\beta_2 = 0.16 \pm 0.03$ obtained by Garnier[662] from studies of absorption spectra in the visible region. In neither the Raman nor the visible spectroscopic studies could the presence of the 1:1 complex be detected. However, infrared data indicated the more usual step-wise formation of complexes $Ni(NO_2)(H_2O)_5^+$, $Ni(NO_2)_2(H_2O)_4$, $Ni(NO_2)_3(H_2O)_3^-$ with $\beta_1 = 2.2 \pm 0.5$, $\beta_2 = 0.45 \pm 0.2$, $\beta_3 = 0.65 \pm 0.2$, and higher-order complexes could not be excluded. To rationalize the difference between the infrared and Raman (and visible) results it was postulated that rapid photochemical aquation altered the chemical equilibrium for light in the 400–600 nm region. In support of this explanation it may be noted that Ivin et al.[665] have observed the photochemically-induced conformational change from square-planar to octahedral exhibited by the reaction of the complex formed between Ni(II) and 1,4,8,11-tetraazoundecane with water. Eaton and Zaw[666] have observed equilibria between nickel(II) complexes of tetrahedral, square-planar, and octahedral geometries. Measurement of the stability constants for $Ni(NO_2)_2$ by non-spectroscopic methods would help to resolve the problem created by the conflicting vibrational spectroscopic data.

In most of the Raman studies it was observed that the total integrated intensity of bands in the 800 cm^{-1} region was directly proportional to total nitrite concentration, which implied that $J_b = J_f$; however, for the aqueous $Cd(NO_2)_2$ system the molar scattering efficiency of the bound nitrite band at approx. 861 cm^{-1} increased considerably and a value of $J_b \approx 2J_f$ could be inferred from the data.[22] Anomalous intensity losses in the ν_1 and ν_3 regions were noted in the infrared spectrum of $Ni(NO_2)_2$[57] and the Raman spectra of $Cd(NO_2)_2$[22] and $Hg(NO_2)_2$.[664]

The ion-pair equilibrium was relatively insensitive to temperature changes over the range 25–95°C.[57] The ratio of free to bound nitrite remained almost constant; however, for aqueous $Ni(NO_2)_2$ the band at ca. 871 cm^{-1} increased slightly with increased temperature. If this band is due to a nitrito-coordinated nitrite ion, it suggests that higher temperatures favour nitrito-coordination, which is in agreement with the results of Goodgame and Hitchman[667] who obtained values of $\Delta H = (-2.3 \pm 0.6)$ kcal mol^{-1} (i.e. (-9.6 ± 2.5) kJ mol^{-1}) and $\Delta S = (-7.2 \pm 1.3)$ cal K^{-1} mol^{-1} (i.e. (-30 ± 5.4) J K^{-1} mol^{-1}) from visible spectroscopic studies of the process: $NiD_2(ONO)_2 \rightleftharpoons NiD_2(NO_2)$.

7.8   Thiocyanates

In aqueous solution the linear thiocyanate ion SCN^- generates a three-band spectrum: ν_1(C—N) stretch, at 2066 cm^{-1}; ν_2(SCN) bend, at 470 cm^{-1}; and ν_3(C—S) stretch, at 747 cm^{-1}.[668] It acts as an ambidentate ligand, i.e. it can coordinate through the (hard) nitrogen or the (softer) sulfur atom; bridging SCN groups are also known to occur. The bonding mode is subject to a number of influences. In solution the dielectric constant (permittivity) of the medium affects the softness or hardness of the coordinating atoms. As the dielectric constant increases, a soft cation will change its preference from N-bonding to S-bonding. For a hard cation the reverse is true.[669] Because of solvent effects, the structures of the species in the solid state will not necessarily be the most stable ones in solutions. Steric requirements of other ligands are also important because the M—S—CN group is often bent whereas the M—N—CS group is linear. The amount of research done to identify the controlling factors is substantial and Bailey et al.[670] have reviewed much of it up to 1970.

Strommen and Plane[671] have reported Raman spectra for aqueous solutions of $Zn(ClO_4)_2$ and KNCS. As the ratio of $[NCS^-]$ to $[Zn^{2+}]$ increased, new polarized Raman bands were observed in the spectrum at 823 cm^{-1} and 793 cm^{-1}. The variation of intensity with composition led them to conclude that the 793 cm^{-1} line is indicative of mono- and di-substituted aquated zinc ions with octahedral coordination and that the 823 cm^{-1} line arises from tri- and tetra-substituted zinc complexes with tetrahedral structures. Only N-bonding is apparent. Generally, as the number of ligands increases, the frequency is expected to decrease; the contrary observation was interpreted in terms of a change in the geometry of the complex from octahedral to tetrahedral. The C—N stretching modes of coordinated NCS^- at approx. 2100 cm^{-1} are virtually insensitive to the number of ligands for the aqueous solutions, and are unlike those obtained from nitromethane solutions.[672] In the latter case the t_2 band is, surprisingly, more intense in the Raman spectrum than the a_1 band and the two bands are more separated than for the aqueous solutions.

An octahedral to tetrahedral conversion—$Co(SCN)(DMSO)_5^+$ to $Co(NCS)_4^{2-}$—has also been found to be favoured by increasing the temperature.[673] From subsequent spectrophotometric studies, equilibrium quotients and enthalpy values were deduced.[674]

Infrared spectra of LiSCN in aprotic solvents have been interpreted in terms of Li^+SCN^- ion pairs and $(LiSCN)_n$ aggregates.[675] In dimethylacetamide the ion-pair generates a band at approx. 2071 cm^{-1} which loses intensity on dilution, leaving only the approx. 2060 cm^{-1} band of the free ion. For dimethylcarbonate with a dielectric constant of 3.09 another band at 2040 cm^{-1} is assigned to the aggregates. This band can be made to disappear by addition of solvent with a higher dielectric constant. When LiSCN is molten or dissolved in water only free ions have been detected.[676]

Infrared spectra suggest that in carbon tetrachloride, thiocyanic acid, HSCN, forms 1:1 complexes with water and 1:1:1 or 1:1:2 complexes with water and methylisobutylketone (MIK). These species are believed to be involved in the extraction of thiocyanic acid from aqueous solutions by MIK.[677]

For a series of mixed thiocyanate complexes of platinum(II), infrared vibrational frequencies for the coordinated NCS^- ion have been assigned using ^{15}N

isotopically substituted compounds.[678] Both solids and solutions were studied and solution data were in qualitative agreement with the observations of Burmeister et al.[669] mentioned above.

7.9 Cyanides

The vibrational frequency of the free CN^- ion occurs at 2079 cm^{-1}. When cyanide ions bind to cations markedly different spectra are observed and these have been well documented.[1,2,551] A thorough infrared and Raman study of crystalline $K_2Zn(CN)_4$, $K_2Cd(CN)_4$, and $K_2Hg(CN)_4$ has recently been reported.[679] In another study, spectra of two isotopically different forms, $[^{64}Zn(CN)_4]^{2-}$ and $[^{68}Zn(CN)_4]^{2-}$, have been obtained and force constants evaluated.[680] No recent, quantitative, spectral investigation of solutions containing these species, to complement the potentiometric study of Persson,[681] has come to our attention. From infrared spectra of dilute solutions of alkali metal cyanides in dimethylformamide and dimethylsulphoxide it has been concluded that virtually all of the electrolyte is in the form of associated ion pairs.[682]

8 CONCLUDING REMARKS

It is abundantly clear from the very large number of reports that vibrational spectroscopy is seen to be a powerful approach to the study of electrolyte solutions. The number of publications, the new and more quantitative procedures for measurement and analysis of data, and the greater depth of understanding which have materialized in the five years since our earlier review[1] are truly impressive. Despite the volume of literature surveyed we do not pretend to be exhaustive and apologize to those whose work has been overlooked. If students new to the subject gain insight and inspiration and if those active in the field conceive of new approaches or interpretations from reading this review we consider our task worthwhile.

REFERENCES

(1) D. E. Irish, in *Ionic Interactions*, Vol. 2 (S. Petrucci, Ed.), Academic Press, New York, 1971, p. 188.
(2) R. S. Tobias, in *The Raman Effect*, Vol. 2 (A. Anderson, Ed.), Marcel Dekker, Inc., New York, 1973, p. 405.
(3) R. E. Verrall, in *Water, A Comprehensive Treatise*, Vol. 3 (F. Franks, Ed.), Plenum Press, New York/London, 1973, p. 211.
(4) T. H. Lilley, *ibid.*, p. 265.
(5) D. E. Irish, in *Physical Chemistry of Organic Solvent Systems* (A. K. Covington and T. Dickinson, Eds.), Plenum Press, London/New York, 1973, p. 433.

(6) A. K. Covington and T. H. Lilley, in *Electrochemistry, A Specialist Periodical Report*, Vol. 1, The Chemical Society, Burlington House, London, 1969, p. 1.
(7) R. E. Hester, *Anal. Chem.* **44**, 490 R (1972).
(8) W. E. L Grossman, *Anal. Chem.* **46**, 345 R (1974).
(9) R. A. Robinson and R. H. Stokes, *Electrolyte Solutions*, 2nd ed., Butterworths, London, 1968, p. 37.
(10) J. G. Kirkwood, *Chem. Rev.* **24**, 233 (1939).
(11) L. C. Bateman, M. G. Church, E. D. Hughes, C. K. Ingold and N. A. Taker, *J. Chem. Soc.* 979 (1940).
(12) J. D. Riddell, D. J. Lockwood and D. E. Irish, *Can. J. Chem.* **50**, 2951 (1972).
(13) A. R. Davis, D. E. Irish, R. B. Roden and A. J. Weerheim, *Appl. Spectrosc.* **26** 384 (1972).
(14) F. J. C. Rossotti and H. S. Rossotti, *The Determination of Stability Constants*, McGraw-Hill, New York, 1961.
(15) M. T. Beck, *Chemistry of Complex Equilibria*, Van Nostrand-Reinhold, London, 1970.
(16) M. M. Jones, *Elementary Coordination Chemistry*, Prentice-Hall, Englewood Cliffs, 1964).
(17) A. M. Bond, *Coord. Chem. Rev.* **6**, 377 (1971).
(18) F. J. C. Rossotti, H. S. Rossotti and R. J. Whewell, *J. Inorg. Nucl. Chem.* **33**, 2051 (1971).
(19) W. A. E. McBryde, *Talanta* **21**, 979 (1974).
(20) D. E. Irish and H. Chen, *Appl. Spectrosc.* **25**, 1 (1971).
(21) R. S. Tobias and M. Yasuda, *Inorg. Chem.* **2**, 1307 (1963).
(22) D. E. Irish and R. V. Thorpe, *Can. J. Chem.* **53**, 1414 (1975).
(23) I. Leden, Dissertation, University of Lund, Lund, Sweden (1943).
(24) A. Swinarski and A. Grodyicki, *Rocz. Chem.* **39**, 1155 (1965).
(25) J. T. Bulmer, T. G. Chang, P. J. Gleeson and D. E. Irish, *J. Solution Chem.* **4**, 969 (1975).
(26) D. J. Leggett and W. A. E. McBryde, *Anal. Chem.* **47**, 1065 (1975).
(27) J. J. Kankare, *Anal. Chem.* **42**, 1322 (1970).
(28) I. G. Sayce, *Talanta* **15**, 1397 (1968).
(29) P. J. Burchill and J. A. McRae, *Aust. J. Chem.* **24**, 187 (1971).
(30) T. Jarv, M.Sc. Thesis, University of Waterloo, Waterloo, Ontario, Canada (1975).
(31) J. Nixon and R. A. Plane, *J. Amer. Chem. Soc.* **84**, 4445 (1962).
(32) J. Bjerrum, in *Coordination Chemistry in Solution* (E. Högfeldt, Ed.), *Transactions of the Royal Institute of Technology, Stockholm, Sweden*, No. 248–296. Swedish Natural Science Research Council, Stockholm, Sweden, 1972, p. 69.
(33) M. H. Brooker and B. De Young, presented to the 58th Canadian Chemical Conference of the Chemical Institute of Canada, Toronto, May 1975.
(34) H. A. Berman and T. R. Stengle, *J. Phys. Chem.* **79**, 1001 (1975).
(35) L. Johansson, *Coord. Chem. Rev.* **12**, 241 (1974).
(36) G. M. Armitage and H. S. Dunsmore, *J. Inorg. Nucl. Chem.* **34**, 2811 (1972).
(37) V. A. Fedorov, A. M. Robov, V. P. Plekhanov, V. V. Kudruk, M. A. Kuzneckikhina and G. E. Chernikova, *Zh. Neorg. Khim.* **19**, 1225 (1974). [*Russ. J. Inorg. Chem.* **19**, 666 (1974)].
(38) Du Pont 310 Curve Resolver, *Chem. Eng. News* **43** (Nov. 15), 50 (1965).
(39) R. N. Jones, *Appl. Optics* **8**, 597 (1969).
(40) W. F. Murphy and H. J. Bernstein, *J. Phys. Chem.* **76**, 1147 (1972).
(41) J. Pitha and R. N. Jones, *Can. J. Chem.* **45**, 2347 (1967).
(42) J. Pitha and R. N. Jones, *Can. J. Chem.* **44**, 3031 (1966).
(43) D. B. Siano and D. E. Metzler, *J. Chem. Phys.* **51**, 1856 (1969).
(44) W. L. Butler and D. W .Hopkins, *Photochem. Photobiol.* **12**, 439, 451 (1970).

(45) J. T. Bulmer and H. F. Shurvell, *J. Phys. Chem.* **77**, 256 (1973).

(46) J. J. Kankare, *Anal. Chem.* **42**, 1322 (1970) and references therein.

(47) J. T. Bulmer and H. F. Shurvell, *Can. J. Chem.* **53**, 1251 (1975).

(48) J. T. Bulmer and H. F. Shurvell, *J. Phys. Chem.* **77**, 2085 (1973).

(49) P. J. Burchill and J. A. McRae, *Aust. J. Chem.* **24**, 187 (1971).

(50) R. N. Jones, communicated to the *XIIth European Congress of Molecular Spectroscopy*, Strasbourg, France, July 1–4 (1975).

(51) D. E. Irish, in *Molecular Spectroscopy of Dense Phases*, Proceedings of the XIIth European Congress on Molecular Spectroscopy, Strasbourg, France, July 1–4, 1975, Elsevier, Amsterdam, p. 595.

(52) R. N. Jones, K. S. Sehadri, N. B. W. Jonathan and J. W. Hopkins, *Can. J. Chem.* **41**, 750 (1963).

(53) D. Ferri, *Acta Chem. Scand.* **26**, 733 (1972).

(54) S. A. Al-Baldawi, M. H. Brooker, T. E. Gough and D. E. Irish, *Can. J. Chem.* **48**, 1202 (1970).

(55) A. T. G. Lemley and R. A. Plane, *J. Chem. Phys.* **57**, 1648 (1972).

(56) R. M. Chatterjee, W. A. Adams and A. R. Davis, *J. Phys. Chem.* **78**, 246 (1974).

(57) M. H. Brooker, *J. Chem. Soc., Faraday Trans. I* **71**, 647 (1975).

(58) T. Fujiyama, *Bull. Chem. Soc. Japan* **46**, 87 (1973).

(59) S. A. Kirillov, *Opt. Spectrosc.* **38**, 310 (1975).

(60) W. H. Leung and F. J. Millero, *J. Solution Chem.* **4**, 145 (1975).

(61) H. Taube and F. A. Posey, *J. Amer. Chem. Soc.* **75**, 1463 (1953).

(62) V. A. Federov, G. E. Chernikova and V. E. Mironov, *Russ. J. Inorg. Chem.* **15** 1082 (1970).

(63) R. G. De Carvalho and G. R. Choppin, *J. Inorg. Nucl. Chem.* **29**, 725 (1967); **29**, 737 (1967).

(64) G. R. Choppin and W. F. Strazik, *Inorg. Chem.* **4**, 1250 (1965).

(65) S. Ahrland, *Coord. Chem. Rev.* **8**, 21 (1972).

(66) J. Beer, D. R. Crow, R. Grzeskowiak and I. D. M. Turner, *Inorg. Nucl. Chem. Lett.* **9**, 35 (1973).

(67) R. Larsson, *Acta Chem. Scand.* **18**, 1923 (1964).

(68) Y.-K. Sze, Ph.D. Thesis, University of Waterloo, Waterloo, Ontario, Canada, 1973.

(69) D. L. Nelson and D. E. Irish, *J. Chem. Soc. Faraday Trans. I* **69**, 156 (1973).

(70) R. E. Hester and R. A. Plane, *J. Chem. Phys.* **40**, 411 (1964).

(71) J. P. Mathieu and M. Lounsbury, *Disc. Faraday Soc.* **9**, 196 (1950).

(72) J. Lewis and R. G. Wilkins, *Modern Coordination Chemistry*, Interscience, New York, 1960.

(73) N. Bjerrum, *Kgl. Danske Vid. Selsk. Mat. Fys. Medd.* 9 (1926).

(74) R. M. Fuoss, *J. Amer. Chem. Soc.* **80**, 5059 (1958).

(75) A. S. Quist and W. L. Marshall, *J. Phys. Chem.* **73**, 978 (1969); **72**, 684 (1968); **70**, 3714 (1966).

(76) T. R. Griffiths and R. K. Scarrow, *J. Chem. Soc. A* 827 (1970).

(77) A. S. Quist and W. L. Marshall, *J. Phys. Chem.* **69**, 3165 (1965).

(78) W. L. Marshall and A. S. Quist, *Proc. Nat. Acad. Sci. U.S.A.* **58**, 901 (1967).

(79) M. V. Ramana-Murti and R. C. Yadav, *Electrochim. Acta* **17**, 643 (1972).

(80) W. L. Marshall, *J. Phys. Chem.* **74**, 346 (1970); **76**, 720 (1972).

(81) J. W. Cobble, *Science* **152**, 1479 (1966).

(82) R. A. Matheson, *J. Phys. Chem.* **73**, 3635 (1969).

(83) W. R. Gilkerson, *J. Phys. Chem.* **74**, 746 (1970).

(84) J. Braunstein, *Ionic Interactions: From Dilute Solutions to Molten Salts*, Vol. 2 (S. Petrucci, Ed.), Academic Press, New York, 1971, p. 243.

(85) D. E. Irish, D. L. Nelson and M. H. Brooker, *J. Chem. Phys.* **54**, 654 (1971).

(86) S. H. Mehdi, D. A. Brisbin and W. A. E. McBryde, *J. Solution Chem.* **4**, 497 (1975).
(87) E. U. Franck, *J. Solution Chem.* **2**, 339 (1973).
(88) M. Buback, *Ber. Bunsenges. Physik. Chem.* **78**, 1230 (1974).
(89) V. M. Valyashko, *Zh. Neorg. Khim.* **20**, 748 (1975).
(90) B. B. Owen and S. R. Brinkley, Jr., *Chem. Rev.* **29**, 461 (1941).
(91) S. D. Hamann, *Physico-Chemical Effects of Pressure*, Butterworths, London, 1957, p. 144.
(92) R. A. Horne, *Marine Chemistry*, Wiley/Interscience, New York, 1969, p. 166.
(93) R. A. Horne, in *Advances in High Pressure Research*, Vol. 2 (R. S. Bradley, Ed.), Academic Press, London, 1969, p. 204.
(94) E. Whalley, *Rev. Phys. Chem. Japan* **45**, 35 (1975).
(95) A. Distèche, in *The Sea, Vol. 5: Marine Chemistry* (E. D. Goldberg, Ed.), Wiley, New York, 1974, p. 81.
(96) G. E. Walrafen, *J. Chem. Phys.* **55**, 768 (1971).
(97) A. R. Davis and A. W. Adams, *Spectrochim. Acta*, **27A**, 2401 (1971).
(98) A. R. Davis, W. A. Adams and M. J. McGuire, *J. Chem. Phys.* **60**, 1751 (1974).
(99) M. Nicol, Y. Ebisuzaki, W. D. Ellenson and A. Karim, *Rev. Sci. Instrum.* **43**, 1368 (1972).
(100) R. Cavagnat, J. J. Martin and G. Turrell, *Appl. Spectrosc.* **23**, 172 (1969).
(101) J. C. Cornut and P. V. Huong, *Appl. Spectrosc.* **27**, 55 (1973).
(102) R. A. Horne, R. A. Courant and G. R. Frysinger, *J. Chem. Soc.* 1515 (1964).
(103) A. R. Davis and B. G. Oliver, *J. Phys. Chem.* **77**, 1315 (1973).
(104) F. H. Fisher, *J. Phys. Chem.* **66**, 1607 (1962).
(105) F. J. Millero and W. L. Masterton, *J. Phys. Chem.* **78**, 1287 (1974).
(106) J. O. Lephardt and G. Vilcins, *Appl. Spectrosc.* **29**, 221 (1975).
(107) M. Delhaye, *Appl. Optics* **7**, 2195 (1968); (Inst. Petroleum Mol. Spectr. Congress, Brighton, 1968 [*Proc. Inst. Pet.*, 1968]).
(108) M. Bridoux, A. Chapput, M. Crunelle and M. Delhaye, *Advan. Raman Spectrosc.* **1**, 65 (1973). (Abstracts of the 3rd International Conference on Raman Spectroscopy, Reims, France, 1972.)
(109) M. Manfait, J. L. Beaudoin and L. Bernard, *Advan. Raman. Spectrosc.* **1**, 76 (1973). (Abstracts of the 3rd International Conference on Raman Spectroscopy, Reims, France, 1972.)
(110) M. Bridoux, A. Chapput, M. Delhaye, H. Tourbez and F. Wallart, *Laser Raman Gas Diagnosis, Proj. Squid Laser Raman Workshop Meas. Gas. Prop.*, **1973** (M. Lapp and C. M. Penney, Eds.), Plenum, New York, 1974, p. 249.
(111) B. Sombret and F. Wallart, *Compt. Rend. Acad. Sci. (Paris)* **227B**, 663 (1973).
(112) Y.-K. Sze and D. E. Irish, *Can. J. Chem.* **53**, 427 (1975).
(113) P. K. Glasoe and C. N. Bush, *Anal. Chem.* **44**, 833 (1972).
(114) J. B. Bates, J. P. Young, M. M. Murray, H. W. Kohn and G. E. Boyd, *J. Inorg. Nucl. Chem.* **34**, 2721 (1972).
(115) G. E. Walrafen, *J. Chem. Phys.* **62**, 297 (1975).
(116) W. H. Woodruff and T. G. Spiro, *Appl. Spectrosc.* **28**, 576 (1974).
(117) H. J. Clase, A. J. Cleland and M. J. Newlands, *J. Organomet. Chem.* **93**, 231 (1975); *J. Chem. Soc., Dalton Trans.* 2546 (1973).
(118) C. J. Clemett, *J. Chem. Soc. B* 2202 (1971).
(119) J. Bukowska and Z. Kęcki, *J. Mol. Struct.* **26**, 289 (1975).
(120) M. Kinugasa, K. Kishi and S. Ikeda, *J. Phys. Chem.* **77**, 1914 (1973).
(121) D. H. Turner, G. W. Flynn, N. Sutin and J. V. Beitz, *J. Amer. Chem. Soc.* **94**, 1554 (1972).
(122) E. E. Genser and R. E. Connick, *J. Chem. Phys.* **58**, 991 (1973).
(123) S. Sykora, *J. Chem. Phys.* **57**, 1795 (1972).

(124) W. G. Rothschild, G. J. Rasasco and R. C. Livingston, *J. Chem. Phys.* **62**, 1253 (1975); W. G. Rothschild, *ibid.* **57**, 997 (1972).

(125) J. Yarwood, *J. Chem. Soc., Faraday Trans. II* **74**, 714 (1975).

(126) J. E. Griffiths, *J. Chem. Phys.* **59**, 751 (1973).

(127) J. DeZwaan, D. W. Hess and C. S. Johnson, Jr., *J. Chem. Phys.* **63**, 422 (1975).

(128) P. Van Konynenburg and W. A. Steele, *J. Chem. Phys.* **62**, 2301 (1975).

(129) J. P. Perchard, W. F. Murphy and H. J. Bernstein, *Mol. Phys.* **23**, 499 (1972); *ibid.*, 519, 534.

(130) G. Birnbaum, *Mol. Phys.* **25**, 241 (1973).

(131) J. F. Dill, T. A. Litovitz and J. A. Bacaro, *J. Chem. Phys.* **62**, 3839 (1975).

(132) J. H. R. Clarke and L. V. Woodcock, *J. Chem. Phys.* **57**, 1006 (1972).

(133) A. H. Jamieson and A. R. Maret, *Quart. Rev. Chem. Soc.* **2**, 325 (1973).

(134) Y. Yeh and R. N. Keeler, *J. Chem. Phys.* **51**, 1120 (1969).

(135) J. H. R. Clarke, G. J. Hills, C. J. Oliver and J. M. Vaughan, *J. Chem. Phys.* **61** 2810 (1974).

(136) M. M. Kreevoy and C. A. Mead, *J. Amer. Chem. Soc.* **84**, 4596 (1962); *Disc. Faraday Soc.* **39**, 166 (1965).

(137) H. Chen and D. E. Irish, *J. Phys. Chem.* **75**, 2672 (1971); D. E. Irish and H. Chen, *ibid.* **74**, 3796 (1970).

(138) D. E. Irish and R. C. Meatherall, *J. Phys. Chem.* **75**, 2684 (1971).

(139) D. E. Irish and M. H. Brooker, *Trans. Faraday Soc.* **67**, 1916 (1971).

(140) M. H. Brooker, *J. Chem. Soc., Faraday I* **71**, 647 (1975).

(141) E. F. Caldin and H. P. Bennett, *J. Solution Chem.* **2**, 217 (1973).

(142) J. P. Hunt, *Coord. Chem. Rev.* **7**, 1 (1971).

(143) E. G. Weidemann and G. Zundel, *Z. Naturforsch.* **28a**, 236 (1973); R. Janoschek, E. G. Weidemann, H. Pfeiffer and G. Zundel, *J. Amer. Chem. Soc.* **94**, 2387 (1972); R. Lindemann and G. Zundel, *J. Chem. Soc., Faraday Trans. II* **68**, 979 (1972).

(144) C. J. Montrose, J. Bucaro, J. Marshall-Coakley and T. A. Litovitz, *J. Chem. Phys.* **60**, 5025 (1974).

(145) J. S. Bodenheimer, B. J. Berenblut and G. R. Wilkinson, *Chem. Phys. Lett.* **14**, 533 (1972).

(146) W. Kiefer, *Appl. Spectrosc.* **27**, 253 (1973).

(147) D. J. Gardiner, R. B. Girling and R. E. Hester, *J. Chem. Soc. Faraday Trans. II* **71**, 709 (1975).

(148) J. W. Amy, R. W. Chrisman, J. W. Lundeen, T. Y. Ridley, J. C. Sprowles and R. S. Tobias, *Appl. Spectrosc.* **28**, 262 (1974).

(149) S. Mansy, T. E. Wood, J. C. Sprowles and R. S. Tobias, *J. Amer. Chem. Soc.* **96**, 1762 (1974).

(150) S. Mansy and R. S. Tobias, *J. Amer. Chem. Soc.* **96**, 6874 (1974).

(151) S. Mansy, J. P. Frick and R. S. Tobias, *Biochim. Biophys. Acta* **378**, 319 (1975).

(152) A. K. Covington and J. M. Thain, *Appl. Spectrosc.* **29**, 386 (1975).

(153) G. E. Walrafen and J. Stone, *Appl. Spectrosc.* **26**, 585 (1972).

(154) G. E. Walrafen, *Phys. Blätter* **12**, 540 (1974).

(155) G. E. Walrafen, *Appl. Spectrosc.* **29**, 179 (1975).

(156) M. Fleischmann, P. J. Hendra and A. J. McQuillan, *J. Chem. Soc., Chem. Commun.* **80** (1973).

(157) M. Fleischmann, P. J. Hendra and A. J. McQuillan, *Chem. Phys. Lett.* **26**, 163 (1974).

(158) R. G. Greenler and T. L. Slager, *Spectrochim. Acta* **29**A, 193 (1973).

(159) J. S. Clarke, A. T. Kuhn and W. J. Orville-Thomas, *Electroanal. Chem. Interfacial Electrochem.* **54**, 253 (1974).

(160) T. Higashiyama and T. Takenaka, *J. Phys. Chem.* **78**, 941 (1974).

(161) I. S. Shamina, O. G. Malandin, S. M. Rakhovskaya and L. A. Vereshchagina, *Elektrokhimiya* **10**, 1745 (1974).
(162) M. J. D. Low, *Progr. Nuclear Energy*, Ser. 9, **11**, 179 (1972).
(163) J. L. Koenig, *Appl. Spectrosc.* **29**, 293 (1975).
(164) M. J. D. Low and R. T. Yang, *Spectrochim. Acta* **29A**, 1761 (1973).
(165) R. T. Yang and M. J. D. Low, *Spectrochim. Acta* **30A**, 1787 (1974).
(166) R. T. Yang and M. J. D. Low, *Anal. Chem.* **45**, 2014 (1973).
(167) E. F. Rissman, *Anal. Chem.* **44**, 644 (1972).
(168) M. H. Brooker and D. E. Irish, *Can. J. Chem.* **46**, 229 (1968).
(169) G. Kraus and M. Maier, *Appl. Phys.* **7**, 287 (1975).
(170) W. Kiefer, *Appl. Spectrosc.* **28**, 115 (1974).
(171) A. Davis, M. Bristow and J. Koningstein, in *Remote Sensing and Water Resources Management* (K. P. B. Thomson, R. K. Lane and S. C. Csallany, Eds.), Proc. No. 17, American Water Resources Association, 1973.
(172) W. Kiefer and H. J. Bernstein, *Mol. Phys.* **23**, 835 (1972).
(173) K. Machida, B.-K. Kim, Y. Saito, K. Igarashi and T. Uno, *Bull. Chem. Soc. Japan* **47**, 78 (1974).
(174) G. Braunlic, G. Gamer and M. S. Petty, *Water Res.* **7**, 1643 (1973).
(175) P. C. Li and J. P. Devlin, *J. Chem. Phys.* **59**, 547 (1973).
(176) *Structure of Water and Aqueous Solutions*, Proc. Internat. Symp. Structure of Water and Aqueous Solutions, July 1973 (W. A. P. Luck, Ed.), Verlag Chemie, Weinheim, Germany, 1974.
(177) *Water and Aqueous Solutions, Structure, Thermodynamics and Transport Processes* (R. A. Horne, Ed.), Wiley, New York, 1972.
(178) D. Eisenberg and W. Kauzman, *Structure and Properties of Water*, Oxford University Press, London, 1969.
(179) H. S. Frank, *Science* **169**, 635 (1970).
(180) D. E. O'Reilly, *Phys. Rev.* **A17**, 1659 (1973).
(181) G. E. Walrafen, in *Hydrogen Bonded Solvent Systems* (A. K. Covington and P. Jones, Eds.), Taylor and Francis, London, 1968, p. 9.
(182) *Water: A Comprehensive Treatise* (Felix Franks, Ed.), Plenum Press, New York, Vol. I, *The Physics and Physical Chemistry of Water* (1972). Vol. II, *Water in Crystalline Hydrates, Aqueous Solutions of Simple Nonelectrolytes* (1972). Vol. III, *Aqueous Solutions of Simple Electrolytes* (1973). Vol. IV, *Aqueous Solutions of Macromolecules: Disperse Systems* (1974).
(183) B. V. Derjaguin and N. V. Churaev, *Nature* **244**, 430 (1973).
(184) J. J. Bikerman, *Nature* **245**, 343 (1973).
(185) L. Allen, *New Scientist* **59**, 376 (1973).
(186) F. Vaslow, *J. Phys. Chem.* **73**, 3745 (1969).
(187) G. Andaloro, M. B. Palma-Vittorelli and M. U. Palma, *J. Solution Chem.* **4**, 215 (1975).
(188) R. Oder and D. A. I. Goring, *Can. J. Chem.* **48**, 3790 (1970).
(189) W. Drost-Hansen, *Fed. Proc. Fed. Amer. Soc. Exp. Biol.* **30**, 1539 (1971).
(190) T. F. Young, *18th Annual Mid-American Symposium on Spectroscopy*, Chicago, May 1967; M. Glos, *Scientific Research*, August 1967, p. 71.
(191) C. A. Angell, J. Shuppert and J. C. Tucker, *J. Phys. Chem.* **77**, 3092 (1973); C. A. Angell and J. C. Tucker, *Science* **181**, 342 (1973).
(192) B. M. Dolgonosov and V. G. Pechnikov, *Biofiz. Aspekty. Zagryazneniya Biosfery* 48 (1973).
(193) A review of the older Russian literature is given in Ref. 196.
(194) M. A. Ryazanov, *Zh. Fiz. Khim.* **49**, 789 (1975).
(195) A. V. Karyakin, G. A. Kriventsova and N. V. Sobaleva, *Dokl. Akad. Nauk. SSSR.* **221**, 1096 (1975).

(196) D. J. Lockwood and D. E. Irish, *Chem. Phys. Lett.* **24**, 123 (1974).
(197) S. O. Mirumyants, E. A. Vandyukov and R. S. Tikhvatullin, *Zh. Fiz. Khim.* **46**, 210 (1972).
(198) F. Aussenegg, M. Lippitsch, R. Moller and J. Wagner, *Phys. Lett.* **50A**, 233 (1974).
(199) E. V. Chisler and V. Y. Davydov, *Fiz. Tverd. Tela.* (Leningrad) **15**, 884 (1973).
(200) G. E. Walrafen, *J. Chem. Phys.* **52**, 4176 (1970); **50**, 567 (1969).
(201) G. R. Choppin and M. R. Violante, *J. Chem. Phys.* **56**, 5890 (1972).
(202) R. A. M. O'Ferrall, G. W. Koeppl and A. J. Kresge, *J. Amer. Chem. Soc.* **93**, 1 (1971).
(203) E. C. W. Clarke and D. N. Glew, *Can. J. Chem.* **50**, 1655 (1972).
(204) B. Curnutte and J. Bandekar, *J. Mol. Spectrosc.* **41**, 500 (1972).
(205) H. R. Wyss and M. Falk, *Can. J. Chem.* **48**, 607 (1970).
(206) M. Falk and T. A. Ford, *Can. J. Chem.* **44**, 1699 (1966).
(207) J. Schiffer and D. F. Hornig, *J. Chem. Phys.* **49**, 4150 (1968).
(208) T. T. Wall, *J. Chem. Phys.* **51**, 113 (1969).
(209) K. M. Cunningham, Ph.D. Thesis, Yale University, New Haven, Conn., 1971.
(210) A. Rahman and F. H. Stillinger, *J. Chem. Phys.* **55**, 3336 (1971).
(211) F. H. Stillinger and A. Rahman, *J. Chem. Phys.* **60**, 1545 (1974); **61**, 4973 (1974); F. H. Stillinger and H. L. Lemberg, *J. Chem. Phys.* **62**, 1340 (1975).
(212) B. R. Lentz and H. A. Scheraga, *J. Chem. Phys.* **58**, 5296 (1973).
(213) B. Curnutte and J. Bandekar, *J. Mol. Spectrosc.* **49**, 314 (1974).
(214) C. A. Angell, *J. Phys. Chem.* **75**, 3698 (1971).
(215) O. Weres and S. A. Rice, *J. Amer. Chem. Soc.* **94**, 8983 (1972); D. Denley and S. A. Rice, *J. Amer. Chem. Soc.* **96**, 4369 (1974).
(216) J. W. Perram, *Mol. Phys.* **21**, 1077 (1971).
(217) F. F. Abraham, *J. Chem. Phys.* **61**, 1221 (1974); A. I. Michaels, G. M. Pound and F. F. Abraham, *J. Appl. Phys.* **45**, 9 (1974); also see K. Binder, *J. Chem. Phys.* **63**, 2265 (1975) and F. F. Abraham and J. A. Barker, *ibid.*, 2266.
(218) I. N. Kochnev, I. A. Sidorova and A. I. Khaloimov, *Mol. Fiz. Biofiz. Vodn. Sist.* **2**, 79 (1974).
(219) J. G. David, *Spectrochim. Acta* **28A**, 977 (1972).
(220) J. R. Scherer, M. K. Go and S. Kint, *J. Phys. Chem.* **77**, 2108 (1973).
(221) J. R. Scherer, M. K. Go and S. Kint, *J. Phys. Chem.* **78**, 1304 (1974).
(222) D. F. Smith and J. Overend, *Spectrochim. Acta* **28A**, 471 (1972).
(223) W. S. Benedict, N. Gailar and E. K. Plyler, *J. Chem. Phys.* **24**, 1139 (1956).
(224) P. Dryjanski and Z. Kęcki, *J. Mol. Struct.* **12**, 219 (1972).
(225) In an infrared study of pure H_2O a broad maximum was observed at ca. 3450 cm⁻¹ with shoulders at 3230 and 3630 cm⁻¹. M. H. Brooker, unpublished work.
(226) G. P. Ayers and A. D. E. Pullin, *Chem. Phys. Lett.* **29**, 609 (1974).
(227) P. V. Huong and J. C. Cornut, *J. Chim. Phys., Phys. Chim. Bio.* **72**, 534 (1975).
(228) V. B. Mann, T. Neikes, E. Schmidt and W. A. P. Luck, *Ber. Bunsenges. Phys. Chem.* **78**, 1236 (1974).
(229) D. P. Strommen, D. M. Gruen and R. L. McBeth, *J. Chem. Phys.* **58**, 4028 (1973).
(230) J. R. Downey, Jr. and G. R. Choppin, *Spectrochim. Acta* **30A**, 37 (1974).
(231) D. Olander and S. A. Rice, *Proc. Nat. Acad. Sci. U.S.A.* **69**, 98 (1972).
(232) V. Bontempo, *Phys. Lett.* **A42**, 17 (1972).
(233) A. H. Hardin and K. B. Harvey, *Spectrochim Acta* **A29**, 1139 (1973).
(234) C. G. Ventatesh, S. A. Rice and J. B. Bates, *J. Chem. Phys.* **63**, 1065 (1975).
(235) G. E. Walrafen, *J. Solution Chem.* **2**, 159 (1973).
(236) P. T. T. Wong and E. Whalley, *J. Chem. Phys.* **64**, 2359 (1976).
(237) P. T. T. Wong and E. Whalley, *J. Chem. Phys.* **62**, 2418 (1975).
(238) G. E. Walrafen and L. A. Blatz, *J. Chem. Phys.* **56**, 4216 (1972).

(239) W. C. Mundy, L. Gutierrez and F. H. Spedding, *J. Chem. Phys.* **59**, 2173 (1973).
(240) G. E. Walrafen, *J. Chem. Phys.* **48**, 244 (1968).
(241) H. R. Wyss and M. Falk, *Can. J. Chem.* **48**, 607 (1970).
(242) E. C. W. Clarke and D. N. Glew, *Can. J. Chem.* **50**, 1655 (1971).
(243) G. E. Walrafen, *J. Phys. Chem.* **55**, 5137 (1971).
(244) G. V. Bondarenko and Y. E. Gorbatyi, *Dokl. Akad. Nauk. SSSR* **210**, 132 (1973).
(245) B. Z. Gorbunov and Y. I. Naberukhim, *Zh. Strukt. Khim.* **13**, 20 (1972).
(246) G. E. Walrafen and L. A. Blatz, *J. Chem. Phys.* **59**, 2646 (1973).
(247) R. Oder and D. A. I. Goring, *Spectrochim. Acta* **27A**, 2285 (1971).
(248) M. A. Gray, T. M. Loehr and P. A. Pincus, *J. Chem. Phys.* **59**, 1121 (1973).
(249) D. W. James and R. Irmer, *J. Raman Spectrosc.* **3**, 91 (1975).
(250) E. Whalley, *Nature* **251**, 217 (1974).
(251) J. J. Péron, C. Bourderon and C. Sandorfy, *Can. J. Chem.* **49**, 3901 (1971).
(252) L. M. Kleiss, H. A. Strobel and M. C. R. Symons, *Spectrochim. Acta* **A29**, 829 (1973).
(253) A. Burneau and J. Corset, *J. Chem. Phys.* **58**, 5188 (1973).
(254) G. R. Choppin and M. Violante, *J. Chem. Phys.* **58**, 5189 (1973).
(255) S. Subramanian and H. F. Fisher, *J. Phys. Chem.* **76**, 452 (1972); W. C. McCabe, S. Subramanian and H. F. Fisher, *J. Phys. Chem.* **74**, 4360 (1970).
(256) O. D. Bonner, *Infrared Physics* **12**, 109 (1972).
(257) O. D. Bonner, *J. Phys. Chem.* **76**, 1228 (1972).
(258) P. A. Giguère, *J. Phys. Chem.* **76**, 3675 (1972).
(259) M. J. Colles, G. E. Walrafen and K. W. Wecht, *Chem. Phys. Lett.* **10**, 621 (1970); G. E. Walrafen, *Adv. Mol. Relax.* **3**, 43 (1972).
(260) M. G. Sceats, S. A. Rice and J. E. Butler, *J. Chem. Phys.* **64**, 2701 (1976) and references therein.
(261) G. E. Walrafen, *J. Chem. Phys.* **55**, 768 (1971).
(262) G. E. Walrafen, *J. Chem. Phys.* **52**, 4176 (1970).
(263) O. D. Bonner and C. F. Jumper, *Infrared Physics* **13**, 233 (1973).
(264) T. Takamura, *Nip. Kag. Kai.* 375 (1974).
(265) S. Subramanian and H. F. Fisher, *J. Phys. Chem.* **76**, 84 (1972).
(266) C. Jolicoeur, N. D. The and A. Cabana, *Can. J. Chem.* **49**, 2008 (1971).
(267) C. DeVisser and G. Somsen, *J. Chem. Soc. Faraday Trans. I* **69**, 1440 (1973).
(268) D. W. James and R. L. Frost, *J. Phys. Chem.* **78**, 1754 (1974).
(269) J. L. MacDonald, J. Serphillyss and J. J. Guerrera, *J. Phys. Chem.* **77**, 370 (1973).
(270) D. N. Glew and N. S. Rath, *Can. J. Chem.* **49**, 837 (1971).
(271) D. W. James and R. F. Armishaw, *Aust. J. Chem.* **28**, 1179 (1975).
(272) A. de Trobriand, M. Ceccaldi, M. Henry, M. M. Marcracq-Rousselot and M. Lucas, *Comp. Rend. Acad. Sci.* (Paris) **274C**, 919 (1972).
(273) S. Taniewsk and R. Grochowss, *Soc. Sci. Lodz.* **17**, 15 (1972).
(274) W. Luck, A. P. Zhukovskii, *Mol. Fiz. Biofiz. Vodn. Sist.* **2**, 131 (1974).
(275) M. J. D. Low and R. T. Yang, *Spectrosc. Lett.* **6**, 299 (1973).
(276) J. Francois, *Comp. Rend. Acad. Sci.* (Paris) **275C**, 725 (1972).
(277) P. R. Philip and C. Jolicoeur, *J. Phys. Chem.* **77**, 3071 (1973).
(278) M. Lucas, A. DeTrobriand and M. Ceccaldi, *J. Phys. Chem.* **79**, 913 (1975).
(279) G. Brink and M. Falk, *Can. J. Chem.* **48**, 3019 (1970).
(280) D. M. Adams, M. J. Blandamer, M. C. R. Symons, and D. Waddington, *Trans. Faraday Soc.* **67**, 611 (1971).
(281) M. C. R. Symons and D. Waddington, *J. Chem. Soc. Faraday Trans. II* **71**, 22 (1975).
(282) M. H. Baron and C. de Lozé, *J. Chim. Phys., Phys.-Chim. Biol.* **68**, 1299 (1971); **68**, 1293 (1971); **69**, 1084 (1972).
(283) C. de Lozé and M. H. Baron, *Chem. Phys. Lett.* **9**, 103 (1971).

(284) O. D. Bonner, R. K. Arisman and C. F. Jumper, *Infrared Physics* **14**, 271 (1974).
(285) E. Gentric, A. Le Narvor and P. Saumagne, *J. Chem. Soc. Faraday Trans. II* **70**, 1191 (1974).
(286) W. C. Mundy and F. Spedding, *J. Chem. Phys.* **59**, 2183 (1973).
(287) P. Dryjanski and Z. Kęcki, *J. Mol. Spectrosc.* **12**, 219 (1972).
(288) A. Sakolowska and Z. Kęcki, *Rocz. Chem.* **46**, 1107 (1972).
(289) P. Dryjanski and Z. Kęcki, *Adv. Mol. Relax.* **5**, 261 (1973).
(290) P. Dryjanski and Z. Kęcki, *Rocz. Chem.* **46**, 671 (1972).
(291) K. R. Plowman and J. J. Lagowski, *J. Phys. Chem.* **78**, 143 (1974).
(292) M. Schwartz and C. H. Wang, *J. Chem. Phys.* **59**, 5258 (1973).
(293) A. T. Lemley and J. J. Lagowski, *J. Phys. Chem.* **78**, 708 (1974).
(294) D. J. Gardiner, R. E. Hester and W. E. L. Grossman, *J. Raman Spectrosc.* **1**, 87 (1973).
(295) A. T. Lemley, J. H. Roberts, K. R. Plowman and J. J. Lagowski, *J. Phys. Chem.* **77**, 2185 (1973).
(296) J. H. Roberts, A. T. Lemley and J. J. Lagowski, *Spectrosc. Lett.* **5**, 271 (1972).
(297) J. H. Roberts and B. J. DeBettignies, *J. Phys. Chem.* **78**, 2106 (1974); **79**, 1852 (1975).
(298) D. J. Gardiner, R. E. Hester and W. E. L. Grossman, *J. Chem. Phys.* **59**, 175 (1973).
(299) T. Birchall and I. Drummond, *J. Chem. Soc.* (*A*), 1859 (1970).
(300) J. W. Lundeen and W. H. Koehler, *J. Phys. Chem.* **79**, 2957 (1975).
(301) M. Buback and E. U. Franck, *J. Chim. Phys., Phys.,-Chim. Biol.* **72**, 601 (1975).
(302) J. A. Cugley and A. D. E. Pullin, *Spectrochim. Acta* **29A**, 1665 (1973).
(303) B. S. Ault and G. C. Pimentel, *J. Phys. Chem.* **77**, 1649 (1973).
(304) J. W. Lundeen and R. S. Tobias, *J. Chem. Phys.* **63**, 924 (1975).
(305) P. Gans and J. B. Gill, *J. Chem. Soc. Chem. Comm.*, 914 (1973).
(306) B. L. Smith and W. H. Koehler, *J. Phys. Chem.* **76**, 2481 (1972); **77**, 1753 (1973).
(307) P. F. Rusch and J. J. Lagowski, *J. Phys. Chem.* **77**, 210 (1973).
(308) G. Herzberg, *Molecular Spectra and Structure*, Van Nostrand, New York, 1945, Vol. 2, Chapters 2 and 3, p. 295.
(309) B. G. Cox, *Chem. Soc. Annual Reports* **70A**, 24 (1973).
(310) K. Szezepianak and W. J. Orville-Thomas, *J. Chem. Soc. Faraday Trans. I* **70**, 1175 (1974).
(311) P. K. Glasoe, S. Hallock, M. Hove and J. M. Duke, *Spectrochim. Acta* **27A** 2309 (1971).
(312) Y. Sassa and T. Katayama, *J. Chem. Eng.* (*Japan*) **7**, 1 (1974).
(313) G. Fini and P. Mirone, *J. Chem. Soc. Faraday Trans. II* **70**, 1767 (1974).
(314) J. E. Katon and M. D. Cohen, *Can. J. Chem.* **53**, 1378 (1975).
(315) Y. Omura and T. Shimanouchi, *J. Mol. Spectrosc.* **55**, 430 (1975).
(316) G. R. Choppin and J. R. Downey, Jr., *Spectrochim. Acta* **30A**, 43 (1974).
(317) A. Burneau and J. Corset, *J. Chem. Phys.* **56**, 662 (1972); *J. Phys. Chem.* **76**, 449 (1972).
(318) P. Hindle, S. Walker and J. Warren, *J. Chem. Soc. Faraday Trans. II*, **71**, 756 (1975).
(319) C. H. Wang and R. B. Wright, *J. Chem. Phys.* **55**, 3300 (1971).
(320) M. Schwartz and C. H. Wang, *Chem. Phys. Lett.* **29**, 383 (1974).
(321) I. W. Larkin, *J. Chem. Soc. Faraday Trans. II* **69**, 1278 (1973).
(322) J. F. Coetzee and W. R. Sharpe, *J. Solution Chem.* **1**, 77 (1972).
(323) Z. Kęcki and J. Wojtczak, *Rocz. Chem.* **44**, 847 (1970).
(324) I. S. Perelygin and A. B. Shaikhova, *Opt. Spectrosc.* **31**, 110 (1971).
(325) A. L. Narvor, E. Gentric and P. Saumagne, *Can. J. Chem.* **49**, 1933 (1971).
(326) T. G. Chang and D. E. Irish, *J. Solution Chem.* **3**, 161 (1974).

(327) G. J. Janz and M. A. Muller, *J. Solution Chem.* **4**, 285 (1975).
(328) O. H. Ellestad, P. Klaboe and G. Hagen, *Spectrochim. Acta* **27A**, 1025 (1971).
(329) S. C. Mohr, W. D. Wilk and G. M. Barrow, *J. Amer. Chem. Soc.* **87**, 3048 (1965).
(330) G. R. Choppin and M. R. Violante, *J. Chem. Phys.* **56**, 5890 (1972).
(331) A. Burneau and J. Corset, *J. Chem. Phys.* **58**, 5188 (1973).
(332) J. C. Barnes and C. S. Duncan, *J. Chem. Soc.* (*A*) 1732 (1972).
(333) S. F. Lincoln, *Coord. Chem. Rev.* **6**, 309 (1971).
(334) J. F. Hinton and E. S. Amis, *Chem. Rev.* **71**, 627 (1971).
(335) P. S. Leung and G. J. Safford, *J. Solution Chem.* **2**, 525 (1973).
(336) E. S. Amis and J. F. Hinton, *Solvent Effects on Chemical Phenomena*, Vol. I, Academic Press, New York, 1973.
(337) G. Zundel and E. G. Weidemann, *Z. Physik. Chem. Neue Folge* **83**, 327 (1973).
(338) H. Kistenmacher, H. Popkie and E. Clementi, *J. Chem. Phys.* **59**, 5842 (1973).
(339) M. Falk, C. H. Huang and O. Knop, *Can. J. Chem.* **53**, 51 (1975).
(340) L. D. Vinh, L. Martin, J. A. de Saja and R. Lafont, *Compt. Rend. Acad. Sci.* (*Paris*) **277B**, 91 (1973).
(341) R. Alonso, L. D. Vinh and J. A. de Saja, *Krist. Tech.* **8**, 457 (1973).
(342) L. Schropfer, *Z. Anorg. Chem.* **401**, 1 (1973).
(343) H. D. Lutz, H. J. Klueppel, W. Pobitschka and B. Baasner, *Z. Naturforsch.* **29b**, 723 (1974).
(344) T. G. Chang and D. E. Irish, *Can. J. Chem.* **51**, 118 (1973).
(345) J. Guillermet, A. Novak and E. Foglizzo, *J. Mol. Struct.* **17**, 91 (1973).
(346) G. S. Karetnikov, O. V. Bazileva and T. V. Gerzha, *Zh. Fiz. Khim.* **49**, 815 (1975).
(347) J. Jager and G. Schaack, *Z. Natursforsch.* **28a**, 738 (1973).
(348) D. M. Adams and W. R. Trumble, *Inorg. Chim. Acta* **10**, 235 (1974).
(349) D. M. Adams and W. R. Trumble, *J. Chem. Soc. Faraday Trans. II* **70**, 1967 (1974).
(350) D. R. Cogley, J. N. Butler and E. Grunwald, *J. Phys. Chem.* **75**, 1477 (1971).
(351) A. L. Van Geet, *J. Amer. Chem. Soc.* **94**, 5583 (1972).
(352) N. Smyrl and J. P. Devlin, *J. Phys. Chem.* **77**, 3067 (1973).
(353) N. Smyrl and J. P. Devlin, *J. Phys. Chem.* **76**, 3093 (1972).
(354) G. Ritzhaupt and J. P. Devlin, *J. Phys. Chem.* **79**, 2265 (1975).
(355) G. Pollard, N. Smyrl and J. P. Devlin, *J. Phys. Chem.* **76**, 1826 (1972).
(356) A. H. Narten, F. Vaslow and H. A. Levy, *J. Chem. Phys.* **58**, 5017 (1973).
(357) G. Licheri, G. Piccaluga and G. Pinna, *Chem. Phys. Lett.* **35**, 119 (1975).
(358) P. A. Kollman and I. D. Kuntz, *J. Amer. Chem. Soc.* **96**, 4766 (1974).
(359) K. Heinzinger and P. C. Vogel, *Z. Naturforsch.* **29a**, 1164 (1974).
(360) L. Leifer and E. Högfeldt, *Acta Chem. Scand.* **27**, 4007 (1973).
(361) J. T. Bulmer, D. E. Irish and L. Odberg, *Can. J. Chem.* **53**, 3806 (1975).
(362) J. T. Bulmer, D. E. Irish, F. W. Grossman, G. Herriot, M. Tseng and A. J. Weerheim, *Appl. Spectrosc.* **29**, 506 (1975).
(363) M. Peleg, *J. Phys. Chem.* **76**, 1019 (1972).
(364) T. G. Chang and D. E. Irish, *J. Phys. Chem.* **77**, 52 (1973).
(365) R. D. Green and N. Sheppard, *J. Chem. Soc. Faraday Trans. II* **68**, 821 (1972).
(366) A. D. Covington and A. K. Covington, *J. Chem. Soc. Faraday Trans. I* **71**, 831 (1975).
(367) D. E. Irish, in Ref. 176.
(368) F. Bertin and J. Derouault, *Compt. Rend. Acad. Sci.* (*Paris*) **280C**, 973 (1975).
(369) A. I. Grigor'ev, V. A. Sipachev and A. V. Novoselova, *Dokl. Akad. Nauk. SSSR* **160**, 383 (1965).
(370) M. A. Marques, B. Oksengorn and B. Vodar, *Advan. Raman Spectrosc.* **1**, 65 (1973). (Abstracts of the 3rd International Conference on Raman Spectroscopy, Reims, France, 1972.)

(371) D. J. Gardiner, R. E. Hester and E. Mayer, *J. Mol. Struct.* **22**, 327 (1974).
(372) T. G. Spiro, *Inorg. Chem.* **4**, 731 (1965).
(373) F. H. Spedding, P. F. Cullen and A. Habenschuss, *J. Phys. Chem.* **78**, 1106 (1974).
(374) M. L. Mitchell, T. Montag, J. Espenson and E. L. King, *Inorg. Chem.* **14**, 2862 (1975).
(375) R. K. Wharton, R. S. Taylor and A. G. Sykes, *Inorg. Chem.* **14**, 33 (1975).
(376) A. Regis and J. Corset, *J. Chim. Phys., Phys.-Chim. Biol.*, **69**, 707 (1972).
(377) S. Isotani, W. Sano and J. A. Ochi, *J. Phys. Chem. Solids* **36**, 95 (1975).
(378) T. M. Loehr, J. Zinich and T. V. Long II, *Chem. Phys. Lett.* **7**, 183 (1970).
(379) W. F. Edgell, in *Ions and Ion Pairs in Organic Reactions*, Vol. 1, Chapter 4 (M. Szwarc, Ed.), Wiley/Interscience, New York, 1972.
(380) A. I. Popov, *Pure Appl. Chem.* **41**, 275 (1975).
(381) R. G. Baum and A. I. Popov, *J. Solution Chem.* **4**, 441 (1975).
(382) R. H. Erlich, M. S. Greenberg and A. I. Popov, *Spectrochim. Acta* **29A**, 543 (1973).
(383) M. S. Greenberg, R. L. Bodner and A. I. Popov, *J. Phys. Chem.* **77**, 2449 (1973).
(384) J. B. Kinsinger, M. M. Tannahill, M. S. Greenberg and A. I. Popov, *J. Phys. Chem.* **77**, 2444 (1973).
(385) M. S. Greenberg, D. M. Wied and A. I. Popov, *Spectrochim. Acta* **29A**, 1927 (1973).
(386) P. R. Handy and A. I. Popov, *Spectrochim. Acta* **28A**, 1545 (1972).
(387) H. L. Yeager, J. D. Fedyk and R. J. Parker, *J. Phys. Chem.* **77**, 2407 (1973).
(388) T. L. Buxton and J. A. Caruso, *J. Phys. Chem.* **77**, 1882 (1973).
(389) E. C. Ashby, F. R. Dobbs and H. P. Hopkins, *J. Amer. Chem. Soc.* **95**, 2823 (1973).
(390) R. C. Paul, P. Singh and S. L. Chadha, *Ind. J. Chem.* **9**, 1160 (1971).
(391) A. Regis and J. Corset, *J. Chim. Phys. Phys.-Chim. Biol.* **69**, 1508 (1972).
(392) J. Rouviere, B. Dimon, D. Brun and J. Salvinien, *Compt. Rend. Acad. Sci. (Paris)* **274C**, 458 (1972).
(393) Z. Kecki, *Adv. Mol. Relaxation* **5**, 137 (1973).
(394) I. S. Perelygin and M. A. Klimchuk, *Zh. Fiz. Khim.* **49**, 138 (1975).
(395) J. A. Olander and M. C. Day, *J. Amer. Chem. Soc.* **93**, 3584 (1971).
(396) M. H. Baron, J. Corset, C. DeLozé and M. L. Josien, *Compt. Rend. Acad. Sci. (Paris)* **274C**, 1321 (1972). Also see C. DeLozé, P. Combelas, P. Bacelon and C. Garrigou-Lagiarge, *J. Chim. Phys., Phys.-Chim. Biol.* **69**, 397 (1972).
(397) B. M. Rode, *Chem. Phys. Lett.* **32**, 38 (1975).
(398) A. Regis and J. Corset, *Can. J. Chem.* **51**, 3577 (1973).
(399) A. K. Covington, I. R. Lantzke and J. M. Thain, *J. Chem. Soc. Faraday Trans. I*, **70**, 1869 (1974).
(400) C. Moreau and G. Douheret, *J. Chim. Phys. Phys.-Chim. Biol.* **71**, 1313 (1974).
(401) H. Kelm, J. Klosowski and E. Steger, *J. Mol. Struct.* **28**, 1 (1975).
(402) Y. M. Cahen and A. I. Popov, *J. Solution Chem.* **4**, 599 (1975).
(403) Y. M. Cahen, J. L. Dye and A. I. Popov, *J. Phys. Chem.* **79**, 1292 (1975).
(404) M. C. R. Symons and D. Waddington, *J. Chem. Soc. Faraday Trans. II* **71**, 22 (1975).
(405) A. R. Davis, J. W. Macklin and R. A. Plane, *J. Chem. Phys.* **50**, 1478 (1969).
(406) T. J. V. Findlay and M. C. R. Symons, *J. Chem. Soc. Faraday Trans. II* **72**, 820 (1976).
(407) D. E. Irish and A. R. Davis, *Can. J. Chem.* **46**, 943 (1968).
(408) D. J. Lockwood, *J. Chem. Soc. Faraday Trans. II* **71**, 1440 (1975).
(409) J. D. Payzant, R. Yamdagni and P. Kebarle, *Can. J. Chem.* **49**, 3308 (1971).
(410) H. G. Hertz, *J. Solution Chem.* **2**, 239 (1973).
(411) K. M. Harmon and I. Gennick, *Inorg. Chem.* **14**, 1840 (1975).

(412) H. P. Hayward and J. Schiffer, *J. Chem. Phys.* **62**, 1473 (1975).
(413) S. Pinchas and J. Shamir, *J. Chem. Phys.* **56**, 2017 (1972); *Israel J. Chem.* **9**, 477 (1971).
(414) S. Pinchas, *J. Chem. Phys.* **51**, 2284 (1969).
(415) A. P. Zhukovskii, A. N. Diep and A. I. Sidorova, *Mol. Fiz. Biofiz. Vodn. Sist.* **1**, 74 (1973).
(416) The values of $\bar{V}°$ ($cm^3 \, mol^{-1}$) are: OH^-, -5.23; F^-, -1.9; CO_3^{2-}, -3.5; SO_4^{2-}, $+15.0$; NO_3^-, $+29.7$. E. A. Moelwyn-Hughes, *Physical Chemistry*, Pergamon, New York, 1957, p. 851.
(417) A. K. Covington, M. L. Hassall and D. E. Irish, *J. Solution Chem.* **3**, 629 (1974).
(418) A. K. Covington, J. G. Freeman and T. H. Lilley, *J. Phys. Chem.* **74**, 3773 (1970).
(419) O. D. Bonner, H. B. Flora and H. W. Aitken, *J. Phys. Chem.* **75**, 2492 (1971).
(420) A. K. Covington and R. Thompson, *J. Solution Chem.* **3**, 603 (1974).
(421) R. M. Fuoss, *J. Chem. Educ.* **32**, 527 (1955).
(422) J. E. Prue, *Proc. 3rd Symposium on Coordination Chemistry* (M. T. Beck, Ed.), Debrecen, Hungary, 1970, Vol. 1, p. 25.
(423) D. E. Irish and O. Puzic, presented to the 21st Canadian Spectroscopy Symposium, Ottawa, Oct. 7–9, 1974.
(424) D. J. Turner, *J. Chem. Soc. Faraday Trans. II* **68**, 643 (1972).
(425) D. J. Turner, *J. Chem. Soc. Faraday Trans. I* **70**, 1346 (1974).
(426) A. S. Gilbert and N. Sheppard, *J. Chem. Soc. Faraday Trans. II*, **69**, 1628 (1973).
(427) L. J. Basile, P. LaBonville, J. R. Ferraro and J. M. Williams, *J. Chem. Phys.* **60**, 1981 (1974).
(428) B. Desbat and P. V. Huong, *Spectrochim. Acta* **31A**, 1109 (1975).
(429) P. V. Huong and B. Desbat, *J. Raman Spectrosc.* **2**, 373 (1974).
(430) J. Rozière and J. Potier, *J. Mol. Struct.* **13**, 91 (1972).
(431) J. Rozière and J. Potier, *J. Inorg. Nucl. Chem.* **35**, 1179 (1973).
(432) P. A. Giguère and C. Madec, presented at the Spectroscopy Society of Canada Symposium, Montreal, October, 1975; *Chem. Phys. Letts.* **37**, 569 (1976).
(433) I. Pernoll, U. Maier, R. Janoschek and G. Zundel, *J. Chem. Soc. Faraday Trans. II* **71**, 201 (1975).
(434) D. Schioberg and G. Zundel, *J. Chem. Soc. Faraday Trans. II* **69**, 771 (1973).
(435) R. Janoschek, E. G. Weidemann and G. Zundel, *J. Chem. Soc. Faraday Trans. II* **69**, 505 (1973).
(436) J. P. Perchard, W. F. Murphy and H. J. Bernstein, *Mol. Phys.* **23**, 519 (1972).
(437) D. Richon, D. Patterson and G. Turrell, *Chem. Phys. Lett.* **36**, 492 (1975).
(438) Y. LeDuff and W. Holzer, *J. Chem. Phys.* **60**, 2175 (1974).
(439) H. Touhara, H. Shimoda, K. Nakanishi and N. Watanabe, *J. Phys. Chem.* **75**, 2222 (1971).
(440) M. Kinugasa, K. Kishi and S. Ikeda, *J. Phys. Chem.* **77**, 1914 (1973).
(441) W. A. Guillory and M. L. Bernstein, *J. Chem. Phys.* **62**, 1058 (1975).
(442) R. D. Gillard and R. Ugo, *J. Chem. Soc. (A)*, 549 (1966).
(443) D. M. Palade, Yu. L. Popov and E. S. Il'ina, *Russian J. Inorg. Chem.* **17**, 228 (1972).
(444) R. Gunde, T. Solmajer, A. Ažman and D. Hadži, *J. Mol. Struct.* **24**, 405 (1975).
(445) R. Audinos, *Rev. Chim. minérale*, **10**, 701 (1973).
(446) R. Audinos, *J. Chim. Phys. Phys.-Chim. Biol.* **71**, 117 (1974).
(447) (a) B. G. Oliver and A. R. Davis, *Can. J. Chem.* **51**, 698 (1973); (b) A. R. Davis and B. G. Oliver, *J. Solution Chem.* **1**, 329 (1972).
(448) F. S. Nakayama, *J. Phys. Chem.* **74**, 2726 (1970).
(449) L. Fredin, B. Nelander and G. Ribbegard, *Chemica Scripta* **7**, 11 (1975).
(450) R. Foglizzo and A. Novak, *J. Chim. Phys. Phys.-Chim. Biol.* **71**, 1322 (1974).

(451) M. Deporcq-Stratmains, C. Josson and P. Vast, *Compt. Rend. Acad. Sci. (Paris)* **C280**, 513 (1975).
(452) R. L. Redington and K. C. Lin, *Spectrochim. Acta* **27A**, 2445 (1971).
(453) J. Guilleme, M. Chabanel and R. Wojtkowiak, *Spectrochim. Acta* **27A**, 2355 (1971).
(454) P. K. Glasoe, S. Hallock, M. Hove and J. M. Duke, *Spectrochim. Acta* **27A**, 2309 (1971).
(455) G. R. Alms, D. R. Bauer, J. I. Brauman and R. Pecora, *J. Chem. Phys.* **59**, 5321 (1973).
(456) F. Harbach and F. Fischer, *J. Phys. Chem. Solids* **36**, 601 (1975).
(457) B. A. Phillips and W. R. Busing, *J. Phys. Chem.* **61**, 502 (1957).
(458) S. K. Sharma and S. C. Kashyap, *J. Inorg. Nucl. Chem.* **34**, 3623 (1972).
(459) S. K. Sharma, *J. Chem. Phys.* **58**, 1626 (1973).
(460) E. R. Lippincott, J. A. Psellos and M. C. Tobin, *J. Chem. Phys.* **20**, 536 (1952).
(461) J. S. Fordyce and R. L. Baum, *J. Chem. Phys.* **43**, 843 (1965).
(462) D. E. Irish, B. McCarroll and T. F. Young, *J. Chem. Phys.* **39**, 3436 (1963).
(463) A. G. Briggs, N. A. Hampson and A. Marshall, *J. Chem. Soc. Faraday Trans. II* **70**, 1978 (1974).
(464) F. Ichikawa and T. Sato, *J. Inorg. Nucl. Chem.* **35**, 2592 (1973).
(465) R. Hoppe and P. Kastner, *Z. Anorg. Allgem. Chem.* **393**, 105 (1972).
(466) L. A. Carreira, V. A. Maroni, J. W. Swaine, Jr. and R. C. Plumb, *J. Chem. Phys.* **45**, 2216 (1966).
(467) E. A. Kopylova, L. P. Ni, M. V. Zakharova and Yu. F. Klyuchnikov, *J. Appl. Chem. USSR* **47**, 2396 (1974). [Translation of *Zh. Prikl. Khim.* **47**, 2336 (1974)].
(468) E. A. Kopylova, M. V. Zakharova, L. P. Ni and Yu. F. Klyuchnikov, *Tr. Inst. Met. Obogashch. Akad. Nauk Kaz. SSR*, **49**, 11 (1973); *Chem. Abstr.* **80**, 41573j.
(469) E. A. Kopylova, L. P. Ni, Yu. F. Klyuchnikov and M. V. Zakharova, *Tr. Inst. Met. Obogashch. Akad. Nauk Kaz. SSR*, **49**, 18 (1973). *Chem. Abstr.* **80**, 20138f.
(470) M. M. Iannuzzi and P. H. Rieger, Sixteenth International Conference on Coordination Chemistry, Dublin, Ireland, 1974. M. M. Iannuzzi, Ph.D. Thesis, Brown University, Rhode Island, U.S.A., 1974.
(471) E. Freund, *Bull. Soc. Chim. France*, 2238, 2244 (1973).
(472) G. E. Walrafen and J. P. Luongo, *The Spex Speaker* **20**(3), 1 (1975). (Spex Industries Inc., 3880 Park Ave., Metuchen, N.J.)
(473) E. Högfeldt, *Chemica Scripta* **8**, 23, 57, 104 (1975).
(474) A. Holmgren and P. Beronius, *Acta Chem. Scand.* **26**, 3881 (1972).
(475) O. Fischer, M. Vrbova and Z. Zubalik, *Coll. Czech. Chem. Comm.* **40**, 2733 (1975).
(476) A. S. Solovkin, *Zh. Strukt. Khim.* **14**, 921 (1973).
(477) A. S. Quist, J. B. Bates and G. E. Boyd, *J. Phys. Chem.* **76**, 78 (1972).
(478) M. H. Brooker, *J. Chem. Phys.* **63**, 3054 (1975).
(479) R. E. Mesmer and C. F. Baes, Jr., *Inorg. Chem.* **8**, 618 (1969).
(480) M. G. Hogben, K. Radley and L. W. Reeves, *Can. J. Chem.* **48**, 2960 (1970).
(481) J. Havel and E. Högfeldt, *Acta Chem. Scand.* **27**, 3323 (1973).
(482) A. Snelson, B. N. Cyvin and S. J. Cyvin, *J. Mol. Struct.* **24**, 165 (1975).
(483) D. White, G. V. Calder, S. Hemple and D. E. Mann, *J. Chem. Phys.* **59**, 6645 (1973).
(484) M. L. Lesiecki and J. W. Nibler, *J. Chem. Phys.* **64**, 871 (1976).
(485) J. B. Bates, *J. Chem. Phys.* **55**, 489 (1971).
(486) J. B. Bates, A. S. Quist and G. E. Boyd, *J. Chem. Phys.* **54**, 124 (1971).
(487) J. B. Bates and A. S. Quist, *Spectrochim. Acta* **31A**, 1317 (1975).
(488) R. E. Mesmer, K. M. Palen and C. F. Baes, *Inorg. Chem.* **12**, 89 (1973).
(489) M. C. Dhamelincourt and M. Migeon, *Compt. Rend. Acad. Sci. (Paris)* **C281**, 79 (1975).

(490) G. Torsi, G. Mamantov and G. M. Begun, *Inorg. Nucl. Chem. Lett.* **6**, 553 (1970).

(491) E. Rytter, H. A. Øye, S. J. Cyvin, B. N. Cyvin and P. Klaboe, *J. Inorg. Nucl. Chem.* **35**, 1185 (1973).

(492) B. Gilbert, G. Mamantov and G. M. Begun, *J. Chem. Phys.* **62**, 950 (1975). Also see S. J. Ratkje and E. Rytter, *J. Phys. Chem.* **78**, 1499 (1974).

(493) Y. S. Yang and J. S. Shirk, *J. Mol. Spectrosc.* **54**, 39 (1975).

(494) R. G. S. Pong, R. A. Stachnik, A. E. Shirk and J. S. Shirk, *J. Chem. Phys.* **63**, 1525 (1975).

(495) S. F. Lincoln, A. C. Sandercock and D. R. Stranks, *J. Chem. Soc. Dalton Trans.*, 66 (1975).

(496) L. A. Woodward and A. H. Nord, *J. Chem. Soc.* 3721 (1956).

(497) K. Schug and L. Katzin, *J. Phys. Chem.* **66**, 907 (1962).

(498) M. P. Hanson and R. A. Plane, *Inorg. Chem.* **8**, 726 (1969).

(499) T. G. Spiro, *Inorg. Chem.* **4**, 731 (1965).

(500) R. A. Work and M. L. Good, *Spectrochim. Acta* **28A**, 1537 (1972).

(501) H. A. Øye and W. Bues, *Inorg. Nucl. Chem. Lett.* **8**, 31 (1972); *Acta Chem. Scand.* **A29**, 489 (1975).

(502) H. A. Øye, E. Rytter and P. Klaboe, *J. Inorg. Nucl. Chem.* **36**, 1925 (1974).

(503) J. E. Davies, L. G. Waterworth and I. J. Worrall, *J. Inorg. Nucl. Chem.* **36**, 805 (1974).

(504) A. N. Campbell, *Can. J. Chem.* **53**, 1761 (1975).

(505) V. A. Maroni and P. T. Cunningham, *Appl. Spectrosc.* **27**, 428 (1973).

(506) S. Stafford, H. J. Haupt and F. Huber, *Inorg. Chim. Acta* **11**, 207 (1974).

(507) V. B. Ramos and R. S. Tobias, *Inorg. Chem.* **11**, 2451 (1972).

(508) C. E. Freidline and R. S. Tobias, *Inorg. Chem.* **5**, 354 (1966).

(509) G. J. Piermarini and A. B. Braun, *J. Chem. Phys.* **58**, 1974 (1973).

(510) F. P. Daly, A. G. Hopkins and C. W. Brown, *Spectrochim. Acta* **30A**, 2159 (1974).

(511) J. E. Griffith, *Spectrochim. Acta* **30A**, 169 (1974).

(512) J. A. Creighton and T. J. Sinclair, *Spectrochim. Acta* **29A**, 817 (1973).

(513) H. F. Shurvell, *J. Mol. Spectrosc.* **38**, 431 (1971).

(514) R. J. H. Clark and P. D. Mitchell, *J. Chem. Soc. Chem. Comm.* 762 (1973).

(515) E. S. Stoyanov, Y. B. Spikakov and L. A. Gribov, *Koord. Khim.* **1**, 228 (1975).

(516) P. T. Cunningham and V. A. Maroni, *Appl. Spectrosc.* **27**, 54 (1975).

(517) R. A. Work and M. L. Good, *Spectrochim. Acta* **29A**, 1547 (1973).

(518) T. Østvold, *High Temp. Sci.* **4**, 51 (1972).

(519) L. S. Smith and D. L. Wertz, *J. Amer. Chem. Soc.* **97**, 2365 (1975).

(520) M. H. Hutchinson and W. C. E. Higginson, *J. Chem. Soc. Dalton Trans.* 1247 (1973).

(521) *Stability Constants of Metal-ion Complexes*, Special Publication No. 17, 1964; No. 25, 1971; The Chemical Society, London.

(522) M. H. Kennedy and M. W. Lister, *Can. J. Chem.* **44**, 1709 (1966).

(523) Yu. A. Makashev, M. I. Shalaevskaya, V. V. Blokhim and V. E. Mironov, *Zh. Fiz. Khim.* **48**, 2066 (1974).

(524) J. K. Rowley and N. Sutin, *J. Phys. Chem.* **74**, 2043 (1970).

(525) M. Ohlson and N. G. Vannerberg, *Acta Chem. Scand.* **A28**, 1021 (1974).

(526) I. R. Beattie, T. R. Gilson and G. A. Ozin, *J. Chem. Soc. (A)*, 534 (1969).

(527) J. T. R. Dunsmuir and A. P. Lane, *J. Chem. Soc. (A)*, 404, 2781 (1971).

(528) H. D. Ludemann and E. U. Franck, *Ber. Bunsenges. Physik. Chem.* **72**, 514 (1968).

(529) B. Scholz, H. D. Ludemann and E. U. Franck, *Ber. Bunsenges. Physik. Chem.* **76**, 406 (1972).

(530) T. R. Griffiths and P. J. Potts, *J. Chem. Soc. Dalton Trans.* 344 (1975).

(531) A. L. Marston and S. F. Bush, *Appl. Spectrosc.* **26**, 579 (1972).
(532) S. K. Sharma, *J. Chem. Phys.* **60**, 1368 (1974).
(533) Y. Inoue, S. Deki, M. Yokoyama, N. Masaie and Y. Kanaji, *Nippon Kogaku Kaishi*, 2297 (1974).
(534) H. A. Andreasen and N. J. Bjerrum, *Inorg. Chem.* **14**, 1807 (1975).
(535) G. M. Begun, J. Brynestad, F. W. Fung and G. Mamantov, *Inorg. Nucl. Chem. Lett.* **8**, 79 (1972).
(536) P. T. T. Wong, *J. Chem. Phys.* **64**, 2186 (1976).
(537) J. W. Macklin and R. A. Plane, *Inorg. Chem.* **9**, 821 (1970).
(538) J. A. McGinnety, *Inorg. Chem.* **13**, 1057 (1974).
(539) C. A. Angell, G. H. Wegdam and J. van der Elsken, *Spectrochim. Acta* **30A**, 665 (1974).
(540) R. M. Nikolic and I. J. Gal, *J. Chem. Soc. Dalton Trans.* 985 (1974).
(541) J. H. R. Clarke and P. J. Hartley, *J. Phys. Chem.* **78**, 595 (1974).
(542) J. H. R. Clarke, P. J. Hartley and Y. Kuroda, *Inorg. Chem.* **11**, 29 (1972).
(543) N. Yellin and Y. Marcus, *J. Inorg. Nucl. Chem.* **36**, 1325 (1974); *ibid* p. 1331; *Israel J. Chem.* **10**, 919 (1972).
(544) J. Breckenridge, W. Warzecha and T. Surles, *Inorg. Nucl. Chem. Lett.* **9**, 437 (1973).
(545) J. P. Coignac and M. Debeau, *Spectrochim. Acta* **30A**, 1551 (1974).
(546) K. R. Loos and A. C. Jones, *J. Phys. Chem.* **78**, 2306 (1974).
(547) F. H. Herbstein and M. Kapon, *J. Chem. Soc. Chem. Comm.* 677 (1975).
(548) J. P. Coignac and M. Debeau, *Spectrochim. Acta* **30A**, 1365 (1974).
(549) M. Delhaye, P. Dhamelincourt, J.-C. Merlin and F. Wallart, *Compt. Rend. Acad. Sci. (Paris)* **B272**, 1003 (1971).
(550) P. Dawson, M. M. Hargreave and G. R. Wilkinson, *Spectrochim. Acta* **31A**, 1055 (1975).
(551) S. D. Ross, *Inorganic Infrared and Raman Spectra*, McGraw-Hill, London, 1972.
(552) H. Schulze, N. Weinstock, A. Müller and G. Vandrish, *Spectrochim. Acta* **29A**, 1705 (1973).
(553) D. M. Hwang, *Phys. Rev.* **89**, 2717 (1974).
(554) C. M. Hartwig, D. L. Rousseau and S. P. S. Porto, *Phys. Rev.* **188**, 1328 (1969).
(555) J. B. Bates, *J. Chem. Phys.* **55**, 494 (1971).
(556) B. J. Berenblut, P. Dawson, P. Morse and G. R. Wilkinson, *J. Raman Spectrosc.* **1**, 523 (1973).
(557) I. I. Kondilenko, P. A. Korotkov and N. G. Golubeva, *Opt. Spektrosk.* **38**, 689 (1975).
(558) H. D. Lutz and H. J. Klueppel, *Ber. Bunsenges. Phys. Chem.* **79**, 98 (1975).
(559) T. G. Balicheva and G. A. Petrova, *Probl. Sovrem. Khim. Koord. Soedin.* **4**, 266 (1974).
(560) N. Smyrl and J. P. Devlin, *J. Chem. Phys.* **60**, 2540 (1974); **61**, 1596 (1974).
(561) N. Smyrl and J. P. Devlin, *J. Chem. Phys.* **62**, 1982 (1975).
(562) B. G. Oliver and G. J. Janz, *J. Phys. Chem.* **75**, 2948 (1971).
(563) D. J. Gardiner, R. B. Girling and R. E. Hester, *J. Mol. Struct.* **13**, 105 (1972).
(564) D. J. Gardiner, R. B. Girling and R. E. Hester, *J. Phys. Chem.* **77**, 640 (1973).
(565) J. C. Sprowles and R. A. Plane, *J. Phys. Chem.* **79**, 1711 (1975).
(566) R. E. Hester, R. A. Plane and G. E. Walrafen, *J. Chem. Phys.* **38**, 249 (1963).
(567) I. S. Perelygin and M. A. Klimchuk, *Zh. Fiz. Khim.* **47**, 2486 (1973).
(568) S. A. Al-Baldawi and T. E. Gough, *Can. J. Chem.* **47**, 1417 (1969).
(569) A. Diamond, A. Fanelli and S. Petrucci, *Inorg. Chem.* **12**, 611 (1973).
(570) V. Gutmann and H. Schmidt, *Monats. Chem.* **105**, 653 (1974).
(571) M. H. Brooker and J. B. Bates, *J. Chem. Phys.* **54**, 4788 (1971); *Spectrochim. Acta* **30A**, 2211 (1974).

(572) G. Lucazeau and A. Novak, *J. Raman Spectrosc.* **1**, 573 (1973).
(573) J. B. Bates, M. H. Brooker, A. S. Quist and G. E. Boyd, *J. Phys. Chem.* **76**, 1565 (1972).
(574) R. C. Patel, R. J. Boe and G. Atkinson, *J. Solution Chem.* **2**, 357 (1973).
(575) B. Taravel, G. Chauvet, P. Quintard and P. Delorme, *Compt. Rend. Acad. Sci. (Paris)* **273B**, 85 (1971).
(576) R. C. Patel, F. Garland and G. Atkinson, *J. Solution Chem.* **4**, 161 (1975).
(577) F. S. Nakayama, *J. Phys. Chem.* **74**, 2726 (1970).
(578) C. C. Addison, N. Logan, S. C. Wallwork and C. D. Garner, *Quart. Rev.* **25**, 289 (1971).
(579) J. P. Devlin and R. Frech, *J. Chem. Phys.* **63**, 1663 (1975).
(580) D. W. James and J. P. Devlin, *J. Chem. Phys.* **56**, 4688 (1972); J. P. Devlin, D. W. James and R. Frech, *J. Chem. Phys.* **53**, 4394 (1970); *Chem. Phys. Lett.* **12**, 602 (1972).
(581) E. V. Chisler, *Fiz. Tverd. Tela.* **11**, 1272 (1969) [*Soviet Physics—Solid State* **11**, 1032 (1969).]
(582) M. Peleg, *J. Phys. Chem.* **77**, 2252 (1973).
(583) K. Balasubrahmanyam and G. J. Janz, *J. Chem. Phys.* **57**, 4089 (1972).
(584) J. P. Devlin, G. Ritzhaupt and T. Hudson, *J. Chem. Phys.* **58**, 817 (1973).
(585) M. H. Brooker, A. S. Quist and G. E. Boyd, *Chem. Phys. Lett.* **9**, 242 (1971); **5**, 357 (1970).
(586) Y. K. Delimarskii and S. A. Kirillov, *Teor. Eksp. Khim.* **10**, 201 (1974); S. A. Kirillov and Y. K. Delimarskii, *Teor. Eksp. Khim.* **11**, 124 (1975).
(587) H. D. B. Jenkins and T. C. Waddington, *J. Inorg. Nucl. Chem.* **34**, 2465 (1972).
(588) F. Bigoli, A. Braibanti, A. Tiripicchio and M. T. Camellini, *Acta Cryst.* **B27**, 1427 (1971).
(589) A. Leclaire and J. D. Monier, *Compt. Rend. Acad. Sci. (Paris)* **271C**, 1555 (1970).
(590) A. Leclaire, *Acta Cryst.* **B30**, 605 (1974); **B30**, 2259 (1974).
(591) A. Braibanti, A. Tiripicchio, A. M. M. Lanfredi and F. Bigoli, *Acta Cryst.* **B25**, 354 (1969).
(592) B. Ribar, B. Matkovic and M. Sljukic, *Z. Krist.* **135**, 137 (1972).
(593) B. Ribar, V. Divjakovic and A. Petrovic, *Z. Krist.* **136**, 159 (1972).
(594) P. Cherin, W. C. Hamilton and B. Post, *Acta Cryst.* **23**, 455 (1967).
(595) C. S. Gibbons and J. Trotter, *J. Chem. Soc. (A)*, 2058 (1971).
(596) J. M. Bijvoet and J. A. A. Ketelaar, *J. Amer. Chem. Soc.* **54**, 625 (1932).
(597) D. E. Irish, A. R. Davis and R. A. Plane, *J. Chem. Phys.* **50**, 2262 (1969).
(598) J. H. R. Clarke and P. J. Hartley, *J. Chem. Soc. Faraday Trans. II* **68**, 1634 (1972).
(599) D. Harold-Smith, *J. Chem. Phys.* **59**, 4771 (1973); **60**, 1405 (1974).
(600) M. H. Brooker, unpublished work.
(601) J. P. Devlin, P. C. Li and G. Pollard, *J. Chem. Phys.* **52**, 2267 (1970).
(602) M. Tsuboi, A. Y. Hirakawa and S. Muraishi, *J. Mol. Spectrosc.* **56**, 146 (1975).
(603) T. G. Chang, Ph.D. Thesis, University of Waterloo, Ontario, 1972.
(604) D. E. Irish, T. G. Chang and D. L. Nelson, *Inorg. Chem.* **9**, 425 (1970).
(605) R. G. DeCarvalho and G. R. Choppin, *Inorg. Chem.* **4**, 1250 (1965).
(606) M. H. Brooker and J. B. Bates, *Spectrochim. Acta* **29A**, 439 (1973).
(607) M. H. Brooker and D. E. Irish, *Can. J. Chem.* **48**, 1183 (1970).
(608) D. E. Irish and G. E. Walrafen, *J. Chem. Phys.* **46**, 378 (1967).
(609) Y. Sze, M.Sc. Thesis, University of Waterloo, Waterloo, Ontario, 1970.
(610) H. Brintzinger and R. E. Hester, *Inorg. Chem.* **5**, 980 (1966); R. E. Hester and W. E. Grossman, *ibid.* **5**, 1308 (1966).
(611) J. Drummond and J. S. Wood, *J. Chem. Soc. (A)*, 226 (1970).
(612) L. J. Blackwell, T. J. King and A. Morris, *J. Chem. Soc. Chem. Comm.* 644, (1973).

(613) C. C. Addison, L. J. Blackwell, B. Harrison, D. H. Jones, N. Logan, E. K. Nunn and S. C. Wallwork, *J. Chem. Soc. Chem. Comm.*, 347 (1973).
(614) D. W. Amos and G. W. Flewett, *Spectrochim. Acta* **30A**, 453 (1974).
(615) M. H. Brooker, *Spectrochim. Acta* **32A**, 369 (1976).
(616) B. Hutchinson and M. Stewart, *Spectrochim. Acta* **30A**, 2173 (1974).
(617) D. W. James and G. M. Kimber, *Aust. J. Chem.* **22**, 2287 (1969); **23**, 829 (1970).
(618) A. N. Khodchenkov, V. P. Spiridonov and P. A. Akishin, *Zh. Strukt. Khim.* **6**, 765 (1965); *J. Struct. Chem.* **6**, 724 (1965).
(619) A. A. Ishchenko, V. P. Spiridonov and E. Z. Zasorin, *Zh. Strukt. Khim.* **15**, 300 (1974).
(620) A. Shapovalov, V. F. Shevel'kov and A. A. Mal'tsev, *Vestnik. Moskov. Univ. Khim.* **14**, 151 (1973).
(621) A. R. Davis and R. A. Plane, *Inorg. Chem.* **7**, 2565 (1968).
(622) A. R. Davis and C. Chong, *Inorg. Chem.* **11**, 1891 (1972).
(623) A. R. Davis and D. E. Irish, *Inorg. Chem.* **7**, 1699 (1968).
(624) T. G. Chang and D. E. Irish, *J. Solution Chem.* **3**, 175 (1974).
(625) B. G. Oliver and G. J. Janz, *J. Phys. Chem.* **74**, 3819 (1970).
(626) G. J. Janz, K. Balasubrahmanyam and B. G. Oliver, *J. Chem. Phys.* **51**, 5723 (1969).
(627) B. Bolshaw and S. I. Smedley, *J. Phys. Chem.* **79**, 1323 (1975).
(628) R. E. Hester and R. A. Plane, *J. Chem. Phys.* **40**, 411 (1964).
(629) J. P. Mathieu and M. Lounsbury, *Disc. Faraday Soc.* **9**, 196 (1950).
(630) J. H. R. Clarke and L. A. Woodward, *Trans. Faraday Soc.* **62**, 3022 (1966).
(631) H. G. M. Edwards and L. A. Woodward, *J. Raman Spectrosc.* **2**, 423 (1974).
(632) B. Strauch and L. N. K. Komissarova, *Collect. Czech. Chem. Comm.* **32**, 1484 (1967).
(633) S. K. Sharma, *J. Inorg. Nucl. Chem.* **35**, 3831 (1973); *J. Chem. Phys.* **61**, 1748 (1974).
(634) R. P. Oertel and R. A. Plane, *Inorg. Chem.* **7**, 1192 (1968).
(635) D. L. Nelson and D. E. Irish, *J. Chem. Phys.* **54**, 4479 (1971).
(636) J. T. Miller and D. E. Irish, *Can. J. Chem.* **45**, 147 (1967).
(637) B. G. Oliver and A. R. Davis, *J. Inorg. Nucl. Chem.* **34**, 2851 (1972).
(638) A. S. Solovkin, *Zh. Fiz. Khim.* **48**, 2655 (1974).
(639) W. L. Masterton, H. Welles, J. H. Knox and F. J. Millero, *J. Solution Chem.* **3**, 91 (1974).
(640) A. M. Fedorenko and E. A. Gyunner, *Zh. Neorg. Khim.* **19**, 2560 (1974).
(641) M. Peleg, *Israel J. Chem.* **11**, 534 (1973).
(642) V. A. Fedorov, A. M. Robov, I. I. Shymd'ko, N. A. Vorontsova and V. E. Mironov, *Zh. Neorg. Khim.* **19**, 1746 (1974).
(643) Y. I. Ramankov and T. A. Komarova, *Zh. Fiz. Khim.* **47**, 2159 (1973).
(644) N. G. Zunjurwad and S. V. Tagare, *J. Shivaji Univ.* **6**, 1 (1973). *Chem. Abstr.* **83**, 21050v.
(645) D. F. Peppard, G. W. Mason and I. Hucher, *J. Inorg. Nucl. Chem.* **24**, 881 (1962).
(646) A. V. Stepanov, *Russ. J. Inorg. Chem.* **18**, 194 (1973).
(647) N. A. Coward and R. W. Kisir, *J. Phys. Chem.* **70**, 213 (1966).
(648) A. Anagnostopoulos and P. O. Sakellaridis, *J. Inorg. Nucl. Chem.* **32**, 1740 (1970).
(649) V. A. Shchurov and T. M. Romanova, *Uch. Zap., Permsk. Gos. Univ.* **289**, 42 (1973). *Chem. Abstr.* **81**, 141739g.
(650) T. I. Turtseva and V. I. Glizerman, *Vestn. Mosh. Univ. Khim.* **14**, 51 (1973).
(651) F. H. Spedding, P. F. Cullen and A. Habenschuss, *J. Phys. Chem.* **78**, 1106 (1974).
(652) J. A. Rard and F. H. Spedding, *J. Phys. Chem.* **79**, 257 (1975); *J. Chem. Eng. Data* **20**, 81 (1975).

(653) A. Apelblat, D. Azoulay and A. Sahar, *J. Chem. Soc. Faraday Trans. I* **69**, 1618, 1624 (1973).

(654) S. Hietanen and L. G. Sillén, *Arkiv Kemi.* **10**, 103 (1956).

(655) K. Balasubrahmanyam and G. J. Janz, *J. Solution Chem.* **1**, 445 (1972).

(656) J. L. Burmeister, *Coord. Chem. Rev.* **3**, 225 (1968).

(657) M. H. Brooker and D. E. Irish, *Trans. Faraday Soc.* **67**, 1923 (1971).

(658) R. W. Green and B. Bell, *Aust. J. Chem.* **26**, 1663 (1973); R. W. Green, *ibid.* **26**, 1841 (1973).

(659) M. H. Brooker and D. E. Irish, *Inorg. Chem.* **8**, 219 (1969).

(660) J. Tummavouri, *Suom. Kemi.* **B45**, 169 (1972); **B44**, 343, 350 (1971).

(661) D. W. James and M. J. Nolan, *Aust. J. Chem.* **26**, 1433 (1973).

(662) A. Garnier, *J. Chim. Phys. Phys.-Chim. Biol.* **67**, 1458 (1970).

(663) A. Garnier, *J. Chim. Phys. Phys.-Chim. Biol.* **67**, 1440 (1970).

(664) A. G. Cram and M. B. Davies, *J. Inorg. Nucl. Chem.* **37**, 1693 (1975).

(665) K. J. Ivin, R. Jamison and J. J. McGarvey, *J. Amer. Chem. Soc.* **94**, 1763 (1972).

(666) D. R. Eaton and K. Zaw, *Can. J. Chem.* **53**, 633 (1975).

(667) D. M. L. Goodgame and M. A. Hitchman, *Inorg. Chem.* **5**, 1303 (1966).

(668) L. J. Jones, *J. Chem. Phys.* **25**, 1069 (1956).

(669) J. L. Burmeister, R. L. Hassel and R. J. Phelan, *Inorg. Chem.* **10**, 2032 (1971).

(670) R. A. Bailey, S. L. Kozak, T. W. Michelsen and W. N. Mills, *Coord. Chem. Rev.* **6**, 407 (1971).

(671) D. P. Stommen and R. A. Plane, *J. Chem. Phys.* **60**, 2643 (1974).

(672) D. Forster and W. De W. Horrocks, Jr., *Inorg. Chem.* **6**, 339 (1967).

(673) J. R. Dickinson, T. R. Griffiths and P. J. Potts, *J. Inorg. Nucl. Chem.* **37**, 511 (1975).

(674) T. R. Griffiths and P. J. Potts, *J. Inorg. Nucl. Chem.* **37**, 521 (1975).

(675) M. Chabanel, C. Ménard and G. Guihéneuf, *Compt. Rend. Acad. Sci.* (*Paris*) **272C**, 253 (1971).

(676) C. B. Baddiel and G. J. Janz, *Trans. Faraday Soc.* **60**, 2009 (1964).

(677) L. Schriver and J. Corset, *J. Chim. Phys. Phys.-Chim. Biol.* **70**, 1463 (1973).

(678) Y. S. Wong, S. Jacobson, P. C. Chieh and A. J. Carty, *Inorg. Chem.* **13**, 284 (1974).

(679) Y. Morioka, I. Nakagawa and T. Shimanouchi, *Spectrochim. Acta* **30A**, 479 (1974).

(680) A. Müller, K. H. Schmidt and G. Vandrish, *Spectrochim. Acta* **30A**, 651 (1974).

(681) H. Persson, *Acta Chem. Scand.* **25**, 543 (1971); **28A**, 885 (1974).

(682) A. Loupy and J. Corset, *Compt. Rend. Acad. Sci.* (*Paris*) **279C**, 713 (1974).

AUTHOR INDEX

Authors' names are given followed by the page numbers where each reference is cited, with the reference numbers in parentheses. Italicized numbers indicate pages on which the full reference is given.

A

Abe, M., 249 (28); *249*
Abel, E. W., 31 (52); *51*
Abouaf-Marguin, L., 42 (66); 44 (71); 45 (71); 46 (71, 73); *52*
Abraham, F. F., 237 (217); *300*
Adams, D. M., 242 (280); 256 (348, 349); *301*; *303*
Adams, W. A., 223 (56); 224 (56), 225 (56); 228 (56, 97, 98); 229 (98); 230 (56); *296*; *297*
Addison, C. C., 275 (578); 280 (578); *308*
Ahrland, S., 226 (65); *296*
Aitken, H. W., 263 (419); *305*
Akhmedzhanov, R., 248 (10); *248*
Akiskin, P. A., 157 (21); 165 (21); *208*; 281 (618); *309*
Akkison, G. H., 146 (13); *152*
Al-Baldawi, S. A., 223 (54); 224 (54); 225 (54); 226 (54); 233 (54); 258 (54); 274 (54, 568); 282 (54); 288 (54); *296*; *308*
Allavena, M., 4 (12); 5 (12); 8 (12); *50*
Allen, L., 236 (185); *299*
Alms, G. R., 267 (455); *305*
Alonso, R., 256 (341); 285 (341); *303*
Amis, E. S., 254 (334, 336); *303*
Amos, D. W., 281 (614); *309*
Amy, J. W., 234 (148); *298*
Anagnostopoulos, A., 287 (648); *310*
Andaloro, G., 236 (187); *299*
Anderson, J. S., 9 (17); 17 (17); *50*
Andreasen, H. A., 272 (534); *307*

Andrews, L., 1 (6); 14 (24); 15 (24); *50*; *51*; 249 (33); *249*
Angell, C. A., 179 (72); 185 (72, 91); 191 (72); 193 (72); 203 (138); 206 (138, 139); *209*; *210*; *211*; 236 (191); 237 (214); 272 (539); *299*, *300*; *308*
Antion, D. J., 249 (29); *249*
Apelblat, A., 288 (653); *310*
Arisman, R. K., 242 (284); *301*
Arkell, A., 1 (7); *50*
Armishaw, R. F., 242 (271); *301*
Armitage, G. M., 220 (36); *295*
Arnau, J. L., 249 (28); *249*
Ashby, E. C., 259 (389); 260 (389); *304*
Atkinson, G., 275 (574, 576); *308*
Attwood, J. D., 36 (56); *51*
Audinos, R., 249 (33); *249*; 266 (445, 446); *305*
Aussenegg, F., 236 (198); *300*
Ault, B. S., 155 (14); *208*; 243 (303); 245 (303); *302*
Austin, G., 176 (67); 177 (67); *209*
Auton, J. P., 117 (34); *139*
Avery, J. S., 62 (10); *79*
Ayers, G. P., 240 (226); *300*
Ažman, A., 266 (444); *305*
Azoulay, D., 288 (653); *310*

B

Baasner, B., 256 (343); *303*
Bacaro, J. A., 232 (131); *298*
Bacelon, P., 260 (396); *304*

313

FORMULA INDEX

SUBJECT INDEX

A

Absolute intensities, 11
Acetone, 260, 269
Acetonitrile, 232, 246, 250, 251, 259, 260, 288
Acidity constant, 263
Acoustic, modes, 67
  phonons, 65
Activity coefficient, 213–215, 218, 230
Adiabatic approximation, 58, 59
Ageing, 268
Alkali metal–ammonia solutions, 246
Aluminates, 267
Ammonia, 93, 243–245, 261, 277
  solvation of ion pairs, 169
Ammoniates, 258
Analysers for solids, 107
Analytical precision, 82
Angular overlap model, 57
Anharmonic, force constants, 23, 36
  frequencies, 5
  localized modes, 48
Anharmonicity, 4
  constants, 26
Anion
  distortion, 158
  hydration, 262
  perturbations, 154
  solvation, 261
Anomalous, spectra, 184
  water, 236
Antifluorite, K_2PtCl_6, 65, 75
Aprotic solvents, 260, 261, 293
Aquodimethyllead(IV) ion, 270
Associating matrices, 168
Atmospheric, absorption, 130
  pollution, 93, 129
Attenuated total reflectance (a.t.r.), 100, 176, 235

B

Band-fitting, 220–222, 230
Band intensities of metal carbonyls, 27
Band overlap, 222
Band-shapes, 232, 233, 237, 250, 263, 265
Bicarbonates, 274
Blast furnace, 91
Bond
  angle, 4, 7–9, 30, 34, 36, 37
  dipole moment, 14
  derivatives, 35
Born–Oppenheimer approximation, 54, 58
Brewster angle, 117
Brillouin zone, 65

C

Carbonate melts, 188
Carbonates, 274
Carbon dioxide, 90–93, 104
Carbon monoxide, 90–93
Carbonyl fragments, 39
Cascade image-intensifier, 145
Cassegrainian collector, 128
Cation polarizability, 161, 200, 256
  polarization, 158, 166, 168
  polarizing power, 160, 161, 168
  solvation, 254
Cauchy–Gauss shape ratios, 220–222
Cell design, 197
Cells, 228
Central field approximation, 55
Chemical potentials, 213, 214
Chemical process streams, 92, 93
Chlorate melts, 186
Chloroaluminate melts, 269
Circular dichroism, 70
Cluster model of Satten, 65